WEEKEND GETAWAYS
IN ALABAMA

Cahaba lily at Cheaha State Park. (Photo courtesy Charlene Wells)

WEEKEND GETAWAYS
IN ALABAMA

By Joan Broerman

PELICAN PUBLISHING COMPANY
Gretna 2000

Library of Congress Cataloging-in-Publication Data

Broerman, Joan.
  Weekend getaways in Alabama / by Joan Broerman.
    p. cm.
  Includes bibliographical references and index.
  ISBN 1-56554-676-8 (alk. paper)
    1. Alabama—Guidebooks. I. Title.
  F324.3 .B76 2000
  917.6104'64—dc21
                          00-035966

Information in this guidebook is based on authoritative data available at the time of printing. Prices and hours of operation of businesses are subject to change without notice. Readers are asked to take this into account when consulting this guide.

Printed in the United States of America
Published by Pelican Publishing Company, Inc.
1000 Burmaster Street, Gretna, Louisiana 70053

*To the real treasure in Alabama: its people.
And to those who share this diverse and delightful state
with me, my husband, Neal, my children and grandchildren,
and dear friends. They make Alabama home.*

CONTENTS

ACKNOWLEDGMENTS

Tourism representatives across Alabama were an unfailing source of information and support. Many thanks to Ami Simpson, Peggy Collins, Patty and Michael Tucker, Squee Bailey, Rick Roden, Darlene Wheeler, Margaret Day, BeBe Gauntt, Tinsley Gunby, Lisa Stockton, Debbie Wilson, Heather Green, Georgia Turner, Monica Tidwell, Jennifer Lindsay, Lauri Cothran, Pam Powers, Kitty Leverett, Scott Moreland, Kristi Nichols, Leah Stokes, and Liz Ramsey. The Shades Valley Camera Club in Homewood, Alabama, and their president, Ron Bowen, gave technical assistance.

Friends, family, and fellow writers suggested places that enriched our travels. I'd especially like to thank Michael Vigliotti, Carol Mader, Julie Klein, Bob Roberts, Lou and Pat Williams, Steven Biggs, Jo Kittinger, Debbie Sanders, Han Holan, Brenda Moore, Karen Cronin, Annie Laura Smith, Shirley Bingham, Lynn Rich, Ellen Mason, Mary Ann and Charles Taylor, Tracy McMahan, Gay Martin, Lynn Fullman, Ottie Newsom, Tom Lane, Evelyn Coleman, Irene Sexton, Paula Rhea, Kathye Marsh, Marilyn Shank, Anne Dalton, and the Lara family, Eduardo, Pilar, Antonia, and Valentina. May their own travels be blessed.

INTRODUCTION

This book isn't finished. It never will be. To gather information, my husband drove and I tapped away on my laptop, which plugs into the cigarette lighter in the car. We motored from sandy beaches to flatlands to mountains, jolted down little dirt roads, and inched through traffic lights in crowded cities. In cafes, coffee shops, gourmet restaurants, campgrounds, motels, inns, museums, parks, art studios, and flea markets, we talked with spelunkers, rock climbers, fishermen, golfers, picnickers, shop clerks, librarians, curators, waitresses, switchboard operators, innkeepers, and many others. Everyone had a story to tell or a place we had to see. The road kept stretching ahead. It still does.

In shaping lists of places to see and stories that should be shared into a form you could use, I decided to begin this book with the beaches, as the first explorers and settlers did, and work my way up the rivers that flow through Alabama's land and history. My husband and I grew in ways we never expected and in some we wish we had not. As you travel along with us in these pages, you will not be able to resist Southern cooking any more than you can help melting in the warmth and charm of a Southern smile.

May you enjoy the discoveries I'm eager to share and find many of your own as you plan your *Weekend Getaways in Alabama.*

HOW TO USE THIS BOOK

Each getaway is designed to fit into a two- or three-day stay. For many, a weekend means Friday through Sunday. However, others take their getaways in the middle of the week when the crowds are smaller. With that in mind, references are often made to weekday hours, too.

Because interests and energy levels vary, I've tried to provide options for side trips or contrasting activities. For example, one member of the family might want to spend the day in a museum, but another would prefer being outdoors. Most areas offer opportunities to do both.

Alabama's climate and the abundance of rivers and lakes lure golfers and fishermen alike for well-known tournaments or personal pursuits. Golfers can pick up a comprehensive map and listing of state golf courses at most pro shops or at the **Edwin Watts Golf Shop** (see below).

Additional sources of information are the **Alabama Golf Association** and **Robert Trent Jones Reservations Coordinators.**

Fishing enthusiasts have several sources of information. A helpful Web site is Alabama State Owned and Operated Public Fishing Lakes, http://www.dcnr.state.al.us/agfd/lakes.html. *The Complete Alabama Fisherman,* by Mike Bolton, is a great guide book, and Mike's Web page gives hunting, fishing, and boating information for all outdoorspeople, including those who are physically challenged. His Web page is http://members.aol.com/aloutdoors/home.html. Note: Any person aged twelve years or older must have a valid Alabama fishing permit in possession to fish.

The national headquarters for B.A.S.S., the Bass Anglers Sportsman Society, is in Montgomery, and to receive information about tournaments, call (334) 272-9530 or see the Web page: http://www.bassmaster.com/misc/opus12.html. *Watching* bass-fishing tournaments is a sport, too, and this is free.

Known as *the* handbook for those who want to float the rivers and streams is *Alabama Canoe Rides and Float Trips,* by John H. Foshee.

Conservation Media Public Information is a source of information on hunting seasons, boating laws, and where to go fishing.

Hikers can get rails to trails information by writing Trail Manager, P.O. Box 112, Piedmont, AL 36272. Or call (256) 447-3363 or (256) 447-9007.

The Alabama Coastal Birding Guide (from the U.S. Fish & Wildlife Service) contains maps, a suggested trail, and native birds to watch for in specific areas.

An excellent informational booklet that should be carried along with the traveler is *Alabama's Black Heritage,* coordinated by Frances Smiley, Black Heritage Coordinator, Alabama Bureau of Tourism and Travel. To get one, call 1-800-ALABAMA (252-2262).

A summary of necessary information is included at the end of each chapter. Major annual events are listed at the end of chapters, too. For a much more detailed listing, *Alabama Calendar of Events* is available at any Alabama Welcome Center. Web pages listed were accessed and up to date at the time this book went to press. No attraction, accommodation, or shop has paid to be included.

To make the most of your getaway, call ahead to confirm days and hours an attraction or restaurant is open. On more than one occasion, we have found a restaurant closed to the public to accommodate a private celebration.

Throughout the state, chain restaurants, hotels, and motels cluster around interstate exits. These are easy to find and so I have concentrated on looking for the more secluded spots. One gift shop or small cafe in an area will take the traveler into a section that may invite hours of exploring. For that reason, this book of 36 weekends may become a guide to three times that many getaway adventures.

Bed and breakfasts offer several advantages. Innkeepers are knowledgeable and enthusiastic, and they want you to come back. A **Bed and Breakfast Association of Alabama** listing is available at the state tourism department at 1-800-ALABAMA (252-2262). Their Web site lists all members and has links to those with home pages.

Drive carefully while you enjoy Alabama. If your windshield wipers are on, your headlights should be on, too. And, of course, buckle up! These are state laws.

Did I miss anything? Undoubtedly. Alabama overflows with surprises. Allow for the fact that what seems noteworthy to me may not be of interest to everyone. My hope is that a few directions and suggestions will give even the most reluctant tourist an opportunity to make discoveries of his own. New events will debut, exciting restaurants and museums will open, and others will find what I overlooked. Let me know what you find. Send comments or updates to me at Pelican Publishing Company, P.O. Box 3110, Gretna, LA 70054.

Information:

1st Traveler's Choice, National Listing of Bed and Breakfast Inns.
                        Web site: www.virtualcities.com
Alabama Vacation Guide, call 1-800-ALABAMA (252-2262).
Alabama Automobile Association, 2400 Acton Rd., Birmingham, AL 35243. Mon.-Fri., 8 A.M.-6 P.M.; Sat. 9 A.M.-2 P.M.; drive-through windows open 24 hours for pickups, maps, and guides. (205) 978-7000; (800) 521-8224.   Web site: www.aaa.com
Alabama Bed and Breakfast Association
                        Web site: www.bbonline.com/al/bbaa
Alabama Bureau of Tourism and Travel, 401 Adams Ave., Montgomery, AL 36104. (800) 252-2262.
                        Web site: www.touralabama.org
Alabama Coastal Birding Guide, U.S. Fish & Wildlife Service. (800) 566-2453.
Alabama Department of Conservation and Natural Resources
                        Web site: www.dcnr.state.al.us
Alabama Forestry Commission
                        Web site: www.forestry.state.al.us/
Alabama Golf Association, (205) 979-1234.
                        Web site: www.bamagolf.com
Alabama Gulf Coast Convention and Visitors Bureau, Drawer 457, Gulf Shores, AL 36547. Mon.-Fri., 8 A.M.-5 P.M.; Sat.-Sun., 9 A.M.-5 P.M. (334) 974-1510; (800) 745-7263.
Alabama Highway Construction
        Web site: www.dot.state.al.us/bureau/construction/bulletin/
Alabama Highway Patrol, 322-4691; from a cellular phone: *47 or *HP.   Web site: www.dps.state.al.us
Alabama Mountain Lakes Tourist Association, 25062 North St., Mooresville, AL 35649. (256) 350-3500.
Alabama Restaurant Association, P.O. Box 241413, Montgomery, AL 36124. (334) 244-1320.
Alabama State Parks, 64 N. Union St., Montgomery, AL 36130. (800) 252-7277.   Web site: www.dcnr.state.al.us or www.vten.com
Alabama Weather
        Web site: www.weather.com/weather/us/states/alabama/

Conservation Media Public Information, (800) 262-3151.

Edwin Watts Golf Shops, 189 State Farm Pkwy., Birmingham, AL 35209. Mon.-Fri., 9:30 A.M.-6 P.M.; Sat., 9:30 A.M.-5 P.M. (205) 942-7083.
                                                    Web site: www.ewgs.com/bhm

Fishing Information
            Web site: www.dcnr.state.al.ul/agfd/lakes.html or
            hometown.aol.com/aloutdoors/home.html

Jefferson County Library Cooperative   Web site: www.jclc.org

National Forests in Alabama, 2946 Chestnut St., Montgomery, AL 36107. (334) 832-4470.

National Park Service   Web site: www.nps.gov/parklists/al/

Rails to Trails Information, P.O. Box 112, Piedmont, AL 36272. (256) 447-3363.

Rare Bird Alerts, Alabama Ornithological Society, (205) 987-2730.

Robert Trent Jones Golf Trail. For tee times at any RTJ course: (800) 949-4444.   Web site: golf.jsu.edu

Traveler Discount Guide   Web site: roomsaver.com

WEEKEND GETAWAYS
IN ALABAMA

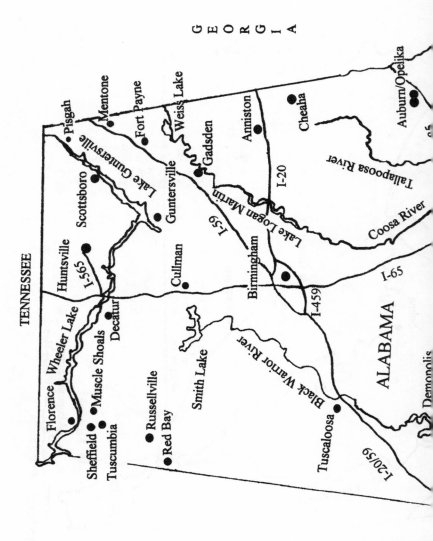

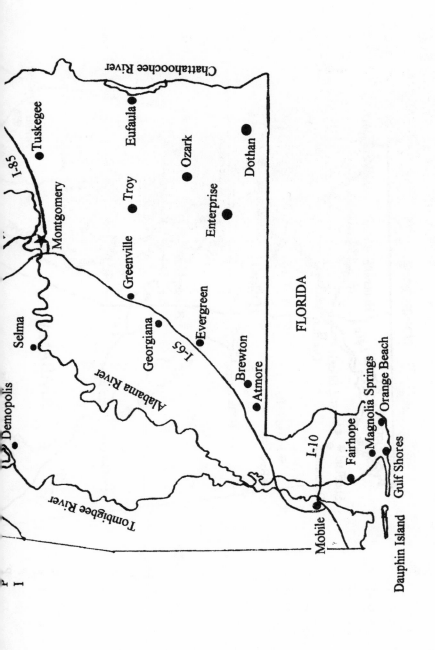

Pool, beach, and gulf waves. (Photo courtesy Charlene Wells)

1

WINTER AT THE BEACH

Winter fires blaze and snow falls softly on homes shuttered against the winter cold. Birds have migrated south months ago. Well, not all the birds. Shortly after the new year begins, a new kind of bird flies south. These are wise birds. Flocks of them land in parking lots, and their metal licensing bands identify their point of origin. Michigan. Indiana. Canada. These are the snowbirds who discovered the white beaches and off-season rates of Gulf Shores years ago. Thanks to their annual migrations, hotels, restaurants, and other places that thrive on tourists in the summer season are able to stay open and prosper. As you drive into Gulf Shores or Orange Beach, be alert for signs welcoming the snowbirds. You don't have to be part of the flock to share in the greetings from shop and restaurant owners, innkeepers, and nearby churches.

Gulf Shores and Orange Beach, which merge gracefully as you drive along Alabama 182, are known as Alabama's Gulf Coast or "the island." Bordered on the south by the Gulf of Mexico, on the east by Perdido Bay, on the north by the Intracoastal Waterway, and on the west by Mobile Bay, this 30,000-acre island has 32 miles of sparkling white beaches on the Gulf.

Gulf State Park Resort Hotel is so tuned in to winter vacationers that special events are offered all year, including a Valentine Package. What better place to celebrate a warm heart! All rooms in the motel open onto the beach. Sea oats wave in greeting, and the sounds of water breaking on the shore work magic on your jangled nerves the minute you toss your car keys on the bedside table. Lists of restaurants and other activities that have winter hours and are just a few miles away should be in your room or at the lodge desk, as close as a phone call while you slip out of those tight shoes. Eat at the lodge, always a great possibility, or scout the area. Jake's Steakhouse, known for steaks and seafood, is highly visible—no guessing about whether it's open during the winter months—and has two locations, one in Gulf Shores and one in Orange Beach. You'll spot other "open" signs as you drive the uncrowded streets.

Wherever you head for supper, know that breakfast at **Gulf State Park** is considered one of the best values for miles around. After a brisk early walk on the beach, you'll catch a whiff of sausage and bacon. Follow that tantalizing aroma to the lodge for a full Southern breakfast. "Full" means something other than how you feel when you leave. Scrambled eggs, fruit, sausage, bacon, grits, and rolls and biscuits, are what Southerners mean when they talk about a "full Southern breakfast."

Before you leave the lodge dining room for a day on the beach or for that good book you tossed into your suitcase, step into the gift shop. It's well stocked in case you packed in a hurry or need to have guilt gifts to take home. It seems almost wicked to have such a great time when your friends are at home slogging through slush.

Young families know about the less-crowded beaches in cooler months, and children are always somewhere laughing, flying kites, or building sand castles. January and February temperatures may be in the fifties and sixties, but with the warm sun on your back, you'll soon shed that sweater. For those who live close enough, a Friday night drive and Sunday afternoon ride home means an entire wonderful Saturday for strolling up and down the sandy stretches.

If you want to swim as well as walk on the beach, and you'd prefer warmer water, two other places to consider staying are the **Lighthouse Resort Motel** on East Beach Boulevard and **Quality Inn Beachside on the Gulf** on West Beach Boulevard. Both have indoor heated pools. The Quality Inn is also the location of a small restaurant and lounge, so the traveler who wants to park the car and forget about driving until the trip home will find this friendly place to be just right.

Budget-minded travelers can pick up coupon booklets at the **Gulf Shores Welcome Center** at the **Gulf Shores Convention and Visitors Bureau**, in the freebie racks at Shoney's in Foley, or the markets in any of the shopping strips along the highway. Coupons for dollars off lodging and other attractions could help you shave the expense of your winter getaway.

Maybe you'd like to have that old-time beach house feeling but be pampered at the same time. The **Original Romar House** lives up to its listing as "A Seaside Bed and Breakfast Inn." The genial manager, Darrell Finley, showed me through Alabama's first gulfside B&B, and I mentally picked out the spot I would claim, a hammock just beyond the cozy sitting area and the famous Purple Parrot Bar. Would it ever be too chilly to curl up with a good book in that spot? Built in 1924, this sturdy house has withstood a number of hurricanes and was purchased by today's owner, Jerry Gilbreath, after Hurricane Frederick. He vacationed there from 1980 until 1991, when bed and breakfast fever struck and he decided to share this serenity with others.

Gilbreath and Finley combined talents to give each of the five rooms, a suite, and the guest cottage an individual personality. Stained-glass windows and antiques compete with the view of the beach at its best—and that's any time you are there. Leave the children and pets at home if you decide to reserve a room at the Romar. The only sounds you will hear in the morning are the gulls searching for a bit of breakfast—and you won't have to search for yours! Finley, who has won awards for his hospitality, will see that your day at the beach begins with a satisfied appetite.

Golf is always great at the beach, due to the moderate climate. Opportunities for the golfer will only increase as future course development is planned. **Gulf State Park Golf Course** on Alabama 35 is well-maintained and is popular with golfers of all skill levels. **Kiva Dunes Country Club** is easy to find. **Orange Beach Golf Course** is on Canal Road. Take Alabama 182 to Alabama 161 and Canal Road is on your right.

If a souvenir from the beach is something you'd like to make yourself, consider a visit to basket weaver Esther Hellmich at **Hellmich's Hampers.** Call her first to find out how you can participate in one of her classes, but be prepared to take lunch and spend most of the day. If you'd rather purchase one of Mrs. Hellmich's own artistically crafted baskets and learn a little about the history and art of basket weaving, a shorter time will do. A retired fifth-grade teacher, Mrs. Helmich holds classes for enthusiastic and willing students on the enclosed front porch of her home. This is a true cottage industry. The artist herself and the chance to learn a craft under her guidance make this a place to keep in mind for each trip to the beach.

Esther Hellmich, basket weaver. (Photo by Neal Broerman)

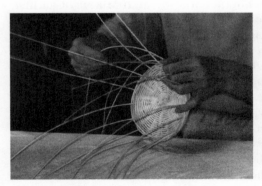

Hands of Esther Hellmich, basket weaver.
(Photo by Neal Broerman)

Sculpture by Steven Burrow. (Photo courtesy Chris Keifer)

When your appetite alarm sounds, if you are at **Hellmich's Hampers,** you are not far from the **Back Porch Seafood and Oyster House,** which has indoor or outdoor porch dining and overlooks **Bear Point Marina.** In this pleasant spot, sandwich platters for lunch will beat peanut butter and jelly any day. Another choice is **Mikee's Seafood,** which is two blocks east of Alabama 59. The dark, cool interior makes a nice contrast to the reflections of a bright beach and water, and the service and seafood will suit your lunch or dinner interests.

Steven Burrow, a Gulf Shores artist, potter, and sculptor, says the beach has its own four seasons: the summer tourist season, which ends with one quarter of a million people attending the **Shrimp Festival;** a lull from mid-October to mid-December; arrival of the Snow Birds; and Spring Break. Then the cycle begins again.

Steven and his wife, Dee, also an artist, own **Sea Oat Studio.** Dee teaches art to local children and Steven digs his own clay in favorite places on the island and throws pots in the back of the family car port. A piece my husband and I especially admired was a lidded decorative pot that Steven calls a round form with dolphins. Finished work is available at the studio as well as at many local gift shops such as **Seacrets at Zeke's Landing** on Orange Beach Boulevard. You are not far from **Sea Oat Studio** after your meal at **Mikee's.** Call first, however, as Steven may be out digging clay.

When it's time to think about eating again, the strip along Alabama 182 is lined with choices. **Hazel's Family Restaurant** is part of a group of locally owned restaurants, and the waitresses seem especially helpful to parents with young children. Another good choice is **Desoto's Seafood Kitchen,** in the heart of Gulf Shores. This is also a family restaurant on everybody's list for lunch or dinner at least once during a beach getaway. Impromptu reunions happen here when you spot a friend and family two tables away. And you thought you were the only one who knew about this place!

I've saved **Dauphin Island** for a later getaway, but an event that takes place there in early January should be noted. **"Fury on the Gulf"** at **Fort Gaines Historic Site** gives visitors a spine-tingling opportunity to go back over 140 years in time to the Civil War and the **Battle of Mobile Bay,** when the Union won what many consider the most important Civil War action in the state. You've probably used Admiral Farragut's famous quote, "Damn the torpedoes! Full steam ahead!" You'll have to fight your own battle, however, when it's time to load the car and leave the beach behind.

Why is the sun always so bright on the day you go home?

Area Code: (334)

Getting There:

Gulf Shores can be easily reached from Interstate 65 or Interstate 10. From Interstate 65, take Exit 37. For a short distance it will be Alabama 287 and become U. S. 31 and Alabama 59—Gulf Shores Parkway. From Interstate 10, take Exit 44 to Alabama 59—Gulf Shores Parkway. The Parkway crosses the Intracoastal Waterway as you enter Gulf Shores and crosses Alabama 180 (Fort Morgan Parkway). It ends at the beach. Turn left to go to Orange Beach or Gulf State Park. Turn right to the heart of Gulf Shores.

Major airlines serve Pensacola Regional Airport, a 45-minute drive from Orange Beach, and the Mobile airport, which is one hour from Gulf Shores.

Where and When:

Fort Gaines Historic Site, 51 Bienville Boulevard, Dauphin Island, AL 36528. Open daily, summer, 9 A.M.-6 P.M.; winter, 9 A.M.-5 P.M. 861-6992.   Web site: www.dauphine.net

Gulf State Park Golf Course, Alabama 35, Gulf Shores, AL 36547. 948-4853; (800) 544-4853.

Hellmich's Hampers, 5438 Mobile Avenue, Gulf Shores, AL 36561. Mon.-Wed., Fri.-Sat., 9 A.M.-5 P.M. 981-3226.

Kiva Dunes Country Club, Plantation Road, Gulf Shores, AL 35999. 540-7000.

Orange Beach Golf Course, Canal Road, Orange Beach, AL 36561. 981-3279.

Sea Oat Studio, 1009 E. Canal Road, Gulf Shores, AL 36547. Open by appointment or by chance. 968-6744.

Seacrets at Zeke's Landing, 26619 Perdido Beach Boulevard, Orange Beach, AL 36561. Daily, 9 A.M.-9 P.M. 981-5600.

Transportation:

The Pleasure Island Trolley (PIT). Purchase PIT tokens at Gulf Shores City Hall or Orange Beach City Hall, or local businesses, hotels, and restaurants. PIT runs in Orange Beach only during winter months.

Information:

Orange Beach Fishing Association, P.O. Box 1202, Orange Beach, AL 36561. 981-2300.

Alabama Gulf Coast Convention and Visitors Bureau, Drawer 457, Gulf Shores, AL 36547. Mon.-Fri., 8 A.M.-5 P.M.; Sat.-Sun., 9 A.M.-5 P.M. 974-1510; (800) 745-7263.

Foley Convention and Visitors Bureau, P. O. Box 448, Foley, AL 36536. 943-1200.   Web site: www.foleycvb.com
Gulf Coast Golf Planner, Gulf Shores/Orange Beach, AL 36547. (877) 475-1530.   Web site: www.golfgulfshores.com or www.forebettergolf.com
Gulf Shores Island Wide Activities, P.O. Box 437, Gulf Shores, AL 36547. 948-4853, (800) 544-4853.
                    Web site: www.gulfshores.com/things_to_do/
South Baldwin Chamber of Commerce, P. O. Box 1117, Foley, AL 36536. 943-3291.   Web site: www.southbaldwinchamber.com
Accommodations:
The Alabama Bed and Breakfast Association
                    Web site: www.bbonline.com/al/
Gulf State Park Resort Hotel, Alabama 182 E, Gulf Shores, AL 36547. 948-4853; (800) 544-4853.
Lighthouse Resort Motel, 455 E. Beach Boulevard, Gulf Shores, AL 36547. 948-6188.
Original Romar House, 23500 Perdido Beach Blvd., Orange Beach, AL 36561. 974-1625; (800) 487-6627.
                    Web site: www.bbonline.com/al/romarhouse
Quality Inn BeachSide on the Gulf, 931 W. Beach Boulevard, Gulf Shores, AL 36547. (800) 844-6913..
Restaurants:
Back Porch Seafood and Oyster House, 5749 Bay La Launch Avenue, Orange Beach, AL 36561. Sun.-Thurs., 11 A.M.-10 P.M.; Fri.-Sat., 11 A.M.-11 P.M. 981-2225.
DeSoto's Seafood Kitchen, 138 W. First Avenue, Gulf Shores, AL 36547. Winter daily, 11 A.M.-9 P.M.; Summer daily, 11 A.M.-10 P.M. 948-7294.
Hazel's Family Restaurant, 25311 Perdido Beach Boulevard, Orange Beach, AL 36547. Winter daily, 6 A.M.-7 P.M.; Summer daily 6 A.M.-9 P.M. 981-4628.
Jake's Steakhouse, Alabama 59, Gulf Shores, AL 36547. Mon.-Thurs., 10:30 A.M.-9 P.M.; Fri.-Sat., 10:30 A.M.-10 P.M.; Sun., 11 A.M.-9 P.M. 968-2777.
Jake's Steakhouse, Alabama 182, Orange Beach, AL 36561. Mon.-Thurs., 10:30 A.M.-9 P.M.; Fri.-Sat., 10:30 A.M.-10 P.M. 968-2777.
Mikee's Seafood, 201 E. 2nd Avenue & First Street, Gulf Shores, AL 36547. Daily, 11 A.M.-11 P.M. 948-6452.
Major Annual Events:
"Fury on the Gulf", Historic Fort Gaines, Dauphin Island. 861-6992.

Seagulls, Mobile Bay. (Photo by Neal Broerman)

2

WARMING UP

Spring comes to Alabama beaches a little differently than it comes to the roadsides and gardens in other parts of the state. In towns along the Coosa and Cahaba Rivers, and in backyards just off Interstate 65 and U.S. 280, green shoots break through the earth. Buds turn into blossoms in a chorus of color and a profusion of fragrances. In **Gulf Shores** and **Orange Beach**, however, boarded-up ice cream stores open doors to the sun. Fresh breezes blow through the souvenir shops and painted T-shirt stands. The great shark with his mouth wide open looked a little out of place in an empty parking lot, but spring ushers in families and other lucky ones who kept their eyes on the calendar and their sun screen and beach towels ready for traveling. The shark looks as if he's smiling again. Spring just before the tides of student spring breakers arrive is a great time to plan a getaway to the Gulf.

All the restaurants and places to stay you read about in "Winter at the Beach" are still there for you to enjoy. Lodging rates will inch up a bit, but summer season rates do not begin to appear until the first spring break weekend, usually in early March. What you discover in this chapter will add to your list of must-do's. It's time to practice the sandy feet shuffle, shaking sand from shoes before climbing in the car.

It will take a little adventuring off the main road through Gulf Shores, but if you want to stay at a place you won't soon forget, take County Road 6 to the **Oar House Riverside Inn.** George and Debbie Rudolph run the inn and the **Oar House Restaurant**, a restaurant and motel decorated with fun and whimsy. The food is fantastic and plentiful. Ask your waiter if you can share an entrée. Some restaurants charge a "split" fee for this; others do not. In many generous restaurants, it can ease your guilty conscience and your waistband to pay the split fee and go halves with your dinner partner. If you elect to package leftovers in a to-go box, your room at the inn is equipped with a refrigerator and microwave.

Put a boat in your future if the weather is smiling on you when the new day begins. More than 100 boats make up the charter fishing fleet in Gulf Shores and Orange Beach, and they offer trolling, bottom fishing, back bay, sport, fly, and light tackle fishing. To begin your fishing plans, write, call, or e-mail for the Orange Beach Fishing Association's Charter Boat Directory. It's free and can be picked up at welcome centers, the **Alabama Gulf Coast Convention and Visitors Bureau,** and many hotels and stores that have racks of freebies advertising area attractions.

Charters can be booked for half-day or full-day trips. On a charter you will NOT need an Alabama state fishing license. Everywhere else you drop a line, that fishing license needs to be tucked into a pocket. For freshwater fishing, the **Bon Secour River** is not far from your Riverside Inn pillow, and the 700-acre **Lake Shelby** and 395,000 acres of other watery hiding places for speckled trout, black and striped bass, bream, and red drum keep weekend anglers coming back for more. At the **Gulf State Park**'s fishing pier, which allows you to stroll out 824 feet into the Gulf and still keep your boots dry, fishermen can rent bait, tackle, and supplies.

Would another kind of boat tour suit you better? A little preparation will get you ready to sail the *Daedalus*, a 50-foot, 23-ton United States Coast Guard-certified sailboat. Bring lunch or favorite snacks, an ice chest, swim suit and towel, sunscreen and mosquito repellent, camera, and binoculars. Add plenty of curiosity about dolphins and the wildlife you will be able to wade close to if Captain Fred tells you it's safe. There is a bathroom on board, and families love the three-hour trip on the back bays to dolphin habitats.

The *Daedalus* is in Elberta. To go there from the Oar House, take Highway 59 north to Lambert's, go right on Baldwin County Road 20, and turn right on Baldwin County Road 95 to South Bayou Drive.

Before or after your trip aboard the *Daedalus,* see the pitcher plants, insect-eating Venus flytraps, butterflies breaking free of their chrysalises, and the resident 11-foot alligator that keeps visitors looking where they step at the **Biophilia Nature Center,** native nursery, and bookstore. Since late 1991 Captain Fred Saas, his wife, research biologist Carol Lovell-Saas, and others have been working to restore the swamp, pitcher plant bog, forests, and wildflower meadows of the 20-acre center with hundreds of southeastern native species. Their Web site and a newsletter keep enthusiasts informed. An hour at the Biophilia may not be enough.

For dinner you have another choice on County Road 6, just past the Oar House, at the **Fish Camp Restaurant.**

The road rambles, but you'll see signs and lights. Sunday can begin with packing up and heading for the weekend brunch at **Perdido Pass Restaurant.** They say it is "The Best on the Island." Make your own test of that confident claim and walk off the calories with a hike on the beach or in **Bon Secour National Wildlife Refuge.** Wear your favorite scent of mosquito repellent and enter a world trimmed in Spanish moss. This refuge covers 6,200 acres, and more than two miles of beach front can be reached from the nature trails. Follow the path that opens up to the lagoon and continues on to the beach. Carry your camera. For help planning your hike, stop by the ranger's office on Ft. Morgan Road. Maps and brochures are placed outside in case a real person is not available.

Take a hike or bike! More than 36 miles of bike paths thread a scented and scenic path throughout the Gulf Shores and Orange Beach area. Pick up a map at a welcome center.

Whenever it's time to stop for lunch or dinner, it's a good time to head for **Wolf Bay Lodge,** owned by Charlie and Sandy Bretz. Take 59 toward Foley, turn right at Lambert's, and go over two small bridges. Stay on County Road 20, and at the gas station take a right. You'll soon see signs for Wolf Bay. If you go for dinner, go between 5 P.M. and 6 P.M. After 7 P.M. there is a wait. We went there for lunch and the first door we came to was locked. The recommendation for this seafood restaurant was so strong that we were not about to give up easily. Besides, the parking lot overlooking the bay was so full we knew a great meal was being served somewhere. A brisk walk around the building brought us to another door and the unmistakable aromatic invitation of fish frying. Come on in! Our taste buds soon told us why this out-of-the-way place is so popular among the locals. No credit cards are accepted here. If you don't have enough cash, don't leave. It would be worth washing dishes to enjoy the seafood platter.

Yes, earlier I did preface the list of things to see and do with *"if"* the weather is smiling on you this weekend. What if it drizzles all day Saturday? No need to be gloomy. Fishermen still cast their lines from the shore, so the fish must not care if it's raining. However, for people who do care, hop on the **Pleasure Island Trolley** (PIT) and see what you can see. Pick up a map and list of designated stops at most hotels or restaurants and plan your tour. Stand by Trolley Stop signs to board. Sometimes you can get off the trolley earlier than at a set stop. This depends on the driver, who has to pay attention to the traffic. Two trolleys operate in Gulf Shores and two run in Orange Beach, looping routes 20-30 minutes behind each other. The exchange point between routes is at the Gulf State Park Resort. The route change will cost an additional 50¢ or PIT token. For the money, this is one of the least-expensive ways to enjoy a beach vacation. Well, it's inexpensive if you are able to resist stopping in the gift shops placed far enough off the main street that you have to know where to hunt or you'll miss them.

Bayou Village is a boardwalk of small shops and a few places to pick up nibbles or a cool drink. Enjoy your snack while you look over the end deck railing and wonder why it's called an alligator lookout. For more substantial fare, the **Original Oyster House** is located at the other end of the row of shops, and many regular beachgoers make this restaurant part of their vacation routine. Travel east toward Florida on Perdido Beach Boulevard (Highway 182) and look for **Tootie Green's Yellow Broom.** Once you finish touring Tootie's wares, you'll find it absolutely necessary to step into the other gift shops along the short side drive.

Whether you travel up Perdido Beach as far as San Roc Cay for lunch or to shop, this new area will make itself a part of any weekend you spend at the beach. At the **San Roc Cay Delicatezza International Grocery,** which fronts on Perdido Beach Boulevard, we bought ham-and-cheese wraps and raspberry tea for a lunch to take with us. While we waited for our sandwiches, a walk through the back sidewalks and courtyards convinced us we'd come back to try out other shops and eat lunch or dinner at **Café Grazie** or **Louisiana Lagniappe**. Either could be the setting for a special night out.

Turn around and head away from the bridge, but don't miss **Secrecy** on your right, at the Perdido Pass Building. Pat Wright, a transplant from Ohio, shared the secrets of three gift shops on the island, all owned by Linda St. Charles and each with its own personality. Secrecy is a feast for the collector. Swarovski crystal, Limoges boxes, and Margaret Furlong Ornaments sparkle atop the glass shelves. Farther down the boulevard, but still on the right, **Seacrets at Zeke's Landing**—and this is another gift shop set back from the highway—features condo accessories, nautical gifts, and T-shirts. **St. Charles Place,** in the Delchamps Shopping Center, is easier to find and offers gifts and cards with a lighter touch.

After you leave Seacrets, be sure to stop by **Page and Palette** and pick up a book for the trip home—or to bring you back to that deck rocker overlooking the changing colors of a whispering sea.

Area Code: (334)

Getting There:

Gulf Shores can be easily reached from Interstate 65 or Interstate 10. From Interstate 65, take Exit 37. For a short distance it will be Alabama 287 and become U. S. 31 and Alabama 59-Gulf Shores Parkway. From Interstate 10, take Exit 44 to Alabama 59-Gulf Shores Parkway. The Parkway crosses the Intracoastal Waterway as you enter Gulf Shores and crosses Alabama 180 (Fort Morgan Parkway). It ends at the beach. Turn left to go to Orange Beach or Gulf State Park. Turn right to the heart of Gulf Shores.

Major airlines serve Pensacola Regional Airport, a 45 minute drive from Orange Beach, and the Mobile airport, which is one hour from Gulf Shores.

Where and When:

Bayou Village, U. S. 98, Gulf Shores, AL.

Biophilia Nature Center, 12695 Baldwin County Road 95, Elberta, AL 36530. 987-1200. Admission.
                                    Web site: www.gulftel.net/daedalus

Bon Secour National Wildlife Refuge, 12295 Alabama 180, Gulf Shores, AL 36547. 540-7720.   Web site: www.fws.gov/~r4eao

Seacrets at Zeke's Landing, 26619 Perdido Beach Boulevard, Orange Beach, AL 36561. Daily, 9 A.M.-9 P.M. 981-5600.

Secrecy, Perdido Pass Bldg. at Alabama Point, Orange Beach, AL 36561. Daily, 10 A.M.-9 P.M. 981-5500.

St. Charles Place, 25241 Perdido Beach Boulevard, Orange Beach, AL 36561. Daily, 9 A.M.-9 P.M. 981-6400.

Tootie Green's Yellow Broom, 25122 Perdido Beach Boulevard, Orange Beach, AL 36561. 981-7377.

Page and Palette, 26651 Perdido Beach Boulevard, Orange Beach, AL 36561. Open daily. 981-2073.

Transportation:
The Pleasure Island Trolley (PIT). Sun.-Thurs., 9 A.M.-10 P.M.; Fri.-Sat., 9 A.M.-midnight (Runs in Orange Beach only during winter months). 968-2425.

Information:
Alabama Gulf Coast Convention and Visitors Bureau, Drawer 457, Gulf Shores, AL 36547. Mon.-Fri., 8 A.M.-5 P.M.; Sat.-Sun, 9 A.M.-5 P.M. 974-1510; (800) 745-7263.
Fishing Information, Orange Beach.
Web site: www.orangebeach.com
Foley Convention and Visitors Bureau, P. O. Box 448, Foley, AL 36536. 943-1200.   Web site: www.foleycvb.com
Gulf Shores Island Wide Activities, P.O. Box 437, Gulf Shores, AL 36547. 948-4853; (800) 544-4853.
Web site: www.gulfshores.com/things_to_do/
South Baldwin Chamber of Commerce, P. O. Box 1117, Foley, AL 36536. 943-3291.   Web site: www.southbaldwinchamber.com

Guide Services:
Daedalus Sail Boat, 6816 S. Bayou Dr., Elberta, AL 36530. 987-1228
Web site: www.gulftel.net/daedalus

Accommodations:
The Alabama Bed & Breakfast Association
Web site: www.bbonline.com/al/
Gulf State Park Resort Hotel, Alabama 182 E, Gulf Shores, AL 36547. 948-4853; (800) 544-4853.
Lighthouse Resort Motel, 455 E. Beach Boulevard, Gulf Shores, AL 36547. 948-6188.
Oar House Riverside Inn, 5587 Baldwin County Road 6, Gulf Shores, AL 36542. 967-7478.
Quality Inn BeachSide on the Gulf, 931 W. Beach Boulevard, Gulf Shores, AL 36547. (800) 844-6913.
Romar House, 23500 Perdido Beach Boulevard, Orange Beach, AL 36561. 974-1625; (800) 487-6627.
Web site: www.bbonline.com/al/romarhouse

Restaurants:
Café Grazie, 27267 Perdido Beach Boulevard, Orange Beach, AL 36561. Sun.-Thurs., 5 P.M.-9:30 P.M.; Fri.-Sat., 5 P.M.-10:30 P.M. 981-8466.
Fish Camp Restaurant, 4297 Baldwin County Road 6, Gulf Shores, AL 36542. Daily, from 11 A.M. 968-2267.

Louisiana Lagniappe, 27267 Perdido Beach Boulevard, Orange Beach, AL 36561. Sun.-Thurs., 5 P.M.-9:30 P.M.; Fri.-Sat., 5 P.M.-10:30 P.M. 981-2258.

Oar House Restaurant, 5587 Baldwin County Road 6, Gulf Shores, AL 36542. Tue.-Sat., 11 A.M.-9 P.M.; Sun., 5 P.M.-9 P.M. 967-2422.

Original Oyster House, Bayou Village, Gulf Shores, AL. Sun.-Thurs., 11 A.M.-10 P.M.; Fri.-Sat., 11 A.M.-11 P.M. 948-2445.

Perdido Pass Restaurant, 27501 Perdido Beach Boulevard, Orange Beach, AL 36561. Daily lunch, 11 A.M.-4 P.M.; Brunch, Sat.-Sun., 11 A.M.-2 P.M. 981-6312.

San Roc Cay Delicatezza International Grocery, 27267 Perdido Beach Boulevard, Orange Beach, AL 36561. Winter, Sun.-Thurs., 8 A.M.-8 P.M.; Fri.-Sat., 8 A.M.-9 P.M.; Summer, daily, 7 A.M.-10 P.M.

Wolf Bay Lodge, 9050 Pinewood Ave., Elberta, AL 36530. Tue.-Thurs., 11 A.M.-9 P.M.; Fri.-Sat., 11 A.M.-10 P.M.; Sun., noon-8 P.M. 987-5129.

Shark store entrance. (Photo by Neal Broerman)

3

PERFECTLY
PERFECT

Spring or fall at an Alabama beach comes close to perfection. Under cloudless skies, turquoise water shimmers from emerald to amethyst, washing the sand with gentle waves. The voice of the sea is a siren song, calling the weary weekender to leave real time behind. April and May, tucked in between bustling spring break and the humming summer season, are great months for stealing a few days to travel to the beach. Fall is a fine time to be there, too, but keep your eyes on the weather channel and plan with the idea of changing your direction if a tropical disturbance flexes its muscles. Summer? Everything mentioned in these first three chapters will be open and booming from June through early August. However, to plan a weekend at the beach in the summer, call before you pack. During the summer months, many rental properties require at least a one-week commitment.

You might get lucky and find a motel or hotel with room for a consecutive Friday and Saturday or a nontraditional weekend of two days in the middle of the week, but let your fingers do the walking and use the phone to make reservations in advance. If you are one who enjoys living on the edge, try walking up to a beach motel in July and asking for a room. The chances of getting one are slim.

If you haven't been to Gulf Shores in the summer, imagine a carnival and set it spinning in a sandy setting. Miniature golf, water slides, ferris wheels, arcades—all vie for your attention along the main roads. Dozens of delicious aromas beg the traveler to follow them. Tropical department stores offer an amazing variety of air-brushed T-shirts and festive beach towels. You'll understand immediately why the whole area is called Pleasure Island. However, if you want to spend your weekend getaway with fewer people and a more flexible choice of places to stay, head for the beach before Memorial Day or after the middle of August.

To help you get the most out of a stolen spring or fall weekend, I've crammed a lot of activities into this chapter. I don't want you to miss anything, but please don't forget that the real reason for a beach weekend is to recover from busy-ness. What looks fine on paper may not translate into the time and energy you have available. If you pack shorts and long pants, a sweater and face-shading hat, your favorite sneakers, and a collection of comfortable T-shirts, you'll have plenty to wear. Add insect repellant, a thirsty beach towel, and take off.

On Friday night, if you are coming from the north and hunger for that first seafood dinner, stop at **Street's Seafood Restaurant** in **Bay Minette** for a buffet that will turn "Are we there yet?" to a definite "Almost" answer. Eugene Overstreet and his six sisters, Joyce, Sharon, Carrie, Carolyn, Rebie, and Linda, oversee Street's.

For your place to stay, the Winfield Resort Properties offer excellent choices on the edge of Orange Beach: a **Windemere Condominiums & Conference Center** right on the beach (it still smells new!) or the **Hampton Inn Orange Beach,** next door on Orange Beach Boulevard (Highway 182). Except under certain circumstances, the condominium must be rented for a minimum number of nights, and this may suit your plans. However, staying only one night gives you the option of planning a stay in a second setting. But first things, first. If you haven't eaten yet and before you collapse from the drive, enjoy a relaxing supper at **Calypso Fish Grille and Market** or **Mango's on the Island,** at **Orange Beach Marina.** They are close enough together that you can park and then decide. However, Mango's suggests calling for reservations.

To find the Orange Beach Marina, go toward Florida on Alabama 182 to Alabama 161. Turn left on Alabama 161 and then turn right again on Marina Road. The marina will be on your left.

Saturday dawns slowly. Along with the light tiptoeing into your dreams comes the realization that you have an entire day ahead to loaf around or pick and choose from a list of things to do.

For the golfer in the family, courses in Gulf Shores are open to the public, but here are a couple of suggestions to add to your growing

Sailing on Mobile Bay. (Photo courtesy Alabama Bureau of Tourism & Travel)

list of Southern links: **Gulf Links Golf Club** in nearby Foley and **Peninsula Golf and Racquet Club.** Peninsula not only has fine golf available, but it also has a fitness center on site. (Keep this in mind for future visits!)

Eco-tourism is the current buzzword, and birding has become a popular sport. Add the adventure of exploring and you can't spend a better morning than taking a **Caribiana Birding Cruise** on Perdido Bay with Captain Joanne McDonough. Go early in the day. Afternoons tend to get stormy when the weather is hot.

Perdido Bay is home to dolphins that feed off the mullet, and the small inlets offer access to diversity. The captain is a naturalist who enjoys sharing her knowledge and enthusiasm with children and families. She and her husband design and sell the boats available for her personally-conducted cruises—although during busy times you may get a captain personally chosen by this intrepid seeker of small sea creatures. Nothing has been spared in making your introduction to ecosystems a memory you'll want to re-create.

Captain McDonough's boat is unusual, and the cruise offers full service: binoculars, sunscreen, and lunch if the adventurer requests it. What is unusual about the Caribiana coastal yachts is the upswept bow, which even at high speeds slices smoothly through the waves and keeps pilot and passengers dry. A choice of birding tours gives the seeking environmentalist a closeness to a variety of wading birds, migratory birds, raptors, and communities of nesting egrets, great blue herons, pelicans, and little green herons. Fees vary with the length and needs of each planned trip.

After you get your land legs back, head for lunch in Foley. **Sweetie Pies** has daily lunch specials and old-fashioned deli sandwiches, but the sweet in its name is found in the tantalizing bakery. Save room.

Next, stretch your legs for an afternoon of shopping and sightseeing. You could get started on both lunch and antiquing at the **Gift Horse Restaurant & Antiques,** which feeds the body and senses. Another lunch spot that serves such substantial portions that you may want to think about sharing an order is **Amelia's Gourmet Deli** in Orange Blossom Square. Everything is homemade, Southern, and delicious.

After lunch, tour the **Holmes Medical Museum,** which is upstairs over the **Baldwin County Museum of Art** and down the street from the Gift Horse. All are on West Laurel Avenue, which is also Highway 98. From 1936 to 1958 a hospital stood on the spot now occupied by the museum. See the operating suite, private patient rooms, male and female wardrooms, and x-ray room equipped to show how medicine was practiced in the early half of this century in rural Baldwin County.

By now you are surely ready to eat again. Stop by **Stacey Rexall Drugs & Olde Tyme Soda Fountain.** The furnishings are 1920, but the kids watching the train above their heads as it circles the store from the soda fountain to the pharmacy are all ages. On a warm day you'll have to get in line to place your order, so make it worth the wait. Chat with the children or the retirees or the lucky people who live there. Enjoy a sundae or a banana split. Sure, you could get an ice cream cone, but you're on a short vacation, so splurge!

In contrast with the small gift shops in the heart of Foley is a great complex of bargain-stuffed buildings just off the highway leading into town, the **Riviera Center.** More than 100 outlet stores carry favorite designer and brand names. This is a great place for a rainy day, because most of the walkways are covered.

After so much walking, looking, buying, and package lugging, you'll be ready for a hearty supper at **Lambert's Café,** home of the throwed rolls. It would spoil the fun to tell you about those throwed rolls, so I'll leave it at that. Know that you are in for a feast of food and hilarity in the midst of décor that defies description.

Sunday morning church services are held across the island. Pick up one of the many beach guides in restaurants, motels, and shops to see a listing. If your weekend at the beach falls between Mother's Day and Labor Day, you can attend the beachside services sponsored by Foley United Methodist Church, east of the Gulf State Park Pavilion. People of all denominations, from across the country and out of the country, too, have been gathering among the dunes since 1951. The **Galilean Beach Service** is early—7:30 A.M.—but you can come in beach attire. Pull on a sweater and jeans and you'll be comfortable enough to go from the service to the **Gulf State Park Lodge** for brunch. I've mentioned this in an earlier chapter. Brunch at the lodge is a good start to your day, no matter what the season.

After breakfast head for **Fort Morgan** and stop at the **Shellbanks Southern Baptist Church,** which is built near the location of **Achuse,** the first Indian village in America visited by a white man. The white man was one of De Soto's officers, Admiral Maldonado. We do not know what kind of impression he made.

While you are on Fort Morgan Parkway, you can end your beach weekend with a hike into **Bon Secour National Wildlife Refuge.** This is one of over 500 refuges in the National Wildlife Refuge System, which is administered by the U.S. Fish and Wildlife Service. Stop at the kiosk near the parking lot for trail information and bird cards, or drive west to the end of the peninsula on the mouth of Mobile Bay and visit **Fort Morgan,** which was constructed during the War of 1812 between the United States and England. Fort Morgan Parkway is really a winding country road that offers its own opportunities to explore. Take a few side roads and make a list of the places you want to visit the next time you come. A beach weekend always ends with thoughts of "next time."

Area Code: (334)

Getting There:

Gulf Shores can be easily reached from Interstate 65 or Interstate 10. From Interstate 65, take Exit 37. For a short distance it will be Alabama 287 and become U.S. 31 and Alabama 59-Gulf Shores Parkway. From Interstate 10, take Exit 44 to Alabama 59-Gulf Shores Parkway. The Parkway crosses the Intracoastal Waterway as you enter Gulf Shores and crosses Alabama 180 (Fort Morgan Parkway). It ends at the beach. Turn left to go to Orange Beach or Gulf State Park. Turn right to the heart of Gulf Shores.

Major airlines serve Pensacola Regional Airport, a 45-minute drive from Orange Beach and the Mobile airport, which is one hour from Gulf Shores.

Where and When:

Many hotels, motels, and condominium rental groups offer golf packages at area courses. Call 1-800-SAND.

Web site: www.golfgulfshores.com

Baldwin County Museum of Art, 111 W. Laurel Ave., Foley, AL 36535. Tue.-Sat., 10 A.M.-4 P.M. 979-1818.

Bon Secour National Wildlife Refuge, 12295 Alabama 180, Gulf Shores, AL 36547. 540-7720.   Web site: www.fws.gov/~r4eao

Fort Morgan, 51 Alabama 180 W (Ft. Morgan Pkwy.), Gulf Shores, AL 36542. Daily, 9 A.M.-5 P.M. 540-7125. Admission.

Gulf Links Golf Club, 3901 S. McKenzie Street, Foley, AL 36535. 970-1441.

Gulf State Park Golf Course, Alabama 35, Gulf Shores, AL 36547. 948-4853; (800) 544-4853.

Holmes Medical Museum, 111 W. Laurel Ave., Foley, AL 36535. Tue.-Sat., 10 A.M.-4 P.M. 979-1818.

Peninsula Golf and Racquet Club, Peninsula Boulevard, Gulf Shores, AL 36542. 968-8009; (800) 391-8009.

Riviera Center, Alabama 59, Foley.

Shellbanks Southern Baptist Church, Fort Morgan Road, Gulf Shores, AL. Sunday service at 9:30 A.M.

South Baldwin Community Theatre, 2022 W. Second Ave., Gulf Shores, AL 36542. 968-6721.   Web site: www.sbct.com

Stacey Rexall Drugs & Old Tyme Soda Fountain, 121 W. Laurel Ave., Foley, AL 36535. Mon.-Fri., 8 A.M.-6 P.M.; Sat., 9 A.M.-6 P.M. 943-7191.

Information:

Foley Convention and Visitors Bureau, P. O. Box 448, Foley, AL 36536. 943-1200.   Web site: www.foleycvb.com

Gulf Coast Convention and Visitor Bureau, Gulf Shores, AL 36547. (800) 745-7263.

Gulf Coast Golf Planner, Gulf Shores/Orange Beach. (877) 475-1530.   Web site: www.golfgulfshores.com or www.forebettergolf.com

Gulf Shores Island Wide Activities, P.O. Box 437, Gulf Shores, AL 36547. 948-4853; (800) 544-4853.

Web site: www.gulfshores.com/things_to_do/

South Baldwin Chamber of Commerce, P. O. Box 1117, Foley, AL 36536. 943-3291.   Web site: www.southbaldwinchamber.com
Guide Services:
Caribiana Birding Cruise, Orange Beach. 981-4442; (888) 2034883.   Web site: www.caribiana.com
Accommodations:
The Alabama Bed & Breakfast Association.
     Web site: www.bbonline.com/al/bbaa
Hampton Inn Orange Beach, 22988 Perdido Beach Boulevard, Orange Beach, AL 36561. 974-1598; (800) 981-6242.
Windemere Condominiums & Conference Center, P.O. Box 2933, Orange Beach, AL 36561. 974-1120; (888) 974-1120.
     Web site: www.winfieldresorts.com
Restaurants:
Amelia's Gourmet Deli, 119 W. Orange Ave., Foley, AL 36535. Mon.-Sat., 10 A.M.-3 P.M. 970-1200.
Bayside Grill, 27842 Canal Road, Orange Beach, AL 36561. Mon.-Sat., 11:30 A.M.-10 P.M.; Sun., 11 A.M.-9 P.M. 981-4899.
Calypso Fish Grille and Market, 27075 Marina Road, Orange Beach, AL 36561. Sept.-Feb, Tue.-Sat., 11 A.M.-9 P.M.; Mar.-Aug. daily, 11 A.M.-11 P.M. 981-1415.
Gift Horse Restaurant & Antiques, 209 W. Laurel Ave., Foley, AL 36535. Daily, 11 A.M.-9 P.M. 943-3663.
Lambert's Café, Alabama 59, Foley, AL 36535. Daily, 10 A.M.-9:30 P.M. 943-7655.   Web site: www.throwedrolls.com/lamberts/
Mango's on the Island, 27075 Marina Road, Orange Beach, AL 36561. Sept.-Feb; Tue.-Sat., 11 A.M.-9 P.M.; Mar.-Aug., Sun.-Thurs., 11 A.M.-10 P.M.; Fri.-Sat., 11 A.M.-11 P.M. 981-1415.
Pompano's Restaurant, 931 W. Beach Road, Gulf Shores, AL 36547. Daily, 7 A.M.-9 P.M. 948-6874.
Street's Seafood Restaurant, 251 U.S. 31 S, Bay Minette, AL 36507. Serves breakfast, lunch buffet, and dinner; seafood buffet, Fri.-Sat., 5 P.M. 937-4096.
Sweetie Pies, 109 S. McKenzie Street, Foley, AL 36535. Mon.-Fri., 8:30 A.M.-3 P.M. 943-8119.
Major Annual Events:
Galilean Beach Service, East of Gulf Shores State Park Pavilion— Sunday Morning, Mother's Day-Labor Day, 7:30 A.M. 943-4393.
     Web site: www.foleyumc.org
National Shrimp Festival, Gulf Shores—October, Thurs.-Sat., 10 A.M.-10 P.M.; Sun., 10 A.M.-5 P.M. 968-6904.

4

MAIL BY BOAT

In a day of e-mail and the Internet, what would it be like to have your mail delivered by boat? Ask the residents of Magnolia Springs.

Before you go looking for the townsfolk, however, check into the **Magnolia Springs Bed & Breakfast** and let innkeeper David Worthington give you the tour of this historical 1898 home. Worthington is also the president of the **Bed and Breakfast Association of Alabama.** He knows B&Bs inside-out and is rightly proud of this one. It's on the National Register of Historic Places and was built entirely with bead board, heart pine floors, and rare curly pine trim. The authentically restored elephant trunk toilet is a must-see and will charm the children (and adults who haven't grown up).

Unpack and then take time at the end of the day to stroll through the **Moore Bros. Fresh Market** on Oak Street. It's fragrant with fruits that almost beg you to sample them, and it shares the building with **Jesse's Deli, Restaurant & Bakery,** an establishment people travel great distances to enjoy. One look at the menu and you'll see why. While you wait for your dinner, here is a little tidbit about the good choice you've made for dining. Jesse's is named for a man who reportedly never missed a day of work during the 60 years he worked for the Moore Bros. Gen'l Merchandise, which stood on the same spot from 1922 until 1993.

Magnolia Springs is central to bird sanctuaries such as the **Weeks Bay National Estuarine Research Reserve,** 3,000 acres of bays, marshes, and lowlands. A critical nursery for fish and shellfish, this sub-estuary (a mix of fresh water from rivers and salt water from the oceans) of Mobile Bay offers glimpses of the great blue heron and the brown pelican. A nature trail might lead beneath a nest of ospreys. Some guests at the Magnolia Springs B&B come specifically to pursue this burgeoning sport of birding, which needs very little equipment. A handbook, binoculars, and comfortable sneakers (plus the always-helpful insect repellent) make a short list of what is necessary.

Another treat for the naturalist is the **Weeks Bay Pitcher Plant Bog,** between Highway 17 and Fish River. It's part of the **Weeks Bay National Estuarine Research Reserve** but is across the river. Four species of pitcher plants are native to this bog. Bogs are not as wet as other wetland habitats, such as swamps and marshes. Actually, a bog needs to be dry enough to burn at different times, or some species will grow quickly and become so dense that orchids, sundews, lilies, pitcher plants, and other low-growing bog plants will not get enough light. Be sure to stay on the boardwalk here, because the surface of the bog is fragile. All parts of the estuary boardwalk make viewing from a wheelchair easy.

For a change of pace, hop back in the car and go to Point Clear to visit the **Punta Clara Kitchen.** The kitchen is part of **Miss Colleen's House** and is located on U.S. 98, across from **Ye Olde Post Office Antiques and Militaria.** Miss Colleen's House was built in 1897 and is still furnished as it was in the early days of the twentieth century. After viewing the rooms, step into the kitchen where the candy is homemade and you might be lucky enough to be offered a sample. Gather a few boxes of fudge and pecan butter crunch to take home as gifts—if you have self-discipline.

Next move the car to **Ye Olde Post Office Antiques and Militaria.** If you have a few wiggly boys in your entourage—and the age doesn't matter—this is a great stop-off to see Civil War memorabilia as well as other historic artifacts. You'll see World War I and II items as well as Civil War uniforms, belts, and buckles. Are coins your passion? Antique toys? Owner Jim Mitchell can show you rare and out-of-print books and documents, historic maps, and newspapers from long ago. Whether you want to buy, sell, or wander back in time, this is the place.

Continue north on U.S. 98 until you reach Fairhope, a charming town of streets filled with flowers. In the spring, the entry to town is well marked with hundreds of golden daffodils bobbing their greetings to passersby. Meander into Fairhope for dinner, and you'll see many choices from casual to formal dining. **Chandler's Café** on

Section Street offers hearty soups and thick sandwiches. If you want more atmosphere, go three blocks south to **Aubergine.**

Sunday in Fairhope is always lovely. The same is true of Fairhope any day in the week, but Sunday mornings are a little softer, the light is a little kinder to the eyes, and a morning walk in the park along the bay before church is a tradition. Choose a church and join the townspeople, then amble down the pleasant streets and you'll understand why **Fairhope** is proclaimed the "Historic Village of Flowers on Mobile Bay." Even the utility poles are trimmed with hanging pots of blossoms. Murals adorn city buildings and when we dropped into the **Church Street Café,** we found artistic touches everywhere, including the colorful presentation of the crab and artichoke bisque, special of the day.

Art galleries, coffee shops, and tearooms within easy walking distance guarantee a full afternoon of looking and choosing. Follow the cobblestone path into Fairhope's French Quarter on Section Street and see a familiar name, another place to sample candy from the **Punta Clara Kitchen.**

The **Eastern Shore Art Center** is located at the corner of Oak and Section Streets, across from the Civic Center. You can view some of the South's best visual artists in all media here. Artwork changes monthly, and pieces by nationally recognized artists are also exhibited. Visitors can tour the galleries and the five working art studios. The Center is now in its fourth decade and was founded to provide art education to the community. Classes in painting, drawing, pottery, sculpture, photography, and other visual arts are offered, and a weekend introduction to this thriving art colony might bring the traveler back to stay a little longer just to participate in these classes. During the winter months, you can wander among the galleries and gift shops and enjoy a series of classical music concerts hosted by the Center.

Not far from the Center is the **Jim Gray Gallery,** which features original watercolors, oils, limited edition reproductions, bronze sculpture, and note paper by renowned American artist Jim Gray. You'll also see artwork by artist/gallery manager **Laurie Gray Schmohl**. Stroll among the displays of pottery by ten different potters, woodcarving and turned wood by four different woodworkers, and handcrafted jewelry, sand casting, weaving, porcelain sculpture, and unique kaleidoscopes. This gallery is a banquet for the senses.

To fully immerse yourself in this outstanding arts community, make your weekend getaway here on the third weekend of either

March or October. Outdoor art shows are held and the streets are limited to foot traffic.

The third weekend of October will keep the art enthusiast scurrying back and forth from Fairhope to the **Grand Festival of Art,** which is held on the grounds of the five-star **Marriott's Grand Hotel Resort & Golf Club** in **Point Clear,** about four miles south of Fairhope. The hotel and the lovely bed and breakfast inns in the area are booked early for these art festivals, so plan accordingly.

Fairhope has no municipal sales tax, which makes the temptation to buy easier to satisfy. We had a long list of unique gift shops friends told us not to miss, and they are easy for you to find and explore. The one we slipped into had not been open very long and it was actually three stores in one. It was newer than it might have been because a hurricane had delayed the opening. With such a beginning, you know the determined owners will be interesting to meet. Patsy Deakle, the Patsy of **Peppermint Patsy's Antiques, Art & Accessories,** paints and gathers antiques, art, and accessories, which she calls "delectable collectables" and displays them for browsers' enjoyment. Anita Sharpless and Cynthia Turner are partners in **Two Antique Broads,** which has "Old" crossed out and "Antique" written above it. Anita says she is one of the old broads and it's clear she loves meeting the people who are drawn into this eclectic store. **Nanny's Antiques** is owned by Jean and Jerry Bernhardt. They all live together happily ever after in one store. Well, actually, they take turns being there.

Nothing fuels the appetite like shopping. A quiet place to enjoy a break—or continue enjoying blissful solitude if you've been a guest in the hotel—is the restaurant at the **Fairhope Inn.** We stopped for crème brûlée and coffee and wished we could return to this oasis for an entire weekend.

Unless you are a wildflower aficionado, you will probably not know about the **Minamac Wildflower Bog.** Having sampled the **Weeks Bay Pitcher Plant Bog,** you are ready to carry your powers of observation deeper into the woods. An article written about this bog by **Steve Bender** in *Southern Living* ten years ago calls it "a vision of loveliness sculpted by nature." The vision continues to intensify and is open to visits April through September.

Southern Living is a glamorous full-color magazine based in Birmingham. For 35 years this publication has made readers sigh for the gracious South it describes. To be featured in *Southern Living* is a sign of stature, and this bog has lots of stature. The owners, Min and Mac MacCartee, moved from Maryland to Alabama with the intention

Wisteria in bloom. (Photo by Neal Broerman)

of raising cattle. Burning off the land to clear it produced a surprise of magnificent proportions. Acre upon acre of rare and unusual wildflowers responded to the removal of the brushy cover that had hidden them. The bog is thousands of years old, and nature's painting of rare orchids, pine lilies, and enticing pitcher plants changes daily. Garden clubs, school groups, and commercial tours make reservations ahead of time. An individual tourist should make an appointment, too, and ask for directions. It's out of the way and worth the extra time. The MacCartees could have kept this treasure to themselves, but they share it and their knowledge generously.

You've left the bog, your green thumb is itching, and you want something to take home to the neighbor who fed your cat. The place to stop is **Good Scents Herbs & Flowers,** on Highway 59 in **Loxley.** Ask for help from the very knowledgeable owner, Loraine Keane. But take a walk up and down the rows of plants first and breathe in the perfume. What's one more simple pleasure before you head home?

Area Code: (334)

Getting There:

Fairhope can be easily reached from Interstate 65 or Interstate 10. From Interstate 65, take Exit 31, Alabama 255. Alabama 255 joins

U.S. 98 at Spanish Fort. From Interstate 10, take Exit 35, U.S. 98. Point Clear and Magnolia Springs are also on U.S. 98.
Weeks Bay National Estuarine Research Reserve. From Magnolia Springs take Route 98, go 5 miles west and cross the Louis Brannon Bridge.
Where and When:
Baldwin County Museum of Art, 111 W. Laurel Ave., Foley, AL 36535. Tue.-Sat., 10 A.M.-4 P.M. 979-1818.
Eastern Shore Art Center, Oak and Section Streets, Fairhope, AL 36532. Mon.-Sat., 10 A.M.-4 P.M. 928-5188.
Fairhope Antiques (Nanny's Antiques), 52 N. Section Street, Fairhope, AL 36532. 928-9321.
Good Scents Herbs & Flowers, 26175 Alabama 59, Loxley, AL 36551. Mon.-Sat., 9 A.M.-5 P.M.; Sun., 11 A.M.-5 P.M. 964-5661.
Jim Gray Gallery, 61 N. Section Street, Fairhope, AL 36532. Tue.-Sat., 10 A.M.-5 P.M.; Nov.- Dec 24th, Tue.-Sat., 10 A.M.-6 P.M.; Sun., 1 P.M.-5 P.M. 928-8446.
Minamac Wildflower Bog, 13199 MacCartee Ln., Silverhill, AL 36576. 945-6157. Admission.
Miss Colleen's House, Scenic Alabama 98, Point Clear, AL 36564. 928-8477.
Moore Bros. Fresh Market, 14770 Oak Street, Magnolia Springs, AL 36555. Mon.-Sat., 11 A.M.-2:30 P.M., 5 P.M.-9 P.M. 965-3827.
Nanny's Antiques, 5 N. Church Street, Fairhope, AL 36532. 990-0080.
Peppermint Patsy's Antiques, Art & Accessories, 5 N. Church Street, Fairhope, AL 36532. 990-0080.
Punta Clara Kitchen, Section Street, Fairhope, AL 36532. Tues.-Sat., 10 A.M.-5 P.M. 928-1548.
Punta Clara Kitchen, one mile south of Grand Hotel, Point Clear, AL 36564. 990-9962; (800) 437-7868.
Web site: www.puntaclarakitchen.com
Two Antique Broads, 5 N. Church Street, Fairhope, AL 36532. 990-0080.
Weeks Bay National Estuarine Research Reserve, 11300 Alabama 98, Fairhope, AL 36532. Mon.-Sat., 9 A.M.-5 P.M.; Sun., 1 P.M.-5 p.m; Closed on Federal and state holidays, but you can still access the boardwalk. 928-9792. Admission.
Weeks Bay Pitcher Plant Bog, 11300 Alabama 98, Fairhope, AL 36532. Open dawn to dusk all year.
Ye Olde Post Office Antiques and Militaria, 17070 Scenic Alabama 98, Point Clear, AL 36564. Mon.-Sat., 9 A.M.-5 P.M. 928-0108.

Information:

Eastern Shore Art Center and art festivals in Fairhope, 928-2228.
Eastern Shore Chamber of Commerce, 327 Fairhope Avenue,
Fairhope, AL 36532. 621-8222.   Web site: www.eschamber.com
Alabama Welcome Centers, Interstate 10, Exit 66, Seminole.
Eastern Shore Chamber of Commerce, 29750 Larry Dee Cawyer
Dr., Daphne, AL 36526. 621-8222. Write for a full list of accommodations, gift shops, and restaurants.

Accommodations:

Away at the Bay, 557 N. Mobile Street, Fairhope, AL 36533. 928-9725.
Web site: www.awayatthebay.com
Bay Breeze Guest House, 742 S. Mobile Street, Fairhope, AL
36533. 928-8976.   Web site: www.bbonline.com/al/baybreeze
Church Street Inn, 51 S. Church Street, Fairhope, AL 36533.
928-8976.   Web site: www.bbonline.com/al/churchstreet
Fairhope Inn, 63 S. Church Street, Fairhope, AL 36532. 928-6226.
Magnolia Springs Bed & Breakfast, 14469 Oak Street, Magnolia
Springs, AL 36555. 965-7321; (800) 965-7321.
Web site: www.bbonline.com/al/magnolia
Marriott's Grand Hotel Resort & Golf Club, P.O. Box 639, Point
Clear, AL 36564. 928-9201; (800) 544-9933.

Restaurants:

Aubergine, 315 DeLaMare, Fairhope, AL 36532. Open Mon.-Sat.
for lunch and dinner. 928-9541.
Chandler's Café, Section Street, Fairhope, AL.
Church Street Café, 9 N. Church Street, Fairhope, AL 36532.
Mon.-Wed., 11 A.M.-9 P.M.; Thurs.-Sat., 11 A.M.-9:30 P.M. 928-6611.
Fairhope Inn, 63 S. Church Street, Fairhope, AL 36532. Closed
Mon. 928-6226.
Jesse's Deli, Restaurant & Bakery, 14770 Oak Street, Magnolia
Springs, AL 36555. Mon.-Sat., 11 A.M.-2:30 P.M.; 5 P.M.-9 P.M. 965-6020.

Major Annual Events:

Arts & Crafts Festival, Fairhope—Third weekend in March.
Strawberry Festival, Loxley—First Saturday in May.
Grand Festival of Art, Marriott Grand Hotel, Point Clear—Third
weekend in October. 928-5188.

5

SNEAKER TIME

After a lot of week-in and week-out rushing, take a long weekend at the **Beach House,** a bed and breakfast by the sea. An old beach house retreat with huge porches, double hammocks, and fantastic views right on the beach is hard to find, but this is one of them. Check the Web site for details or call innkeepers Carol and Russell Shackelford and ask about their plans and packages, especially "The Long Weekend Plan." This is a couples retreat, so leave the pets and kids at home. To get there, take Fort Morgan Road from Alabama 59 in Gulf Shores. The sign to the ferry may catch your eye before you see the road sign.

When it's time for dinner and you want to match the elegant but casual atmosphere at the Beach House, go back to the main road leading to **Fort Morgan** and turn left. The **Restaurant at the Beach Club** may look private and perhaps a bit formal and forbidding, but stroll in the front door on the left side of the parking lot and ascend the staircase. The restaurant is on the second floor and you have your choice of eating inside or on the balcony overlooking the pool. We entered at the same time as a wedding party and discovered that our table was closer to the ceremony than we'd been at the last wedding we attended in church. Kids splashed in the pool, diners enjoyed pasta and seafood specialties, and the happy couple and their families began a new life together.

An early morning walk to greet the dawn and smell the fresh sea breezes gets any day started with euphoria. Go ahead. After the full

Southern breakfast served by the Shackelfords, spend the whole day in that hammock with a great book.

If you've opted for a different place to stay, maybe in one of the many hotels and motels in Gulf Shores or Orange Beach, and the family is along, too, **Fort Morgan** is at the end of Highway 180 West (Fort Morgan Road), 21 miles from Gulf Shores. This fort has stood up to the War of 1812, the Civil War, the Spanish American War, and World Wars I and II. It should still be standing after you and yours tour the site and the museum. Take a lunch and enjoy the picnic tables.

Bon Secour National Wildlife Refuge stands waiting for you to explore the **Pine Beach Trail** or the one-mile loop of the **Jeff Friend Trail.** Within minutes you can be in the midst of some of Alabama's last remaining undisturbed coastal barrier habitats. Or you can drive to Orange Beach and visit the **Orange Beach Indian & Sea Museum.**

Check your watch and be sure to arrive at the Sea Museum at least an hour before it closes at 2:00. It is not open on Sunday. Use **Orange Beach Drugs** as your landmark. It's on Alabama 161 (4098 Orange Beach Boulevard) at the light. Turn left if the drugstore is on your right and you will see the museum, a small white building that has served the community as a church and a school. Gail Walker Graham, assistant at the museum, comes from a long line of deepwater fishermen. She can point out homemade lures from the 1900s and sugar canes that did double duty as fishing poles. This is a family history, too, of the eight Walker boys and their lives on the sea.

Now you're ready for a killer milkshake at **Orange Beach Drugs.** This is not your usual drugstore. It is also a gift shop called the **Mermaid's Purse.** The pharmacist is Don Roberts, and his wife Donna manages the gift shop and soda fountain and makes those killer milkshakes.

The next stop will be a short one, but it's fun. Did you notice the mattress company with the flowers and plants painted on the pink walls? You don't have to buy a mattress, but drop in and meet Cyndi Brewer of **Creative Energy,** an eclectic art studio. Cyndi paints furniture and gives it a personality. We liked what she did with a wrought-iron table and chairs set. She paints murals, too. In fact, whatever art challenge you have in mind will give Cyndi and her husband, whose sense of the possible complements Cyndi's creativity, the chance to stop and ponder, "Well, what if . . .?"

By now you may be ready to stretch your legs on the beach. Take along a handful of breadcrumbs or breakfast cereal for the hungry

Cyndi Brewer, painter. (Photo by Joan Broerman)

Table and chair painted by Cyndi Brewer. (Photo by Neal Broerman)

gulls. Average temperatures on the beach are over 60 degrees, March through November, and even February temperatures have been known to climb into the 80s during the day. Slip into those comfortable jeans and sneakers and nod hello to the friendly people you pass on your beach stroll.

Have you watched a sunset from the deck of the **Bayside Grill** yet? Maybe now is the time. Take Alabama 182 East to Alabama 161 and the Grill is two miles on the right at **Sportsman Marina.** Dress is casual and the cuisine is Creole, Caribbean, and cause for celebration. If you'd rather come when the sun is up, this is also a great place for brunch.

To start the next day of this weekend, pack a picnic lunch and board the *Mobile Bay Ferry* from **Fort Morgan** for a day of strolling through history, adding to your knowledge of the rich sea life around you, bird watching, or just plain relaxing. You might want to bring a bike and take it on the ferry with you, as many locals do. **Dauphin Island** is a 14-mile-long barrier island, but the main road is only seven miles long. The **Audubon Bird Sanctuary and Trail,** which is almost in the middle of the island, is 164 acres of maritime forests, marshes, and dunes, and includes a lake, swamp, and the beach. Trails cover 160 of those acres. Exhausted migratory birds find food and rest here as they travel south and when they return, too. It's ranked as one of the most important sites for bird migration. Glorious butterflies also use this sanctuary. To keep yourself from being a treat to the mosquito population, wear insect repellent.

The web page for **Dauphin Island** will give you a fine introduction to this warm, sandy paradise. It will also keep you up-to-date on events. If you spend an afternoon biking or hiking on the island, you are sure to want to come back. The next chapter will take you there.

Area Code: (334)

Getting There:

Gulf Shores can be easily reached from Interstate 65 or Interstate 10. From Interstate 65, take Exit 37. For a short distance it will be Alabama 287 and become U.S. 31 and Alabama 59—Gulf Shores Parkway. From Interstate 10, take Exit 44 to Alabama 59-Gulf Shores Parkway. The Parkway crosses the Intracoastal Waterway as you enter Gulf Shores and crosses Alabama 180 (Fort Morgan Parkway). It ends at the beach. Turn left to go to Orange Beach or Gulf State Park. Turn right to the heart of Gulf Shores.

Major airlines serve Pensacola Regional Airport, a 45-minute drive from Orange Beach, and the Mobile airport, which is one hour from Gulf Shores.

Where and When:

Audubon Bird Sanctuary and Trail, Bienville Ave., Dauphin Island, AL 36528. 861-2120.

Biophilia Nature Center, 12695 Baldwin County Road 95, Elberta, AL 36530. 987-1200. Admission.
Web site: www.gulftel.net/daedalus

Bon Secour National Wildlife Refuge, 12295 Alabama 180, Gulf Shores, AL 36547. 540-7720.   Web site: www.fws.gov/~r4eao

Creative Energy, 4161 Orange Beach Boulevard, Orange Beach, AL 36561. Winter Tue.-Fri, 10 A.M.-5 P.M.; Sat., 11 A.M.-2 P.M.; Summer also open Mon. 981-1852.   Web site: www.creativenrg.net

Fort Morgan, 51 Alabama 180 W, Ft. Morgan Pkwy., Gulf Shores, AL 36542. Daily, 9 A.M.-5 P.M. 540-7125. Admission.

Isle Dauphine Golf Club, Bienville Road, Dauphin Island, AL 36528.

Orange Beach Drugs, 4098 Orange Beach Boulevard, Orange Beach, AL 36561. Mon, Wed.-Fri., 8:30 A.M.-6 P.M.; Tue., 8:30 A.M.-5 P.M.; Sat., 9 A.M.-1 P.M. 981-8778.

Orange Beach Indian & Sea Museum, Bonita Drive off Alabama 161, Orange Beach AL 36561. Tue.-Fri., 7:30 A.M.-4 P.M.; Sat., 9 A.M.-2 P.M. 981-8545.

Mermaid's Purse, 4098 Orange Beach Boulevard, Orange Beach, AL 36561. Tue.-Fri., 7:30 A.M.-4 P.M.; Sat., 9 A.M.-2 P.M. 981-8778.

Seacrets at Zeke's Landing, 26619 Perdido Beach Boulevard, Orange Beach, AL 36561. Daily, 9 A.M.-9 P.M. 981-5600.

Secrecy, Perdido Pass Bldg. at Alabama Point, Orange Beach, AL 36561. Daily, 10 A.M.-9 P.M. 981-5500.

St. Charles Place, 25241 Perdido Beach Boulevard, Orange Beach, AL 36561. Daily, 9 A.M.-9 P.M. 981-6400.

Tootie Green's Yellow Broom, 25122 Perdido Beach Boulevard, Orange Beach, AL 36561. 981-7377.

Transportation:

Pleasure Island Trolley. Purchase PIT tokens at Gulf Shores City Hall or Orange Beach City Hall, or local businesses, hotels, and restaurants.

Mobile Bay Ferry, Ft. Morgan Pkwy., Gulf Shores, AL 36542. Daily, 8 A.M.-7:15 P.M.; Nov.-Feb., last ferry at 5 P.M. 540-7787.

Information:
Alabama Vacation Guide, call 1-800-ALABAMA (252-2262).
Island Wide Activities Web site:www.gulfshores.com/things_to_do
Alabama Gulf Coast Convention and Visitors Bureau, P.O. Drawer
457, Gulf Shores, AL 36547. 974-1510.
Fishing information   Web site: www.orangebeach.com
Dauphin Island Development Network, P.O. Box 610, Dauphin
Island, AL 36528. 861-5524.   Web site: gulfinfo.com/ditown
Tide information, 968-TIDE (8433).
Rare Bird Alerts, Alabama Ornithological Society, 987-2730.

Accommodations:
Alabama Bed & Breakfast Association
                    Web site: www.bbonline.com/al/bbaa
Beach House, 9218 Dacus Ln., Gulf Shores, AL 36542. 540-7039;
(800) 659-6004.   Web site: www.bigbeachhouse.com
Gulf State Park Resort Hotel, Alabama 182 E., Gulf Shores, AL
36547. 948-4853; (800) 544-4853.
Lighthouse Resort Motel, 455 E. Beach Boulevard, Gulf Shores,
AL 36547. 948-6188.
Oar House Riverside Inn, 5587 Baldwin County Road 6, Gulf
Shores, AL 36542. 967-7478.
Quality Inn BeachSide on the Gulf, 931 W. Beach Boulevard, Gulf
Shores, AL 36547. (800) 844-6913.
Romar House, 23500 Perdido Beach Boulevard, Orange Beach,
AL 36561. 974-1625; (800) 487-6627.
                    Web site: www.bbonline.com/al/romarhouse
Restaurants:
Back Porch Seafood and Oyster House, 5749 Bay La Launch Ave.,
Orange Beach, AL 36561. Sun.-Thurs., 11 A.M.-10 P.M.; Fri.-Sat., 11
A.M.-11 P.M. 981-2225.
Bayside Grill, 27842 Canal Road, Orange Beach, AL 36561. Mon.-
Sat., 11:30 A.M.-10 P.M.; Sun., 11 A.M.-9 P.M. 981-4899.
Café Grazie, 27267 Perdido Beach Boulevard, Orange Beach, AL
36561. Sun.-Thurs., 5 P.M.-9:30 P.M.; Fri.-Sat., 5 P.M.-10:30 P.M. 981-8466.
Calypso Fish Grille and Market, 27075 Marina Road, Orange
Beach, AL 36561. Sept.-Feb; Tue.-Sat., 11 A.M.-9 P.M.; Mar.-Aug. daily,
11 A.M.-11 P.M. 981-1415.
DeSoto's Seafood Kitchen, 138 W. First Ave., Gulf Shores, AL 36547.
Winter daily, 11 A.M.-9 P.M.; Summer daily, 11 A.M.-10 P.M. 948-7294.

Fish Camp Restaurant, 4297 Baldwin County Road 6, Gulf Shores, AL 36542. Daily, from 11 A.M. 968-2267.

Hazel's Family Restaurant, 25311 Perdido Beach Boulevard, Orange Beach, AL 36547. Winter daily, 6 A.M.-7 P.M.; Summer daily 6 A.M.-9 P.M. 981-4628.

Jake's Steakhouse, Alabama 59, Gulf Shores, AL 36547. Mon.-Thurs., 10:30 A.M.-9 P.M.; Fri.-Sat., 10:30 A.M.-10 P.M.; Sun 11 A.M.-9 P.M. 968-2777.

Jake's Steakhouse, Alabama 182, Orange Beach, AL 36561. Mon.-Thurs., 10:30 A.M.-9 P.M.; Fri.-Sat., 10:30 A.M.-10 P.M. 968-2777.

Mikee's Seafood, 201 E. Second Ave. and First Street, Gulf Shores, AL 36547. Daily, 11 A.M.-11 P.M. 948-6452.

Louisiana Lagniappe, 27267 Perdido Beach Boulevard, Orange Beach, AL 36561. Sun.-Thurs., 5 P.M.-9:30 P.M.; Fri.-Sat., 5 P.M.-10:30 P.M. 981-2258.

Mango's on the Island, 27075 Marina Road, Orange Beach, AL 36561. Sept.- Feb; Tue.-Sat., 11 A.M.-9 P.M.; Mar.-Aug.; Sun.-Thurs. 11 A.M.-10 P.M.; Fri.-Sat., 11 A.M.-11 P.M. 981-1415.

Oar House Restaurant, 5587 Baldwin County Road 6, Gulf Shores, AL 36542. Tue.-Sat., 11 .am.-9 P.M.; Sun., 5 P.M.-9 P.M. 967-2422.

Original Oyster House, Bayou Village, Gulf Shores, AL. Sun.-Thurs., 11 A.M.-10 P.M.; Fri.-Sat., 11 A.M.-11 P.M. 948-2445.

Perdido Pass Restaurant, 27501 Perdido Beach Boulevard, Orange Beach, AL 36561. Daily lunch, 11 A.M.-4 P.M.; Brunch, Sat.-Sun., 11 A.M.-2 P.M. 981-6312.

Restaurant at the Beach Club, Ft. Morgan Pkwy., Gulf Shores, AL 36542. Sun. Brunch 11 A.M.-3 P.M. 540-2525.

San Roc Cay Delicatezza International Grocery, 27267 Perdido Beach Boulevard, Orange Beach, AL 36561. Winter Sun.-Thurs., 8 A.M.-8 P.M.; Fri.-Sat., 8 A.M.-9 P.M.; Summer daily, 7 A.M.-10 P.M.

Wolf Bay Lodge, 9050 Pinewood Ave., Elberta, AL 36530. Tue.-Thurs., 11 A.M.-9 P.M.; Fri.-Sat., 11 A.M.-10 P.M.; Sun., noon-8 P.M. 987-5129.

Dauphin Island pier. (Photo by Joan Broerman)

6

CITY AND SEA

Many consider **Dauphin Island** to be the undiscovered treasure of the Gulf of Mexico. Maybe that's because there are no hotels there. However, there is a campground that has 150 sites with power and water and the bathhouse has hot showers and a washer and dryer. This can be your base of operations or, if you prefer a hotel or motel, stay in **Theodore,** on the other end of the scenic three-mile Dauphin Island Bridge. Either way, you can fill this weekend with the beauty of the sea and take in a few historical and educational city sights, too.

Dauphin Island has a golf course, tennis courts, and sport fishing charters, which you can find out more about through the Dauphin Island Development Network. The web page is excellent and you can take a trip across the island without ever setting foot on the sand.

For simply sitting in the sun and dropping a line, the **Dauphin Island Fishing Pier** is a gathering spot for all ages and is comfortable for those in wheelchairs, too. The pier is equipped with lights for night fishing. It also has restrooms, a tackle shop, concessions, and rods you can rent if you forgot yours.

Isle Dauphine Golf Club is open to the public and offers fairways that run beside Gulf Beaches. Keep in mind that dinner on the island can be enjoyed in **Barnacle Bill's,** the club's dining spot.

The entire island is now officially a bird sanctuary. Thousands of migrating songbirds and shorebirds make a final stop on Dauphin Island before they leave for their winter homes, and this makes the fall an ideal time to visit. The chorus of birdsong in the **Audubon**

Bird Sanctuary and Trail, 160 acres of woodlands with a freshwater lake and miles of walking trails, is always a treat for the ears, no matter what time you go. Begin your day here, just listening.

Mobile Bay, which you may have crossed on the ferry if that was the way you elected to arrive at this point, is the fourth-largest estuary system in the United States. The recently-opened **Estuarium at the Dauphin Island Sea Lab** shows sea life up close and explains the ecological interactions that take place among the Barrier Islands, the Gulf of Mexico, the Delta, and Mobile Bay. All are key habitats of coastal Alabama.

It takes five minutes to walk to the left of the ferry and reach the handsome grey deck of the Estuarium. See the short movie to get an overview. A family of four with middle-grade children can walk through in 45 minutes to an hour—but don't be surprised if it takes longer. One trip around may not be enough. Just one tank of streaming jellyfish can arrest your interest for several minutes.

For contrast, visit the past at **Fort Gaines Historic Site.** See where soldiers lived and worked from the 1800s to 1946. Touch the actual cannons fired in the Civil War during the three-week naval and land battle that ended with the capture of Fort Gaines and the Confederate fleet by Union forces. The fort is across the road from the Estuarium, and you don't have to repark the car.

Next take a short drive to the other end of the island and park near the **Lighthouse Bakery.** Walk up and order great sandwiches at the outside window. Eat in the park or in a pavilion overlooking the beach.

Take your time and stroll up and down the island. Browse in the gift shops. Stop for ice cream or have a cup of coffee. Note the Little Red Schoolhouse. Some kids have all the luck—imagine going to school with the gulf outside your window!

If you elected to stay in Theodore, across the Dauphin Island Bridge, take your appetite to **Dick Russell's BBQ.** This place is known for steaks and seafood. Biscuits, which are served at every meal, also star in an old-fashioned country breakfast.

Saturday you could drive over the bridge into **Dauphin Island** to spend a morning or the day. Then travel in another direction to see how one family took nature's loveliest productions and gave them a more formal setting.

From Theodore, take Bellingrath Gardens Road and follow the signs to **Bellingrath Gardens and Home.** Built for Walter and Bessie

*Fishermen and boats,
Dauphin Island.* (Photo by
Neal Broerman)

Above and right:
*Christmas at Bellingrath
Gardens.* (Photos by Neal
Broerman)

Bellingrath in 1935, this 15-room home was constructed with hand-made brick salvaged from the birthplace of Alva Vanderbilt in Mobile. While Walter made his fortune with Coca-Cola in Mobile, Bessie collected fine antiques, which still furnish the home. In one of the three dining rooms you can see the Chippendale banquet table and chairs once possessed by Sir Thomas Lipton of tea fame. Look up! The chandeliers are Baccarat and Waterford crystal. The collection of porcelain includes Meissen and Dresden, and the silver must have kept many servants polishing. The Bellingraths had no children of their own, but they had many relatives and loved to entertain. The house is listed on the National Register of Historic Places, but it still feels as if it could be lived in.

The gardens, home, and scenic river cruise (**Southern Belle River Cruiser**) have separate tickets, but a tour of the gardens alone is a camera buff's delight. The profuse plant life, no matter what the season, draws the traveler around the next bend and the next. Included in the gardens tour is the **Delchamps Gallery of Boehm Porcelain,** the largest public collection of the works of Edward Marshall Boehm. This is housed in what was once the Bellingraths' six-car garage. Plan on one to two hours for the Garden, about 40 minutes for the home tour, and 45 minutes for the river cruise.

For lunch or supper, eat in the **Magnolia Cafe,** which sits handily beside the **Gazebo Gift Shop.** Be glad your car is not parked very far away. A full meal and hands full of purchases could take the energy you need for the next part of your trip.

Ready for more? Travel to Mobile and stay along Interstate 65, where you will be ready to shop or see **Spring Hill College,** the first institution of higher learning in Alabama. Founded in 1830, this is the third oldest of the 28 Jesuit colleges and universities in the United States. The 500-acre campus is criss-crossed by oak-lined avenues and azalea-bordered walkways and overlooks the city of Mobile. The campus also boasts the oldest collegiate ball field still in use.

Somewhere in your day of traveling along **Spring Hill Avenue,** plan a stop at the **Visitation Monastery and Gift Shop.** The gift shop offers many unusual items, and specializes in new and vintage linens (perfect for celebrating weddings or new babies). The kindly salespeople will wrap and mail your purchases, too. This is a soothing place in which to think about special occasions in your future. For a longer stay, consider a personalized retreat. This modernized monastery has been a retreat center for more than 35 years, offering amenities such as private, air-conditioned rooms, tiled baths, and meals served in the large dining room. Men and women, individuals and groups are all welcome to retreat.

Dinner at **Dreamland** will leave you with quite an impression and probably the need to change clothes, too. How can you enjoy ribs drenched in "Big Daddy's" secret sauce without spilling a little? This is one place you don't mind getting sauce everywhere because it's O.K. to lick your fingers. You'll be glad bibs and packaged wet towels are furnished, too. John "Big Daddy" Bishop founded Dreamland in Tuscaloosa in 1958, and this one in Mobile features the same hickory-smoked ribs that made the name Dreamland famous. Some people call this "hog heaven," but you can have barbecued chicken, too.

Sunday would be a good day to take in the **Mobile Museum of Art.** This is one of those rare museums open on Mondays if your weekend stretches into an extra day. The permanent collection has more than 5000 works of art and spans 2000 years of cultural history. You may spend several hours here and in the gift shop browsing through a fine collection of books on art and artists.

Go left out of the Museum, toward the water tower (on Museum Drive); turn left onto McGregor Drive and right on Old Shell; pass in front of Spring Hill College again and see **Carpe Diem Coffee and Tea Company** on the left. Surely you have an excuse to stop for breakfast, lunch, or a light supper. No? Then how about a cup of coffee? This small gem of a discovery is fragrant with the fresh-brewed aroma of specialty coffees, teas, and pastries. All coffees are roasted in the shop. You can buy gifts and books here, too. Take a table near the window and contemplate your drive home. Maybe you'll want a second cup for the road.

Area Code: (334)

Getting There:

Easily accessible from Interstates 65 and 10. Take Interstate 65 south to its end at Interstate 10 and continue on Interstate 10 to Alabama 193, which becomes Dauphin Island Parkway. From downtown Mobile, take Government Street to its intersection of Dauphin Island Parkway. The island is about 30 miles from Mobile.

Where and When:

Audubon Bird Sanctuary and Trail, Bienville Ave., Dauphin Island, AL 36528. 861-2120.

Bellingrath Gardens and Home, 12401 Bellingrath Gardens Road, Theodore, AL 36582. Open 8 A.M.-one hour before dark. 973-2217; (800) 247-8420. Admission.   Web site: www.bellingrath.org/

Dauphin Island Fishing Pier, P.O. Box 610, Dauphin Island, AL 36528. Open 24 hours daily. 861-6972.

Dauphin Island Sea Lab, 101 Bienville Ave., Dauphin Island, AL 36528. 861-2141.   Web site: www.disl.org

Estuarium at the Dauphin Island Sea Lab, 101 Bienville Ave., Dauphin Island, AL 36528. Summer, Tue.-Sun., 9 A.M.-6 P.M.; Winter, Tue.-Fri., 11 A.M.-5 P.M.; Sat.-Sun., 9 a.m-5 P.M. 861-7500. Admission.
                                    Web site: sites.gulf.net/sealab

Fort Gaines Historic Site, 51 Bienville Boulevard, Dauphin Island, AL 36528. Open daily, summer, 9 A.M.-6 P.M.; winter, 9 A.M.-5 P.M. 861-6992.   Web site: www.dauphine.net

Isle Dauphine Golf Club, Bienville Road., Dauphin Island, AL 36528.

Mobile Museum of Art, 4850 Museum Dr., Mobile, AL 36689. Mon.-Sat., 10 A.M.-5 P.M.; Sun., 1 P.M.-5 P.M. 343-2667. Admission.
                              Web site: www.MobileMuseumOfArt.com

Sacred Heart Retreat House, 2300 Spring Hill Ave., Mobile, AL 36607. 473-2321.

Spring Hill College, 4000 Dauphin Street, Mobile, AL 36608. 380-3094.   Web site: www.shc.edu/

Visitation Monastery and Gift Shop, 2300 Spring Hill Ave., Mobile, AL 36607. Mon.-Sat., 10 A.M.-5 P.M. 471-4106.

Information:

Alabama Gulf Coast Convention and Visitors Bureau, Drawer 457, Gulf Shores, AL 36547. Mon.-Fri., 8 A.M.-5 P.M.; Sat.-Sun, 9 A.M.-5 P.M. 974-1510; (800) 745-7263.

Alabama Welcome Center, Interstate 10, Exit 1, Grand Bay.

Dauphin Island Development Network, P.O. Box 610, Dauphin Island, AL 36528. 861-5524.   Web site: www.gulfinfo.com/ditown

Fishing Information   Web site: www.orangebeach.com

Gulf Shores Island Wide Activities, P.O. Box 437, Gulf Shores, AL 36547. 948-4853; (800) 544-4853.
                        Web site: www.gulfshores.com/things_to_do/

Accommodations:

Dauphin Island Campground, P.O. Box 97, Dauphin Island, AL 36528. 861-2742.

Riverhouse, 13285 Rebel Road, Theodore, AL 36582. 973-2233; (800) 552-9791.   Web site: www.bbonline.com/al/riverhouse

Restaurants:

Barnacle Bill's, 100 Orleans Dr., Dauphin Island, AL 36528. Daily from 5 P.M. 861-5255.

Carpe Diem Coffee and Tea Company, 4072 Old Shell Road, Mobile, AL 36608. Mon.-Thurs., 7 A.M.; Fri., 7 A.M.-11 P.M.; Sat., 8A.M.-10.P.M.; Sun., 1 P.M.-10 P.M. 304-0448.

Dick Russell's BBQ, 5360 U. S. 90 W, Mobile, AL 36619. Sun.-Thurs., 6 A.M.-9 P.M.; Fri.-Sat., 6 A.M.-10 P.M. 661-6090.

Drayton Place, 101 Dauphin Street, Mobile, AL 36602. Mon.-Sat. for lunch and dinner. 432-7438.

Dreamland, 3314 Old Shell Road, Mobile, AL 36607. Mon.-Thurs.,10 A.M.-10 P.M.; Fri.-Sat., 10 A.M.-midnight; Sun., 11 A.M.-9 P.M. 479-9898; (800) 752-0544. Web site: www.dreamlandbbq.com/ribs

Lighthouse Bakery, Bienville Road, Dauphin Island, AL 35628.

Major Annual Events:

Fury on the Gulf, 51 Bienville Boulevard, Dauphin Island—January. 861-6992.

Dauphin Island Regatta—April.

Alabama Deep Sea Fishing Rodeo, Dauphin Island —July.

Blessing of the Fleet, Bayou La Batre—May. 824-2415.

Mother's Day at Bellingrath Gardens, 12401 Bellingrath Gardens Road, Theodore—Second Sunday in May 973-2217; (800) 247-842.

Web site: www.bellingrath.org/

Deep Sea Fishing Rodeo, P.O. Box 610, Dauphin Island—July. 861-6972.

Damn the Torpedoes Commemorative Battle of Mobile Bay, Fort Gaines Historic Site, Mobile—August. 861-6992.

Alabama Pecan Festival, Community Center, Tillmans Corner—November, 9 A.M.-6 P.M. 666-3575.

Magic Christmas in Lights at Bellingrath Gardens, 12401 Bellingrath Gardens Road, Theodore—December. 973-2217; (800) 247-8420.   Web site: www.bellingrath.org/

Above and right: *Fort Conde.* (Photos by Neal Broerman)

7

MOBILE,
OUR OLDEST CITY

Come flirt with 300 years of our country's past. Author, historian, and native Mobilian **Caldwell Delaney** notes that Mobile has had a part in all the major events of American history. **Mobile Bay** was one of the first North American bodies of water seen by European eyes. Originally founded on the 27 Mile Bluff above the **Mobile River,** the city was moved to its present location where the river meets the bay in 1711. **Fort Conde** was built, and even though the old fort has long since disappeared, the reconstructed fort now serves as Mobile's official welcome center, where you can discover 300 years of Mobile and 300 years of America. On your first full day in historic Mobile, make **Fort Conde Visitor Center** your first stop.

The city is small enough to be absorbed slowly and savored, but with so many museums and historical homes to pack into one weekend, downtown hotels or nearby bed and breakfasts are convenient places to stay for the weekender who wants to see it all—or as much as possible.

Two downtown hotels many find convenient and comfortable for touring historic Mobile are the **Adam's Mark Hotel** and the restored **Radisson Admiral Semmes Hotel.** You will find others and you will have many choices of restaurants, too. The **Towle House Bed and Breakfast** has been featured on television and the personalities of the innkeepers, Felix and Carolyn Vereen, seem warm and personable even coming across a television screen. Mobile's oldest B&B, the Towle House is located in the heart of Mobile's Historic District, and serves a gourmet breakfast.

If you drive to **Fort Conde,** park free across the street. The fort was built from 1724-1735 by the French and was the headquarters for colonial governments of the French, British, and Spanish. Americans seized it in 1813; Congress declared the fort "surplus," and it was sold at public auction in 1820. The City of Mobile partially reconstructed the fort with local funds during the American Revolution Bicentennial. Today educational tours of the fort are offered to visitors by guides dressed in eighteenth-century military uniforms. The guides will be happy to fire their muskets, which kids say are louder than any firecracker. Don't flinch, and you can see the spark.

If you're interested in a commercial tour to give yourself an overview of the city, ask a knowledgeable welcome center staff member about tours and fees and pick up a schedule. Set tours run for one to three hours or longer. You can also request a customized tour.

After my husband and I peeked over the brick walls of the fort at the river in the distance, we gathered a stack of brochures and maps and headed on foot for the **Phoenix Fire Museum.** In 1964 this museum was two blocks away. When it was moved to its present location, Lady Bird Johnson christened the structure, "The Museum of the City of Mobile." It's free and unguided, but we were lucky to find a fireman there polishing one of the vehicles. He was happy to share tales of the 1880s, when the firemen's elaborate balls were attended by United States presidents, wealthy businessmen, and other celebrities. The volunteer fire companies were made up of young businessmen who bought their own equipment and furnished their fire stations themselves. Pride and rivalry among companies made the competition fierce, and sometimes buildings burned down while the men debated as to whose company would get there first!

In the first half of the nineteenth century there were several disastrous fires, and most of the original French, British, and Spanish buildings were destroyed. On the first floor of the museum you'll see an array of vehicles showing the progression from people and horse-drawn fire wagons to those driven by steam and gas engines. Don't miss climbing the long set of steps to the second floor. That's where the firemen become real people, represented by articles of clothing, letters, certificates, and awards. The firemen didn't live on the second floor as in later days, but reserved this space for parties. As we prepared to leave, the fireman who welcomed us to this step back in the city's past told us the **Mobile Fire Department** is one of the oldest in the United States, older than the one in New Orleans. He reminded us, as many Mobilians did throughout our weekends in the city, that the Mobile Mardi Gras is also older than the one in New Orleans.

Because Mobile is the oldest city in the state, it is indeed a city of firsts. It is home to the oldest Protestant church in Alabama, **Christ Episcopal,** and boasts the oldest newspaper, the *Mobile Register.* Mobile also hosts **America's Junior Miss,** the oldest and largest scholarship program for high school senior women in the country, and the **Senior Bowl.** The Junior Miss program began in Mobile over 40 years ago, and the national finals take place here. The national headquarters is located on Government Street.

The Senior Bowl is the only NFL-sanctioned postseason game and pits the best senior collegiate football stars from the North and the South against each other. The real prize is not who wins the game, but who gets noticed. The Junior Miss competition takes place in June and the Senior Bowl, which is now in its fifth decade, is a January event. If you schedule your weekend getaway around either of these times, you can still see the city, and a good way to tour the city without wearing out your shoe leather is by boat.

The ***Cotton Blossom* Riverboat** takes daily lunch and dinner cruises on the Mobile River. The cabins on the first and second decks are climate controlled. (This means air conditioning!) Watch the massive sternwheeler and imagine days gone by. You might also glimpse an alligator. The boat is 70 years old and is one of only four boats in the nation to have National Register of Historic Places recognition. This is noted on the bronze plaque in the main cabin. One of the few survivors of the paddlewheel-towing era of the 1920s, the *Cotton Blossom* is beautifully refurbished and docks at the **Mobile Convention Center,** the handsome glass building overlooking the Mobile River. Narrated sightseeing cruises are scheduled at 1 P.M. daily and depart from the Convention Center. Outside seating is covered and if you didn't have time for lunch, you can buy sodas and hot dogs aboard.

If you'd rather see a different kind of ship, go through the Bankhead Tunnel under the Mobile River and turn right. Take Highway 98 to **Battleship Memorial Park** to see the **Battleship USS *Alabama*** and the submarine, **USS *Drum*.** The battleship was in every major sea battle of World War II, and neither the ship nor the crew members were ever injured. However, the submarine had recently taken a hit from a hurricane the day we were there.

A huge bell hangs just outside the entrance to the complex, and it's a challenge to the kids to ring the bell. As you walk up the ramps

USS Alabama. (Photo by Neal Broerman)

Ship's bell on USS Alabama. (Photo by Joan Broerman)

and steps on the battleship, you hear the bell ringing and almost feel as if the ship might pull away from the dock. The main deck is fine for wheelchairs and strollers, but that's as far as anything on wheels can go. The steps between decks are steep.

After you've toured the ship, see the **Aircraft Pavilion** nearby. It houses military bombers and fighter planes, Jeeps, and other military exhibits.

Hungry? You will be! Bring a picnic lunch to eat on the grounds, or leave the park and turn right. Go east on U.S. 98 to the **Original Oyster House** for lunch. You'll have a good view of the water, and the food is worthy of the appetite you just worked up while touring the deck of the USS *Alabama*. We spotted happy young diners coloring their own menus featuring a smiling Wally, the Gator Chef, in the center. The gumbo has real crab claws and is a meal in itself. Peanut chocolate chip pie is a specialty. As in many restaurants in the south, the manager circulates among the patrons to see if they are satisfied. Stuart Livingston was no exception. He got smiles for answers.

Mobile to **Daphne** on Interstate 10 is a scenic drive over the water. You'll see fishermen trolling from their boats and hungry birds waiting for a fishy treat. You could keep driving until you reach **Spanish Fort** and drive through two parks, one historic and the other a pleasant place to hike or fish. **Meaher State Park** is located on Mobile Bay, and **Blakeley State Park** is a well-preserved battlefield, the site of the last major battle of the Civil War. Turn around and head back toward Mobile and take a side trip to the **Malbis Plantation** where you can visit a **Greek Orthodox Church** of Byzantine architecture, replete with vivid stained glass, and murals depicting the life of Christ.

As you retrace your steps on I-10 toward the city, stop for dinner at **Pier 4 Restaurant.** See if those fishermen you saw earlier are still at it!

Begin Sunday with the comfortable ambience of brunch at **Spot of Tea,** owned by Tony and Michelle Moore. You may have to stand in a short line, but take the time to look around the gift shop and sniff the soaps and special teas and flavored coffees. Slices of fruity soaps are packaged and beribboned for quick gift choices, or you can choose something out of the ordinary. So popular that it's sold out by Christmas is the Mardi Gras soap, which is like the King Cake. The person who gets the baby in a slice of **King Cake** at a Mardi Gras Party has to give the next party. The Mardi Gras soap has a baby in every slice.

Once you are called to your seat, you'll enjoy reading the menu and notes on the ritual of afternoon tea. This restaurant is smoke-

Cutting novelty soap at Spot of Tea. (Photo by Neal Broerman)

and alcohol-free. There's just enough elegance for parents, but it's not too stuffy for kids. My husband ordered Belgian waffles and I chose eggs Benedict. The portions were generous. You might prefer paying the $2 split fee and sharing.

We stepped out into a warm Mobile morning and walked across Cathedral Square to visit the **Cathedral of the Immaculate Conception.** The first Catholic parish on the Gulf Coast was established at Mobile in 1703, one year after the founding of the city. When the city was relocated to its present site in 1711, the parish church was rebuilt. The cornerstone for the new cathedral was laid in 1835. It was consecrated as the **Cathedral of the Immaculate Conception** in December 1850 and has suffered war, fire, and modifications. The word "cathedral" comes from the Latin word *cathedra,* which means throne. The archbishop's throne or chair is located in the sanctuary and symbolizes his governing and teaching roles.

Are you ready for an experience the entire family will enjoy? Make your last stop for this weekend the **Gulf Coast Exploreum Museum of Science.** Part of the building housing this interactive science museum and IMAX dome theatre dates back to the first settlement.

Look for original staircases and locks on the doors. Parents, grandparents, and kids swarm into intriguing exhibits like 1001 Gears, the Circuit Lab, Mirror Magic, Animal Tools, Wheel Race, and Pulley Power. Throughout the spacious halls, kids' voices echoed, "Me next!" One nine and a half-year-old boy (he was specific about the half) described the museum this way: "It's awesome. I love it so much, I wish I could live here."

The **IMAX** theater program will add one more brush with the extraordinary. Buy your tickets and get there before the theater is darkened for the show. You will want to feel that you have tightened your pretend safety belt in time to take off on a roller coaster ride or spacecraft or whatever adventure is offered.

After you return to reality, no need to leave the building if you want to eat before you head home. **Carpe Diem Coffee and Tea Company** runs the food area and serves the same mouthwatering sandwiches and desserts as at their coffee house near **Spring Hill College.**

Area Code: (334)

Getting There:

Mobile is at the southern end of Interstate 65 and on Interstate 10. Interstate 165 is Exit 9 from Interstate 65 and comes into downtown Mobile at Water Street. The Mobile airport is served by major airlines and is located on Airport Highway, about 12 miles from downtown.

Where and When:

Battleship USS *Alabama*, Battleship Memorial Park, U.S. 98, Mobile, AL 36601, Daily from 8 A.M. 433-2703. Admission.

Bellingrath Gardens and Home, 12401 Bellingrath Gardens Road, **Theodore,** AL 36582. March. 973-2217; (800) 247-8420. Admission.
Web site: www.bellingrath.org/

Blakeley State Park, 33707 Alabama 225, Spanish Fort, AL 36527. 626-0798.

Cathedral of the Immaculate Conception, 2 S. Claiborne Street, Mobile, AL 36602. 434-1565.

Christ Episcopal Church, 115 S. Conception Street, Mobile, AL 36604. 438-1822.

***Cotton Blossom* Riverboat,** 1 S. Water Street, Mobile, AL 36601. Sightseeing cruise 1 P.M. daily. 438-3060. Admission.

Gulf Coast Exploreum Museum of Science, 65 Government Street at Water Street, Mobile, AL 36602. June-Aug., Sun.-Thurs., 9 A.M.-8 P.M.,

Fri.-Sat., 9 A.M.-9P.M.; Sept.-May, Sun.-Thurs., close at 5 P.M. 208-6873; (800) 262-3151. Admission.   Web site: www.exploreum.com
Malbis Plantation and **Greek Orthodox Memorial Church,** Baldwin County Road 27, Malbis, AL. Daily, 9 A.M.-noon, 2 P.M.-5 P.M. 626-3050.
Meaher State Park, U.S. 90 W., Spanish Fort, AL 36527. 626-5529.
Phoenix Fire Museum, 54 S. Claiborne Street, Mobile, AL 36604. Tue.-Sat., 10 A.M.-5 P.M.; Sun., 1 P.M.-5 P.M. 434-7554.

Information:
Fort Conde Visitor Center, 150 S. Royal Street, Mobile, AL 36602. 434-7304.

Guide Services:
Bay City Tours (formerly Gray Line), 210 S. Washington Avenue, Mobile, AL 36602. 432-2229.
Landmark Tours, 22873 U.S. 98, Fairhope, AL 36532. 928-0207.
Web site: www.landmarktours.com

Accommodations:
Adam's Mark Hotel, 64 S. Water Street, Mobile, AL 36602. 438-4000; (800) 444-2326.
Radisson Admiral Semmes Hotel, 251 Government Street, Mobile, AL 36602. 432-8000; (800) 333-3333.
Towle House Bed and Breakfast, 1104 Montauk Avenue, Mobile, AL 36604. 432-6440; (800) 938-6953.
Web site: www.towle-house.com

Restaurants:
Original Oyster House, near Battleship Park on U.S. 98, Mobile, AL 36601. Sun.-Thurs., 11 A.M.-10 P.M.; Fri.-Sat., 11 A.M.-11 P.M. 626-2188.
Pier 4 Restaurant, 1420 Battleship Pkwy., Mobile, AL 36616. Sun.-Thurs., 11 A.M.-9 P.M.; Fri.-Sat., 11 A.M.-10 P.M. 626-6710.
Roussos Seafood Restaurant, 166 S. Royal Street, Mobile, AL 36601. 433-3322.
Spot of Tea, 310 Dauphin Street, Mobile, AL 36602. Daily, 7 A.M.-2 P.M. 433-9009.

Major Annual Events:
Senior Bowl All Star Classic, Mobile—January. 438-2276.
Battle of Mobile Bay Living History Program, Fort Gaines Historic Site, Dauphin Island—February. 450-0517.

Medieval Hit List, Fort Gaines Historic Site, Dauphin Island—March. 450-0517.

Blessing of the Fleet, Bayou La Batre—May.

Prichard Juneteenth Celebration, Prichard—June. 452-7893.

All Star Classic Mississippi and Alabama High School Senior Football Game, Mobile—Late June. 208-2500.

Junior Miss Pageant, Mobile Civic Center, Mobile—Late June. 438-3621.

Bayfest Music Festival, Downtown Mobile—October. 470-7730.

8

HAMMERING
HISTORY IN PLACE

At night, when you drive down the side streets of **Mobile,** porch lights turn dark streets into neighborhoods. Historic neighborhoods may have their ghosts, but today's residents are renewing and restoring the old homes and preserving the memories of those who walked the area decades or centuries ago. In many of the historic districts, dumpsters stand in front yards of dilapidated shells, but the house next door and the one across the street could be completed restoration projects sporting white wicker rockers and ferns on the wraparound porches. Preservation fever is contagious in Mobile. The lucky tourist gets to enjoy the results without having to clear away the dust of the rescue efforts.

A downtown hotel or bed and breakfast will put you in good position to start your weekend with a visit to the glamorous glass **Mobile Convention and Visitors' Bureau,** which overlooks Mobile River at the foot of Government Street. Pick up all the historic walking tours brochures and maps you can find. Use them for taking notes on what you discover.

Take a good look around the Convention Center before you venture into Mobile's past. The center opened in 1993 on the site of the old banana docks, and in a relatively short time has won many awards. Notice the light fixtures, crafted with a nautical flair. The color of the building, inside and out, reflects the native color of the area. Enjoy the magnificent view of the river and count the different kinds of ships dotting the water. Surprisingly, a double set of train tracks runs through the building.

For Friday supper or Saturday breakfast, you'll find the **House of Seafood Restaurant** to be a neighborhood kind of place. The restaurant fronts on Government Street, but the street behind it separates its parking lot from a residential section. Families gather here to relax, and tourists wander in to make new friends. Perfect strangers seated at nearby tables find themselves making conversation with each other. Every night a special is described on a chalkboard by the back door. Lightly-seasoned shrimp marinara served over angel hair pasta convinced us that ordering the special not only spared us from struggling to make a decision from the menu, but also turned out to be exactly what we wanted, whether we realized it at the time or not. Louise Radcliff and her partners from Panama City opened this, their second seafood restaurant, in Mobile in 1997. For a breakfast you'll tell your friends about, try the crabmeat omelet, grits, and biscuits that have to be grasped firmly or they will float away.

On Saturday the **Dauphin Street Historic District Walking Tour** will make you feel as if you are on a scavenger hunt trying to spot architectural landmarks. This is the city's main commercial street, and in the past, when a native wanted to describe anything of exceptional quality, he'd say it was "...like walkin' down Dauphin Street." After a few hours of "I Spy," sit down in **Cathedral Square** and watch others amble by.

The oldest surviving residential area in Mobile is found within the nine-block area known as **De Tonti Square Historic District.** This is located three blocks north of the central business district. A few buildings date from the 1830s, but many were built during Mobile's "Golden Era" in the 1850s. Examples of Greek Revival, Gulf Coast Cottage, and Victorian architecture are found here, as well as the dominant styles of Federal and Italianate.

Here is a note on Mobile's **Historic Building Markers.** On the houses you might see two separate plaques-the shield and the banner. The shield represents the six flags that have flown over Mobile: French, Spanish, English, Republic of Alabama, Confederate, and United States of America. The banner displays the construction date of the building and either the name by which the building is popularly known or the names of both the original and current owners. These markers will tell you that a building is of historic importance and is an excellent example of the architectural heritage of Mobile.

As you continue your tour, you'll see much of the city's history reflected in its street and park names. If the two French brothers who moved from Canada and played the biggest part in settling Mobile could return and look for signs of the city's gratitude, they'd find it in **Bienville Square,** which is named for Jean Baptiste Le Moyne, Sieur de **Bienville.** His older brother, Pierre Le Moyne, Sieur **D'Iberville,** brought the teen-aged Bienville to Louisiana as a reward for his bravery in manning a gun during battle. Bienville's bravery seems to have stayed with him all his life. He explored the Gulf Coast and located the mouth of a mighty river that turned out to be the Mississippi. Later he set up the first colony of Mobile at the 27 Mile Bluff. Still later, in 1711, Bienville participated in the move to the city's present site, and he laid out the streets of Royal, Dauphin, Conti, St. Francis, and St. Louis, which retain those names today. Dauphin Street, a principal street in the new settlement, was named for the son of Louis XIV. The Spaniards changed the name, but the Americans changed it back.

Most of the museums and historic buildings you are able to tour today will not be open during **Mardi Gras,** so make the most of your time on Government Street. The **City of Mobile Museum** will soon move to the Southern Market/Old City Hall complex, a designated National Landmark dating to 1855, at 111 South Royal Street. The current building will become a Mardi Gras Museum and will continue to display the elegant gowns and robes worn by Mardi Gras royalty. This is part of the **Church Street East Historic District.**

Oakleigh Period House Museum is the magnificent Greek antebellum mansion located in the center of the **Oakleigh Garden Historic District,** which is largely residential in character. The area was developed mostly after the Civil War and Reconstruction and represents the new growth and economic prosperity that the city enjoyed starting in the last quarter of the nineteenth century and continuing into the first quarter of the twentieth century. Notice the grand live oaks. The house was begun in 1833 by Mobile merchant James W. Roper, who acted as his own architect and devised a number of unique and practical features. Oakleigh, two and a half blocks south of Government Street between Roper Street and George Street, is furnished with fine period collections, and gives a peek into a household that enjoyed prosperous times.

Not far from Oakleigh is **La Pizzeria,** on Monroe Street. The aroma invites you in, and the menu proclaims "Sumptuous, succulent, to die for." See if the menu is right.

The library on Government Street is in the center of much you

Mardi Gras gowns on display at the Museum of Mobile. (Photo by Karim Shamsi-Basha, courtesy Alabama Bureau of Tourism & Travel)

will want to see. The **Mobile Public Library** was built in 1928, but due to segregation, African Americans were not allowed to use it. Two years later, eight blocks from the library, another library was built. This is now the **African-American Archives,** and the surrounding area is known as the **Martin Luther King Historic District.** Both libraries were designed by the same architect. The archives, listed in the National Register of Historic Places, has portraits and biographies of famous African Americans, a section of African-American carving, artifacts, books, records, and other documents pertaining to historical places, events and occasions.

Church Street Cemetery is located behind the Mobile Public Library. This is Mobile's oldest resting place. **Joe Cain,** who is credited with reviving Mardi Gras after the Civil War, is buried here. People toss Mardi Gras beads across his marker—even when it is not Mardi Gras! **Charles Boyington** is also buried here. He was convicted of murder and not only proclaimed his innocence until his last breath but told the crowd gathered to watch his hanging that upon his burial an oak tree with 100 roots would grow out of his grave to prove his innocence. He was right about the oak, which marks his grave today. It's called the **Boyington Oak**.

Across from the Boyington Oak on South Bayou you will see a church on the corner, the **Big Zion African Methodist Episcopal Church.** At this church, built in 1867 and remodeled in 1896, the first ordination in Alabama of a black minister by a black bishop took place.

Another cemetery of interesting historical importance is the **Magnolia Cemetery.** To get there from Government Street, take Ann Street to Virginia Street. This burial place for the citizens of Mobile was established in 1836, and the elaborate monuments and unusual funerary sculpture reflect the romantic attitudes toward death during that period. The Bellingrath-Morse colonnade (the Bellingrath family founded Bellingrath Gardens) is one of the cemetery's tallest and most well-known monuments.

Segregation was not practiced in this cemetery, and African-American burial sites are located throughout Magnolia. Those who visit this cemetery are reminded that new burials still take place here, and respect is expected. Rubbings are not allowed. A warning: snakes and ant hills make footing somewhat precarious.

If a morning of following history was enough for you and your family and you want to do something really different, follow the advice of noted river photographer **Beth Maynor Young,** who says the **Mobile-Tensaw Delta** scenery must not be missed. One way to venture into this swamp is to take a **Wildland Expedition Swamp Tour** in the capable hands of Captain Gene Burrell, a U.S. Coast Guard master captain. On these swamp tours you can explore one of America's most diverse wildlands and see water lilies, cypress trees, and lush vegetation. More than 250 species of birds and 230 species of fish thrive here. The **Mobile-Tensaw Delta** is 200,000 acres of marshland and forested wetlands, the largest inland delta in the U.S. It begins at the northern end of Mobile Bay and extends 40 miles up the Mobile-Tensaw system. Other wildlife you might see include the American alligator, black bear, bald eagle, and osprey.

Each two-hour narrated expedition has rest stops and leaves from **Chickasaw Marina,** on U.S. 43 in Chickasaw, Alabama. To get there, take Interstate 165 from Mobile to Interstate 65 and go 13 miles to Exit 13. Turn right on Alabama 158 and go two miles to U.S. 43. You are half a mile from the Marina. Even though mosquitoes are not supposed to travel on these tours, be prepared for those no see-ums, and wear insect repellent.

You may not have seen a black bear on your wetlands tour, but you'll return to your Mobile getaway room as hungry as one. For a fun supper you could go to **Picklefish,** downtown on Dauphin. If you want more formality, go to the **Pillars Restaurant** on Government Street, not far from the **House of Seafood Restaurant.** At one time, two houses stood where The Pillars is now located. One house was torn down in the 1940s and the other was turned into a boarding house. The current owner bought it and remodeled it into an elegant restaurant. Our waitress told us that the most popular dessert is the bread pudding, served with a Southern Comfort cinnamon sauce.

If Sunday finds you eager to get out on the links, you have a number of choices: **Spring Hill College Golf Course, Azalea City Golf Course** (which overlooks the lakes at Municipal Park and is owned by the city), and **Magnolia Grove Golf Course,** a **Robert Trent Jones Golf Trail** member.

To get to the Azalea City Golf Course, go west on Airport Boulevard, then north on University and right onto Gaillard Drive.

Magnolia Grove features 54 holes, and the main tract is the Falls Course. On the tenth hole, a 570-yard par five, a waterfall flows across stairsteps beneath a green falling eight feet from front to back. The rest of the property includes creeks, marshlands, and lakes.

For the traveler, the marshes, swamps, rivers, and bays of Mobile offer memories easy to record with a camera. As you leave the city, you may find yourself pulling over onto a gravel parking lot beside the water and leaning out the window to snap pictures of gulls flocking on the sand. Listen to their soft cries. Jean Baptiste Le Moyne, Sieur de Bienville, may not recognize this city he started, but the gulls still speak the same language.

Area Code: (334)

Getting There:

Mobile is at the southern end of Interstate 65 and on Interstate 10. Interstate 165 is Exit 9 from Interstate 65 and comes into downtown Mobile at Water Street. The Mobile airport is served by major airlines and is located on Airport Highway, about 12 miles from downtown.

Where and When:

African-American Archives, 564 Dr. Martin Luther King, Jr. Avenue, Mobile, AL 36603. Tue.-Fri., 9 A.M.-4 P.M. 433-8511. Donations accepted.

Azalea City Golf Course, Gaillard Drive, Mobile, AL. 342-4221.

Big Zion African Methodist Episcopal Church, 112 S. Bayou Street, Mobile, AL 36602. 433-8431.

Bragg Mitchell Mansion, 1906 Springhill Ave., Mobile, AL 36607. Mon.-Fri., 10 A.M.-4 P.M.; Sun., 1 P.M.-4 P.M. 471-6364. Admission.

Conde-Charlotte Museum House, 104 Theatre Street, Mobile, AL 36604. Tue.-Sat., 10 A.M.-4 P.M. 432-4722. Admission.

Magnolia Cemetery, 1202 Virginia Street, Mobile, AL 36604. 432-8672.

Magnolia Grove Golf Course, 7000 Lamplighters Drive, Semmes, AL 36575. 645-0075.

Mobile Public Library, Government Street, Mobile, AL.

Mobile Symphony. 432-2010.

City of Mobile Museum, 355 Government Street, Mobile, AL 36604. Tue.-Sat., 10 .am.-5 P.M.; Sun., 1 P.M.-5 P.M. 434-7569.

Oakleigh Period House Museum, 350 Oakleigh Place, Mobile, AL 36604. Mon.-Sat., 10 A.M.-4 P.M. 432-1281. Admission.

Southern Market/Old City Hall complex, 111 South Royal Street, Mobile, AL.

Spring Hill College Golf Course, Dauphin Street, Mobile, AL 36608. 380-4655.

Information:

Mobile Convention and Visitors' Bureau, P.O. Box 204, Mobile, AL 36601. 208-2000; (800) 566-2453.

Mobile Office of Special Events, 2900 Dauphin Street, Mobile, AL 36606. Weekdays, 8 A.M.-5 P.M. 470-7730.

Guide Services:

Memorable Mobile Tours, P.O. Box 81852, Mobile, AL 36608. 344-8687.

Wildland Expeditions Swamp Tours. Office: 7536 Tung Ave. N., Theodore, AL 36582. Tue.-Sat., tours leave at 8 A.M., 10 A.M., and 2 P.M. from Chickasaw Marina, U.S. 43. 460-8206. Admission.

Accommodations:

Adam's Mark Hotel, 64 S. Water Street, Mobile, AL 36602. 438-4000; (800) 444-2326.

Radisson Admiral Semmes Hotel, 251 Government Street, Mobile, AL 36602. 432-8000; (800) 333-3333.

Towle House, 1104 Montauk Ave., Mobile, AL 36604. 432-6440; (800) 938-6953.   Web site: www.towle-house.com

Restaurants:

House of Seafood Restaurant, 1960 Government Street, Mobile, AL 36606. Mon.-Thurs., 6 A.M.-9 P.M.; Fri.-Sat., 6 A.M.-10 P.M. 478-3031.

La Pizzeria, 1455½ Monroe Street, Mobile, AL 36604. Tue.-Thurs., 11 A.M.-9 P.M.; Fri.-Sat., 11 A.M.-10 P.M. 473-5003.

Picklefish, 251 Dauphin Street, Mobile, AL 36602. Mon.-Wed.,11 A.M.-11 P.M.; Thurs., 11 A.M.-2 A.M.; Fri.-Sat., 11 A.M.-4 A.M.

Pier 4 Restaurant, 1420 Battleship Pkwy., Mobile, AL 36616. Sun.-Thurs., 11 A.M.-9 P.M.; Fri.-Sat., 11 A.M.-10 P.M. 626-6710.

Pillars Restaurant, 1757 Government Street, Mobile, AL 36604. Open daily for lunch and dinner. 478-6341.

Wintzell's Oyster House, 605 Dauphin Street, Mobile, AL 36602. 432-4605.

Major Annual Events:

Historic Mobile Homes Tour, Mobile—Second week in March. 433-0259.

Fort Mims Presents Living History, Tensaw—August, Sat, 9 A.M.-5 P.M.; Sun, 9 A.M.-4 P.M. 937-9464.

Oakleigh Period House Museum Candlelight Christmas, Mobile—First weekend in December. 432-1281.

9

WHOSE IDEA
WAS IT?

This entire chapter is devoted to **Mardi Gras** in Mobile. Do not plan to do anything else during this time in the Port City. Mardi Gras becomes a way of life.

Because there are so many Mardi Gras events, you can choose to come in February for some of the first parades for a sampling of this effervescent time. You might come the weekend before the actual Mardi Gras or plan to stay Monday and Tuesday. On Tuesday, the event is supercharged.

The city's first Mardi Gras celebration dates back to 1703, one year after Mobile's founding. Historians can't agree on who started this festival of fun, but does it really matter? Joe Cain revived it after the Civil War by dressing in full Chickasaw Indian regalia, climbing atop a decorated coal wagon pulled by a mule, and holding a one-float parade through the streets. He was really snubbing the Union soldiers who watched the whole thing, not realizing they were being insulted. Joe Cain chose to dress like a Chickasaw Indian because the Chickasaws had never been defeated in battle. This sly renewal of Carnival humor stirred the townsfolk to action, and Mardi Gras fever returned.

To honor Joe, the **Joe Cain Procession,** or the People's Parade, is held the Sunday before Mardi Gras. A related event is the tribute to Joe Cain at the Church Street Cemetery (behind the Mobile Public Library) sponsored by **"Cain's Merry Widows,"** who dress in black, carry white lilies, and ride in funeral hearses in the procession.

Mardi Gras parade. (Photo by Neal Broerman)

University of Alabama Million Dollar Band. (Photo by Neal Broerman)

In *Let the Good Times Roll!*, the history of Mardi Gras socialites and the **Carnival** season in Mobile, recorded by **Emily Staples Hearin** and available at most gift shops in Mobile, Mrs. Hearin asks, "What is a Mardi Gras Parade?" She answers that it takes just three Mobilians— two to march and one to watch. Actually, a parade is a procession of eight, ten or more floats, mounted by costumed riders. The floats form a tableau, and the central theme is carried over to the masked ball that follows by members of the Mystic organizations who keep their identities secret—even after the ball ends. The theme of the parade is usually a Classic legend. Watch closely and see if you find this to be true today.

Daytime floats usually appeal to children, and children ride on the floats in the Floral Parade. Children also have their own royalty and Junior Court.

What makes the Mardi Gras parade distinctive is that the masked riders toss candies and trinkets into the crowd of parade watchers. A story is told of then-President Richard Nixon paying a visit to Mobile. Children were excused from their classes in order to watch the presidential parade. Lining the streets on a weekday in order to watch a procession was familiar, as Mardi Gras was an official school holiday. What was not familiar was the disappointment the children felt after the smiling, waving president and his motorcade had passed. "He didn't throw anything!" the children exclaimed.

Mardi Gras is for fun. But where did the idea come from? French settlers founded the city that is now Mobile in 1711. Since settling new land is hard work, they had to have time to play, too. From their old country, the French brought their customs of Carnival and Mardi Gras.

Twelfth Night, the evening before Epiphany is celebrated (on January 6th), marks the end of the Christmas season and the beginning of the Carnival season. Most people call the whole Carnival season Mardi Gras, French for Fat Tuesday. Mardi Gras is supposed to take place only one day in the season of Carnival and traditionally refers to an individual's "farewell to meat." Many people give up eating meat for Lent, the forty-day period before Easter. Before Lent begins, it is common practice to throw a party to formally say goodbye to eating meat.

According to historian **Caldwell Delaney,** "It was on New Year's Eve of 1830 that Michael Krafft and a group of his friends went about the city with cowbells and rakes making a great noise in celebration of the happy season, and from their spree grew the first of Mobile's Mystic societies, the Cowbellion de Rakin Society. These societies put on street parades, which were the first theme parades to be presented in America and out of them grew the Mardi Gras celebrations of Mobile and New Orleans."

Bennett Wayne Dean, another noted Mardi Gras historian, says that although Michael Krafft and George Huggins of the Cowbellion de Rakin Society are buried in Magnolia Cemetery, Krafft may not be in his grave during Mardi Gras but is one of the more active revelers on one of the floats. Dean also says the Joe Cain buried in the Church Street Cemetery is not the same Joe Cain who brought the Mardi Gras back after the Civil War.

While Krafft and company started the celebration on New Year's, New Orleans held its Mardi Gras celebration before Lent. After the Civil War, citizens in both cities wondered if they could recover the old customs. Doubt was dispelled in Mobile by Chief Slackabamirimico, who said he lived in Wragg Swamp and had come to the city to put an end to the gloom of the war years. This was Joseph Cain, a clerk at the city market, and the superhero of Mobile. Wherever the real Joe Cain might be buried, Mardi Gras crowds are grateful.

Begin making Mardi Gras plans four to six months ahead. It's almost impossible to get a hotel room downtown, because so many revelers return year after year. They even request the same rooms! Motels on the perimeter of the city fill quickly, too. The *Mobile Register* publishes a Mardi Gras guide and gives daily coverage and parade routes.

Walk down Government Street the weekend before Fat Tuesday and you will see a city living outdoors. Families squeeze dining tents, charcoal cookers, folding chairs, and coolers into the space between sidewalks and old historic buildings. Many families use this festive weekend to plan family reunions, and reunite they do, from Friday to Tuesday night, when the last float rolls by. At that point the tents come down, the cars are loaded up, and choruses of, "See ya' next year" sound throughout the neighborhoods on the side streets.

If it's your first Mardi Gras, your senses will be overloaded. The smells of charcoal, beer, and grilling meat are thick, and the sounds of drums, shuffling feet, and cheers of the crowd when the rocking floats pass by will fill your ears to the point of exploding. Costumed riders and mounted police prance by. Then another brightly lit, multicolored float rocks into view, and then another, and another.

Look out! "Throws" or showers of trinkets, toys, candy, beads, and

Comic Cowboys float, Mardi Gras parade. (Photo by Neal Broerman)

McGuire's. Irish Pub float, Mardi Gras parade. (Photo by Neal Broerman)

coins will bounce off your head and send those next to you scrambling over your toes. Especially prized among the throws are the original Moon Pies from Chattanooga Bakery Co. in Chattanooga, Tennessee, but others that look like them and are called names like Mardi Gras pies, party pies, and marshmallow pies are plucked from the air and eaten with gusto, too. Peanuts, wrapped candies and bubble gum, plastic cups, giant plastic toothbrushes, coins with the crest of the Mystic society, and glittery beads in the Mardi Gras colors of gold, green, and purple tumble from the hands of the masked riders on the floats that are like stories come to life.

Those who have made a study of such things say the best places to watch the parade—and catch a good collection of throws—are at the start of the parade and at the end. As the float journeys down the first section of the route, the revelers atop the floats are enthusiastic and throw beads and marshmallow pies wildly. At the end they are tired and want to toss out everything they have left. Don't stand under a tree. Tree limbs can catch or deflect your treasures. Carry a large paper bag to hold your catches, a fish net for scooping, and a child's plastic rake to reach under the barricades and capture candies and beads that fall inches too far away.

Another parade expert suggests keeping an eye on TV crews. Follow those cams! Bands show off more for the media and the float riders toss more goodies. There is also a special area set aside for the handicapped. Ask where that will be.

To have a safe, enjoyable Mardi Gras experience, follow these safety rules:

1) Stay behind barricades.

2) Don't throw anything at the floats, band members, or parade participants.

3) City ordinance forbids beverages in glass containers in public. Violators may be arrested.

4) Spectators at turns in the parade route need to be ready to move back quickly. Floats often need extra room for turning.

5) Choose a well-lit area to view night parades and a designated meeting place for gathering your group after the parade.

6) Parade routes are well marked. Pay attention to the signs. Don't park along the route two hours before the scheduled parade starting time and not until two hours after the parade ends.

There are so many secret clubs in Mobile that the city is called "Mother of Mystics." The Mystics build floats privately and all floats are new every year. None are refurbished from the year before. Even if you don't belong to a Mystic Society, coronations and other royal festivities held by the **Mobile Carnival Association,** Mobile Area Mardi Gras Association, and the Prichard Mardi Gras Association are open to the public, and tickets can be purchased.

Mardi Gras in Mobile has a particular charm. Layers of history and tradition strengthen this city that refused to give up its good times in spite of wars, hurricanes, or depressions. Mobilians say, "Let the Good Times Roll," and they do . . . right down Government Street.

When you arrive back home and sort out your bag of Mardi Gras treasures, share the fun with your friends. You'll have plenty of beads to toss their way, and you'll impress them with your surprise dessert. For each serving, place one of those leftover marshmallow cookies or original Moon Pies in the microwave for a minute, remove, and top with ice cream and chocolate sauce. Sounds like a good way to make the Mardi Gras feeling last.

Area Code: (334)

Getting There:

Mobile lies at the southern end of Interstate 65 and on Interstate 10. Interstate 165 is Exit 9 from Interstate 65 and comes into downtown Mobile at Water Street. The Mobile airport is served by major airlines and is located on Airport Highway, about twelve miles from downtown.

Information:

Mobile Carnival Association, P.O. Box 2488, Mobile, AL 36652. Offices inside the Mobile Chamber of Commerce. 432-3324.

Prichard Mardi Gras Association, 432-3050.

Mobile Register   Web site: www.mobileregister.com

St. Stephens reenactment. (Photo by Neal Broerman)

10

ITCHY FEET

Pull on your travel boots and get ready for a weekend of variety. Pack a cooler with bottled water and soda and a few snacks to nibble on the way. Choose a hotel or motel on Interstate 65 near Saraland for your Friday night stay, and be sure you have plenty of film for your camera.

Begin your day with a visit to **Grand Oak Wildlife Park,** one mile east of Interstate 65, eight miles north of Mobile. This is home to the Grand Oak, which is not only believed to be the second-largest live oak in the United States, but as far as anyone has been able to determine is the only living thing in Alabama that was alive two millennia ago. While you are roaming the grounds, you will see emus, rheas, llamas, and black turkeys roaming, too. You can even feed some of them at feeding stations in various locations throughout the park. Walk through Australian, Indo-Pacific, South China, African Madagascan, and New World rain forest plantings. The paths are natural and navigable by wheelchair, and visitors in wheelchairs are admitted free.

Now you are ready to travel from the oldest tree to the oldest above-ground historic structure in Alabama. Andrew Ellicott mapped the Mississippi Territory, and the so-called Ellicott's Stone marked the beginning of the United States' rule over the land that is now Alabama. This stone also symbolizes a crucial turning point for the Indian nations that once controlled the land. The decades that followed Ellicott's demarcation saw Indian culture begin to disappear, as natives were forced out by soldiers and settlers from the East.

St. Stephens flag ceremony reenactment. (Photo by Neal Broerman)

Take Interstate 65 about 15 miles north of Mobile to U.S. 43, Exit 19.
Go toward the Bucks community and at the steam plant you will see a
historic marker on the east side of the highway, at a parking lot set for
visitors of the **Ellicott Stone.** A mulched trail about .25-mile long will
take you into the woods to the stone. When you get there, note that on
one side the Spanish inscription marking the territory under the rule
of King Charles IV appears. On the other side, an English inscription
proclaims that the territory is held by the United States.

To continue this historic trail, take U.S. 43 to Washington County
Road 34. Turn west and go about 5 miles to St. Stephens. Then follow the signs. **St. Stephens** is the oldest of Alabama's five capitals. In
St. Stephens, Native Americans and European colonials interacted.
When the fort at San Esteban was evacuated by the soldiers of Spain,
the first American flag to fly over the state of Alabama was raised
here. You can visit the site of the old fort, even though it is at the end
of a little dirt road, but it is worth spending a few hours exploring.

The best route to your next stop, **Perdido Vineyards,** the first farm
winery in the state, is to retrace your steps down U.S. 43 to Interstate
65 and go north. When you reach Interstate 65, take time for lunch,
as that intersection will probably give you the greatest selection. The

Perdido Vineyards are located less than 50 miles out of Mobile. Signs to the vineyard are easy to find, but when you pull up in the parking area, you will wonder if you are in the right place. Enter the small building on your right, and you will probably find one of the owners, Jim or Marianne Eddins, stocking the refrigerator or the jelly and jam shelf.

Perdido wines are made exclusively from the finest varieties of muscadine and scuppernong grapes. You will be offered a taste, and even if you are not a wine drinker, you will appreciate the fruity aroma. The vineyards produce premium white, red, and rosé table wines, and wines are also made from Alabama apples. In addition to wine, the small gift shop carries homemade, mouthwatering fruit preserves, jams, and peach butter under the label **"Rachel's Recipe."** The winery accepts no credit cards and is closed on Sunday, so bring your checkbook and make this a Saturday stop.

Next on your road trip is a leisurely drive through the town of **Brewton,** which has that old Southern town feeling. Most of the historic homes on Belleville Avenue are still occupied by descendants of the original builders. Drive through and continue to **Monroeville,** made famous by acclaimed writers **Harper Lee** and **Truman Capote.** This, too, seems like a sleepy Southern town, but it is known as the Literary Capital of Alabama and is probably not sleepy. Many writers work at night, and the area may just be catching up on its rest after a night of creating. Works by Lee and Capote are presented on special occasions throughout the year, including an annual production of Lee's Pulitzer-prize winning novel, *To Kill a Mockingbird.* This two-act play features a local cast and the jury is drawn from the audience. The first act begins on the back lawn of the county courthouse, and the second act continues in the historic courtroom where Atticus Finch proved his mettle. Even though the play runs during two weekends in May, the first day of ticket sales is March 1. This popular play has experienced a first-day sellout, so you will want to make arrangements for tickets early.

Park near the downtown square in Monroeville and wander into the **Monroe County Heritage Museum.** You can spend a short time here, but if you are lucky enough to find one of the townspeople in a talkative mood, you may want to stay awhile. When you leave the museum, go to Alabama Avenue, just off the square and across from the courthouse, and see the mural of Scout, Jem, and Dill peeking through the fence at "Boo" Radley, as well as other scenes from *To Kill a Mockingbird.*

These murals are the work of artist **William Harrison** of Foley, Alabama, and are part of a downtown **Monroeville Walking Tour.**

Now that you can face driving some more, get back in the car and look for signs to **Ricard's Mill,** an operating water-powered grain mill established in 1845. It's nearby, located on Flat Creek between Camden and Monroeville, five miles north of Beatrice on Alabama 265. This is a living history park open April through mid-December, and you can witness grist milling, cane syrup making, and black-smithing. The original mill was washed out by flooding, and the one you will see was relocated in 1858, just south of the first site.

You won't want to miss driving through **Camden.** Enjoy the lovely old homes just waiting for admirers. The courthouse square architecture displays an Italianate influence and features one of only four courthouses in Alabama that has been in continual use since the antebellum period.

The next stop on this day of history tracking is **Andalusia.** Spanish explorer Ponce de Leon allegedly came here looking for the fountain of youth. It's rumored that De Soto settled for a time on the Conecuh River nearby. Still later, it's possible that Andrew Jackson marked a trail through the area on his way to New Orleans by cutting three notches on the trees—thus the name of the **Three Notch Museum,** located in a nineteenth-century railroad depot in downtown Andalusia.

Modern history is made in this town every July when the **World Championship Domino Tournament** is held. This is a family event with three divisions: children 5-12, teens, and adults. The age groups overlap when teams are set up and some of the most formidable pairs are teens and grandparents. Some of the grandparents are in their nineties. People from across the southeastern part of the country come for this event, as well as players from the great domino-appreciating state of California. The 25th annual World Tournament will be held in 2000.

Hikers and mountain bikers may want to return to the **Conecuh National Forest** and take the Conecuh Trail, 20 miles of forest rich in dogwoods, holly, longleaf pine, magnolia, and cypress. Picturesque cypress ponds delight photographers. Blue Springs is a large natural spring of clear, icy-blue water that lies just off the trail. The trail crosses streams at several points and skirts Blue Pond, Five Run Creek, Nellie Pond, and Mossy Pond. The ponds provide good bass fishing.

The entire trail is open to foot traffic and can be hiked in two days. Mountain biking is allowed only on the Open Pond and Blue Lake loops. Hikers not interested in overnight camping can take two major loop trails for one-day trips.

Since these are one- and two-day hikes, for your trip from Saraland to Greenville (or Mobile to Montgomery), spend a few minutes driving into the forest for a few restful views. Hunting season is October through April, and it's suggested that hikers wear hunter-orange.

For country music fans, **Georgiana** is more than a name on the map, it's the site of the **Hank Williams, Sr., Boyhood Home and Museum.** The exhibits in his home and museum at 127 Rose Street follow this country music legend from his birth on a farm to the Grand Ole Opry, national fame, and his death at 29. He learned to play the guitar in Georgiana, and this is believed to be the only house Williams lived in that is still standing. You'll see art, clothes, guitars, and personal memorabilia.

By early evening, you should reach **Greenville,** known as the Camellia City. Begin your stay here by checking into the **Martin House,** a B&B that was built in 1895 and is listed on the National Register. Call ahead a few days and request dinner. By the time you get there, you will be ready to be pampered by innkeeper Jo Weitman.

On Sunday in Greenville, you can amble through this town that is the oldest one in Alabama *not* located on a river. The Federal Road passed five miles northeast of the area, and many people who arrived in 1818 were brave enough to travel farther south, where they settled in the wilderness and built a courthouse. The current courthouse in Greenville is of late Victorian vintage, built in 1903, and is the fourth courthouse building to stand on that site. The area surrounding the courthouse is the earlier town. Ask at the Martin House for the **Main Street Walking Tour** brochure and explore. The Pioneer Cemetery is on this tour, and the oldest grave you will see was dug there in 1827. There are many historical homes here, all private residences.

If you'd like to hear more about this historic area and Tom Braxton is in town, you can make arrangements through Ms. Weitman to meet this knowledgeable man, who often volunteers to tell visitors about his town. You can also stop by the Train Depot, which was built in 1910. It houses the Chamber of Commerce, another source of information.

For dinner, **Nanny's Fine Dining** is located in an old family home, and the home cooking and homemade pies will add to your enjoyment of the weekend, not to mention your waistline. It is on Alabama 185 North, between Greenville and Fort Deposit, but it's just open for the church crowd, which means between 11 and 2. If you miss that window of opportunity, try the **Smokehouse,** which has a country store atmosphere, can satisfy the biggest bear of an appetite, and is open every day, all day.

There are many gift shops in Greenville, but all of them are closed on Sunday. If gift-store sleuthing is your favorite activity, reverse this weekend getaway, begin with your stay in Greenville, and then travel south.

Golf lovers will want to head for the **Robert Trent Jones Golf Trail** and the Greenville delight, **Cambrian Ridge.** If you've played any of the other courses on the trail, you know this one will be exciting, too. It boasts three distinct championship courses, and one short nine-hole course.

To complete this getaway, you may want to explore a little of the Federal Road that brought settlers to Greenville. The road had its genesis as an old Indian trail, or group of trails, which the Creeks called "the wolf trail" or "the great trading path." The naturalist **William Bartram** followed these trails in 1776, and in 1805 Congress provided funds for opening the **Federal Road,** which was by then a horse path that followed the Indian trails along the crests of ridges. In 1815 the clatter of horse's hooves sounded across the countryside from this road when Sam Dale made his famous 600-mile ride in eight days to reach General Andrew Jackson at New Orleans with the news that the War of 1812 had ended.

The **Butler County Historical Landmarks Foundation** has marked a 4.5-mile section of the Bartram Trail and old Federal Road along Alabama 185 and Butler County Road 54. Except for some widening and paving, this stretch of the state looks much as it did when Bartram and Dale passed this way 200 years ago. Return to Alabama 263 and Interstate 65 for your route home. If home is 600 miles away, you will be glad your trail is paved and your horse will not tire.

Before you leave the area, you will surely want to take Exit 142 on Interstate 65 (Alabama 185) and pay a visit to **Priester's Pecans and Candies.** If you are searching for a gift that will represent Alabama, pecans do so deliciously. Priester's has been in business since 1935, and the gourmet candies are still made by hand in small batches stirred with wooden paddles in copper pots. You can watch the process yourself from the second-floor viewing area. Then take a trip to the sampling table. The free samples are supposed to help you make up your mind about what you'd like to purchase. This doesn't work. You will want a little of everything. If you arrive between 11 A.M. and 3 P.M., you can eat lunch. If you are too late for lunch, you'll have to fill up on ice cream and candy. Sorry.

Area Code: (334)

Getting There:

Mobile lies at the southern end of Interstate 65 and on Interstate 10. Interstate 165 is Exit 9 from Interstate 65 and comes into downtown Mobile at Water Street. The Mobile airport is served by major airlines and is located on Airport Highway, about 12 miles from downtown. All of the towns and cities mentioned in this chapter lie along Interstate 65 like charms on a bracelet.

Grand Oak Wildlife Park. From Mobile, take Interstate 65 to Exit 13 E. The park is one mile east of the interstate, about 8 miles north of Mobile.

St. Stephens. Take Interstate 65 about 15 miles north from Mobile to Exit 19 N. Take U.S. 43 to Washington County 34. Turn west and go about five miles to St. Stephens. The site is about 46 miles from Interstate 65.

Perdido Vineyards. Take Interstate 65, Exit 45 S. The vineyards are less than one mile from the exit.

Brewton. Take Interstate 65, Exit 77 S. Take Alabama 41 S about seventeen miles to the center of Brewton.

Monroeville. Take Interstate 65, Exit 93 N. It is about eighteen miles to Alabama 21 N, then about five miles to Monroeville.

Ricard's Mill. Located on Flat Creek between Camden and Monroeville. Go north on Alabama 21 from Monroeville about 18 miles to Beatrice, then five miles on Alabama 265 North.

Camden. Continue north on Alabama 265 from Beatrice for about 21 miles.

Andalusia. Take Interstate 65, Exit 93 S. It is about 38 miles to Andalusia.

Conecuh National Forest. The forest lies south of Andalusia on U.S. 29.

Georgiana. From Interstate 65, take Exit 114 S. Georgiana is about three miles from the Interstate.

Greenville. Greenville straddles Interstate 65 at exit 128.

Where and When:

Cambrian Ridge Golf Course, 101 SunBelt Pkwy., Greenville, AL 36037. 382-9787.

Claude D. Kelley State Park, 580 H. Kyle Road, (Alabama 21, north of Interstate 65), Atmore, AL 36502. 862-2511.

Conecuh National Forest, U.S. 29, Andalusia, AL.

Grand Oak Wildlife Park, Interstate 65, Exit 13 east one mile, Saraland, AL. Open daily at 9 A.M.; close summer, 5:30 P.M.; spring and fall, 5 P.M.; winter, 4 P.M.. 679-5757. Admission.

Hank Williams, Sr., Boyhood Home and Museum, 127 Rose Street (Interstate 65, Exit 114), Georgiana, AL 36033. Mon.-Sat., 10 A.M.-5 P.M.; Sun., 1 P.M.-5 P.M. 376-2555. Admission.

Monroe County Heritage Museum, P.O. Box 1637, Monroeville, AL 36461. Mon.-Fri., 8 A.M.-4 P.M.; Sat., 10 A.M.-2 P.M. 575-7433. Admission.

Old St. Stephens Historic Site, Washington County Road 34, St. Stephens, AL.

Perdido Vineyards, Interstate 65, Exit 45, Perdido, AL 36562, Mon.-Sat., 10 A.M.-5 P.M. 937-9483.

Ricard's Mill, Alabama 265, north of Beatrice, Monroeville, AL 36461, Mon.-Fri., 8 A.M.-4 P.M.; Sat., 10 A.M.-2 P.M. 575-2781. Admission.

River Heritage Museum, Clairborne Lock and Dam, Monroe County Road 17, Clairborne, AL. Fri.-Sat., 9 A.M.-4 P.M.; Sun., 1 p.m-5 P.M. 282-4206.

Three Notch Museum, Central Street, Andalusia, AL 36420. 222-0674.

Pineapple, 132 W. Commerce Street, Greenville, AL 36037. 382-7240.

Teacher's Pet, 130 W. Commerce Street, Greenville, AL 36037. 382-0349.

Elizabeth Wilson Florist, 105 Adams Street, Greenville, AL 36037. 382-3041.

Information:

Alabama Vacation Guide. Call 1-800-ALABAMA (252-2262).

Alabama Welcome Center, U.S. 331, Exit 14, Florala, AL.

Atmore Chamber of Commerce, 501 S. Pensacola Avenue, Atmore, AL 36502. 368-3305.

Web site: www.frontiernet/~commerce

Brewton Chamber of Commerce, 1010-B Douglas Avenue, Brewton, AL 36426. 867-3224.

Web site: www.brewtonchamber.com

Foley Convention and Visitors Bureau, P. O. Box 448, Foley, AL 36536. 943-1200.   Web site: www.foleycvb.com

Georgiana City Chamber of Commerce, P. O. Box 310, Georgiana, AL 36033. 376-2555.   Web site: www.hankmuseum.com
Georgiana Information, Georgiana, AL 36033. 376-2396.
Greenville Chamber of Commerce, 110 Cedar Street, Greenville, AL 36037. 382-3251; (800) 959-0717.
Web site: www.alabamasbest.com
Monroeville Chamber of Commerce, P. O. Box 214, Monroeville, AL 36461. 743-2879.
South Baldwin Chamber of Commerce, P. O. Box 1117, Foley, AL 36536. 943-3291.   Web site: www.southbaldwinchamber.com

Accommodations:

Chain and independent motels are available along Interstate 65. See the *Alabama Vacation Guide*. Call 1-800-ALABAMA (252-2262).

Martin House, 212 E. Commerce Street, Greenville, AL 36037. 382-2011.   Web site: www.bbonline.com/al/martin/rooms.html

Restaurants:

Nanny's Fine Dining, 430 Barganier, Greenville, AL 36037. Sun., 11 A.M.-2 P.M. 382-5689.

Priester's Pecans and Candies, Interstate 65, Exit 142, Fort Deposit, AL. Daily, 8 A.M.-6 P.M. 227-8355; (800) 277-3226.
Web site: www.priester.com

Smokehouse, 315 Pineapple Highway at Exit 128 off I-65. Open 7 days a week, 5:30 A.M.-9 P.M. 382-5868.

Major Annual Events:

Heritage Arts Festival. Old Courthouse Museum, Monroeville— February. 575-7433.

To Kill A Mockingbird, Old Courthouse Museum, Monroeville— March. 575-7433.

Ricard's Mill Reopening. Alabama 265 N, Beatrice—April. 575-7433.

Alabama's Blueberry Festival, Brewton—Third Saturday in June.

Hank Williams Day Celebration, Georgiana—First Saturday in June. 376-2396.

World Championship Domino Tournament. Andalusia—July. Sponsored by the Rotary Club. To play or be a spectator, write the World Championship Domino Tournament, PO Box 276, Andalusia, AL 36420. 222-3528.

Fountain in Eufaula. (Photo by Neal Broerman)

11

COTTON'S
CHRONOLOGY

One look at **Kendall Manor Inn** at night and suddenly you aren't riding in a car anymore. You rustle your satin skirts in the swaying carriage and wonder who will greet you at the door of that festive mansion lit up from front door to belvedere. Guests drawn to this gracious antebellum home set on the bluff above Lake Eufaula find themselves slipping back in time. And that's exactly how Barbara and Tim Lubsen want it. They've been inviting guests to "capture a memory" at this magnificently restored home for six years, and in that short period of time their bed and breakfast has been recognized for its excellence by *Country Inns Magazine*.

If you've ever built a house, you will understand the feelings of the man who built Kendall Manor Hall. When the cost reached thirty thousand dollars, he just quit keeping track. Of course, that was in the 1800s when cotton was king, and this cotton broker was able to continue building after he passed that dollar landmark. The curved walls and the moldings that had to be shaped to fit them bespeak wealth. So does the brightly patterned cranberry window glass made in Bohemia. The ceilings are 16 feet high, and the floors are heart of pine taken from original forests. Floor-to-ceiling windows grace the front parlor, and the focal point is the mantle made of white, carved Italian marble. Cornices and mirror surrounds are original to the house. Pocket doors that divide the front and back parlors feature Tiffany glass. The front parlor rosewood and walnut settee and side chair backs are upholstered in scarlet and carved to represent parts of the family crest. Listed on the National Register, the house has been featured in *Southern Living.*

If you have come to Kendall Manor to relax, delve into the many interesting books spread throughout the house. Have morning coffee on the second-floor porch and watch the squirrels play in the tulip poplar tree. Or climb to the belvedere, the place servants were sent long ago to look for the smoke of a riverboat. Be sure to sign the attic wall with your name and date. It's a tradition!

Once you descend to the main floor, you may want to leave by the side door and stroll through the historic town of Eufaula.

No one knows for sure the meaning of **Eufaula.** Some say it means "High Bluff." Others recall the popular Indian legend about two lovers: a young brave who, having been exposed to the white man's language, is believed to have uttered, "You fall-uh!" as he rescued his love from what could have been a fatal accident. History records a Chief Eufaula and the Eufaula Indians, so perhaps that influenced the name choice for this town of nearly 14,000 citizens.

Eufaula has more than 500 registered landmarks dating to 1836. A walking tour in the downtown area will introduce you to a gracious past. Take the **Historic Eufaula Walking-Driving Tour.** An excellent guide is available at the Chamber of Commerce, which is on Orange Street.

The downtown area was developed in 1834 by **Captain Seth Lore,** who named the four main north-south avenues by using the letters in his last name: Livingston, Orange, Randolph, and Eufaula. At that time the town was named Irwinton in honor of General William Irwin, a hero in the War of 1814. However, the mail kept getting confused and misdelivered to Irwinton, Georgia. In 1843, the town name was changed to Eufaula, but the history lives on in the Seth Lore and **Irwinton Historic District,** which encompasses most of the oldest part of the city. This is also the second-largest historic district in Alabama and includes the state's most extensive collection of Italianate architecture. If you can spare enough time to hunt them up, you can see over 700 historical and architecturally significant structures.

In spite of the serenity of its graceful mansions, the people who came to claim the land in earlier times saw their share of conflict. Disputes over the land led to the bloody Creek Indian War. Then, with forests cleared, fields planted, and Native Americans removed, the boom began. This boom was interrupted by the War Between the States, but the town, though occupied, did not suffer damage.

Following the fall of Montgomery to Union troops, Eufaulians wondered what would happen to them. The war ended before an approaching Union general and his 4000 cavalrymen arrived in the town, and townspeople and their property were treated with respect.

One family with concerns about the approaching Union troops was the Young family. Edward and Ann Fendall Beall Young began their new home, now known as **Fendall Hall,** in the fashionable area of "The Hill" west of downtown in 1859. They lived on their property in temporary cabins, using a small brick structure as their parlor, while the new house was under construction. The Youngs had just begun to settle the new rooms and enjoy their prosperity when the Civil War began. Since that time the house has seen many changes, not only in the country around it, but within its walls.

During the 1880s, descendants of the original owners made plans to present their daughter to Eufaula society. Just as today's families see their houses differently before they entertain for a special occasion and paint, paper, or spruce up before the guests arrive, so did Anna Beall Young Dent and her husband, Stouten Hubert Dent. The Victorian style was "in," and the Dents hired a traveling French artist to create decorative murals in the entry hall and two parlors. The painter is remembered as being somewhat temperamental, yet he managed to complete his Victorian-inspired murals within six months. Can you imagine two generations preparing for an important social event while a high-strung artist holds forth in the middle of the house for six months? Ah, tension! Through five generations and a long process of restoration and preservation by the Alabama Historical Commission, what you see today at Fendall Hall is still one of the finest Alabama Italianate style homes.

In downtown Eufaula, one of the first handsome homes you will notice is also, happily, one you can tour. Built in 1884 by cotton planter Eli S. Shorter, and his wife Wileyna Lamar of Macon (heiress to the SSS Tonic fortune), **Shorter Mansion Museum** was remodeled in 1906 with the addition of the front porch and seventeen Corinthian columns to create an outstanding example of Neoclassical Revival architecture.

What catches your eye as you walk up the steps (and there is a wheelchair lift on the side of the house if you need assistance) is the lotus blossom design in the beveled glass sidelights around the front doors. Step into the entry hall, which is decorated with hand-flocked wallpaper, and the parquet floor leads you toward a handsome staircase. First, however, you will want to see the double parlors, sparkling with original mirrors and Waterford chandeliers and lusters. Our guide through the house was Mrs. Bette Singer, whose grandparents lived next door. She played in the house as a child.

In 1965 the home was purchased at auction from the Shorter heirs by the **Eufaula Heritage Association.** The next year the first Eufaula Pilgrimage was held, and the mansion became headquarters for both the association and the tour. In buying the home and rescuing it from demolition, the Heritage Association spent all its money. It owned a lovely, historic, albeit empty house. The museum on the second floor of the Shorter Mansion is what enabled the townspeople to furnish the house. The Alabama legislature appropriated funds to establish a museum honoring the six governors of Alabama who had come from Barbour County *and* to furnish the home. The Governors' Room is only one part of the museum, however. You will enjoy wandering among the displays and picturing a town flowing through its founding families from generation to generation.

Continue your tour by venturing farther downtown to the **Bluff City Inn,** which has seen grander days but is now undergoing restoration. Built in 1885 and recently placed on Alabama's list of endangered historical sites, this was once one of the most modern and well-equipped hotels in the south. The current owners, Jack and Ardis Rusch, are spearheading the revitalization of this grand old hotel, hoping to restore it "as close to original as possible." Small shops and a restaurant have spaces on the first floor and the second floor is closed.

If you crave hot and spicy foods, **Old Mexico** and **Boux Rae's Four Beans Café,** which serves Cajun dishes, are located in the Inn building. When you leave either restaurant and turn left, you will soon come to **Folk Treasures,** an airy, fragrant gift shop that carries Collegiate Collectables made in Phenix City, Alabama. This shop also carries three-dimensional shelf sitters of college buildings such as the Auburn University clock tower. Continue to your left, and pass the BP service station. Keep looking to your left, and you will see **Design Detail,** occupying space in a comfortable old house. The owner and staff were bustling about, setting up giftwares for the holidays when we were there, and the warmth of the season settled around us the minute we walked through the doors.

It's Saturday afternoon, and you are ready to travel to Dothan. Before you do, however, let's consider an alternate plan for your time in Eufaula.

Eufaula's second boom period followed the construction of the

Walter F. George Lock and Dam on the Chattahoochee River. This created Lake Eufaula, but because a lake in another state was given that name first, Lake Eufaula, Alabama, is known officially by the Corps of Engineers as **Lake Walter F. George.** Call it Lake George or Lake Eufaula or call it by its third name, "The Bass Capital of the World."

Crappie, bass, and many other species of fish lure sportsmen to this lake that covers 46,000 acres and has 640 miles of shoreline. There are 22 public-use areas and two full-service marinas around the lake. **Lakepoint State Park** is situated so that most of its 101 rooms overlook the lake, and you can either stay in cabins or camp. If you'd rather hike or play golf instead of fish, you can do that, too. That's not all. Nearby is the **Eufaula National Wildlife Refuge,** home to almost 300 species of birds, forty mammal species, reptiles, and amphibians. Pick up a copy of the *Interpretive Auto Tour* brochure and see the sights along a 5- to 7-mile route. Take binoculars and a camera; you can stop your car and get out for a closer look.

Finally, before you say goodbye to this town by the Chattahoochee River, you must take time to see **Tom Mann's Fish World,** the largest freshwater aquarium in the state. You'll want to allow about two hours here so you won't feel rushed. Several rooms and displays of early Native American life require time to fully appreciate them. This 1000-acre complex, which backs up to the Eufaula National Wildlife Refuge, is the result of one man's vision. Tom Mann is a legend in these parts and wherever else a great fish tale is told. As a boy Tom learned to make his own lures out of what he could find on the family farm. This early creativity led to an entire industry of plastic worm manufacturing, with the "Jelly Worm" and "Little George" making Tom's name famous.

Tom is quick to give credit. His bait tester, a bass named **Leroy Brown,** lived in a tank outside Tom's office. Tom knew when he pulled Leroy Brown from the water that this was a special bass. He had the same work ethic as his owner. Tom says that if Leroy didn't like the bait he made, "neither did the fishermen." If Leroy showed the slightest interest in a new creation, Tom put it on the market. When Leroy died, Tom gave him the best funeral a fish ever had. It was probably attended by more mourners than any other funeral in town. Step behind the aquarium to see Leroy's monument, carved from Georgia marble.

Tom Mann has designed over 3600 lures and founded and sold several businesses. He's been inducted into the Fishing Hall of Fame, holds the Dolphin Award, and has taken President Carter, Porter Waggoner, Dolly Parton, Bobby Knight, and Hank Williams, Jr., fishing. It's nice to see all of these people from various professions looking happy in Tom's pictures.

Tom isn't sitting on the riverbank with a line trailing lazily in the water, however. He's still dreaming and making plans for more ways to enable others to enjoy the outdoors. "Make every hour count," he says. "You'll live longer."

With that advice ringing in our ears, we turned our car toward Dothan. The first stop was the Welcome Center, and just south of the Welcome Center you should be able to see the above-ground marker on what was the southern boundary of the United States from 1795-1819. You'll also see a monument to the peanut proclaiming Dothan the Peanut Capital of the World.

Like Eufaula, **Dothan** was once called by a different name and ran into difficulties with the postal system. Even after the postal authorities assigned the name of "Dothan," it was also spelled "Dothen." The city fathers finally stepped in and decided to make the spelling consistent with a verse from Genesis 37:17: "For I heard them say, 'Let us go to Dothan.'"

Golfers will head for the nearby **Robert Trent Jones Golf Trail** course, **Highland Oaks,** which seems almost hidden away, but has won much praise from those who know. Shoppers can travel down Ross Clark Circle, pass **Wiregrass Commons Mall,** the intersection with U.S. 84, and the Bruno's Shopping Plaza. Drive to the door of the **Unique Shop,** which lives up to its name. Local people go there for the consulting service on home décor. You can hunt for great housewarming gifts or decorative knickknacks for your own home. Amble down the sidewalk and sample other shops, then let the fountain in front of **Ted's Jewelers** soothe you. Inside you'll find several lines of exquisite jewelry plus Swarovski and Waterford crystal.

Now you're ready for a break. We found the perfect place in the Bruno's Shopping Center at the **Dakota Coffee Works.** Entrepreneur Ron McGhee, who owns the store with his wife, Tana, was getting ready for the Peanut Festival, roasting and flavoring peanut butter-flavored coffee 25 pounds at a time. McGhee is also opening another shop in the Wiregrass Commons Mall, where visitors can watch the coffee bean roasting process. What an aroma that will generate! While you sip your favorite flavored coffee, contemplate a picnic at

Landmark Park. Your sandwiches and salads can be ready for you by the time you have enjoyed the last drop. If you are taking a picnic to Landmark Park, be sure you tuck in a trash bag because the park has a policy: "Pack it in; pack it out."

Landmark Park is a living history museum of agriculture. Visitors can return to the 1890s and wander among the buildings that were part of life in those days. To learn why the area is called the "Wiregrass" region, stop in the interpretive center for a good description of this tough grass and an explanation of what happened to it. Listen to the hum of the honeybees inside the clear frame set up as a hive. You may never have another chance to get so close!

A wide boardwalk smooth enough for wheelchairs leads into the woods. Stop and breathe in the sweet pine before you head across the park to see the newly-opened **Alabama State Agricultural Museum.** We were there in time for the first exhibit, "Retiring the Mule," a progression of farm tractors that serve as a tribute to the hardy Wiregrass peanut farmer and a celebration of the role of machinery in the history of Southern agriculture. William Holman, executive director, said this museum site could change, so when you arrive at the main gate, ask where to find it. You will discover many treasures at the end of little dirt roads in Alabama, and Landmark Park is one of them. So is the agriculture museum. Be sure to see it.

Another choice for your afternoon in Dothan is the **Wiregrass Museum of Art,** across from the Civic Center in the downtown area. To quote the director, Sam W. Kates, "Dothan is a hotspot for art." This art center not only showcases local artists like **Dale Kennington** and **Jeannie Maddox** but encourages artists-to-be. The children's hands-on art section on the second floor vibrates with the sounds of happy young artists learning about color, textures, weaving, and how to read a label on a piece of art work. "Capture your shadow" is fun for all ages.

Before you leave the Museum of Art, pick up a brochure on the **Wiregrass Festival of Murals** and follow a priceless art trail. Again, you will see the importance of the peanut to the region from the early days of **George Washington Carver,** but you will continue backwards in time to the 1540s when **Hernando De Soto** trod the wiregrass.

It's been a full day and your stomach is protesting even more than your feet. To make all of you and your family happy, go to the bypass (Ross Clark Circle) and hunt for **Dobb's Famous Bar B Que Restaurant.** A family restaurant founded in December 1948, this is

Landmark Park. (Photo by Neal Broerman)

Agricultural Museum, Landmark Park. (Photo by Neal Broerman)

Johnny Mack Brown mural, Dothan. (Photo by Neal Broerman)

the oldest barbecue in Dothan. Mrs. Dobb's homemade strawberry shortcake gets four stars.

Choose a motel along the bypass near Dothan or consult the Bed and Breakfast of Alabama Association member booklet and get ready for several interesting side trips on Sunday.

If you have chosen a "non-traditional" weekend (that is, a couple of days during the week), or can start early Friday or extend your weekend until Monday morning, the **Farley Nuclear Visitors Center** is 23 miles southeast of Dothan, has no admission fee, and is easy to enjoy from a wheelchair. Since it is open only during the week, this limits its availability, but it is definitely a fun way to view and learn about electricity.

If you are still close to Dothan, you may want to see the murals in the less crowded Sunday morning atmosphere of downtown before you head for your next stop at the **U.S. Army Aviation Museum.** The museum doesn't open until noon on Sunday. Take U.S. 84 W. to **Daleville,** turn right on Alabama 85, and go into **Fort Rucker.** The museum will be on your left. You will see the world's largest collection of helicopters, more than 160 military aircraft, and you can trace the army's history in aviation from the days of the Wright brothers to the aircraft flown today. Allow at least an hour here. Then travel on to **Enterprise,** the county seat of Coffee County and home of the **Boll Weevil Monument.** Keep an eye out for a little red schoolhouse. If you see one on the U.S. 84 bypass at Alabama 27, you have found the Enterprise Welcome Center. Stop by to pick up information about the area.

In the middle of town, at Main and College Streets, you will see the only monument in the world recognizing the role of a pest, the Boll Weevil Monument. In 1915 boll weevils devoured two thirds of Coffee County's cotton crop. This forced local farmers to diversify and changed poverty to prosperity.

Cotton may no longer be king, but at the end of summer you will still see many fields turning white. A lesser tribute to the insect is found in the light-green boll weevil traps placed at the edges of the fields. An empty trap is good news.

For an afternoon you and your family will treasure, visit a U-Pick farm and experience some of those fields that once suffered the ravages of the boll weevil. Feel the sun on your back, the nurturing earth under your feet. Due to Alabama's mild climate, almost any season could offer possibilities for this kind of country trek. Call ahead for a

U.S. Army Aviation Museum.
(Photo by Neal Broerman)

Boll Weevil Marker. (Photo by Neal
Broerman)

Boll Weevil Monument. (Photo by
Neal Broerman)

Aviator Monument. (Photo by Neal
Broerman)

list of local farms open to travelers and directions for getting there. Coffee County Agent Richard Petcher keeps a list as crops come in and would be pleased to hear from you.

Before you say goodbye to Enterprise, visit the **Aviator Monument** at the intersection of Park and Plaza Drive (U.S. 84 East). This monument is dedicated to army aviators for their gallantry and devotion to duty and will have special meaning for you if you spent part of the day at the Aviation Museum at Fort Rucker.

You might finish this weekend with a side trip to **Ozark**. Drive down the streets lined with antebellum homes under a canopy of huge oaks draped with Spanish moss. See the **Claybank Church,** an original log structure built in 1852, or take a few late afternoon hours to fish for bass and bream in the 92-acre **Dale County Lake.** Any reason to sit on a bank with your toes in the water is a good reason.

Area Code: (334)

Getting There:

Eufaula and Dothan are both in the southeastern part of Alabama. Eufaula looks over the Chattahoochee River at Georgia, while Dothan is near the borders of both Florida and Georgia. To reach Eufaula from Interstate 85 take Exit 62 to U. S 280 and U.S. 431 near Auburn and drive south through Phenix City. It is about 70 miles to Andalusia and another 50 miles to Dothan. Dothan is bisected by U.S. 231 (called the Bee Line Highway) from Montgomery. It is about 100 miles from Montgomery to Dothan.

Where and When:

Alabama State Agricultural Museum, Landmark Park (U.S. 431 N.), Dothan, AL, 36302. Mon.-Sat., 9 A.M.-5 P.M.; Sun., noon-6 P.M.794-3452.

Army Aviation Museum, Alabama 249 (Fort Rucker), Daleville, AL 36362. Mon.-Sat., 9 A.M.-4 P.M.; Sun., noon-4 P.M. 598-2508.

Web site: www.aviationmuseum.org

Blue Springs State Park, 2595 Alabama 10, Clio, AL 36017. 397-4875. Admission.

Bluff City Inn, 114 N. Eufaula Avenue, Eufaula, AL 36027.

Claybank Church, East Andrews Avenue, Ozark, AL.

Dale County Lake, Alabama 123 N., Ozark, AL.

Design Detail, 214 N. Eufaula Avenue, Eufaula, AL 36027. Mon.-Fri., 9 A.M.-5 P.M.; Sat., 10 A.M.-2 P.M. 687-8771.

Eufaula National Wildlife Refuge, 509 Old Alabama 165, Eufaula, AL 36027. 687-4065.

Web site: www.southeast.fws.gov/wildlife/al.html

Farley Nuclear Visitors Center, 7388 Alabama 95 N., Columbia, AL 36319. Mon.-Fri., 8 A.M.-4 P.M. 899-5108; (800) 344-8295.
                    Web site: www.southernco.com/site/southernnuclear
Fendall Hall, 917 W. Barbour Street, Eufaula, AL 36027. Mon.-Sat., 10 A.M.-4 P.M. 687-8469. Admission.   Web site: www.preserveala.org
Folk Treasures, 120 N. Eufaula Avenue, Eufaula, AL 36027. Mon.-Tue., Thurs.-Fri. 9 A.M.-5 P.M.; Wed. and Sat., 9 A.M.-3 P.M. 687-8230.
Highland Oaks, 904 Royal Pkwy., Dothan, AL 36301. 712-2820.
Jeanie's Party Line, 2946 Ross Clark Circle, Dothan, AL 36303. Mon.-Fri., 10 A.M.-5:30 P.M.; Sat., 10 A.M.-5 P.M.
Landmark Park, U.S. 431 N., Dothan, AL 36302. Mon.-Sat., 9 A.M.-5 P.M.; Sun., noon-6 P.M. 794-3452. Admission.
Shorter Mansion, 340 N. Eufaula Avenue, Eufaula, AL 36072. Mon.-Sat., 10 A.M.-4 P.M.; Sun., 1 P.M.-4 P.M. 687-3792. Admission.
Ted's Jewelers, 2956 Ross Clark Circle S.W., Dothan, AL 36301. Mon.-Fri., 9:30 A.M.-5:30 P.M.; Sat., 10 A.M.-5 P.M. 794-0686; (800) 523-2412.
Tom Mann's Fish World and Aquarium, 1951 N. Eufaula Avenue, Eufaula, AL 36027. Daily, 8 A.M.-5 P.M. 687-3655. Admission.
Understudy Dinner Theater, 137 S. Oates Street, Dothan, AL 36301. 792-1268.
Unique Shop, 2944 Ross Clark Circle Dothan, AL 36301. Mon.-Sat., 10 A.M.-5 P.M. 793-7166.
Wiregrass Festival of Murals, Downtown, Dothan, AL 36303. 794-6622; (888) 449-0212.   Web site: www.dothanalcvb.com.
Wiregrass Museum of Art, 126 Museum Avenue, Dothan, AL 36301. Tue.-Sat., 10 A.M.-5 P.M.; Sun., 1 P.M.-5 P.M. 794-3871. Donation.
Guide Services:
Tracy Beall, 1924 N. Eufaula Avenue, Eufaula, AL 36027. 687-2245.
Information:
Alabama Welcome Center, U.S. 231, Dothan, AL.
Coffee County Extension Service (U-Pick Farm Info), 5 Farm Center, New Brockton, AL 36351. 894-5596.
Dothan Area Convention and Visitors Bureau, 3311 Ross Clark Circle, Dothan, AL 36303. 794-6622; (888) 449-0212.
                    Web site: www.dothanalcvb.com
Enterprise Welcome Center and **Little Red Schoolhouse,** U.S. 84 Bypass, Enterprise, AL. 347-0581; (800)-235-4730.
Eufaula Heritage Association, P.O. Box 486, Eufaula, AL 36027. 687-3793, (888) 383-2852.

Eufaula/Barbour County Chamber of Commerce, 102 N. Orange Avenue, Eufaula, AL 36072. Mon.-Fri. 687-7099.
Georgiana Visitors Information, 376-3296.
Ozark Area Chamber of Commerce, 308 Painter Avenue, Ozark, AL 36360. 774-9321; (800) 582-8497.

Web site: www.snowhill.com/ozark

Accommodations:
Kendall Manor Inn, 534 W. Broad Street, Eufaula, AL 36027. 687-8847.   Web site: www.bbonline.com/al/kendall
Lakepoint Resort State Park, U.S. 431 N., Eufaula, AL 36072. 687-8011; (800) 544-5253.

Restaurants:
Boux Rae's Four Beans Café, 114 N. Eufaula Avenue, Eufaula, AL 36027. Mon.-Fri., 11 A.M.-2:30 P.M.; Thurs.-Sat., 5 P.M.-10 P.M.
Boux Rae's Lagniappe, 114 N. Eufaula Avenue, Eufaula, AL 36027. Mon.-Fri., 11 A.M.-2:30 P.M.; Thurs.-Sat., 5 P.M.-10 P.M.
Bread Basket, 330 E. Broad Street, Eufaula, AL 36027. Mon.-Fri., 6 A.M.-2 P.M. 687-5567.
Creek Restaurant, 3301 S. Eufaula Avenue, Eufaula, AL 36027. Mon.-Sat., 4 P.M.-10 P.M.
Dakota Coffee Works, 3074 Ross Clark Circle (also in Wiregrass Commons Mall), Dothan, AL 36072. Mon.-Thurs., 7:30 A.M.-10 P.M.; Fri.-Sat., 7:30 A.M.-midnight; Sun., 2 P.M.-10 P.M. 677-1718.

Web site: www.dakotacoffee.com

Dobb's Famous Bar B Que Restaurant, 231 U.S. 231 S. at Ross Clark Circle, Dothan, AL 36301. Tue.-Sun. 794-5195.
Nanny's Fine Dining, 430 Barganier, Greenville, AL 36037. 382-5689.
Old Mexico, 114 N. Eufaula Avenue, Eufaula, AL 36027. Mon.-Fri., 11 A.M.-2:30 P.M.; Mon.-Sat., 5 P.M.-10 P.M. 687-7770.

Major Annual Events:
Lake Eufaula's Fins, Feathers & Flowers, Lakepoint State Park, Eufaula—February. 242-3334.
Spring Farm Day, U.S. 431, Dothan—March. 794-3452.
Eufaula Pilgrimage, Historic District, Eufaula—April 7-9, 2000; Apr. 6-8, 2001; Fri.-Sat., 9 A.M.-9 P.M.; Sun., 1 P.M.-5 P.M. 687-3793; (888) 383-2852.   Web site: www.zebra.net/~pilgrimage
National Peanut Festival, Downtown Dothan—November. 794-6622; (888) 449-0212.   Web site: www.dothanalcvb.com

Sculpted angel creation. (Photo courtesy Jan Jones)

12

SWEET AUBURN

Even the squirrels are competitive when you get close to Auburn, a town known for its football team and stirring battle cry, "War Eagle!" **Chewacla State Park,** three miles south of Auburn off U.S. 29, is inhabited by squirrels that dare you to drive down their road. Students study here and alumni camp here for game weekends if they are among the lucky ones to call in between 8 A.M. and 5 P.M. Monday-Friday at least four months before the team plays a home game. The 26-acre lake features a waterfall, and the park includes a mountain bike and tree identification trail. Fishing boats and swimming privileges are part of the fee.

In spite of the tempting scenery at the park, we opted to stay in the middle of town in The **Crenshaw Guest House,** a stately Victorian built in 1890 by Auburn mathematics professor Bolling Hall Crenshaw. Fifteen years ago the house, which is listed on the National Register of Historic Places, became one of the first bed and breakfasts in the state. It's owned and run with college town enthusiasm by Fran and Peppi Verma. The guest rooms have high ceilings and are furnished with period antiques, allowing the innkeepers to combine Southern hospitality with Old World charm.

When the university is in full swing, this is one of those places that fills up first with parents and visiting alumni because it is in the **Old Main and Church Street District** and close to everything, yet it has an off-the-street, secluded feeling. We stayed in the carriage house, which was once the good math professor's study. We enjoyed a breakfast basket of fresh fruit, although if your schedule permits, the Verma's can provide you with a full Southern breakfast—with style

Auburn gets its name from Oliver Goldsmith's poem, "The Deserted Village" that reads, "Sweet Auburn, the loveliest village of the plain." The center of the village is marked by **Toomer's Corner,** where College Street and Magnolia Avenue meet. A drugstore on the spot is both a sentimental and historic landmark for the thousands of students who have entered the halls of higher learning here, home to Alabama's largest college, **Auburn University.**

For our first meal in this friendly college town, we chose **Niffer's Place.** The food is fine, but the atmosphere is fun. Above the cashier's head decorative fish dangle from the Victorian street lamp. Each new employee (and most employees are college students) decorates a wooden fish. Years later alumni come back to see their additions to Niffer's decor. The kids' mural at the entrance was painted by schoolchildren in 1993—future Niffer's employees?

The clock in the famous **Auburn Clock Tower** struck 8 P.M. as we walked down College Street. No, that tree on the corner does not have slender streaming white flowers. If you are unaccustomed to football season celebrations, you will not recognize the role played by that household necessity, toilet paper, until you get closer to the graceful limbs of the large tree, which stays decked out in flowing white as long as Auburn is winning. The height from which this tree décor falls is testimony to the exuberance of youth—especially youth celebrating a winning streak. Yes, there is money in the city budget for clean-up. Northern cities have snow removal budgets; this town has a budget for cleanup of a different kind of whiteness—reportedly the only town budget with funds so allocated.

Toomer's Drugs, the cherished landmark, was established in 1896 and featured lemonade that was squeezed fresh daily. When the owner retired, the drugstore closed. However, such a tradition could not be defeated. An alumnus driving through town noticed the store was closed, bought it, acquired the recipe for the lemonade, and reopened the institution. Above the soda fountain, notice the pressed tin ceiling, murals, and an Auburn time line.

You can study the history of the Auburn sports program in a variety of ways, but one of the most unusual ways is by walking with your head down along the downtown streets. Of course, this will tip everyone off that you are a tourist on the **Tiger Walk.** The Tiger Walk is a series of granite squares or plaques set into the sidewalk. Our Saturday began

Toomer's Corner. (Photo
courtesy Robert Smith)

Samford Hall. (Photo courtesy Robert Smith)

with a walk to the corner of College and Magnolia, where we saw the Ralph "Shug" Jordan square. These plaques pay tribute to Auburn University's greatest athletes, coaches, and administrators. Each year the Auburn Chamber of Commerce adds the plaques of new inductees to the city's walk of fame.

Next we ambled down Magnolia between the art building and the side of **Bodega,** a new Mexican Restaurant that has a courtyard, fountain, and live bands in the evenings. It must be difficult for the art students to stay focused when they must work at night against the distractions of the lively scene below. Bodega is housed in a former bank, and you can glance through a window and see the safe.

If you expect a college town to have an abundance of small gift shops interspersed with groups of tables and tasty places to eat, Auburn will not disappoint you. There's more good news. You won't need to drive and park, drive and park. Instead, slip on your comfortable shoes and enjoy the rich concentration of gifts and goodies packed into a few blocks. From Toomer's wander past the **Grille,** a great place for breakfast, and **Traditions,** where you might want to pick up a picnic lunch for a trip to Chewacla State Park. Next you'll pass a barber shop that gives an old-fashioned lather-soap shave. Step into **Heartstrings** and browse among the figurines. Sorority and fraternity members have a source of jewelry and trophies at the Greek shop upstairs. **Ampersand,** next on this sidewalk tour, sells furniture and larger décor and accent items. Your nose will tell you that you are near **Taylor's Bakery and Gourmet Coffee,** which has hours that change with the season. Take note of **Cheeburger Cheeburger,** where eating *all* of the one-pound specialty hamburger will earn your photo a space on the restaurant's wall of fame. Cross the street to see the pottery and small decorative items the **Veranda** has to offer.

Now it's time to see the campus. Thousands tour the **John B. Lovelace Athletic Museum** on game weekends, even if they've already been there many times. It's as close to the feeling of the game as you can get without taking your place among cheering fans in **Jordan-Hare Stadium.** Follow those tiger paws through the museum and your motion triggers a recording of the crowd sounds. What is it like to be an Auburn player on the great day of a game? Close your eyes and imagine.

Each exhibit pulls you closer to the heart of the game. An animated life-size diorama shows Coach **Ralph "Shug" Jordan** and Heisman Trophy winner **Pat Sullivan** discussing plays on the sidelines. They seem so real you might want to offer your own suggestions. You'll also see basketball players **Vickie Orr** and **Charles Barkley.** Auburn grads who are astronauts come back for football games, too, and they are represented in their own section of the museum.

You'll also find Toomer's Drug in the museum, complete with its black-and-white tile mosaic floor. Turn a corner and you'll recognize the streamer-trimmed tree. "What kind of tree is it?" I asked the group around me. Some thought it might be an oak tree, but most were unable to see past the white paper and hazard a guess.

This athletic museum was dedicated in April 1996 to honor Auburn's athletic past, define its present, inspire future generations, and show how Auburn's athletic programs have contributed to Auburn's historical traditions. It's named for a graduate who did not play football. The closest John Lovelace got was to be the assistant faculty manager on "Iron Mike" Donahue's undefeated championship football team of 1913 and 1914. At Auburn, Lovelace learned discipline, desire, determination, dependability, and dedication, and used them all to build a successful and prosperous investment organization. His family and corporate associates honored him with this monument.

Wherever you are in Auburn, even outside on a road leading into town, you can follow the tiger paws and wind up at the stadium. (Note: Auburn now has left turn arrows!) No need to worry that the paws will fade away. Annually the streets are closed and the Auburn Student Government Association re-paints the tiger paws on campus. Even without the paws to lead you, Jordan-Hare Stadium would be difficult to miss. In addition to the crowds moving in the same direction, the newcomer would notice the large etched photograph mural around the stadium and see the blazing tiger eyes. War Eagle!

If you've come for a game, your afternoon is planned. If you haven't, get back in the car and drive to **Opelika.**

It's hard to tell where Auburn ends and Opelika begins. In fact, the Colonial Mall sits in both. The name Opelika is derived from the Creek Indian word that means "Big Swamp." Since Opelika is actually the highest point along the route from Atlanta to New Orleans, the name is probably due to the fact that Opelika is surrounded by five lakes and the Chattahoochee River.

Golf? Of course. One of the five lakes is 600-acre Lake Saugahatchee, and the **Grand National** Golf Course, another fine member of the **Robert Trent Jones Golf Trail,** is set so close to the water that more than half the holes of the Short Course touch the lake. In the year 2000, the Grand National Golf Course will host the NCAA Men's Division 1 National Championship. Look for the signs.

Opelika is the county seat of Lee County. The first courthouse was built after the Civil War by freed slave Horace King, who also built bridges and civic buildings, including the Lee County jail. Neither the jail nor the courthouse stands today. The courthouse built by King was torn down and replaced by the current one, which has already passed its first century. It's easy to picture townsfolk hurrying along the brick side streets toward the handsome courthouse or the **Old Depot,** where the **Opelika Arts Association** has its offices in the historic business district on Railroad Avenue. Absorbing this atmosphere will put you in the mood for stepping through the doors of the **Museum of East Alabama.**

This is not your usual museum. The director, Barbara Barnhill-West, explained that their "open collection" policy allows this museum of general history to exhibit a wide range of objects and subject matter, forming a fascinating picture of life from the 1880s to the present. Exhibits are well documented, and the aisles are wide enough that wheelchairs can move through them easily. You won't want to rush through this museum, which houses an ice cream bicycle with a jingly bell (that was a welcome sound on warm summer evenings), a rather amazing hair curler that came out of a beauty parlor, an extensive doll collection, and everything in between. Many of the items will cause you to remark, "My grandmother had one of those!"

If you stand on the courthouse steps and look across the spacious square, you'll see a French village. Look again. Actually it's the back of the **Jan Jones** studio, **"Creations by Jan."** Jan was inspired by the faux paintings she spied in a small French town, and when she returned from that particular trip, she wasted little time in finding a muralist to bring the charming scene in her mind to her own space in Opelika. The building Jan uses as an art studio has a fascinating history. It used to be a corner building and it has housed a bakery, pool hall, and hardware store. When the hardware store was in business, it was known to have the largest selection of Christmas toys in the area. The Jan Jones studio and showroom has returned the colorful frenzy of the holidays to this spacious building.

For thirty years Jan has designed elves, angels, toy soldiers, and all those whimsical, imaginative characters that populate holiday displays and delight children of all ages. If you are lucky enough to catch Jan at work—and she says her studio is open by appointment and by chance—she will lead you across a painted pathway of flowers through the shop and storeroom. Signs high above your head proclaim "Creativity is not a pretty sight," and "He who dies with the most fabric wins."

Jan's papier-mâché creations go through seven steps from her vision to final figurine. They are molded, shaped, primed, painted, varnished, antiqued, and glazed. The soft, luminous expressions on the faces of her angels will bring a smile to your face, too.

Jan's creativity spills over into one of the most exciting events in Opelika, **Front Porch Christmas.** This four-day event transforms the **North Opelika Historic Neighborhood** into a world of holiday fantasy, and thousands flock to the area to be dazzled by the sights. The event begins when Jan leaves life-size Victorian Santas or other figures she has designed on area front porches. Homeowners wake to the happy discovery and then great fun erupts as they decorate their homes with lights, trimmings, and colors coordinated to a theme inspired by "their" figures. On the Saturday of this event, the streets are closed to automobiles. Carolers and neighbors dress in costume and mingle with the many who walk through and stop to chat. As you drive the route, you will notice **Heritage House.** This bed and breakfast, which is an example of neoclassical architecture, was built in 1913-1914 and is the entry point to the historical neighborhood for the Front Porch Christmas program. Thousands have come and because so many return, the crowd increases every year.

If you plan a fall visit to this area, you might want to go in October and add **Loachapoka** to your itinerary. Take in the **Annual Historical Fair and Ruritan's Syrup Sop.** This is a celebration of folk life. Witness syrup making, quilting, spinning, and more while you listen to live music and enjoy buttermilk biscuits and fritters. Every year this festival brings 10,000 people to a town of 200 residents.

As for me, I elected to end this weekend on the Plains by returning to the state park and standing up to those squirrels.

Area Code: (334)

Getting There:
Auburn and Opelika are just north of Interstate 85 at Exits 51 and 59. U.S. 280 crosses through Opelika.

Where and When:
Ampersand, 116 N. College Street, Auburn, AL 36830. 887-7486.

Chewacla State Park, 124 Shell Toomer Pkwy., Auburn, AL 36830. 821-2439. Admission.

Creations by Jan, 219 N. 8th Street, Opelika, AL 36801. 741-7040.

Grand National, SunBelt Pkwy., Opelika, AL 36801. 749-9042.

Heartstrings, 112 N. College Street, Auburn, AL 36830. 887-7447.

Lovelace Athletic Museum, Donahue Drive (Auburn University Campus), Auburn, AL 36830. Mon.-Fri., 8 A.M.-4:30 P.M.; Football Sat., 9 A.M.-6 P.M.; Football Sun., 9 A.M.-3 P.M. 844-4750.

Web site: www.auburn.edu

Museum of East Alabama, 121 S. Ninth Street, Opelika, AL 36803. Tue.-Fri, 10 A.M.-4 P.M.; Sat., 2 P.M.-4 P.M. 749-2751. Admission.

Opelika Arts Association, 200 S. Sixth Street, Opelika, AL 36803. Mon.-Thurs., 8 A.M.-7:30 P.M.; Fri., 8 A.M.-5 P.M.; Sat., 9 A.M.-6 P.M.; Sun., 1 P.M.-5 P.M. 749-8105.

Veranda, 113 N. College Street, Auburn, AL 36830. 826-6519.

Information:

Auburn/Opelika Convention and Visitors Bureau, 714 E. Glenn Avenue, Auburn, AL 36831. (800) 321- 8880; 887-8747.

Web site: www.auburn-opelika.com

Many events on the Auburn campus are free and open to the general public. Call the **University Information Desk.** 844-4244.

Alabama Welcome Centers, Interstate 85, Exit 79, Lanett, AL.

Accommodations:

Auburn University Hotel and Dixon Conference Center, 241 S. College Street, Auburn, AL 36830. 821-8200; (800) 228-2876.

Crenshaw Guest House, 371 N. College Street, Auburn, AL 36830. 821-1131.   Web site: www.auburnalabama.com

Heritage House, 714 Second Avenue, Opelika, AL 36801. 705-0485.

Restaurants:

Amsterdam Café, 410 S. Gay Street, Auburn, AL 36830. Daily, 11 A.M.-10 P.M. 826-8181.

Bodega, 101 N. College Street at Magnolia Street, Auburn, AL 36830. 887-5990.

Bottchers Restaurant, 1310 Opelika Road, Auburn, AL 36830. Mon.-Thurs., 5:30 P.M.-9 P.M.; Fri.-Sat., 5:30 P.M.-10 P.M. 821-8393.

Cheeburger Cheeburger, 160 N. College Street, Auburn, AL 36830. Open daily from 11A.M. 826-0845.

Cheng Du, 160 N. College Street, Auburn, AL 36830. Daily, 11 A.M.-2:30 P.M.; 4:30 P.M.-10 P.M. 826-3221.

Grille Restaurant, 104 N. College Street, Auburn, AL 36830. Mon.-Sat., 6:30 A.M.-9 P.M.; Sun., 8 A.M.-8 P.M. 826-1933.

Mandarin House, 3800 Opelika Road, Auburn, AL 36830. Daily, 11 A.M.-2:30 P.M.; Sun.-Thurs., 5 P.M.-10 P.M.; Fri.-Sat., 4 P.M.-10:30 P.M. 745-7234.

Niffer's Place, 1151 Opelika Road, Auburn, AL 36830. Mon.-Wed., 11 A.M.-10 P.M.; Thurs.,11 A.M.-10:30 P.M.; Fri.-Sat., 11 A.M.-11 P.M.; Sun., 11 A.M.-8:30 P.M. 821-3118.

Taylor's Bakery and Gourmet Coffee, 132 N. College Street, Auburn, AL 36831. Mon.-Fri., 7 A.M.-6 P.M.; Sat.-Sun., 7 A.M.-2 P.M. 502-1112.

Toomer's Drugs, N. College Street at Magnolia Street, Auburn, AL 36830. Mon.-Sat., 9 A.M.-6 P.M.; Sun., 1 P.M.-6 P.M. 887-3488.

Traditions, 126 N. College Street, Auburn, AL 36830. Mon.-Sat., 9 A.M.-3 P.M. 887-8712.

Major Annual Events:

Auburn Floral Trail, Auburn—Late March and early April. Call 887-8747 or (800) 321-8880.

Summer Swing Concert Series, Opelika Municipal Park—Every Tuesday evening, June through August. 705-5560.

Historical Fair and Ruritan's Syrup Sop, Loachapoka—Fall. 887-8747; (800) 321-8880.

Christmas in a Railroad Town, Opelika—December.

Victorian Front Porch Christmas, North Opelika Historic Neighborhood, N. Eighth and Ninth Streets, Opelika—December. 887-8747; (800) 321-8880.

Tuskegee University. (Photo courtesy Alabama Bureau of Tourism & Travel)

13

TUSKEGEE
ANY SEASON

Fifteen miles from Auburn, another college town bustles with students hurrying to class during the golden days of fall. Of course, springtime in **Tuskegee** is a bustling time, too. The buds and blossoms of roses, camellias, and azaleas gladden the eye and put a spring in the step of students, professors, parents, and those who come to enjoy the culture and history displayed here. When **George Washington Carver** first set foot in this area in 1896, he planned to stay three years, but he stayed until he died, nearly 50 years later. Could spring in Tuskegee have had something to do with that?

Before you enter the campus, stop at the National Park Service Office and ask for a map. For accommodations, you are in luck. The **Kellogg Conference Center** in the middle of the campus is also a hotel. The front entrance is part of the original campus, historic Dorothy Hall. This hotel opened in 1994, and the elegant lobby and friendly staff extend a gracious welcome to the traveler. Take time to get settled and then enjoy a walk on the campus. Pedestrians have the right-of-way on campus roads. Across from the Kellogg Center entrance, you will see the famous monument, "The **Veil of Ignorance,**" which shows **Booker T. Washington** lifting the veil of ignorance from his fellow man. After a pleasant stroll, you may want to drive into the town of Tuskegee, which dates from the mid-1800s. Among other historic buildings, you will see the first site of Tuskegee University, the **Butler Chapel A.M.E. Zion Church.** Return to the Center in time for dinner. Relax. You are among the fortunate few here who will not be expected to take an exam.

The next day, your first stop should be the **George Washington Carver Museum,** which is around the corner from the Kellogg Center. See the 30-minute movie that will give you an excellent overview of the area and an acquaintance with George Washington Carver.

The invitation Carver received from Booker T. Washington to come and help his people was hard to turn down. Washington was the founder, driving force, and director of Tuskegee Institute, an outstanding school for blacks, which had humble beginnings in a couple of dilapidated buildings. Washington had been leading and laboring over his school for 15 years when he invited Carver to create a science and agricultural department. Carver immediately learned that Washington's expectations were vast. His lab, Washington explained, was in Carver's head. Actually, Carver, already a noted college professor by this time, brought a microscope to start his lab. Then he led his eager students to the garbage dump and introduced them to the treasures there.

Carver's insatiable curiosity, and his ability to find the possible hidden deep inside the impossible, linked with Washington's steady and brilliant leadership, made a good match for the nurturing of the fledgling school. By 1915, when Washington died, it was an internationally famous institution.

After the movie ends, you will be ready to climb the steps—or take the elevator—to the main floor of the museum, where you could easily spend an hour reading the display signs and asking questions of the knowledgeable staff.

Carver overcame poverty, poor health, and prejudice, finding solace in the nature he loved. As a man, Carver prioritized and focused. He wore baggy clothes and a fresh flower in his lapel. He had no interest in the business side of agriculture, except how it affected the people who depended on crops for their livelihood. He used a Movable School—an equipped automobile—to take Tuskegee extension services to rural people in Alabama. The "Bulletins" he handed out gave agricultural information in a simple, readable style meant for farmers, teachers, and housewives, rather than for other researchers. Carver was characterized as a true teacher who guided and inspired his students. As for his personal fortune, he turned down industry, took out no patents, and rarely cashed his paychecks unless a student needed his help. He never married.

Carver understood that cotton took nitrogen from the land and depleted the soil. He urged farmers to plant nitrogen-restoring plants such as sweet potatoes. Those whom Carver could not convince changed their minds when the boll weevil reached Alabama in 1915. This forced farmers to burn their infested fields and plant peanuts. Carver learned the secrets of the peanut and made over 300 products from this lowly legume. The end result was a shift from poverty to plenty, especially in the town of Enterprise, which honored the boll weevil with a monument. The peanut is honored by a monument in Dothan.

Dr. Carver's Museum honors him, and his accomplishments are legendary. In 1916 he became a Fellow in the Royal Society of Arts in London, an honor given to few Americans. In 1923 he won the Spingarn medal for distinguished service in agricultural history. The Roosevelt Medal was awarded to Dr. Carver in 1939 for his valuable contributions to society. Not only was he a scientist, but he also enjoyed painting, drawing, and creating textile art. Some of this artwork survived a fire in the museum in 1947. Read the lists of Dr. Carver's sweet potato products, and you will have a new appreciation for your next Thanksgiving sweet potato casserole.

Now it's time to venture outdoors again. Most of the historic buildings on the campus were built by students, as was the home Booker T. Washington shared with his wife, Margaret, and his children. Sadly, Washington's first two wives died shortly after giving birth, leaving him with a daughter and two young sons. **The Oaks** was built on property owned by Washington, adjacent to the campus at that time in 1899. Today the home is in the middle of the campus, only a few blocks from the Carver Museum. The National Park Service manages the property and provides a guide as the schedule permits. You can get details from the guide at the museum.

When you enter the house, the lights will be on. The Oaks was the first house in Macon County with electric lights, and 10-watt light bulbs that were used then are burned now to create a feeling of authenticity. This will seem dim to you, as they did to me, but the guide explained that this is a matter of comparison. Ten-watt electric bulbs are brighter than candles and so were an improvement much enjoyed by the Washington family.

The evening for the Washington family began at 6 P.M. when they dressed in their Sunday clothes and sat down for dinner using their formal china. Daughter Portia often played the piano for the family and guests after dinner, and the remaining evening hours were a time for reading and study. The dim light and shuttered, draped windows also help preserve the Persian rug and Washington's certificate from Hampton Institute, which hangs on the wall in the den on the second floor. The damaging effects of light are limited there.

Mrs. Washington was 4 feet 11 inches tall and had a bad back. The stair railing to the second floor was set lower for her, and the steps were closer together. Chairs in the dining room were built closer to the floor, too. The students customized the furniture and stairs for her, thus carrying out her husband's philosophy, "We ask for nothing we can make for ourselves."

As I left The Oaks, I let my hand slide down the low bannister and pictured Mrs. Washington hurrying to summon her family to dinner. I heard the creak on the stairway and wondered if this was a familiar sound in a household of readers going to bed late.

After lunch at the Center, there may be campus events open to you. Ask at the front desk. Visitors are encouraged to enjoy the campus but respect the first priority of the university, which is to educate students and protect their privacy.

Another fine way to spend an afternoon is to drive out to the **Tuskegee National Forest.** This 11,000-acre forest is one of four national forests within Alabama, and the smallest in the nation. It is not short on enjoyment. You will find a log cabin replica of Booker T. Washington's birthplace in the **Taska Recreation** area and if you have thought to bring a cooler and sandwiches, you can picnic there. The picnic area is fully accessible, and the **Tsinia Wildlife Viewing Area** is accessible but may cause difficulty for persons using a cane or walker. The Big and Little Ponds have an accessible pier, but the slight grade and loose gravel might cause a problem for those with mobility impairments.

Hikers will delight in following the **Bartram National Recreation Trail.** It's named for William Bartram, who was the nation's first naturalist. Bartram observed the birds and other creatures here in the 1700s. The scenic hiking trail threads its way through hardwood bottoms and along pine ridges for 8.6 miles. You can begin this hike at several trailheads and travel for a mile or two or take an entire day to enjoy it.

If horses are your love, ride on the **Bold Destiny/Bedford V. Cash Memorial Trail.** You can observe native species of birds, reptiles, and mammals from trails, an observation tower, or viewing blind in the **Tsinia Wildlife Viewing Area,** or practice firearms skills at the **Uchee**

Gravel road in an Alabama State Park. (Photo courtesy Lynard Stroud)

Firing Range. Primitive camping is available, except during hunting season. Hunting and fishing are allowed for those with valid Alabama hunting and fishing licenses and an up-to-date knowledge of Alabama hunting and fishing regulations. Gun and bow hunting are allowed in season in designated areas.

On your last day of this weekend, you may want to pay your respects to Washington and Carver and other noted persons associated with the university. They are buried in the University Cemetery, near the University Chapel. Ask for a schedule of chapel services before you leave the Kellogg Center.

For your last stop before you head home, drive out to **Moton Field,** where the famed **Tuskegee Airmen** learned to fly. These black aviators were considered among the best fighter pilots of World War II. They are remembered every year with the **Memorial Day Fly-In,** a three-day event that attracts flying enthusiasts from across the country.

Area Code: (334)

Getting There:
To reach Tuskegee, take Exit 32 from Interstate 85 S. or Exit 38 S. Follow Macon County Road 30 for 6 miles to the university.

Where and When:
Butler Chapel A.M.E. Zion Church, 102 N. Church Street, Tuskegee, AL 36083.

George Washington Carver Museum, Tuskegee University, Tuskegee, AL 36083. Daily, 9 A.M.-5 P.M.

The **Oaks,** Tuskegee University, Tuskegee, AL.

Tuskegee Institute National Historic Site, Tuskegee University, Tuskegee, AL 36083. 727-3200.

Tuskegee National Forest, 125 National Forest Road 949, 2 miles east of Interstate 85 on Alabama 186, Tuskegee, AL 36083. Mon.-Fri., 7:30 A.M.-4 P.M. 832-4470. 125-foot wildlife viewing area.

Information:
Office of Information and Public Affairs. Tuskegee University. 727- 8344.

Tuskegee Area Chamber of Commerce, 121 S. Main Street, Tuskegee, AL 36083. 727-6619.

Accommodations:
Kellogg Conference Center, Tuskegee University, Tuskegee, AL 36083. 727-3000; (800) 949-6161.

Restaurants:

Kellogg Conference Center Restaurant, Tuskegee University, Tuskegee, AL 36083. Serves breakfast, lunch, and dinner, Mon.-Sat.; Buffet on Sun., 11 A.M.-3 P.M. 727-3000; (800) 949-6161.

Major Annual Events:

Carver Arts and Crafts Fair—Second Saturday in May.

Memorial Day Fly-In—3-day event sponsored by Negro Airmen International (NAI).

Carver Sweet Potato Festival, On the Square, Tuskegee—3rd Saturday in October. 7:30 A.M.-4 P.M. 727-6390.

Founding Day Celebration, Lake Tuskegee—July 4th .

The Peanut Drop!, Kellogg Conference Center, Tuskegee— December 31. 727-3000; (800) 949-6161.

Hotel Talisi. (Photo by Joan Broerman)

14

TIME TRAVEL

Check into the **Hotel Talisi** in **Tallassee,** and the first hint that you are traveling backward in time is the massive brass cash register, its golden glow dominating the front desk. The desk dates to the hotel's opening in 1928, and the scarlet and velvet lobby maintains the twenties atmosphere, but this is only the beginning of your odyssey. After your feet have left deep footprints on the carpeted steps leading to the spacious second-floor hallway and you have called home from the wooden telephone booth, you are ready to continue the path to the past.

Use the twilight hours remaining in your first weekend evening to drive east across the **Benjamin Fitzpatrick Bridge,** one block past the hotel. This is one of the world's longest curved bridges, and you can get a good overview of the Tallassee Mills, a textile plant built around 1844. The mills prospered and when the Civil War began, they became part of the supply system of the Confederacy, manufacturing uniforms. Then the factory became a Confederate armory, intended to replace a carbine shop in Richmond. The armory was the target of a Union attack led by General James H. Wilson, whose forces were known as **"Wilson's Raiders,"** but even the famous general was not immune to mistakes in direction. He had the guide shot because he suspected treachery and, following another mistaken route, missed the armory by 10 miles, sparing the townsfolk serious trouble. This was the only Confederate armory not destroyed during the Civil War.

Does tracking history make you hungry? Turn around and head back for the **Hotel Talisi,** which is so well known for its fried chicken that nearly 700 people flock through the doors every Sunday. You don't have to be part of the crowd on Sunday, however. The tantalizing smell of Southern-fried chicken has floated from the kitchen every day for more than 37 years. It's estimated that over 8,000 pounds of fried chicken are served every month. You're in luck if you've elected to come on Friday, because the competition for a table is not as great and you can also savor catfish fillet, Friday's special. It's hard not to overdo at the buffet, but save room for dessert, especially the banana pudding, which is almost as famous as the fried chicken.

You'll sleep well in the hotel, which has been restored by its owners Bob Brown and Roger Gaither, and when daylight comes you'll want to see the pair's project across the street, the Roxy Garden. When the Roxy Theatre burned, it was boarded up and vacant for almost 50 years. Then Brown and Gaither bought the theater and turned it into a three-level New Orleans-style garden with fountains, ferns, frogs, and fish. In warm weather, this outdoor setting is perfect for weddings, receptions, and other festive celebrations. Since the hotel dining room does not open until 11 A.M., ask when you check in where you can find an early breakfast on Saturday. You'll want to eat in town, since the next eating opportunity is miles away, and you also want to get an early start.

You have one more important stop on your trek into times past. Nearly 400 years ago, about three miles south of town, one of the larger villages of the Creek nation flourished on the banks of the Tallapoosa River. During the Revolutionary War, it's said the Talisi Indians were friendly to the cause of the colonists in spite of bribe offers from British agents. However, during the War of 1812, the Talisis sided with the British. This came about because of the fiery persuasive abilities of **Tecumseh,** a Shawnee leader who met with **Menawa,** chief of the Creeks, at **Tukabahchi,** the last great capitol of the Creek Confederacy. At one time Tukabahchi was thought to be the second-largest city on the North American continent. It sat almost directly across the river from the Talisi village, and because it was younger than Talisi was thought more likely to be open to Tecumseh's urging. The meeting was held at the Great Council Tree. When the mighty oak was blown down in 1929, the spot was marked by a bronze plaque. The plaque has been moved to a place of honor about six yards from the front door of the present-day Tallassee City Hall, and you can see the Tukabahchi plaque by driving across the bridge again and turning left at the library on Freeman Avenue. City

Hall will be on your right. To get your day off to a brisk start, don't drive across the bridge to see the plaque. Walk. Listen to the roar of the water 143 feet below your shoes. The round trip will be less than a mile, and by the time you've returned to check out of your hotel room, your blood will be pumping and you'll be ready for a day's adventure in Alabama's capitol city.

Take Alabama 229 S. out of town, get back on I-85, and go west to **Montgomery.** When you arrive in downtown Montgomery, follow the signs to the **Montgomery Visitor's Center** in the historic **Union Station,** adjacent to Riverfront Park. The nearby train shed is one of the few surviving structures of its type from the nineteenth century. Gather information in the Visitor's Center and then see the **Hank Williams Museum,** which is near Union Station. Before you leave the area, follow the steps behind the Visitor's Center to the river.

The Alabama River was a major player in the formation of the city that surrounds you today. The Federal Road curved close to the river, and in 1817 a group of Georgia investors laid out the Town of Alabama near a curve in the river. They advertised the sale of lots, commending the high ground as free of swamps and touting this as a healthier area for the future residents.

Competition arrived in the person of a transplanted northerner, **Andrew Dexter.** He and his group of investors laid out the town of New Philadelphia, which the locals called Yankee Town. A national panic and depression halted this fierce competition, and the rivals realized a merger would be in the best interests of both. They put the courthouse on the line that divided them and named the town Montgomery. This convenient location on the river became the spot where cotton was loaded and shipped to Mobile. The town prospered and grew, and the population explosion resulted in change. Alabama moved from territorial status to statehood in 1819.

The new state struggled to choose a capital. From the first territorial capital at **St. Stephens** to a temporary capital at **Huntsville,** to the first permanent state capital at **Cahawba,** the legislators shuffled their papers and discussed options. After a one-vote decision heavily influenced by assemblymen whose interests were outside the Alabama River region, the capital was located at **Tuscaloosa** on the Black Warrior River for more than twenty years.

Thanks to the steamboat, Alabama river towns flourished and the whispers of Dame Fortune traveled on the wind. During the flush times of the 1830s, Montgomery confirmed its place as a major market center. Its growth was a direct result of the rapidly increasing population of the Alabama River region and of the eastern part of the state in general. With the removal of the last remnants of the Creek Nation, the flood of immigration that had poured into the Black Belt pushed eastward to the rich lands between the Coosa and Tallapoosa Rivers. Residents complained that it was difficult to do business with the capital in Tuscaloosa. Now the Alabama River Valley folks had allies and together they forced the capital to Montgomery. Finally, in 1847, with much credit being given to the steamboat, the capital was settled at last in Montgomery.

The city deeded the hill where Andrew Dexter's goats had grazed to the State for the site of the new statehouse, and local businessmen raised $75,000 to build it. The nickname "Goat Hill" remains to this day. By 1847 the statehouse was complete, but two years later it burned and the fight to move the capital erupted again. The move didn't happen. The new statehouse was completed in 1851 and still stands as a testament to the importance of the Alabama River region and the power of its leaders. It is also one of only a few state capitols designated a National Historic Landmark. You'll want to see this symbol of victory next.

Leave the Visitor's Center and turn left on Water Street. Then take Commerce through downtown Montgomery. When it curves to the left, it becomes Dexter and you are headed directly toward the Capitol. You'll find metered parking on Washington Avenue and wheelchair access through the Bainbridge Street entrance. Handicapped parking is available on Adams Avenue.

Two significant events that affected the entire country occurred at the **Alabama State Capitol.** If you climb the steps to the Capitol, you will be reminded of the second one first. This is where the Selma to Montgomery civil rights demonstration ended, on the Capitol steps, in 1965. When you tour the Capitol building and reach the west portico, look for a star marking the spot where **Jefferson Davis** was inaugurated the first and only president of the Confederate States of America in February 1861, a century earlier than the Civil Rights march. To put the Civil War dates in perspective, Alabama seceded from the Union on January 11, 1861, and became the Republic of Alabama until February 8, when it joined the Confederacy. The state was readmitted to the Union on June 25, 1868.

Within walking distance of the Capitol Building (Don't forget to feed your parking meter!) is the **Alabama Department of Archives**

Alabama State Capitol Building. (Photo by Karim Shamsi-Basha, courtesy Alabama Bureau of Tourism & Travel)

and History, the oldest state archival agency in the nation. Likely to be overlooked is the third-floor museum. Many Indian artifacts and early colonial displays create an Alabama timeline, and the chair in which **Jefferson Davis** sat awaiting his inauguration is preserved under glass. Don't miss "Grandma's Attic," the children's hands-on museum on the second floor. In the fall of 2000 the archives will break ground on the addition of a new wing with climate-controlled storage, ensuring the preservation of priceless historical documents.

After your archives visit, another short walk will take you to the **Dexter Avenue King Memorial Baptist Church,** where **Dr. Martin Luther King, Jr.,** started his ministry and where the Civil Rights Movement began. See the mural that depicts events and people associated with Dr. King's career.

You can continue on foot to the **Civil Rights Memorial,** which is outside and bears the names of 40 men, women, and children who died during the Civil Rights Movement. Designed by architect Maya Lin, who also designed the Vietnam Veterans Memorial in Washington, D.C., the memorial makes use of water in two strikingly different ways. Visitors can read with their fingers as well as their eyes the brutal history of anti-civil rights violence in the South between

1954 (the year of *Brown v. Board of Education* in the Supreme Court), and 1968, when Dr. King was assassinated.

Two other attractions that are not open on the weekends but are mentioned in case you start your weekend early or can stay over on Monday are the home and church of Jefferson Davis. The **First White House of the Confederacy** is an Italianate, two-story house built about 1835. It is on the National Register and has been moved from its original site. It features period furnishings and many of Davis's personal belongings. While living in Montgomery, Davis, though not an Episcopalian, attended **St. John's Episcopal Church,** built in 1855 and widely known as the "church of angels." His pew is marked with a plaque.

It's time to move the car and travel over one hundred years again by revisiting the early settlers in Montgomery in a tour of **Old Alabama Town,** a history village of more than forty restored nineteenth-century buildings. With Kathryn Tucker Windham's taped voice accompanying you on your tour, you will feel as though you have chores to do and ought to take a broom to the dirt yard. You'll see Lucas Tavern, the Grange Hall, the doctor's office, the schoolhouse, a drugstore museum, the corner grocery, and a cotton gin. The gardens around the 1840s barn are planted with period trees. It would be easy to spend two hours or more covering the three to four blocks of this detailed display, and it will be difficult to return to present day. Your appetite may help.

If you are touring during the week, an excellent choice for lunch is across the street from Old Alabama Town. The **Young House Restaurant** was built in Lowndes County and moved to the Old Alabama Town area in the early 1990s. The house represents two important periods in Alabama history—the settlement of the 1820s and the flush time of the 1850s. It was perfect for the hot Southern climate because it had a central hall, high ceilings, and large rooms.

Since it is difficult to find a place to eat in the historical section of Montgomery on the weekends, take Interstate 85 to Eastern Boulevard. Eastern Boulevard is U.S. 231 and becomes Northern Boulevard. Along this thoroughfare you will find many choices for lunch. After lunch you could follow U.S. 231 N. to **Wetumpka** and the **Fort Toulouse-Jackson Park.** Or you could take Interstate 65 North to **Prattville** and spend the afternoon playing golf.

In Prattville you'll find the newest member of the **Robert Trent Jones Golf Trail,** aptly dubbed **Capitol Hill.** It's on the banks of the

Capitol Hill, Robert Trent Jones Golf Trail. (Photo by Karim Shamsi-Basha, courtesy Alabama Bureau of Tourism & Travel)

Alabama River and is the largest golf course construction project ever attempted anywhere in the world. **Clyde Bolton,** a sports writer for the Birmingham News, played this course just after it opened—it was his job, after all—and found it worthy of the advance hype. From the comments of Bolton and other avid golfers, it seems clear that anyone who plays a course on this Trail goes home with a feeling of elation—even if the greatest accomplishment is walking to the clubhouse without calling for assistance.

A treat for the whole family or a good reward for a successful golf game is a trip farther north on Interstate 65 to **Chilton County,** the Peach Capital of Alabama. The Welcome Center in **Clanton** is also a museum housed in an old railroad section house. If you are in Clanton between April and Thanksgiving, visit **Peach Park** and sample the homemade ice cream. The **Water Course,** an Alabama center for water and environmental education, is open year-round except for Sunday and Monday. Take the simulated helicopter ride across the Alabama waterways.

If you opted to go to **Fort Toulouse-Jackson Park,** 10 miles north of Montgomery, you are in for a great afternoon of living history. Instead of taking time to eat along the highway, you might want to pick up a lunch for enjoying in the 165-acre park, which is run by the Alabama Historical Commission. Then you will have an overview and be ready to enjoy the tour of the Fort and the reenactments as soon as you've wiped away the catsup and crumbs.

To get to the park, which is also a National Historic Landmark, when you reach the edge of Wetumpka on U.S. 231, turn west at the stoplight near the Food World and SouthTrust Bank onto Fort Toulouse Road. Pass the new Wetumpka Post Office and you will be two miles from Jackson Park.

In 1717 French settlers established Fort Toulouse to be an outpost for Indian trade. Almost one hundred years later, in 1814, Andrew Jackson built Fort Jackson on the site of Fort Toulouse. It's easy to understand the importance of the site because it sits at the foothills of the Blue Ridge Mountains, close to the junction where the Coosa and Tallapoosa Rivers flow into the Alabama. The Creek Indians surrendered here at the end of the Creek War and ceded 20 million acres of land to the United States government.

If you've ever wondered what it was like to live in this country from 1700-1820, you'll find out here. Living history programs focus on the War of 1812 on the first weekend of each month except January. On the third weekend of each month, except in August and December, the French Colonial times live again.

Two major events deepen the historical perspective. Alabama Frontier Days, a five-day event held the first week of November, is considered to be the most authentic living history event in the state. This reenactment focuses on the frontier culture of the South as it was transformed from Creek Indian lands to pioneer forts and homesteads during the period of 1700-1820.

A **French and Indian War Encampment** that will transport you to 1755-1763 is held the second weekend of April. Dedicated to historical accuracy and dramatic authenticity, participants come from all over the country, bringing period equipment and tent gear and leaving modern equipment behind to live for three days as Indians and French, British, and Spanish troops.

The park is also home to the **William Bartram Arboretum,** named after the eighteenth-century naturalist who visited this area more than 200 years ago and described Alabama flora and fauna in *Travels of William Bartram.* If your visit does not coincide with any of the living history programs, you can still breathe in some of the fragrances enjoyed by early Alabamians.

To continue smelling the roses, as you return to Montgomery, stop by **Jasmine Hill Gardens and Outdoor Museum,** "Alabama's little corner of Greece." Begin with the 10-minute video and then wander through 20 acres of year-round floral beauty that serves as a fitting backdrop for the private art collection of Benjamin and Mary Fitzpatrick. What you will see is the result of more than 20 trips to Greece to purchase art objects.

For your Saturday night stay, you have many choices along U.S. 231 (Eastern Boulevard) and this will put you in perfect position to take in a play at the **Alabama Shakespeare Festival.** Call ahead to reserve your choice or take a chance on getting tickets at the last minute. In either event, you will want to start the next day with a trip to the **Wynton Blount Cultural Park,** site of the **Carolyn Blount Theater** and home to the **Alabama Shakespeare Festival.** The **Shakespeare Gardens** may be open at sunrise.

The swans on the lake are also up early. The 240-acre park, which is also shared by the **Montgomery Museum of Fine Arts,** was designed to resemble an authentic English park, including black swans swimming in the lake. Where can you find black swans? Calls were placed to England. Where do they get black swans for the English parks? They use a supplier in **Pike Road,** Alabama, a few minutes drive from the Shakespeare Festival grounds. The **Museum of Fine Arts** is the oldest fine arts museum in Alabama and is therefore rich in works by Southern artists. However, it doesn't open until noon on Sunday, so you may want to go visit the zoo first and see the baby animals when they are their most playful. The **Montgomery Zoo** is home to over 600 animals and covers 40 acres. The habitats are natural and considered barrier-free. A moat might protect the animals from the visitors or vice-versa, but there is little feeling of separation. Wander along the paths and listen to the waterfalls. A whiff of smoke might lead you to the Overlook Café and a circular outdoor eating area. We watched a lion family watching us. It would be easy to spend an hour or more here. For the hungry, there are fast food restaurants nearby and a few picnic tables at the entrance to the zoo.

Take in the sweeping view of Festival Drive one more time and enter Montgomery's masterpiece, the Montgomery Museum of Fine Arts. The museum features more than 15 exhibits each year and strives for variety to intrigue and educate its patrons. "Artworks" is an interactive gallery and art studio for children of all ages. You can find the education wing by listening for happy sounds.

Jasmine Hill Gardens. (Photo by Dan Brothers, courtesy Alabama Bureau of Tourism & Travel)

Alabama Shakespeare Festival Theater. (Photo courtesy Alabama Bureau of Tourism & Travel)

It's a feast for your eyes to roam the galleries filled with art and sculpture that follow the same historical paths as your weekend in the capital city. To reorient yourself for the trip home, a careful search through the gift shop might end with a few discoveries that will fit quite nicely in your suitcase. Before you merge into the traffic on the interstate, slip into the Terrace Café and enjoy a moment of reflection. A view of swans swimming peacefully on a mirror lake is a good memory to take home.

Area Code: (334)

Getting There:

Montgomery lies on Interstate 85 and Interstate 65, in the south central part of Alabama.

To go to downtown Tallassee, get off Interstate 85 at Exit 26 and go 8 miles on Alabama 229 to the United Methodist Church in Tallassee; turn right on Alabama 14 and go almost to the bridge.

Where and When:

Alabama Department of Archives and History, 624 Washington Avenue, Montgomery, AL 36104. 242-4363.

Web site: www.archives.state.al.us

Alabama Shakespeare Festival, Wynton Blount Cultural Park (off Vaughn Road), Montgomery, AL 36117. 271-5353; (800) 841-4273. Admission.

Alabama State Capitol, Bainbridge Street and Dexter Avenue, Montgomery, AL 36104. Open Mon.-Sat. 242-3925.

Capitol Hill, Prattville. (800) 949-4444.

Civil Rights Memorial, Washington and Hull Streets, Montgomery, AL.

Chilton County Welcome Center Mini-Museum, U.S. 31 at Interstate 65, Clanton, AL 35046. Daily 9 A.M.-4 P.M. (205) 755-2400; (800) 553-0493.

Dexter Avenue King Memorial Baptist Church, 454 Dexter Avenue, Montgomery, AL 36104. 263-3970.

First White House of the Confederacy, 644 Washington Avenue, Montgomery, AL 36104. Open Mon.-Fri. 242-1861.

Fort Toulouse, 2521 W. Fort Toulouse Road, Wetumpka, AL 36092. 567-3002. Admission.   Web site: www.wetumpka.al.us/fort

French Colonial Living History, 2521 W. Fort Toulouse Road, Wetumpka, AL 36092. 567-3002.

Hank Williams Museum, 118 Commerce Street, Montgomery, AL 36104. Mon.-Sat, 9 A.M.-5 P.M.; Sun. 1 P.M.-4 P.M. 262-3600. Admission.

Jasmine Hill Gardens and Outdoor Museum, Jasmine Hill Road (off U.S. 231 N), Montgomery, AL 36121. Tue.-Sun., 9 A.M.-5 P.M. 567-6463. Admission.   Web site: www.jasminehill.org

Montgomery **Museum of Fine Arts,** One Museum Drive (off Vaughn Road), Montgomery, AL 36117. Tue.-Sat., 10 A.M.-5 P.M.; Thurs., until 9 P.M.; Sun., noon-5 P.M. 244-5700. Admission.

Web site: www.wsnet.com/~mmfa

Montgomery Zoo, 329 Vandiver Boulevard, Montgomery, AL 36117. Open daily, 9 A.M.-5 P.M. 240-4900. Admission.

Old Alabama Town, 310 N. Hull Street, Montgomery, AL 36104. Mon.-Sat., 9:30 A.M.-3:30 P.M.; Sun., 1:30 P.M.-3:30 P.M. 263-4355. Admission.   Web site: www.mindspring.com/~olaltown

Shakespeare Gardens, Wynton Blount Cultural Park (off Vaughn Road), Montgomery, AL 36117. Tue.-Sun., sunrise-10 P.M. 244-4354.

St. John's Episcopal Church, 113 Madison Avenue, Montgomery, AL 36104. Open Mon.-Fri. 262-1937.

Water Course, 2030 Seventh Street S., Clanton, AL. Tue.-Sat., 9 A.M.-4 P.M. Admission.

Information:

Alabama State Parks, 64 N. Union Street, Montgomery, AL 36130. (800) 252-7277.   Web site: www.dcnr.state.al.us

Chilton County Chamber of Commerce, P. O. Box 66, Clanton, AL 35046. 755-2400; (800)-553-0493.   Web site: www.chilton.al.us

Clanton/Chilton County Welcome Center Mini-Museum, U.S. 31 at Interstate 65, Clanton, AL 35046. Daily, 9 A.M.-4 P.M. (205) 755-2400; (800) 553-0493.

Fish Habitat Enhancement Map. Write Alabama Power Company, P. O. Box 160, Montgomery, AL 36101.

Maps of Alabama Power Company Hydrogeneration, Lakes, Launch sites, and Marinas.   Web site: www.alapower.com/hydro

Fun Phone Tourism Hot Line, Montgomery. 240-9447.

Montgomery Visitor's Center, 300 Water Street (Union Station), Montgomery, AL 36104. Open daily. 262-0013.

Web site: www.montgomery.al.us

Rare Bird Alerts, Alabama Ornithological Society. (205) 987-2730.

Robert Trent Jones Golf Trail, 167 SunBelt Pkwy., Birmingham, AL 35211. (205) 942-0444; (800) 949-4444.

Web site: www.rtjgolf.com

Montgomery Area Chamber of Commerce, 401 Madison Avenue, Montgomery, AL 36104. 240-9455; (800) 240-9452.

Web site: www.montgomery.al.us

Tallassee Chamber of Commerce, 301-A King Street, Tallassee AL 36078. 283-5151.   Web site: www.tallassee.al.us

Wetumpka Chamber of Commerce, P. O. Box 785, Wetumpka, AL 36092. 567-4811.   Web site: www.wetumpka.al.us

Accommodations:

Hotel Talisi, 14 Sistrunk Street, Tallassee, AL 36078. 283-2769.

Jemison Inn, 212 Alabama 191, Jemison, AL 35085. (205) 688-2055.

Web site: www.bbonline.com/al/jemison

Lattice Inn, 1414 South Hull Street, Montgomery, AL 36104. 832-9931; (800) 525-0652.   Web site: hometown.aol.com/latticeinn

Red Bluff Cottage, 551 Clay Street, Montgomery, AL 36101. 264-0056.   Web site: www.bbonline.com/al/redbluff

Rocky Mount, 2364 Rocky Mount Road, Prattville, AL 36066. 285-0490; (800) 646-3831.

Web site: www.bbonline.com/al/rockymount

Restaurants:

Hotel Talisi Colonial Room Café, 14 Sistrunk Street, Tallassee, AL 36078. Mon.-Sat., 11 A.M.-7:50 P.M.; Sun., 11 A.M.-2:50 P.M. 283-2769.

Peach Park, U.S. 31 at I-65, Clanton, AL 35046. Apr. 1- Nov. 26, 8 A.M.-9 P.M. (205) 755-2065.

Riverfront Inn, 200 Coosa Street, Montgomery, AL. 834-4300.

Young House Restaurant, 231 N. Hull Street, Montgomery, AL 36104. Mon.-Fri., 11 A.M.-2 P.M. 262-0409.

Major Annual Events:

Jubilee Cityfest, Montgomery—Memorial Day Weekend.

Alabama Jazz and Blues Federation River Jam, Union Station—September.

Edmund Pettus Bridge (1940). (Photo courtesy Alabama Bureau of Tourism & Travel)

15

QUEEN OF THE BLACK BELT

The **St. James Hotel** sits sedately above the Alabama River. It isn't difficult to believe that this building occupies the land sold for the highest price when the town of **Selma,** the second-oldest surviving city in the state, was first laid out. A silent witness to the arrival of the steamboat bearing travelers and commerce, the St. James is one of the few remaining antebellum riverfront hotels in the United States.

The **Marquis de Lafayette,** his dog Quiz, and his secretary Lavasseur, who recorded the journey, spent the night here when the famous Frenchman traveled to Montgomery in 1825. This visit caused a flurry of preparation and party planning all along the Alabama River. The placement of the Capitol was a hot topic, and it was hoped that the preening of social feathers would so focus attention on the area that the bid to keep the capital at Cahawba or move it to Montgomery and keep it on the Alabama River would work. It didn't. Tuscaloosa won the Capitol by one vote.

With all that partying going on, it's a wonder anyone at the hotel got any sleep. Lavasseur doesn't say whether Lafayette slept, but you can. Selma is known for historic preservation, and the **St. James Hotel** has been meticulously restored to the beauty of its earliest and most glorious days. The **Riverfront Market,** an annual craft show that brings thousands to see the antebellum buildings along the waterfront, further fuels the efforts of preservationists. For your first night of this getaway you can enjoy first-class accommodations while you absorb more than 150 years of history. Move into your comfortably furnished room, and before it gets dark, slip out onto the balcony for a twilight view of the **Edmund Pettus Bridge.**

Begin your visit to the "Queen City of the Black Belt" with dinner in the hotel's elegant **Troupe House Restaurant.** You may want to enjoy a full Southern breakfast there, too, to fortify you for the busy day ahead. Maps of walking and driving tours of the **Civil Rights Trail** and other historic sections should be available at the hotel, so why not plan your itinerary over steaming coffee and buttery biscuits and jam?

As you step out onto historic Water Avenue, imagine 49 different railroads operating in and out of the city. In 1861 Selma was the terminus for the Alabama and Mississippi Railroad coming from the west and for the Alabama and Tennessee Rivers Railroad, which ran north through the coal and iron fields of Bibb and Shelby Counties.

Travel to the end of Water Avenue and visit the **Old Depot Museum** in the former L&N Depot, one of only twelve in Alabama classified as being of historic and architectural importance. It's now an interpretive history museum. The schoolroom even smells authentic! As you walk among the exhibits in the depot, you will revisit Selma's days of serving the entire Confederacy as a distribution point for raw materials. When New Orleans fell in the spring of 1862, the Confederate arsenal was moved to Selma, further embellishing the city's role as a manufacturing center. This, of course, made the city an important strategic target for Union forces, and the "Sacking of Selma" in 1865 is remembered in numerous retellings.

Retreating Confederates are thought to have been the ones who torched more than 30,000 bales of hay in the commercial district, causing the loss of many downtown businesses. However, the Union soldiers destroyed the arsenal, the naval foundry, and other buildings so that two thirds of the city went up in flames, along with any hopes the South had of rallying.

It seems appropriate at this point to call your attention to The **Firefighter's Museum,** behind the depot. You'll also see a law enforcement museum. As you return to the depot, notice the large bale of cotton. The scales show that it weighs 485 pounds—a symbol of the wealth that motivated Southern businessmen and leaders.

Inside the depot you'll see portraits of **Benjamin Sterling Turner** and **Martin Luther King, Jr.** Turner was a slave who was owned by the same man who owned the St. James Hotel. When his master was out of town, Turner managed the hotel, an unusual responsibility, but

Cotton bale at Old Depot Museum. (Photo by Neal Broerman)

Turner's intelligence and ability were well respected. When the Civil War ended, Turner became the first African-American to serve in the United States Congress. You will also see the **Keipp Collection,** a phenomenal collection of photographs by **Mary Morgan Keipp.**

Many people have lunch at the St. James and spend the afternoon strolling through the **Selma Antique and Art Mall** on Water Avenue or other fine antique stores and art galleries. Hours are limited or short, often affording a brief opportunity, so if art and antiques are your priority, call for hours or reservations when you plan your visit to the city.

Major Grumbles is another fine restaurant, located on the river a block from the St. James. It sits at the site of an early 1800 structure that was a three-story wooden building, a slave auction center for buyers and sellers covering the area from New Orleans to Charleston and Savannah. The large, black, iron doors in the entrance hall may be the only authentic slave doors existing today. They were found on the premises underground. Stories about the restaurant's namesake, Major Grumbles, lighten the mood of this grim historical setting a bit. The food is the happier attraction here.

Depending on how much time you spent in the depot, it may be too early for lunch, so take a minute to read the **Bienville Boulder,** near the **National Voting Rights Museum and Institute.** Then, if you have time—and you may want to walk through and return to see the movie—enter the museum. The tour takes about 45 minutes, but the movie shown to enhance the exhibits takes more than an hour. The **Black Belt Heritage Tour** Agency is housed in this museum, and you can add to your growing stack of maps and tour possibilities here. This will give you much to discuss over lunch.

Inside the museum, the first display on your left is the "I Was There Wall," which speaks in many voices of the struggles of the Civil Rights Era. A room with plaster footprints of those who took part in the march from Selma to Montgomery is also a compelling witness to the individual contributions. Another room is dedicated to women, recognizing their sacrifices for the progress of human rights. All women are invited to sign the book of honor placed there.

The Selma room was designed by **Marie Foster,** one of the organizers of the movement in Selma. The clothes she wore on Bloody Sunday are folded neatly on top of a display case. You can also see pictures of Ms. Foster with President Clinton and Vice President Al Gore.

Beginning in 1963, voting rights activity in the city accelerated to the point that a march from Selma to Montgomery was organized in 1965 and **Dr. Martin Luther King, Jr.** came to the area to lead it. Daily demonstrations lasted for months, and world attention was focused here. **Brown Chapel AME Church** was the headquarters for the march, and it is now part of the **Civil Rights Trail.** Today this event is remembered with a weeklong reenactment as marchers cross the now famous **Pettus Bridge,** originally constructed in 1940.

A good time to visit Selma—as is true of many Southern towns—is in the spring when dogwoods and azaleas are in bloom. That's also the time when lovely homes are open to be toured and enjoyed and a special Sunday dress feeling pervades. The **Selma Pilgrimage** offers tours of historical homes and museums and a twilight tour of living history at the **Live Oak Cemetery.** Benjamin S. Turner is one of many well-known citizens buried here. So is Martha Todd, half sister of Mary Todd Lincoln.

Headquarters for this annual event are in the **Joseph T. Smitherman Historic Building** on Union Street. This building is not open on weekends, but if you can find even a short time for a tour during the week, see the highlights of Selma's history as Selma artist Kirk Miller depicts them in his paintings displayed in the pavilion.

A few antebellum homes are open for tour regularly, and the house museums, so named because people lived and entertained there and because the tourist is made to feel like a guest in the house, offer a delightful peek into a long-ago, gracious lifestyle.

You'll notice colored shields on many houses. These are placed to indicate age. Blue denotes a house built in 1865 or earlier. Yellow indicates the period from 1866 to 1910. A green shield means the house was built after 1910 and is at least 50 years old.

Sturdivant Hall is a house museum listed on the National Register of Historic Places, and its formal gardens are the setting of an annual event, the Ball of the Battle of Selma. Stand on the veranda overlooking the back courtyard and imagine the costumed ladies and uniformed gentlemen gathered around the fountain, conversing, choosing dance partners, and enjoying the warm Southern evening. They breathe air perfumed by the fruit of a mock lemon tree just outside a young lady's bedroom. The fruit scents the young lady's room, but the tree's spike-like thorns serve as a constant chaperone.

Inside the house we saw two paintings with shoulders and eyes that turned to follow us as we walked in front of them. This was an artist's illusion, not a Hollywood set. We were even more fascinated by two clocks, one in the hallway at the foot of the stairs and the other in the parlor.

A clue to the age of a clock can be found in the date of repair, and the first date etched on the **George Washington Commemorative Clock** in the parlor is 1702. Fifty of these clocks were made in France originally but the story goes that the ship bearing the timepieces sank and only six or seven were rescued. Of these remaining clocks, it's known that one is in the White House, one is in the Metropolitan Museum of Art in New York, three are privately owned, and one is in Selma and proudly pointed out by the two guides who showed us through the house, Marie Barker and Mary Fields.

The sweet tones of the floor clock in the hall will cause you to hurry there to listen and admire. Many of the antiques in the home

Antique clock, Sturdivant Hall. (Photo by Neal Broerman)

Courtyard fountain, Grace Hall. (Photo by Joan Broerman)

are from the personal collection of Mr. and Mrs. Robert Sturdivant, and this is why the house is named for them. Ascend the stately staircase and look for paintings by Clara Weaver Parrish, a world-renowned, turn-of-the-century artist. If you are not among the timid, ask about the ghost.

John McGee Parkman was an ambitious and industrious young man who climbed the financial ladder from bank teller to president of the First National Bank of Selma when he was still in his twenties. Many well-established commercial houses failed as a result of cotton speculation, and the newly organized bank went under, too. Parkman was imprisoned. Friends tried to break him out, and he was either shot or drowned in the river. His wife and two little girls lived in the house. People who see his ghost say they sometimes see two little girls, too.

The afternoon is waning, and you need to think about where you will spend your second night in Selma. More history and another good ghost story await you at **Grace Hall,** across the street from the Chamber of Commerce. This restored Italianate home was built in 1857 and is a mix of older neoclassicism and newer Victorian trends. It's on the National Register and restoration has been certified by the Department of the Interior. Follow the brick walk lined with fragrant boxwood to the front door. Many feet have preceded you.

Joey and Coy Dillon bought the house in the early 1980s and converted it into this fine bed and breakfast, which has a five paws rating because it has resident dogs and a cat named Morris. They will allow guests to bring well-mannered pets. The house holds 67 pieces of original furniture and is described on the historic marker in front of the mansion as Picturesque Eclecticism, which dominated Alabama architecture after 1850. The pressed-tin ceiling in the first-floor office and den is magnificent. It is painted a pale blue and matches the molding. The owners added a powder room and a wall to create a spacious office. They also added a covered breakfast deck, which overlooks a courtyard and a happy fountain.

When **Wilson's Raiders** rode into town, they arrested the owner of this house, who was the mayor and also the newspaper publisher, and then General James H. Wilson occupied the house. Many of his troops occupied the St. James Hotel. Presumably this is why both structures were spared in the burning of the town.

Now for the ghost. Her name is Miss Eliza, and Mrs. Dillon can show you a photo of a lady in white standing in a window, the background of a picture Mrs. Dillon snapped.

Many old Southern towns with gracious antebellum homes boast of their ghosts. Even the most put-upon hosts say a ghost makes a great scapegoat. If you lost your glasses, the ghost must have taken them. Has the room been rearranged or papers shuffled about? That pesky ghost! Selma seems to have more than its share of ghosts, and many are well known, having been the subject of television shows and books. Write the Chamber of Commerce and ask for the Ghost Tour brochure or become acquainted with famous Selma resident and legendary storyteller **Kathryn Tucker Windham** through her books on the subject, especially *13 Alabama Ghosts and Jeffrey*. Jeffrey is also a ghost, and his spirited companionship has kept Mrs. Windham collecting and preserving ghost stories from all over the South, not just from Selma.

It's been a long day and it's time to relax. Innkeepers are always a wonderful source of information about the best café or dining spot to suit your mood. Confer with the Dillons and spend your evening in one of Selma's finest eating establishments. **Oneal's** overlooks the Alabama River and **Tally-Ho** has been satisfying appetites for over 50 years. Enjoy!

Sunday dawns with sunny promise. After your first cup of coffee on the Dillons' back porch, you will be ready to choose your route for a glorious day outdoors. Wear your trail-hugging walking shoes, dab on insect repellant, and before you head out of town, gather cold drinks and sack lunches. No matter your choice for the day, a picnic is always handy.

The **Paul M. Grist State Park** is just 15 miles north of Selma. Take Alabama 22 East to Dallas County Road 37. This is a scenic drive, and you will be further rewarded when you get your first glimpse of the shimmering lake. Hunting is not allowed in the 1,080-acre park, but there is plenty of great fishing in the 100-acre Paul Grist Lake. Day use includes picnicking, swimming, hiking, a boat launch, and fishing, plus a kiddie play park. Pedal boats, canoes, and flat-bottom boats are available for rent. No reservations are accepted, and peak crowds come on holiday weekends. The rest of the time, this is a real find for serenity seekers. There are six modern hookup sites with water, electricity, and sewers, but primitive camping is also available. The bathhouse has hot showers and facilities are immaculate. The staff seems dedicated to making the park experience a pleasant one so visitors will want to come again. Choose a picnic table in the trees where you will have a good view of the lake and the kiddie park, too.

If a different outdoor experience appeals to you, take Alabama 22 W.

to Dallas County Road 9 and five miles more will lead you to **Old Cahawba,** once Alabama's state capital and, as you've read in earlier chapters, a town that seemed destined to hold power and privilege within its boundaries, but lost all in the floods of water and political pressures. Visit the welcome center and decide where to begin today's hunt for history. Hike the **Clear Creek Nature Trail** or read the inscriptions on the crumbling gravestones in the cemetery—if you can. Moss and wildflowers decorate the ruins, reminders of the resiliency of nature.

The picnic area is shaded and close to restrooms and water. Did I mention ghosts? Well, it is a ghost town, isn't it?

Area Code: (334)

Getting There:
To reach Selma from Interstate 65 take U.S. 80 W. from just south of Montgomery.

Where and When:
Brown Chapel AME Church, 410 Martin Luther King Jr. Street, Selma, AL 36701.

Cahawba, Alabama 22 N., Selma, AL 36701. Open daily. 875-2529.

Edmund Pettus Bridge, U.S. 80, Selma AL.

Firefighter's Museum, 4 Martin Luther King, Jr. Street, Selma, AL 36701. Mon.-Sat., 10 A.M.-4 P.M. 874-2197. Admission.

Grace Hall, 506 Lauderdale Street, Selma, AL 36701. 875-5744. Admission.

Live Oak Cemetery, Dallas Avenue, Selma, AL.

National Voting Rights Museum and Institute, 1012 Water Avenue, Selma, AL 36701. 418-0800. Admission.

Old Cahawba Archaeological Park, 9518 Cahaba Road, Orrville, AL 36767. Open Daily, 9 A.M.-5 P.M. 872-8058. Admission.
Web site: www.olcg.com/selma/cahawbah.html

Old Depot Museum, 4 Martin Luther King, Jr. Street, Selma, AL 36701. Mon.-Sat., 10 A.M.-4 P.M. 874-2197. Admission.

Paul M. Grist State Park. 1546 Grist Road (off Dallas County Road 37), Selma, AL 36701. Daily, 8 A.M.-7 P.M. 872-5846. Admission.

Selma Antique and Art Mall, 1410 Water Avenue, Selma, AL 36701. Mon.-Sat., 9 A.M.-5 P.M.; Sun., 1 P.M.-5 P.M. 872-1663.

Selma Art Guild Gallery, 508 Selma Avenue, Selma, AL 36701. Wed.-Sat., 10 A.M.-4 P.M. 874-9017.

Siegel Gallery, 706 Broad Street, Selma, AL 36701. Mon.-Fri., 10 A.M.-5 P.M.; Sat., 10 A.M.-1 P.M. 875-1138.

Joseph T. Smitherman Historic Building, 109 Union Street, Selma, AL 36701. Mon.- Fri., 9 A.M.-4 P.M. 874-2174. Admission.

Sturdivant Hall, 713 Mabry Street, Selma, AL 36701. Tue.-Sat., 9 A.M.-4 P.M. 872-5626. Admission.

Information:

Alabama Vacation Guide. Call 1-800-ALABAMA (252-2262).

Selma-Dallas County Chamber of Commerce, 513 Lauderdale Street, Selma, AL 36702. 875-7241; (800) 457-3562.

Web site: www.olcg.com/selma

Selma-Dallas County Historic Preservation Society, PO Box 586, Selma, AL 36702. Pilgrimage in March. 875-7241; (800) 457-3562.

Web site: www.olcg.com/selma

Guide Services:

Black Belt Heritage Tours, 1012 Water Avenue, Selma, AL 36701. 418-0800.

Accommodations:

St. James Hotel, 1200 Water Avenue, Selma, AL 36701. 872-3284; (888) 264-6788.

Restaurants:

Major Grumbles, 1 Grumbles Alley, Selma, AL 36701. Daily, 11 A.M.-10 P.M. 872-2006.

Oneal's Restaurant, 8 Mulberry Road, Selma, AL 36701. Dinner, Tue.-Sun. 875-2275.

Troupe House Restaurant, 1200 Water Avenue, Selma, AL 36701. Mon.-Sat., 6 A.M.-10 A.M., 11 A.M.-2 P.M., 5 P.M.-9 P.M. (until 10 P.M., Fri.-Sat.). 872-3284; (888) 264-6788.

Tally-Ho Restaurant, 509 Mangum Avenue, Selma, AL 36701. Mon.-Sat., 5 P.M.-10 P.M. 872-1390.

Major Annual Events:

Festival of Art, Music & History, downtown Selma—March.

Bridge Crossing Jubilee, Water Ave., Selma—March. 418-0800; (800) 457-3562.

Historic Selma Pilgrimage, Selma Antique Show & Sale, Selma— March 17-19, 2000.

Battle of Selma Reenactment, Battlefield Park, Selma—April.

Old Cahawba Festival, Orrville—May. 872-8058. Admission.

Web site: www.olcg.com/selma/cahawbah.html

Riverfront Market, Selma—October. 875-7241. Admission.

Tale Tellin' Festival, Selma—October. 875-7241.

16

LAND OF
WELCOME

Alabama is rich in numbers of preservationists, members of historical societies, and environmental organizations who volunteer countless hours scraping paint, cleaning up creeks, raising funds, and doing whatever needs to be done. They work diligently and sometimes doggedly to make the past accessible to future generations. If only the preservationists were rich!

Nowhere is there a more tireless gathering of preservationists than in **Demopolis.** The **Marengo County Historical Society** is but one group dedicated to the memory of the men and women who settled and developed the "City of the People."

Preservation fever is contagious. Every other spring, April on the Avenue celebrates the town's past. It's a time of tiptoeing across the thresholds of carefully restored private residences and learning who lived there once upon a time, how they lived, and why they left or stayed in this town that can still be enjoyed by people who like to walk through neighborhoods of friendly people.

Demopolis puts on an annual citywide major event, **Christmas on the River,** in December. Christmas on the River brings 40,000 cheering children of all ages to this city of less than 10,000 people to see a festival of lighted, animated "float boats" sail below the white chalk bluffs. These are the same chalk cliffs that witnessed the 1817 arrival of the French Bonapartists who came to plant their vine- and olive-growing culture. The Napoleonic refugees were unsuccessful, and most of them left, but the town grew anyway. Only summer has a calendar free of community festivals, but the welcome mat is still out. If the town had a front door, the note to visitors might read: "Gone to the lake. Come on down."

For a quiet, laid-back weekend, pick a non-event time and check into the **Demopolis Inn.** Built in 1892, modernized in 1986, and locally owned and operated, the inn overlooks **Confederate Square,** one of the oldest public squares in the state. Laid out in 1819, the grassy green square is speckled with fragrant clover and surrounds a cast-iron fountain that was added by the city fathers in 1895 because they wanted to welcome the many visitors to the city. That desire continues one hundred years later.

If you are in time for dinner, go back to U.S. 80 W. and look for the **Foscue House.** Built as a home in 1830, this restaurant offers a menu varied enough to suit a wide range of tastes and get your weekend off to a happy start. The combination of atmosphere and setting is unbeatable.

Breakfast at the inn is Continental. Cappuccino, espresso, and fresh bread are the stars here. Sip your favorite brew and feel the pace of a more leisurely world sink into your bones.

Ambling along the sidewalk is a pleasant way to see Demopolis. You won't even have to cross the street if the **Mustard Seed** is your destination. Joy Collins is the delightful owner of this spacious, sweet-smelling shop that is filled with lovely books and fine gifts. The selection of baby heirlooms and antiques will inspire your creativity. You'll come up with any number of reasons to buy items you just discovered you must have.

Carry your purchases to the car and begin covering a larger area. There are no parking meters in Demopolis, and you won't encounter traffic jams. Drive to the **North-South Main Avenue Historic District,** where you can leave the car and venture forth on foot again.

Trinity Episcopal Church is the only Episcopal church in the world that has its own Jewish Temple. At one time there was a thriving Jewish Community in Demopolis. Flu struck the town in 1917, and the young Jewish people began leaving the area. A smaller temple was built to replace the larger one, which was no longer needed. When the Jewish population dwindled to three in Demopolis, Trinity agreed to accept **Temple B'nai Jeshurun** and promised to maintain it, memorialize contributions of the Jews to the area, and to return it to the Jews when they come back. There are 108 graves in the Jewish Cemetery on land donated by Episcopalians.

Trinity, built in 1833, has more stained-glass windows than any other church in Alabama. These 79 works of art reflect a wide range of subjects and periods of nineteenth- and twentieth-century design.

St. Leo the Great Catholic Church, at the other end of Main Street, traces its roots to the monks and priests who accompanied **Hernando De Soto** to the area in 1540. This church also has noteworthy stained glass windows located in the sanctuary, "The Good Shepherd" and "The Little Flower." These windows were crafted by German artists and were placed when the church was built in 1904.

You will pass **Lyon Hall,** which took three years to be built by slaves of George Gaines Lyon and his wife, Anne Glover Lyon, and may take even longer to be restored. This is the newest project of the **Marengo County Historical Society** (MCHS). The house demonstrates Greek Revival style. After the Lyons built the house, they traveled to New York to buy furniture, and many of these original pieces are still in the house.

Laird Cottage is home to both the **Geneva Mercer Museum** and the MCHS. Geneva Mercer was a local artist and sculptor and you can learn much about the area by studying the exhibits scattered among the artwork. When this building is open, it makes a handy rest stop, because it has public restrooms.

There is no predictable schedule for going inside the above historic structures. Churches are usually open, and sometimes a workman or curator will be on site and willing to show visitors around an unoccupied building.

Nine miles east of Demopolis, in **Prairieville,** you can see the **St. Andrew's Episcopal Church,** a red Gothic church that is rarely open but it is surrounded by an ancient graveyard, the final resting place of early settlers of the Black Belt Canebrake section. This church was consecrated in 1858. Continue on to **Greensboro** and look for the **Greensboro-Magnolia Grove Historic House Museum,** located on the western end of Greensboro's Historic District. This house was built as a town house around 1840 by **Col. Isaac Croom** of Lenoir County, North Carolina. This is hardly like our townhouses today. The setting is a 15-acre park.

This house, now owned by the Alabama Historical Commission, was never abandoned. It was owned by three generations of the same family and then turned over to the State. An architectural feature is the cantilevered, or unsupported, staircase. Almost all of the furnishings belonged to the family.

The last resident wanted to honor her brother, **Richmond Pearson Hobson,** who was one of the most celebrated war heroes in the history

Lyon Hall. (Photo by Neal Broerman)

Lyon Hall gardens. (Photo by Neal Broerman)

of the United States for his exploits during the Spanish-American War. The Hobson family deeded this home to the State as a memorial to Admiral Hobson, and there are many interesting naval photos and letters in the front room of the house. The Hobson family had more than its share of hardy intellectuals. While one was distinguishing himself as a military strategist, another was at work with his pen. He died at the age of 103 in the midst of working on five different writing projects.

By now you are ready to head back to Demopolis and lunch. The **River Bend Restaurant** has a view of the **Demopolis Yacht Basin** and turtles that are hungrier than you are. Boaters tie up in the nearby marina and get a courtesy car or walk from the marina and tour the town, knowing that Demopolis is a great place to stretch those leg muscles.

You'll have to pass the turtles swimming up to the dock in hordes, but they will still be there when you have fed yourself and are ready to feed them. Turtle food vending machines are attached to the deck railing. Here is your chance to cause chaos with just a few coins.

You don't have to limit your spending to a few coins, however. There are still gift shops to explore on U. S. 80. Let the nearby **Designers Showcase** and the **Arbor Shop** help you please the hard-to-please on your gift list.

If the weather is warm and you'd like to spend an afternoon outdoors, you are not far from **Foscue Creek Park Campground** and **Forkland Park Campground.** Boaters and scenery seekers will enjoy either park. Hikers, joggers, and picnickers might prefer the more developed facilities at Foscue Creek, only two miles from downtown Demopolis. Both parks are on the banks of 10,000-acre **Demopolis Lake,** which was created when the Army Corps of Engineers built the Lock and Dam. **Chickasaw State Park** is south of town on U.S. 43, and it's located next to a winter season hunting facility that is handicapped accessible and state-operated.

Spending a few hours enjoying Forkland Creek will put you in position to head north toward **Eutaw,** where you can search out more early history of the state. Go through Eutaw, turn left on Alabama 14 N., and cross Interstates 20/59. Take Alabama 39 S. to Clinton and turn left. Twelve miles ahead, on Alabama 39, you will enter **Gainesville.**

Gainesville began when the Choctaws ceded the area in the Treaty of Dancing Rabbit Creek in 1830. It was named for **Colonel George Strother Gaines,** who helped negotiate the treaty. By 1840 Gainesville was the third-largest town in Alabama. As one of the northernmost Alabama landings on the Tombigbee, the port shipped 6,000 bales of

Kring Coffin Shop. (Photo by Neal Broerman)

cotton to Mobile each year. This made Gainesville a major port town, and its bank was one of the few in the state that issued currency. The town boomed. Its hotel, the American Hotel, completed in 1837, was a social hub known especially for its dance floor on springs. In 1855 fire destroyed most of the town. War and Reconstruction, the end of the riverboat era, and the failure of a local railroad line pushed Gainesville farther into the shadows of other towns along the river.

Today Gainesville is a treasure trove for those who enjoy history hunts. One of Gainesville's first businesses (1830) was the **Kring Coffin Shop,** and that survives. Notice the difference between two doors. One is for people. The other is for coffins. The large door is high enough off the ground that a buggy could back up to it to accept its cargo.

At first the coffin shop was used as a meeting spot for the early organization of the **Presbyterian Church.** The congregation grew and built a sanctuary, which was completed in 1837 and is still in use today. Built of cypress, the interior still includes the original pulpit furniture, organ, and whale oil lamps. It's across the street, a few feet southwest of the coffin shop.

A monument on the old town square marks the spot where

General Nathan Bedford Forrest surrendered the last Confederate army in the east on May 15, 1865. You can also see a hand-pump well and a bandstand.

When you drive through the town, look for early homes with wings on one or both sides of the house. These wings were sometimes used as guestrooms for traveling salesmen or circuit-riding preachers. While a guest was welcome, he did not have full run of the family home. The wing rooms had no entrance to the rest of the house.

The road is a ribbon looping its way along the rolling land back toward Eutaw and some of the best fried chicken you'll find anywhere. The night we ate dinner at the **Cotton Patch** it was raining in torrents, but determined diners filled up the place anyhow. Families ran in from the parking lot with toddlers tucked under their sweaters and others just simply ran. Nobody seemed to mind being drenched. This determination became easier to understand as the meal progressed. We began with crispy fried green tomatoes, plowed through the fried chicken dinner with creamy mashed potatoes and flaky biscuits, and ended with homemade ice cream on apple cobbler.

Early Sunday is a good time to visit the **Demopolis Lock and Dam.** Demopolis is located within the triangle of Tuscaloosa, Mobile, and Montgomery, at the confluence of the Tombigbee-Black Warrior Rivers. It is the gateway to the **Tennessee-Tombigbee Waterway System,** which provides low-cost barge service between mid-America and world markets through the port of Mobile. You've already noted how the efforts of the Army Corps of Engineers resulted in Lake Demopolis and months of summer recreation.

The Demopolis Lock acts like an elevator, permitting large boats and barges to pass up and down the river. It is fascinating to watch fleets of barges, lashed together with metal cables, navigate into the long and narrow channel, stopping just short of the gates. You don't have to stay more than minutes to see the lock fill or empty, but you'll want to watch several barges come and go.

It's time for lunch and time to go to U.S. 80 East, where you probably drove right by the popular **Ellis V Restaurant** as you ventured in and out of town. It's been there for 40 years, and "everybody" knows it's there. Now you do, too. You'll eat well and be within a short distance of **Gaineswood Mansion,** which opens at 1 P.M. Anyone who visits Demopolis must tour this mansion and Bluff Hall. We've saved them for last, like that homemade ice cream and cobbler last night. (Do you need reminding?)

Gaineswood. (Photo by Neal Broerman)

Gaineswood Mansion is a National Historic Landmark listed in the National Register of Historic Places. Like the **Greensboro-Magnolia Grove Historic House Museum,** it is owned by the Alabama Historical Commission.

The mansion was named for the same Indian agent who negotiated the Treaty of Dancing Rabbit Creek with the Choctaws for the town of Gainesville. General Gaines' log cabin is at the very center of the mansion of Gaineswood.

General Nathan Bryan Whitfield brought Gaineswood to the level of elegance described by **Ulrich B. Phillips,** a principal writer on the antebellum South, as an "Alabama Plantation Palace." Over a period of years, Whitfield, serving as his own architect, built a series of suites around the log cabin, connecting them in one architecturally harmonious whole. Whitfield's genius is evident in the mansion and many of his creations within it. In the front parlor of the house visitors can see the one-of-a-kind musical instrument he invented, a flutina. Some say it is a cross between a music box and a player piano. It has also been described as sounding like a riverboat calliope. We don't know what General Whitfield intended.

Whitfield was also an artist. The painting of his daughter, Edith, who died when she was 10 years old, hangs above a Chickering piano in the front parlor. What is even more remarkable about this exquisite painting is that the grieving father painted this picture of his daughter 10 years after she died.

Gaineswood is one of the few house museums in the South that features original furnishings, and each piece, large or small, commands the attention of the visitor. The most breathtaking feature of the house is literally over the heads of anyone who enters the parlor or the dining room. Domed skylights ornamented in plaster bathe the rooms below with soft light. Whitfield added "the lights," as he called them, in 1861, and they are among the most arresting features of the mansion.

It's time for your last stop in Demopolis, **Bluff Hall.** Before you enter the house, go to the back of it and look out over the river. Pause for a minute to consider the first settlers, those French exiles. The white chalk cliffs were more impressive when they saw them, by 40 feet, an expanse that is now covered by water. What did these fine ladies and gentlemen think as they arrived in this new land to start over? What were their hopes? We know they planned to raise grapes and olives. Unfortunately, their lives had not prepared them for farming. Apparently the rich land and mild climate that had led them to this land of promise was not the right combination for their specific crops. So they left, but if their vine and olive colony did not thrive, their tribute to Napoleon did. Marengo County is named for the **Battle of Marengo,** the most important victory of Napoleon's second Italian campaign.

Allow the ghosts of the exiles to evaporate and return to the front of Bluff Hall and the **Canebrake Craft Corner** where you can purchase your admission ticket and engage the knowledgeable services of a guide. It may be a few minutes before you are ready to start your tour, however. The gift shop has several nooks filled with handiwork, quilts, artwork, baskets, and books.

Bluff Hall is listed on the National Register of Historic Places and represents two major trends in the architecture of the antebellum South—Federal and Greek Revival. It takes its name from the high chalk bluff where it sits. From there, the house has had a commanding view of the Tombigbee River since **Allen Glover** had it built by slaves in 1832 as a wedding gift to his daughter. After such a festive beginning, the home became the site of several exciting visits.

Bluff Hall egg mailer. (Photo by Neal Broerman)

Confederate President **Jefferson Davis** was entertained here in October 1963. Another famous guest was **General Leonidas Polk,** who was also the Episcopal bishop of Louisiana.

The Marengo County Historical society owns this house, and, in conjunction with providing a small museum of local history and preserving a fine example of one kind of home in the antebellum South, has added to an increasing collection of period clothing. Our guide, Mary Croom Barley, thought the most unusual feature of the house is that the kitchen is attached. Because of the fear of fire, most antebellum kitchens were apart from the main house.

In later years the house was turned into apartments and the kitchen was walled off. When the house was restored, a couple of teenaged boys were helping move equipment out of the house when one stumbled against the wall and broke through into the original fireplace, complete with original soot!

Ending your tour in a kitchen will turn your thoughts toward home and hearth. If you can't reach your own home in time for supper, you are about an hour or less from **Ezell's Fish Camp** near **Lavaca.** You'll just need directions one time. Your appetite will help you find your way back. Take U.S. 43 to Alabama 10 and turn west. Cross the big Tombigbee Bridge and at the bottom of the bridge take the first paved road to the right. At the end of the road you'll find Ezell's. Ask for a table on the back porch overlooking the river, a flowing pathway that still calls people to a welcoming land.

Area Code: (334)

Getting There:
Demopolis is located at the intersection of U.S. 80 and U.S. 43. From Interstate 20/59 take Exit 40 to Eutaw and follow U.S. 43.

Where and When:
Arbor Shop, 929 U.S. 80 E., Demopolis, AL 36732. Mon.-Sat., 9 A.M.-5:30 P.M. 289-9222.

Bluff Hall, N. Commissioners Avenue, Demopolis, AL 36732. Tue.-Sat., 10 A.M.-5 P.M.; Sun., 2 P.M.-5 P.M., 289-1666. Admission.

Canebrake Craft Corner, Gaineswood, 805 S. Cedar Avenue, Demopolis, AL 36732. 289-4846.

Chickasaw State Park, 26955 U.S. 43, Gallion, AL 36742. 395-8230.

Demopolis Lock and Dam, Demopolis, AL 36732.

Gaineswood Mansion, 805 S. Cedar Avenue, Demopolis, AL 36732. Mon.-Sat., 9 A.M.-5 P.M.; Sun., 1 P.M.-5 P.M. 289-4846. Admission.
Web site: www.demopolis.com/gaineswood/

C. N. Kring Coffin Shop, McKee Street, Gainesville, AL 35464.

Geneva Mercer Museum, 311 N. Walnut, Demopolis, AL 36732.

Laird Cottage, 311 N. Walnut, Demopolis, AL 36732.

Lyon Hall, 102 S. Main, Demopolis, AL 36732. Admission.

Magnolia Grove Historic House Museum, 1002 Hobson Street, Greensboro, AL 36744. Tue.-Sat., 10 A.M.-4 P.M.; Sun., 1 P.M.-4 P.M. 624-8618, Admission.

Mustard Seed, 101 W. Washington Street, Demopolis, AL 36732. Mon.-Sat., 9A.M.-5P.M. 289-2878.

St. Andrew's Episcopal Church, U.S. 80 E, Demopolis, AL 36732.

St. Leo the Great Catholic Church, 309 S. Main, Demopolis, AL 36732. 289-2767.

Temple B'nai Jeshurun, 410 N. Main, Demopolis, AL 36732.

Trinity Episcopal Church, 401 N. Main, Demopolis, AL 36732. 289-3363.

Information:
Alabama Welcome Centers, Interstates 20/59, Exit 1, Cuba.

Demopolis Area Chamber of Commerce, P.O.Box 667, Demopolis, AL 36732. 289-0270.
Web site: www.chamber.demopolis.al.us

Marengo County Historical Society, Bluff Hall, Demopolis, AL 36732. 289-9644.

Accommodations:
   Demopolis Inn, 123 W. Washington Street, Demopolis, AL 36732.
289-7003; (800) 501-4338.   Web site: www.demopolis.com/inn
   Foscue Creek Park Campground, Lock & Dam Road, Demopolis,
AL 36732. 289-5535.
   Forkland Park, Demopolis Lake (off U.S. 43 N.), Demopolis, AL
36732. 289-3540.

Restaurants:
   Cotton Patch Restaurant, Interstate 59, Union Exit 45, Eutaw, AL
35462. Tue.-Thurs., 5 P.M.- 9 P.M.; Fri.-Sat., 5 P.M.-9 P.M. 372-4235.
   Ellis V Restaurant, 708 U.S. 80 E., Demopolis, AL 36732. Daily,
10 A.M.-10 P.M. 289-3446.
   Ezell's Fish Camp, Alabama 10, Lavaca, AL. Sun.-Thurs., 11 A.M.-
9 P.M.; Fri.-Sat., 11 A.M.-10 P.M. 654-2205.
   Foscue House, 21333 U.S. 80 W., Demopolis, AL 36732. Tue.-Sat.,
5 P.M.- 10 P.M. 289-2221.
   Red Barn, 901 U.S. 80 E., Demopolis, AL 36732. Mon.-Sat., 5P.M.-
10 P.M. 289-0595.
   River Bend Restaurant, Alabama 13 N. at the Yacht Basin,
Demopolis, AL 36732.

Major Annual Events:
   April on the Avenue, Downtown Demopolis—April every other
year. 289-0270.
   Main Street Past, Present & Future: A Pilgrimage Tour, Bluff Hall,
Demopolis—April. 289-0282.
   Christmas in the Canebrake, Gaineswood, Bluff Hall, Demopolis—
December. 289-4846.
   Christmas at Magnolia Grove Open House, Greensboro—
December. 624-8618.
   Christmas on the River, Tombigbee River, Demopolis—December.
289-0270.

17

FROM MERCEDES TO MOUNDVILLE

Sleek symbols of a society that reveres speed and style roll down a factory assembly line in a small town 30 miles from a centuries-old prehistoric metropolis. Connecting the two is the town that won the Alabama state capital for two decades but now concentrates more on winning grants. **Tuscaloosa** is home to the **University of Alabama** and serves as an academic bridge between **Mercedes-Benz,** the world's premier automobile manufacturer, and **Moundville,** a powerful city and major ceremonial center that prospered eight hundred years ago yet lies buried beneath the ground today.

Tuscaloosa is also a football-loving town. If you arrive when the Crimson Tide is playing at home, you are surely there to join the ranks of the hearty fans who keep the **Bryant-Denny Stadium** ringing with their shouts of "Roll, Tide!" Either that, or you enjoy a different kind of competition: finding accommodations.

To make plans for a football weekend, reserve your hotel or bed and breakfast room early. The Tuscaloosa Convention and Visitors Bureau has a list of places to stay and will help with reservations. This hospitality holds true no matter when you are coming to Alabama's fifth-largest city. If you can possibly arrive in Tuscaloosa before The Visitor Information Center (in the Visitors Bureau) closes at 5 P.M.— it is not open on Saturday—you will be able to pick up maps, brochures, and schedules. That isn't all. The Visitor Information Center is housed in the **Jemison-Van de Graaff Mansion,** an antebellum home that is one of the finest remaining examples of Italianate architecture in the south. It was begun in 1860 by Robert Jemison

Job One, the first SUV built at the Mercedes plant, at Mercedes-Benz Visitor Center. (Photo by Joan Broerman)

Antique Mercedes Roadster, Mercedes-Benz Visitor Center. (Photo by Joan Broerman)

Antique Mercedes motorcycle, Mercedes-Benz Visitor Center. (Photo by Joan Broerman)

and took two years to complete. Most of the labor was done by trained slaves using timber from the Jemison plantations. Call ahead to let the staff know you are coming and would like to have a tour.

Arrive at the Visitor Center by four, check into your hotel after your tour, and then get ready to enjoy dinner at the "in" place, Henson's **Cypress Inn.** Drew Henson's excellent dining establishment has been overlooking the Black Warrior River for 16 years, serving traditional Southern entrees based on original recipes to 25,000 people every month. All meals are served with homemade yeast rolls and Cypress Inn bran muffins. Doors open for dinner at 5 P.M. on Friday and Saturday, and reservations are not accepted on the weekend. The Crawley Room is wheelchair accessible, but the upstairs Crow's Nest is not. Be early and you may be able to get a table by the window. Imagine the sunset!

Saturday morning should find you at the Mercedes-Benz Visitor Center in **Vance** when it opens at 10 A.M. To tour the factory, you'll have to come during the week and call for advance reservations.

This Visitor Center is like a combination showroom and museum-in-the-round. The wide-open, upbeat atmosphere will give you a wide-awake feeling, and you'll wish your bank account were limitless, too.

Trace the history of this luxury car from the Daimler motorcycle in 1885 to 1886, when Gottlieb Daimler's experiments with internal combustion engines and self-propelled vehicles resulted in the motor carriage. In 1907 the public was still skeptical that a motor car would succeed. The Mercedes "Simplex" was designed and named to reflect its simplicity and lack of complicated equipment and methods. This was the last Mercedes developed by Wilhelm Maybach before he left Daimler Motor Works and it is a Mercedes, not a Mercedes-Benz, because it was produced before the 1926 merger of Daimler Motoren Gesellschaf and Benz & Cie.

Two cars you will find interesting, among several, are the Mercedes-Benz Racing C-Class and "Job One." The racing car has collected all sorts of awards in the International Touring Car (ITC) championship in Europe, similar to the NASCAR series in the United States. "Job One" was the first M-class to roll off the assembly line in Vance, and was autographed by every member of the team that worked on the car.

By now you are ready to take a Mercedes home. Stop by the gift shop and buy one. Prices start at $10. The catch, of course, is it's not big enough to drive away.

Child's bed and antique toys at Battle Friedman House. (Photo by Joan Broerman)

Child's rocking chair and antique toys at Battle Friedman House. (Photo by Joan Broerman)

Daybed at Battle Friedman House. (Photo by Joan Broerman)

Get back in your trusty old-faithful vehicle, thank it for its years of service, and head for Tuscaloosa and the **Battle-Friedman House.** You probably passed this mansion when you went to the Visitor Information Center. Built in 1835 by planter and railroad man Alfred Battle at the time Tuscaloosa was the state capital, this townhouse once occupied an entire block of what was then Tuscaloosa's main residential street. In 1844 an English landscape designer was employed by the wealthy owners to lay out the garden, and he created an intricate pattern of interlocking diamond-shaped beds and paths. The family enjoyed the house and gardens for almost 40 years, but their fortune declined significantly after the Civil War and in 1875 they were forced to sell the home to a wealthy Hungarian immigrant, Bernard Friedman. The Friedmans took excellent care of the house and grounds. They added such decorative touches as a matching pair of ornate chandeliers, which they purchased on a trip to their native country in the late 1800s. In 1965 their youngest son, Hugo, a Tuscaloosa businessman and philanthropist who had never married, donated the house to the city for use as a cultural and social center. The last Mr. Friedman's furniture is still in his room.

Our guide, Mary Neal, had not had time to listen to the soothing sounds of the fountain, a recent addition to the gardens, but we did. The brick pathways led through sweet-smelling juniper to a setting of wrought-iron furniture and statuary, the entrance to the office of the **Tuscaloosa Preservation Society,** which maintains the house and gardens now known as the oldest intact antebellum garden in Alabama. A few more steps, and we were back in the parking lot and ready to search out a place for lunch. **Dreamland** is a Tuscaloosa institution. John "Big Daddy" Bishop founded Dreamland here in 1958, and the hickory-smoked ribs slathered in Big Daddy's famous sauce keep people coming back for more. The signed celebrity photographs decorating the walls will tell you this place is not a secret, even if the sauce ingredients are. To get there from the Battle House, turn left on Greensboro Avenue and follow it past Interstate 20/59 to Jug Factory Road. Turn left and follow it to Fifteenth Avenue and Dreamland.

Another lunch choice might be **Hummer's** in **Northport.** Note that many of the interesting shops and art galleries in Northport have weekday hours and may not be open on Saturday. Hummer's will put you in the center of things, and you can find out what is open. Take Greensboro Avenue north toward the river and cross the bridge. Turn left at the light and then right on Main Avenue. You'll see Hummer's ahead on the left.

After lunch is a good time to drive to Twenty-eighth Street and track down that contested spot Tuscaloosa won by one vote in 1825, the Capitol. From Northport, retrace your steps across the bridge and turn right on University Boulevard, then follow the signs to **Capitol Park,** the location of the Alabama capitol from 1826-1846. The old capitol burned in 1923, but you can still see the stone foundation and columns. Relocated to the site so you can get a taste of the past is the **Old Tavern Museum** (1827), which was frequented by many political leaders.

The building shows the French influence on Alabama architecture. Wide planks were used for flooring and pegs were used to put the structure together. Original furniture, tools, and household items from the early 1800s are on exhibit here. The Tuscaloosa County Preservation Society maintains the complex.

Are you ready to feel like a kid again? Make your next stop the **Children's Hands-On Museum.** (**CHOM**) on University Boulevard in the downtown area. When we arrived, the children were having a great time beating drums and singing in the Choctaw Village. We met Kathleen Hughes, director, who said children's hands-on museums have increased from 200 to 500 in the country in the past 15 years. Nearly all major metropolitan areas have at least one. Tuscaloosa is not that large, and the parents who were shepherding their children down the wide avenue past the bank and apothecary looked quite pleased that this type of experience is available to their youngsters. Carla Bailey, the museum manager, made certain we didn't miss the lower floor. We peeked inside the hospital and noticed that all the doll patients were well cared for. My husband had to bend over to try the houseboat steering wheel, but he said the wheel had plenty of power for an imaginative captain. A small patron and her mother had left their shoes outside the Japanese house and whispered softly inside the painted screen walls. Designed to engage parents, teachers, and children interactively, CHOM is geared for ages 2-12 and it is handicapped accessible. History, science, and the arts are targeted, but the smiles on small faces told us that fun is a major part of the learning process, too. CHOM is in downtown Tuscaloosa, so you are not far from several gift shops if you'd like to browse a bit.

Desperado's has a collection of Amish furniture as well as candles, stained glassware, and gift baskets. **Terra Cotta Co.** features European imports.

If you haven't toured the **University of Alabama,** Saturday afternoon

Children's Hands-On Museum (CHOM). (Photo by Joan Broerman)

on a non-game day would be a fine time. Drive east on University Boulevard. You'll be able to spot the **President's Mansion** on your right. Built in 1840, this is one of four buildings not destroyed by Federal Troops at the close of the Civil War. It is also one of the most outstanding examples of Greek Revival architecture in the nation.

You can continue on to Fourth Avenue, turn right, then right again at Ninth Street and go to the **Paul W. Bryant Museum,** or you can save that for the next day and just follow your campus map back and forth across University Boulevard.

The Paul W. Bryant Museum will put you in touch with more than one hundred years of a proud tradition. The much-loved "Bear" Bryant dominates the museum, and this is why many fans come, to see the five videos of his life from the earliest years until his last game in 1982, and to see the great plays of his and other coaches' successful careers as they are immortalized in original art such as *The Sack,* by Alabama alumnus **Daniel Moore.** Coach Bryant's office is re-created, and the dazzling Waterford crystal reproduction of his trademark houndstooth hat is eye-catching.

If you elect to save the Bryant Museum for tomorrow, you might want to drive through the two other campuses nearby, **Stillman**

The Sack. (Original painting by Daniel A. Moore, courtesy NewLife Art, Inc.)

Paul W. Bryant Museum. (Photo by Joan Broerman)

Methane well in Tuscaloosa County. (Photo by Joan Broerman)

College and **Shelton State Community College.** Founded in 1876 to train black ministers, Stillman College has a campus steeped in history. Its library incorporates Corinthian columns from its first building, the Cochrane Home. Shelton State is the proud home of a new fine arts center with a state-of-the-art theater, recital and rehearsal halls, and an art gallery.

Another possibility for Saturday afternoon or Sunday morning is a trip out Rice Mine Road to see the **North River Restorations.** We took U. S. 82 West (McFarland Boulevard), and crossed the river, went right on Rice Mine Road and turned on Tuscaloosa County Road 87, then saw Lake Tuscaloosa. On the way we passed **Old Center Church,** built in 1870 with huge hand-hewn logs held together with pegs. The church is still used for services. The **Dogtrot** is on the other side of the road and is typical of the design of early Alabama homesteads. It was built in 1837. These structures and others have been preserved by the **Gulf States Paper Corporation.** The national headquarters of the corporation houses one of the finest collections of American art in this country, The **Warner Collection.**

From Tuscaloosa County Road 87 we took Tuscaloosa County Road 42 to Tuscaloosa County Road 89 and went to **Deerlick Creek Campground.** It took us 15-20 minutes to get there after we left the Bryant Museum. On the way we passed several sparkling lakes and two unexpected sights. One was a live armadillo and the other was what looked like an oil well. Alabama motorists can tell you that dead armadillos on the road are common, but a live one is rare. And those structures that looked like oil wells along the scenic country road we traveled are actually methane or natural gas wells.

You'll want to come back another time to Deerlick Creek Campground with a picnic lunch and ride your bike on the **Gobbler Ridge Bicycle Trail** or bring a camera and binoculars and walk the **Beech Tree Hollow Hiking Trail.** Since there isn't even a crumb in your car, turn around and look forward to your next meal at **Harvey's** on McFarland Boulevard between U. S. 82 and The Mall. Harvey's has an early-bird special during the week, but the prime rib is great all the time, especially on this Saturday night, because by now you are famished. Enjoy your steak and get ready for a full day ahead.

You may have saved the Bryant Museum and your trip to the countryside for today, or you may want to go to church in one of the historic Tuscaloosa churches. The **Northport First United Methodist Church** is the third structure at the site, but the first one had a particular moment in history. On April 3, 1865, its bell was rung to sound the alarm that U.S. **General John Croxton** was invading Northport and Tuscaloosa. Not long after, General Croxton burned the University of Alabama.

Unless you are a member of the University Club, you will have to look for a brunch opportunity at the interchange of Interstates 59/20 and Alabama 69. There are several chain restaurants to choose from. Then turn south on Alabama 69 and prepare to go back 1200 years in time.

Your first view of **Moundville Archaeological Park** will overwhelm you. It's like driving into a mammoth topographical map designed by a giant architect. Who built these large grassy mounds? Why? A National Historic Landmark, this 320-acre park preserves 26 prehistoric, Mississippian-era Indian mounds. See the video first to prepare you for the tour, the series of dioramas, and the museum.

In AD 1300, most trees had been cleared and the surrounding lowlands were covered in cornfields. The supreme chief was protected behind a mile-long wall studded with fighting towers. He was surrounded by priests, warriors, and artists, as well as the hundreds of commoners who served him. The Black Warrior River valley provided the water, sun, earth, and nurture the Mississippians needed, especially for the planting of corn. They developed the organization and labor needed to build the mounds basket by basket. It is thought that 3000 people on 300 acres controlled 10,000 living outside this large and powerful city. The fortress shows that war was a way of life. As they dug the earth to build mounds, they also created lakes. They used these lakes for fish farms.

In 1915 a Philadelphian named **Clarence Moore** arrived to dig in Moundville's prehistoric past. In 1938 the Civilian Conservation Corps participated in what became the most extensive archaeological dig in history.

We climbed to the top of Mound B and tried to visualize what the setting below must have been 800 years ago. A trip through the museum further enlightened us. The **Jones Archaeological Museum** contains exhibits on the culture of Native Americans, along with artifacts unearthed during the 1930s excavations. The greatest connection came when we visited a series of dioramas. The lifelike appearance of the people captured in moments of everyday activity was startling.

Our discoveries continued. Before we left, we visited with a University of Alabama archaeology class as they worked under the

Pit-fired pottery making at Moundville Archaeological Park. (Photo courtesy Jo S. Kittinger)

Archaeological dig. (Photo by Joan Broerman)

direction of Dr. Vernon James Knight. They had unearthed parts of a hearth and were polite and professional as they explained their work. What will they uncover next?

Area Code: (205)

Getting There:
    Tuscaloosa is located on Interstate 20/59 in the west-central part of the state, about 50 miles from Birmingham. Downtown Tuscaloosa is at the end of Interstate 359, along University Boulevard.
    The Mercedes-Benz plant is about halfway between Birmingham and Tuscaloosa on Interstate 20/59 at Vance.

Where and When:
    Battle-Friedman House, 1010 Greensboro Avenue, Tuscaloosa, AL 35403. Tue.-Sat., 10 A.M.-4 P.M.; Sun., 1 P.M.-4 P.M. 758-6138. Admission.
    Web site: www.tcvb.org
    Capitol Park, 500 28th Street, Tuscaloosa, AL 35403.
    Children's Hands-On Museum (CHOM), 2213 University Avenue, Tuscaloosa, AL 35401. Tues.-Fri., 9 A.M.-5 P.M.; Sat., 1 P.M.-5 P.M. 349-4235. Admission.   Web site: www.tcvb.org
    Cycle Path Bicycle Shop, University Boulevard, Tuscaloosa, AL 35401. Mon.-Sat., 9 A.M.-6 P.M.
    Desperado's, 1410 University Boulevard, Tuscaloosa, AL 35401. Tue.-Fri., 11 A.M.-7 P.M.; Sat., 10 A.M.-5 P.M. 344-5811.
    Down to Earth, 420 Main Avenue, Northport, AL 35476. Mon.-Sat., 10 A.M.-6 P.M. 758-7470.
    Historic Capitol Park, 2800 Queen City Avenue, Tuscaloosa, AL 35403. Open year-round.
    Holt Lake, Lock, and Dam, P.O. Box 295, Peterson, AL 35478. 553-9373.
    Jemison-Van de Graaff Mansion, 1305 Greensboro Avenue, Tuscaloosa, AL 35403. Mon.-Fri., 8:30 A.M.-5 P.M. 752-2575.
    Web site: www.tcvb.org
    Kentuck Museum and Gallery, 503 Main Avenue, Northport, AL 35476. Mon.-Fri., 9 A.M.-5 P.M. 758-1257.   Web site: www.tcvb.org
    Magnolia Grove Historic House Museum, 1002 Hobson Street, Greensboro, AL 36744. Wed.-Sat., 9 A.M.-4 P.M.; Sun., 1 P.M.-4 P.M., (334) 624-8618. Admission.
    Manna Grocery Natural Gourmet, 2312 McFarland Boulevard E., Tuscaloosa, AL 35404. Mon.-Sat., 9 A.M.-7 P.M. 752-9955.

Mercedes-Benz Visitors Center, 11 Mercedes Drive, off Interstates 20/59, Vance, AL 35476. Mon.-Fri., 9 A.M.-5 P.M.; Sat., 10 A.M.-5 P.M. 507-2252; (888) 286-8762. Admission.

Moundville Archaeological Park, Alabama 69, Moundville, AL 35487; Park open daily, 8 A.M.-8 P.M.; Museum, daily, 9 A.M.-5 P.M. 371-2234. Admission.   Web site: www.ua.edu/musmain.html

North River Restorations, Rice Mine Road, Tuscaloosa, AL 35401. Open by appointment.

Northport First United Methodist Church, 700 Main Avenue, Northport, AL.

A Novel Approach Book Store, 2300 McFarland Blvd E., # 5, Tuscaloosa, AL 35404. Mon.-Sat., 10 A.M.-9 P.M.; Sun., 1 P.M.-5 P.M. 758-3979.

Old Tavern Museum, Capitol Park (500 28th Street), Tuscaloosa, AL 35403. Mon.-Fri., 8 A.M.-4 P.M.; Sat., 10 A.M.-4 P.M.; Sun., 1 P.M.-4 P.M. 758-2238.

Parrot's Perch, 420 Queen City Avenue, Tuscaloosa, AL 35401. Mon.-Fri., 10 A.M.-5:30 P.M.; Sat., 10 A.M.-4:30 P.M. 752-2637.

Paul W. Bryant Museum, 300 Bryant Drive (University Campus), Tuscaloosa, AL 35487. Daily, 9 A.M.-4 P.M. 348-4668. Admission.
                                    Web site: www.ua.edu/pwbryant/

President's Mansion, University Campus, Tuscaloosa, AL 35403. Not open to the public.

Shelton State Community College, 9500 Old Greensboro Road, Tuscaloosa AL 35487. 391-2277.

Shelton State Community College Terrific Tuesday Concerts. Call for performance times. 391-2277.

Stillman College, P. O. Box 1430, Tuscaloosa, AL 35403. (800) 841-5722.   Web site: www.stillman.edu.

Terra Cotta Co., 1907 University Boulevard Tuscaloosa, AL 35401. 345-1806.

Theater Tuscaloosa, 9500 Old Greensboro Road, Tuscaloosa, AL 35403. 391-2277.

Tuscaloosa Symphony Orchestra, P.O. Box 870366, Tuscaloosa, AL 35487. Sept.-May. 752-5515.

University of Alabama Ticket Office, 348-6111.

University of Alabama Moody Music Building, University Campus, Tuscaloosa, AL 35487. Call for performance times. 348-7111.

Warner Collection, Gulf States Paper Corp., 1400 River Road N.E., Tuscaloosa, AL 35404. Mon.-Fri., Tours at 5:30 and 6:30; Sat 10 A.M.-4 P.M.; Sun., 1 P.M.-4 P.M. 553-6200.

Transportation:

Tuscaloosa Trolley. Mon.- Sat., 10 A.M.-2 P.M.; Mon.-Wed., 6 P.M.-midnight; Thurs.-Sat., 6 P.M.- 2 A.M. 556-3876.

Historic Churches:

Christ Episcopal Church, 605 25th Avenue, Tuscaloosa, AL 35401.

First African Baptist Church, 2621 9th Street, Tuscaloosa, AL 35401.

First Baptist Church, 721 Greensboro Avenue, Tuscaloosa, AL 35401.

First Presbyterian Church, 900 Greensboro Avenue, Tuscaloosa, AL 35401.

First United Methodist Church, 800 Greensboro Avenue, Tuscaloosa, AL 35401.

St. John's Catholic Church, 800 25th Avenue, Tuscaloosa, AL 35401.

Information:

Tuscaloosa Convention and Visitors Bureau, 1010 Greensboro Avenue, Tuscaloosa, AL 35403. 391-9200; (800) 538-8696.

Web site: www.tcvb.org

Tuscaloosa Visitor Center, University Mall, McFarland Boulevard E., Tuscaloosa, AL 35403.

Tuscaloosa Arts Hotline, (800) 239-1611.

Guide Services:

Tours Your Way, 1800 McFarland Boulevard N.E., Suite 230-I, Tuscaloosa, AL 35406. 349-1995; (800) 923-1995.

Accommodations:

Crimson Inn, 1509 University Boulevard, Tuscaloosa, AL 35401. 758-9937.   Web site: www.bbonline.com/al/crimsoninn

Deerlick Creek Campground, Holt Lake, Peterson, AL 35478. Daily, 7 A.M.-9 P.M. 553-9373. Admission.   Web site: www.tcvb.org

Restaurants:

15th Street Diner, 1036 15th Street, Tuscaloosa, AL 35406. Mon.-Thurs., 10:30 A.M.- 8:30 P.M.; Fri., 10:30 A.M.-9 P.M. 750-8750.

Arman's, 519 Greensboro Avenue, Tuscaloosa, AL 35401. Mon.-Fri., 11 A.M.-2 P.M.; 5:30P.M.-10 P.M.; Sat., 11 A.M.-6 P.M.

City Café, 408 Main Avenue, Northport, AL. Mon.-Fri., 4 A.M.-3:30 P.M. 758-9171.

Cypress Inn, 501 Rice Mine Road, Tuscaloosa, AL 35406, Sun.-Fri., 11 A.M.-2 P.M.; Sun.-Thurs., 5:30 P.M.-9 P.M.; Fri.-Sat., 5 P.M.-10 P.M. 345-6963.

DePalma's Italian Café, 2300 University Boulevard, Tuscaloosa, AL 35401, Mon.-Sat., 11 A.M.-11 P.M.; Sun., 11 A.M.-10 P.M. 759-1879.

Dreamland, 5535 15th Avenue E. (at Jug Factory Road off U. S. 82 S.), Tuscaloosa, AL 35405. Mon.-Thurs.,10 A.M.-9 P.M.; Fri.-Sat., 10 A.M.-10 P.M.; Sun., 11 A.M.-5 P.M. 758-8135; (800) 752-0544.

Web site: www.dreamlandbbq.com/ribs

Globe, 430 Main Avenue, Northport, AL 35476. Serves lunch and dinner Tue.-Sat. 391-0949.

Harvey's, 2710 McFarland Boulevard E., Tuscaloosa, AL. Mon.-Sat., 11 A.M.-10 P.M.; Sun., 11 A.M.-9 P.M. 553-8466.

Hummer's Restaurant & Wine Shop, 433 Main Avenue, Northport, AL 35476. Tue.-Sat., 11 A.M.-6 P.M.

Kozy's, 3510 Loop Road, Tuscaloosa, AL 35404. Open for dinner Mon.-Sat. 556-0665.

Major Annual Events:

Sakura Festival, University Mall, Tuscaloosa—March. (800) 538-8696.

Web site: www.tcvb.org

International **CityFest and Weindorf,** Downtown Tuscaloosa—August; Fri., 6 P.M.-midnight; Sat., 9 A.M.-midnight.

Web site: www.tcvb.org

Kentuck Festival of Arts, 503 Main Avenue, Northport—October. 758-1257   Web site: www.tcvb.org

Moundville Native American Festival, Moundville—October. 371-2234.

Dickens Christmas in Northport, Downtown Northport—December.

Christmas Afloat, River Road, Tuscaloosa—December.

Web site: www.tcvb.org.

Linn Park Fountain. (Photo courtesy Dr. Helmut Eismann)

18

BIRMINGHAM AND
ITS MAGIC

Born after the Civil War, **Birmingham** grew so quickly that it became known as the **Magic City.** It cut its teeth on steel, tested its adolescence in the communications field, and packed hospitals and universities into its young-adult years. This mix of thinkers shaped the Birmingham of today.

Early in the twentieth century, **Vulcan,** the largest iron statue in the world, became the Iron Man symbol of Birmingham. For most of the century he towered over the city from his perch atop **Red Mountain.** As the new century begins, Vulcan is being repaired, but he is expected to return to his place of honor and continue overseeing the growth and change in the valley below.

The city is not symbol-less in Vulcan's absence, however. Arising from deep within the city is a dragon. This dragon is the creation of the children who hold the future of the city in their small hands. The dragon wears a ceramic skin of colors joined in harmony, and symbolizes leadership into a future beyond the rust and dust of industry and the clamor of a city divided by past racial issues.

You may not be able to look at Vulcan for a few years, but you can look up at the dragon, and in this chapter, when you "see" downtown Birmingham, you will learn more about the urban mural made by the students at **Space One Eleven.**

Birmingham is the county seat of Jefferson County. The county and the state became official entities in 1819, but Birmingham did not become a city until 1871. The rivers that carried early settlers from Mobile to St. Stephens, Cahaba, Selma, Montgomery, Demopolis, and Tuscaloosa did not flow through Birmingham. Indian trails and early military roads were the way in and out, and the soil beneath these pathways was not the rich, Black Belt earth that attracted cotton growers and merchants. This limited access and lack of opportunity isolated the area during the antebellum period. Instead, underneath the hard clay of this region lay another kind of treasure waiting to be discovered.

Birmingham had coal, iron ore and limestone, the three necessary ingredients for making steel. Fortunes made on top of the land near the rivers were surpassed by wealth dug from under the land at the foot of the mountains. Birmingham became an industrial giant, the Pittsburgh of the South, and as it grew, it spread out. Large, fashionable homes dotted Red Mountain. Roads climbed **Shades Mountain,** and people carried their belongings up and put them down, along with their roots. Birmingham became a metropolitan center surrounded by cities that were part of it but yet were separate.

The next eight chapters will introduce you to these small communities and growing towns. With this introduction comes only a sampling of what is available to see and do. It's hoped that the mention of one store or restaurant will lead you to discover others on the same side of the street.

For lodging, only a few hotels are noted, since there are many fine chain hotels throughout the area. Call to make your reservations and inquire about handicap accessibility, and/or whether your children or pets will be welcome, if there are nonsmoking and smoking rooms designated, and if there is shuttle service available to the airport or area attractions. Many have complimentary breakfasts, fitness rooms, and business centers if you must include a few hours of work on your weekend. The nearest bed and breakfast accommodations are 30 miles from Birmingham, but the interstates on weekends are not as rushed as during the week. Since your place to stay may determine the attractions you will visit, you may want to read through the next eight chapters and pick and choose what interests you to design your weekends differently from the ones I've suggested.

Getting around downtown Birmingham is simple if you know the layout of the city. It is bisected from west to east by major railroad tracks between Morris and Powell Avenues. Parallel to the tracks are avenues. Those north of the tracks are labeled "N" and those south are labeled "S." Crossing the avenues are streets, starting with First

Street, about two miles west of the heart of the city. Most of the commercial and banking area is along the north avenues, in the vicinity of Twentieth Street. The University of Alabama at Birmingham and the medical center complex lie along Sixth to Tenth Avenue S. from Tenth Street to Twenty-first Street. Southside is centered around Five Points South, at Twentieth Street and Eleventh Avenue S. and Magnolia Avenue.

However you approach the city, its bigness is obvious. Whether the skyline is lit at night by thousands of colored lights or outlined in the early morning sun, the hustle of trucks and hurrying vehicles shakes you into full alert. This is not a good time to have car trouble. But what if you do?

A.S.A.P. to the rescue. The **Alabama Service and Assistance Patrol** is a service designed to help the motorist, and in just three years of operation A.S.A.P. has amassed several thick three-ring binders of letters of appreciation from motorists who have had their travel plans interrupted by car trouble.

Currently, nine A.S.A.P. trucks, jointly run by the Alabama Department of Transportation and the Alabama Department of Public Safety and under the direction of Captain J. T. Smelley, operate during the work week until 10 P.M. Friday night. To reach ASAP, call *HP from a cellular phone or 322-4691. Shortly, you will see a bright yellow truck bearing an arrow board. The push bumper on the front of the A.S.A.P. truck is designed to nudge a stranded car out of traffic. One minute of lane blockage results in four to seven minutes of delay to motorists, and lane blockage also sets up the possibility for a major accident and injuries. A.S.A.P. acts quickly to clear up trouble before it gets worse. The A.S.A.P. truck is equipped with emergency lights, safety cones, and jumper cable attachments. It carries gas, oil, transmission fluid, and coolant. The patrolman can give the stranded motorist courtesy use of a cellular phone and change a flat tire. If you need them, these "Guardian Angels of the Expressway" will have you on your way as soon as possible.

Where are you headed? The **Tutwiler Hotel** is in the heart of the city. Yes, you can still feel the pulse of the dragon, but you can do it from a serene setting, a AAA 4-Diamond landmark. The hotel was named for Major E. M. Tutwiler, one of this city's great pioneers, who was a major investor in the future of the city along with other visionaries whose names you will see throughout your stay, such as Sloss, Jemison, and DeBardeleben.

Alabama Service & Assistance Patrol (A.S.A.P.). (Photo courtesy Alabama Department of Public Safety)

Tutwiler Hotel lobby. (Photo courtesy Whiting Publicity & Promotions)

When you enter the elegant Tutwiler lobby, you may be so dazzled with the marble floors and beautiful antiques that you might miss the spectacular coffered ceiling over your head. Look up! The first-floor hallways are an art gallery featuring paintings on loan from the **Birmingham Museum of Art.** Your room, a study in luxury, will transport you to turn-of-the-century Southern hospitality. Like the forward-inching dragon, the hotel is looking to the future out of the wealth of its past.

For dinner you may stay in the hotel and enjoy such intriguing dishes as crab-stuffed prawns or grilled portobello mushrooms in the **Grille,** or you might venture forth to **John's Restaurant.**

John's has been a Birmingham tradition for more than half a century. There's a reason—everything is homemade every morning. Corn sticks and cinnamon rolls, original secret sauce recipes, and the famous John's Cole Slaw Dressing are there to enjoy every day. You can buy the salad dressing in the grocery, and while it's true you can't pour this restaurant's atmosphere and friendly Southern service out of the bottle at home, the taste will remind you to hurry back to John's.

Breakfast is served in the **Tutwiler Grille** all weekend. Diners can tweak their taste buds with Tutwiler Pecan Toast, which is Texas toast filled with orange cream, rolled in pecans, fried, and covered with maple syrup. After this treat, it's time to go for a walk.

When you step outside the doors of the Tutwiler, you are within walking distance of a number of attractions. The **Birmingham Public Library** is really two buildings joined by a glass archway that crosses above Twenty-first Street. Enter the newer building—completed in 1984—first. The front entrance is on Twenty-first Street. Artwork in the lobby is a changing exhibit, and it is always eye-catching. Ride the escalator two stories up and enjoy the view both inside and out. As you ascend, you face a wall of windows, and the trees outside are also a changing gallery of nature's art.

On the third floor, leave the escalator, turn left, and cross the skyway into the **Linn-Henley Research Library.** You are entering the first library in Birmingham, built in 1927. By elevator or marble steps, descend to the mezzanine. The view below demands at least a few minutes of awe. Vibrant murals float above the tables and bookshelves. These are the creations of artist **Ezra Winter.** He wanted his murals to conform to architectural style, but they have also enriched it. Ask at the reading room desk for a brochure on the murals, and

Tutwiler Hotel. (Photo courtesy Whiting Publicity & Promotions)

Mural at Linn-Henley Research Library. (Photo by Neal Broerman)

Jefferson County Court House with reflecting pools. (Photo courtesy Dr. Helmut Eismann)

then work your way around the room with the colorful brochure acting as your guide. Each of the 16 scenes is a complete painting, and together they are a celebration of our literary legacy. Winter's Italian Renaissance designs border the panels and lead the eye to the beamed ceiling, another feast for the eyes.

From the reading room, turn left and leave the library by the exit to **Linn Park.** Look back at the Linn-Henley to see if you can read the names of authors and artists etched in the building's limestone facade. Take a minute to make the adjustment from the quiet interior of the library to the breezy, friendly outdoor park. At one time, Linn Park was called Capitol Park. Remember the competition among river towns for the location of the state capitol? When the city of Birmingham was laid out, it had no river running through it, but political ambition ran through it just the same. The park was called Capitol Park with great expectations. However, those hopes did not materialize and today the six-acre stretch of greenery named for an early entrepreneur lies between City Hall and the **Jefferson County Courthouse.** In spring and summer the fountain and reflecting pools of water add shimmer, and the scene of friends chatting at a table, a man reading the *Wall Street Journal,* and pigeons hoping for a hand-out all make the park an enjoyable place to spend a few restful min-utes inside a bustling city. If you stand with the courthouse on your right, **Birmingham Green,** with its elegant stores and shops, will be behind you. The Green, which is Twentieth Street, extends all the way to South Side and the **University of Alabama at Birmingham** cam-pus. Wide sidewalks, shady trees, benches, and some of the city's most interesting historical architecture are found along Twentieth Street.

Read your way throughout the park, pausing at each monument to reflect on the contributions of the people so honored. Birmingham remembers its people, and it is to this park that the peo-ple still come for a variety of gatherings. You may want to step inside the Courthouse to see the *Old South* and *New South* murals created by Chicago artist **John Norton**. These murals have not been restored and sealed as the ones in the Linn-Henley have, and the scenes seem to be fading away. The courthouse, which opened in 1931, is under-going major renovation. Perhaps a newer South is yet to come.

Leave the courthouse murals behind and turn toward Eighth Avenue. In front of you will be the **Birmingham Museum of Art.** Cross Eighth avenue and look to the left as you approach the east wall of Boutwell Auditorium. Now you are looking at the dragon. This sculp-ture wall is Birmingham's largest public art installation. Walk under the trees between the glass window of the Museum of Art and the urban mural that was made by the children of the city at **Space One Eleven,** a nonprofit, community-based cultural center. Space One Eleven houses exhibition and studio facilities and is the parent organ-ization of City Center Art and City Center Art and Brick Company.

It took the hardworking students in the City Center art program five years to hand-cut the bricks from Alabama red clay and individ-ually decorate, paint, glaze and fire, then trim and cement the bricks into a series of 79 two-ton panels. Can you pick out the soccer ball? If you look long enough and hard enough at the designs, you can see references to **Sloss Furnaces,** the city's rolling hills, Vulcan, and the cityscape. Space One Eleven is not open on weekends, but if you can get there before it closes at 6 P.M. on Friday, knock on the door. Someone will be happy to give you a tour of the studios and a small art gallery. Many of the art items can be purchased.

After you have enjoyed studying the dragon, go in the back door of the Museum of Art on your right, and up the stairs to the **Charles W. Ireland Sculpture Garden.** Each paver and brick in the mosaic

The Peanut Depot. (Photo by Neal Broerman)

pool represents monetary support of the new wing and was placed in honor or memory of someone dear to the donor.

You could spend several hours in the museum, and even eat lunch here. The **Wedgwood** display is exceptional, and kids love the room of medieval armor and the **Japanese samurai.** Have them bring sketchpads. This is the largest municipally-owned art museum in the southeast, and it includes American, Renaissance, Oriental, and African art collections.

Walk back to the hotel now to pick up your car. Drive toward the Civic Center and locate the **Alabama Sports Hall of Fame,** on the corner of Tenth Avenue and Twenty-second Street. Metered parking and a parking deck are nearby. In the Hall of Fame you will see Olympic medalist **Jesse Owens,** the Alabama Crimson Tide's football coach "Bear" Bryant, baseball Hall of Famer **Willy Mays,** and other sports heroes with ties to Alabama. After seeing so many sports legends, you may want to continue hearing the sound of the crowds ringing in your ears. How about going out to the ballpark?

First take a short side trip to the **Peanut Depot.** Park in the bank parking lot on Morris Avenue. You will enjoy breathing in the aroma of fresh-roasted peanuts, and you can pick up a bag for nibbling now or buy a container of peanut butter with or without salt to remind you of your visit to Birmingham.

While you are on Morris Avenue, you are not far from what was once called "the heaviest corner on earth." At the corner of First Avenue and Twentieth Street, four skyscrapers with steel beam construction were built from 1903-1913. The **Woodward Building** on the southwest corner was the city's first steel frame skyscraper, and it was built in 1902. On the northeast corner, the **Brown-Marx Building** was built in 1906. In 1909 the **City National Bank** was built on the northwest corner, and on the southeast corner, the **John Hand** First National Bank Building went up in 1912.

From Morris Avenue, go to **Rickwood Field** which is about four miles away. This is the oldest baseball park in America, and indeed the oldest one in the world. It can be counted as a living history museum, because if you've timed your trip correctly, (that is, not during a Sunday afternoon game), you can get out on the field, stand on the mound, and pretend you are facing Babe Ruth and the Yankees. Pick up a brochure and follow the self-guided walking tour. Games are played on summer Sundays, and many have no admission charge. Call or write for a schedule. To reach Rickwood Field from downtown Birmingham, take First Avenue North toward Interstate 65. Follow U.S. 11 signs. Continue under the interstate and follow U.S. 11 on Third Avenue North about two miles to Second Street West. Turn left. Rickwood will be two blocks ahead.

In spring or fall it would be difficult to choose a better place to enjoy lunch than **Cobb Lane Restaurant,** just off Twentieth Street. Cobb Lane parallels Twentieth Street South at Fourteenth Avenue South. For all the fuss made over crabs here, she-crab soup and crab cakes, you wonder what the diners are like. Not crabby, that's for sure. The courtyard is a garden of cherry, laurel, and oak trees. Dine outdoors when skies are warm and clear, but if the weather chases you inside, an Old World atmosphere awaits. Any time is a good time to eat here. Cobb Lane was named for Virginia Jemison Cobb, for her efforts in restoring the area. Go ahead and order dessert. The antique shops and second-floor art galleries nearby result in a fitness walk you'll never notice.

If you are accompanied by children, you may prefer going from the baseball park to **McWane Center,** where parents and grandparents have as much fun as the kids do. After only five months of operation, this interactive science and technology museum was named one of the top ten visitor attractions in the state. You will know why the minute you step through the doors. Young voices rise and fall excitedly as kids scurry from the Ocean's Edge to the HighCycle. Just Mice Size won't let you in unless you are accompanied by a child under five, but you can peek into the activities going on there.

This adventure in science is designed for all age and ability levels, and the staff strives to meet special needs. Two hours would be a good block of time to allow here, especially if you want to experience the thrills in the **IMAX** Dome film presentation. Get there before the lights go out and hold on!

To contrast with the technology in the IMAX, visit the **Alabama Theater for the Performing Arts,** which was built in 1927 for Paramount Pictures. From McWane Center, go to Third Avenue North and turn left. The Alabama Theater is called the "Showplace of the South," and is visited every year by more than 400,000 people of all ages who come for one or more of 250 events. The ornate lobby is glamorous, but the real showpiece is the **Wurlitzer organ.**

It's time for dinner, and a colorful part of Birmingham history can be glimpsed by driving south, away from the city on U.S. 31 (Montgomery Highway). As you travel up the mountain, look to your right into the valley for a view of **Samford University.** At the top of the ridge on your right you will see a gazebo. This Romanesque structure was once on the estate of an early resident, **George Ward.** Ward was mayor of Birmingham from 1905 to 1909, and he was known as the "Fighting Mayor" because of his war against saloons, crime, and old-time political machines. He advanced the causes of education, police, fire protection, and urban planning and started a "City Beautiful" movement. By 1916 more than 25,000 gardens bloomed in Birmingham. In 1925 Ward decided to build his home on the crest of **Shades Mountain.** This wasn't to be just any house, however. It was a replica of the Roman Temple of the Vestal Virgins. Even his dogs lived in houses shaped like little Roman temples.

The **Temple of Sybil** is all that remains of Ward's estate, and when you return later this evening, you may want to drive up to it and enjoy the view from inside the building. There will be other opportunities to enjoy this vantage point in future chapters.

For now, pass by the Temple on your right and go about two and a half miles. Pass Pier 1 on your left. Turn left into the next shopping area (Olde Towne), or left at the next light (Vestavia Parkway), and go to the back row of shops, where you will see **Salvatore's Italian Restaurant.** The least-crowded time of the week to eat here is Monday lunch, but you won't mind a little wait if that's what you must do to find out what is causing that wonderful aroma inviting you in from the parking lot. The menu proclaims this to be "Birmingham's Finest Italian Restaurant," and while you are enveloped in the atmosphere of soft music, excellent service, and that tantalizing aroma, you will be too busy eating to debate which Birmingham Italian restaurant is best, but you will have to put this one on your list of favorites. Desserts are the chef's specialty, and rumor has it that he gets more creative toward the end of the week. Enjoy!

As you head for town and your plump pillow at the Tutwiler, you'll enjoy the return trip view of the valley, even if you decide you are too tired to make the trip up into the Temple of Sybil.

Sunday's pace is a little less hectic in Birmingham, but there are many places yet to see. Historic churches abound, and before or after services you will find the brunch at **Anthony's** much to your liking. You will be well fortified for an afternoon of touring must-see museums.

Anyone who reads front pages knows about the city's darkest hour, the civil rights traumas, tragedies, and struggles of the 1960s. Birmingham as a city missed the Civil War but one hundred years later it suffered deep social wounds. Since that time, city and civic leaders, homemakers and corporate dignitaries, university and high school students—many of today's Birmingham and area citizens— have joined together to work for racial reconciliation.

The **Birmingham Civil Rights Institute** (**BCRI**) documents the civil rights struggle and is a tribute to the progress the city and the United States have made. The intensity of the impact of the exhibits depends on the age of the onlooker. When the introductory film ends, the movie screen moves out of the way to admit viewers into the first gallery. In twelve minutes, almost a half century has disappeared. As the viewer marches through time, other marchers are remembered. The Human Rights Gallery links the Birmingham experience to the rest of the world. It's a vivid reminder that the movement for human rights is international in scope. It touches everyone.

Outside again, follow the **Freedom Trail** through **Kelly Ingram Park** across the street. In the 1960s, marchers gathered to organize and pray here. Dramatic sculpture depicts the events of the era. On

Rosa Parks, Birmingham Civil Rights Institute. (Photo by Dan Brothers, courtesy Alabama Bureau of Tourism & Travel)

Below and right: *Sloss Furnace.* (Photos by Neal Broerman)

the far corner across from the park and Civil Rights Institute you will see the **Sixteenth Street Baptist Church,** which played one of the saddest roles in the history of the civil rights movement, the bombing that resulted in the death of four young children. If the building is not open for tours, knock at the office next door and someone may let you in to read the plaques and framed news clippings.

By four on Sunday afternoon Birmingham seems to close down to await a new week. Depending on whether you spend one or two hours at the BCRI, you may have time to drive across town to see **Sloss Furnaces,** a monument to the Industrial Age. This is the largest preserved industrial plant of its kind in the world. Listen to the "puckety-lumpity" sound of the cars passing over the First Avenue viaduct. See the Duncan House, where famous ghost-tale teller **Kathryn Tucker Windham** has held audiences captive by her own dramatic magic. Read about the ghost of **Theophilus Jowers,** who vowed to stay as long as the furnaces stand. This is where the wealth of the city flowed from the depths of the earth and turned ordinary men into industrial barons.

If your final destination is the airport, let's hope you have time to visit the **Southern Museum of Flight** before you take off. Here you will find the Alabama Aviation Hall of Fame as well as a collection of vintage planes that includes the first Delta Air Lines plane. From downtown take Interstate 20/59 East. Exit at Airport Highway, Exit 129, and turn left. Follow Airport Highway to Thirty-seventh Street and turn right. Follow signs to the museum.

Not ready to leave yet? For those who think Birmingham and see steel mills, here's a contrasting image. Many consider the city a prime destination for fishing. Pass the airport exit and continue out Interstate 20 past Pell City. Before the sun sets, drive out to enjoy the scenery at **Logan Martin Lake,** an 18,000-acre lake built in 1965 by Alabama Power Company. Its nickname is "Lake of a Thousand Coves." Each cove is different, and fishing, boating, and skiing are popular pursuits. Boat and motor rentals are available. You'll be making notes on what you want to do when you come back.

End your day with a hearty seafood dinner at the **Ark** on U.S. 78 at Interstate 20, Exit 162 North. It is about one half of a mile from the exit. Bob and Sylvia Cornett have owned this restaurant for 20 years, and it is obviously a favorite of those who make this Shangri-La their home away from home. It's a fitting place to land your flying carpet after a weekend in a city of magic.

Area Code: (205)

Getting There:
Central Birmingham is bounded by Interstate 65, Interstate 20/59 and U.S. 280 (Red Mountain Expressway).

Where and When:
Alabama Sports Hall of Fame Museum, 2150 Civic Center Boulevard and Twenty-second Street N., Birmingham, AL 35203. Mon.-Sat., 9 A.M.-5 P.M.; Sun., 1 P.M.-5 P.M. 323-6665. Admission.
Web site: www.tech-comm.com/ashof/
Alabama Theatre of the Performing Arts, 1817 Third Avenue N., Birmingham, AL. Box office opens Mon.-Fri., 9 A.M.-4 P.M. 282-2262. Admission.
Barber Vintage Motorsports Museum, 2721 Fifth Avenue S., Birmingham, AL 35233. Wed.-Fri., 9 A.M.-3 P.M. 252-8377. Admission.
Birmingham Civil Rights Institute, 520 Sixteenth Street N., Birmingham, AL 35203.Tue.-Sat., 10 A.M.-5 P.M.; Sun., 1 P.M.-5 P.M. 328-9696. Admission.   Web site: www.bham.net/bcri/ or
www.bcri.bham.al.us
Birmingham Green, Twentieth Street, Birmingham, AL 35203.
Birmingham Museum of Art, 2000 Eighth Avenue N., Birmingham, AL 35203. Tue.-Sat., 10 A.M.-5 P.M.; Sun., noon-5 P.M. 254-2565.
Web site: www.artsbma.org
Birmingham Public Library/Linn-Henley Research Library, 2100 Park Place, Birmingham, AL 35203. Mon.-Tue., 9 A.M.-8 P.M.; Wed.-Sat., 9 A.M.-6 P.M.; Sun., 2 P.M.-6 P.M. 226-3600.
Web site: www.bham.lib.al.us/
Birmingham-Jefferson Civic Center, Civic Center Boulevard and Ninth Avenue N, Birmingham, AL 35201. 458-8400.
City Center Art Urban Mural, 1930 Eighth Avenue N., Birmingham, AL 35203. 254-2820.
Farmer's Market, 344 Finley Avenue W., Birmingham, AL 35204.

Historic Churches:
16th Street Baptist Church, 1530 Sixth Avenue N., Birmingham, AL 35203. 251-9402.   Web site:www.16thstreet.org
Episcopal Cathedral of the Advent, 2017 Twentieth Street N., Birmingham, AL 35201.
First Presbyterian Church, 2100 Fourth Avenue N., Birmingham, AL 35203.

First United Methodist Church, 518 Twentieth Street N., Birmingham, AL 35203.

St. Paul's Catholic Cathedral, 2120 Third Avenue N., Birmingham, AL 35201.

Kelly Ingram Park, Fifth Avenue N. at Sixteenth Street, Birmingham, AL 35203.

Linn Park, Park Place at Twentieth Street N., Birmingham, AL 35203.

McWane Center, 200 Nineteenth Street N., Birmingham, AL 35203. Mon.-Sat., 9 A.M.-6 P.M.; Sun., noon-5 P.M. (closes at 6 P.M. June-Aug.). 714-8300. Admission.   Web site: www.mcwane.org

Metropolitan AME Zion-Scotts Chapel, Fourth Avenue N., Birmingham, AL 35201.

Oxmoor Valley, Shannon Wenonah Road, Birmingham, AL 35211. 942-1177; (800) 949-4444.   Web site: www.rtjgolf.com

Peanut Depot, 2016 Morris Avenue, Birmingham, AL. Mon.- Fri., 8:30-5 P.M.; Sat., 8:30 A.M.-noon. 251-3314.

Red Mountain Museum and Roadcut, 2230 Twenty-second Street S., Birmingham, AL 35205. Call the McWane Center for information. 714-8300.

Rickwood Field, 1137 Second Avenue W., Birmingham, AL. Call for Schedule. 458-8161; (800) 742-5966.

Robert R. Meyer Planetarium, 900 Arkadelphia Road (Birmingham Southern College), Birmingham, AL 35254. First and third Sat. and following Sun. at 2 P.M. each month. 226-4771. Admission.

Web site: www.bsc.edu

Ruffner Mountain Nature Center, 1214 Eighty-first Street S., Birmingham, AL 35206, Tue.-Sat., 9 A.M.-5 P.M.; Sun., 1 P.M.-5 P.M. 833-8112.   Web site: www.bham.net/ruffner/

Sloss Furnaces Historic Landmark, First Avenue N. at Thirty-second Street, Birmingham, AL 35202. 324-1911. Admission.

Web site: www.ci.bham.al.us/sloss/

Southern Environmental Center, Birmingham Southern College, 900 Arkadelphia Road, Birmingham, AL 35254. Mon.-Fri., 9A.M.-5 P.M.; Sat.-Sun., 1 P.M.-5 P.M. 226-4770. Admission.

Web site: www.bsc.edu/sec/

Southern Museum of Flight, 4343 Seventy-third Street N., Birmingham, AL 35206. Tue.-Sat.. 9:30 A.M.-4:30 P.M.; Sun.. 1 P.M.-4:30 P.M. 833-8226. Admission.

Web site: www.bham.net/flight/museum/

Space One Eleven, 2409 Second Avenue N., Birmingham, AL. Mon.-Fri., 9 A.M.-6 P.M. 328-0553.

Vulcan Park, Twentieth Street S., Birmingham, AL 35209. 328-6198; (800) 458-8085. CLOSED FOR RENOVATIONS.

Web site: www.ci.bham.al.us/parks/vulcan.html

Information:

Alabama Golf Association, 1025 Montgomery Hwy., Suite 210, Birmingham, AL 35216. 979-1234.

Birmingham City Park Information, 254-2391.

Birmingham Convention and Visitors Bureau, 2200 Ninth Avenue N., Birmingham, AL 35203. 458-8000; (800) 458-8085.

Web site: www.birminghamal.org

Birmingham Fun Line. 458-8000.

Fish Habitat Enhancement Map. Write Alabama Power Company, P. O. Box 160, Montgomery, AL 36101.

Hotel Special Rates. Weekends, Thanksgiving-Christmas. 458-8000; (800) 458-8085.

Traveler's Aid Society, 322-5426.

Vestavia Hills Chamber of Commerce, P. O. Box 660793, Vestavia Hills, AL 35266. 823-5011.   Web site: www.vestaviahills.org

Accommodations:

Tutwiler Hotel, 2021 Park Place, Birmingham, AL 35203. 322-2100; (800) 996-3426.   Web site: www.wyndham.com

Restaurants:

Anthony's, 2131 Seventh Avenue S., Birmingham, AL 35233. Tue.-Thurs., 11 A.M.-2:30 P.M.; 5 P.M.-9:30 P.M. Fri.-Sat., 5 P.M.-10 P.M.; Sun., 11 A.M.-3:30 P.M. 324-1215.

Ark Restaurant, U.S. 78, Riverside, AL 35135. Mon.-Thurs., 11 A.M.-9 P.M.; Fri.-Sat., 11 A.M.-10 P.M.; Sun., 11 A.M.-8:30 P.M. 338-7420.

Azalea Restaurant (now Kane's Chop House), 1218 Twentieth Street S., Birmingham, AL 35205. Mon.-Thurs., 5 P.M.-10:00 P.M.; Fri.-Sat., 5 P.M.-10:30 P.M.; Sun., 5 P.M.-10 P.M. 933-8600.

Café de France (at the **Birmingham Botanical Gardens**), 2612 Lane Park Road, Birmingham, AL 35223. Mon.-Sat., 11 A.M.-2 P.M., 6 P.M.-8 P.M. 871-1000. Reservations preferred.

Cobb Lane Restaurant, #1 Cobb Lane, Birmingham, AL 35205. Mon.-Sat., 11 A.M.-2:30 P.M. 933-0462.

Grille Pub at the Tutwiler, 2021 Park Place, Birmingham, AL 35203. Daily, 11:30 A.M.-midnight. 322-2100.

Grille at the Tutwiler, 2021 Park Place, Birmingham, AL 35203. Mon.-Sun., 6:30 A.M.-10:30 A.M.; Mon.-Fri., 11:30 A.M.-2 P.M.; Mon.-Sat., 6 P.M.-10 P.M. 322-2100.

John's Restaurant, 112 Twenty-first Street N., Birmingham, AL 35299. Mon.-Sat., 11 A.M.-10 P.M. 322-6014.

Salvatore's Italian Restaurant, 730 Olde Town Road, Vestavia Hills, AL 35216. Mon.-Thurs., 11 A.M.-9:30 P.M.; Fri., 11 A.M.-10:30 P.M.; Sat., 4 P.M.-10:30 P.M. 822-7310.

Social Grill, 231 Twenty-third Street N., Birmingham, AL 35203. Mon.-Fri., 10:45 A.M.-6 P.M.; Sun., 11 A.M.-6 P.M. 252-7081.

Terrace Café, Birmingham Museum of Art, 2000 Eighth Avenue N., Birmingham, AL 35203. Tue.-Sat., 11 A.M.-2 P.M.; Sun. brunch, 11 A.M.-2 P.M. 254-2565.

The Original Whistle Stop Café, 1906 First Avenue N. Irondale, AL 35210. Sun.-Fri., 10:45 A.M.-2:30 P.M. 956-5258.

Major Annual Events:

Alabama Sports Hall of Fame Induction, Birmingham—February. 323-6665; (800) 239-2643.

Black History Month, 520 Sixteenth Street, Birmingham—February. 328-9696.

Festival of the Arts, Downtown, Birmingham—April. 252-7652.

Whistle Stop Festival, Irondale—May. 956-5962.

City Stages, Linn Park, Birmingham—June.

Birmingham Heritage Festival, Kelly Ingram Park, Birmingham—July. 324-3333.

Great Southern Kudzu Festival, Sloss Furnaces, Birmingham—August. 325-2108.

Greek Food Festival, 307 Nineteenth Street S., Birmingham—September. 822-6981.

Birmingham Jam, Sloss Furnaces, Birmingham—October. 323-0569.

19

CLIMBING THE MOUNTAIN

It's 1910, and little specks of light dot Red Mountain at night. A steady parade of fashionable homes in the **Five Points South** area is making its presence known on higher elevations and beyond, "climbing" the mountain and leaving the northern part of the city behind. The air from the mountain is better, the view is fabulous, and the status from that point of view is unmistakable. Those aerie owners have arrived at the top of their world.

To get in touch with this area today, make your way to **Anabel & Lulu's.** The first thing that catches your eye when you enter this corner café facing Highland Avenue is a wall of clocks. Each one is set to a different time, another city in another place in the world. This characterizes the people who make the area their home today. Each person is set to a different clock. Artists, musicians, craftspeople, university students, and many types of individualists make this section of Birmingham a fascinating, enriching mix of personalities. Slide into a back booth at Anabel and Lulu's and warm your inner being with a cup of hot, spicy veggie soup. More adventurous vegetarians might order iswad and be delighted to discover it's baked eggplant smothered in a tasty house sauce. Every item on the menu is reasonably priced and the locals don't miss many meals here.

You could decide to stay on the edge of **Southside** and drive in or choose a hotel in the middle of this eclectic grouping of shops, galleries, restaurants, and pubs. Either way, Southside is a feast for the senses.

Southside begins to wake up around noon, so if you are an early bird and a breakfast eater, too, you may want to go up the mountain to Homewood. (If you opt to search out a breakfast spot on Southside, you can always follow the crowds to the popular **Original Pancake House.**)

Twentieth Street is a continuation of the Birmingham Green. Travel up the mountain until you pass Vulcan Park on your right and Highland Avenue becomes Eighteenth Street. If you turn left on Twenty-eighth Avenue, you'll find that **Demetri's** is open at 5 A.M. Stay on Eighteenth and you can enjoy coffee at **O'Henry's** on your left (this coffee shop opens at 8 A.M.) or go ahead two blocks and treat yourself to a Danish at **Savage's Bakery** which opens at 9 A.M. on Saturdays.

Now you are ready to return to Southside for a walking tour. The center of this area is the fountain known as the Fountain at Five Points. The sculpture is called, "**The Storyteller,**" and across from it is the statue of Brother Bryan. **Brother Bryan** was a graduate of Princeton, but he came to a raw mining town to minister to everyone, regardless of their economic status, race, or denomination. He was the pastor of Third Presbyterian Church from 1889 to 1941. Many people have their "Brother Bryan stories," and remember when he came into a bar or a courtroom and intoned, "Let us pray," and the people did just that. His statue was erected while Brother Bryan was still alive. He didn't much like the idea until he was persuaded that this would remind the people of Birmingham to pray.

Within a two-block area, there are several shops to investigate, and by the time you have walked around and returned to the fountain, you will be ready to stop, rest, and eat an ice cream cone. Choose from the many flavors at **Gorin's,** across from Brother Bryan's statue, and sit at one of the small tables out front while you plan your afternoon.

Wipe your chin and get ready to drive again, this time through the historic and lovely section of town known as **Forest Park.** The architecture ranges from small, neatly kept houses to imposing brick mansions that have been turned into apartments. In-between are large, spacious homes that have been restored or carefully maintained by the same families for generations.

As you drive up and down the hilly streets, you'll notice the **Charlie Boswell Golf Course.** Golfers may want to get out there.

Just as you enter Forest Park on Clairmont Boulevard, you will come to a block that has several choices for lunch and gift browsing, too. Park on the street or in the lot on your left just after you pass **V Richards.** It will be hard to decide what you want for lunch whether you stand at the deli counter in V Richards or cross the street to **Silvertron** and sit down while you read a lengthy menu. After lunch, you can visit the **Birmingham Museum of Art Gift Shop** and find answers to your gift-giving problems. **Smith and Hardwick Book Store,** across the street, exudes the wonderful smell of leather and paper that will make you long for a rainy Saturday afternoon and time to browse among intriguing titles. You can always come back.

Get into your car and drive west (turn right if you are parked in the lot beside V. Richards) until Clairmont becomes University. Turn right on Twenty-eighth Street and you will be in the historic **Lake View District,** which is evolving into an artist's area. **Pepper Place** at Third Avenue South and Twenty-eighth Street is filling with small galleries and art shops. Park on Twenty-eighth Street and explore the shops and antique stores between Second and Seventh.

Although you'll have to call first, you are close to landscape and nature photographer **Beth Maynor Young's Photography Gallery,** which exhibits work from other photographers as well as her own. Her evocative river portraits were showcased in "River Walk," a touring story of Southern waters organized by the **Anniston Museum of Natural History** and written by journalist **Jennifer Greer.**

On Fifth Avenue South, you can look down the street and see the **Barber Motorcycle Museum,** which is usually open Monday through Friday only. Keep that in mind if you are here on a non-traditional "weekend" during the week.

After the city sidewalks, you might enjoy getting above the city and looking at the skyline. **Ruffner Mountain Nature Center** is the largest expanse of natural land in the city. In fact, it has, after a recent acquisition, expanded from 538 acres to more than 1,000 acres—larger than New York's Central Park. Wear insect repellent and your favorite hiking shoes. You may want to time your visit so you can watch the sunset from **Hawk's View Overlook.** Whether you spend your afternoon shopping, golfing, or hiking, your stomach will tell you when it's time for dinner. Southside is the place to be!

Highlands Bar and Grill, Bottega Café, **Bottega Italian Restaurant**, **The Veranda, Assagio!,** and **Azalea** (now **Kane's Chop House**) have their devoted diners who make Saturday evening on Southside a part of their best weekend plans. If you want to dress up a little and don't mind paying for ambiance, choose any one. You can't go wrong.

Lucky ticket holders for a performance of the **Alabama Symphony Orchestra** may want to head for the **Pita Stop,** which isn't far from the **Alys Stephens Recital Hall.** Lebanese-American specialties will put you in the mood for an evening of great music played by an acclaimed body of talented musicians. You will be in your theater seats on time if you arrive at the Pita Stop by 6 P.M. and plan to leave by 7:30.

The Alys Stephens Recital Hall is located on the southwest edge of the University of Alabama at Birmingham campus. It seats 1,330 and is acoustically magnificent. Parking is free in the lot across the street. From classical to contemporary, Bach to Gershwin, an evening spent at the Stephens Center soothes the cultural soul.

There are many annual events in this area, but one that bears special note is the **Greek Food Festival** at the **Greek Orthodox Cathedral,** held each fall. This is the heart of the Greek Community, and you can order dinner and carry it out or eat on the grounds and learn about the Mediterranean culture, music, and food from welcoming church members.

A good way to greet Sunday on Southside is with a walk around one of the pocket parks tucked in among the winding, tree-lined streets. Drive along Highland Avenue and pick a park you like. Join the groups of joggers or dog walkers and get a little exercise. There are many historic churches and temples on Southside, too, and the times of services are posted in easy sight.

When you are ready to eat, you will be glad the **Original Pancake House** is open on Sunday. This is a neighborhood favorite, and "outsiders" have discovered it, too. You will look like an insider if you get there early. Otherwise, get in line and wait around the corner. If you'd rather begin your day with lunch, go down the street to **Surin West** and get in line there. During the week folks gather on the sidewalk, waiting for the doors to open at 11:30. Sunday may be a little lighter, but a line is a line. When you finally get seated, you will not count the cost of standing on the pavement.

After your mid-day meal, you can drive to **Arlington Antebellum Home and Gardens** to see what life was like in the Birmingham area during the Civil War but before the city was born. Take First Avenue North toward Interstate 65 and continue until it curves and becomes Second Avenue North; Arlington will be on the left, about .8 mile farther.

Arlington was built in 1842 by **Judge William. S. Mudd,** and used as headquarters by Union general **James H. Wilson** in 1865 as his raiders moved through Alabama toward Selma. Here is where plans were made to burn the University of Alabama in Tuscaloosa. This house museum is furnished with antiques and displays Confederate relics. The grounds invite strolling in mild weather, and lunch is served on certain days during the summer.

By now it should be around two or three o'clock. There will still be time to see the campus of **Birmingham Southern College** (BSC). Leave Arlington and continue west to Seventh Street (Arkadelphia Road). Turn right and go about one mile. The college will be on the left.

Fifteen thousand visitors come to the BSC campus every year to see the star shows at **Meyer Planetarium.** This is like a giant space platform where the stars seem almost within reach. The circular auditorium seats up to 90, and the star shows last about an hour. Doors open one half hour before each show. No late seating is permitted. Some shows are especially geared to children.

You must call the planetarium to make arrangements to see the **Southern Environmental Center.** Although a minimum group of 10 is preferred, the staff is eager to have this facility seen and appreciated. Great efforts will be made to schedule a guide for you and your family, even if your total number is not 10. Families who are in the city while a parent attends a conference may want to join forces and spend several hours here. Ask for parking directions when you call.

This is a solid afternoon of great fun for the entire family, from kindergarten age to 90. Roald Hazelhoff, the director, showed us around. Hazelhoff is a political scientist, so he brings a different approach to the micro- and macro-management of the environment. His strategy is to focus more on package redesign than recycling, and a bar graph of throwaways demonstrates the need for this kind of thinking. The interactive displays will make you and your family think twice about leaving on a light or taking long showers. Kids love the slide down the sewer pipe. The whole family can learn how to make jewelry from junk. Have you ever wondered about those ugly black strips of rubber that litter the roadside? Truckers call them "road gators." At the environmental center you will see these tire scraps made into high-flying crows.

The first impression of the Environmental Center comes from the front wall of junk arranged with pulleys and levers that mesmerize the viewer as they work together and ultimately water the plants sitting under the display. This was designed by **Steve Cole,** whose work also shows up later when you tour the **Ecoscape.**

Kinetic sculpture at Southern Environmental Center. (Photo by Joan Broerman)

Gator from truck retread at Southern Environmental Center. (Photo by Joan Broerman)

Birmingham skyline. (Photo by Dan Brothers, courtesy Alabama Bureau of Tourism & Travel)

You could spend an hour or even two hours in the Environmental Center if you see the video first and make jewelry from junk last. Then you will be taken to the Ecoscape, which is an outdoor complement to the indoor environmental display. Allow an hour to tour the wetlands, bog, forest trail, and wildflowers. Sniff the herbs and look for the huge spider web and the Mayfly done by **Robert Taylor. Art Price** welded scrap metal into a blue heron and cattails. **Allen Peterson**'s praying mantis represents the good guys in the garden, but his Japanese beetle is a villain. Our guide, Lewis Armstrong, showed us an attractive bench beside the garden path and told us the building material is melted-down plastic milk jugs. He also pointed out other benches made of limestone from this area.

The solar system design on the patio is the first thing visitors will see, but they might not truly appreciate it until they have toured the entire area and are ready to leave. By the end of the visit, everyone's senses are sharper. Come to think of it, isn't an expanded vision one of the best things about any change-of-pace weekend getaway?

Area Code: (205)

Getting There:
    South Side centers on the Five Points South Area at Twentieth Street and Eleventh Avenue S. and Magnolia Avenue. The University of Alabama at Birmingham and its medical center complex lies along Sixth to Tenth Avenue S. from Tenth Street to Twenty-first Street.

Where and When:
    Alys Robinson Stephens Performing Arts Center, 1200 Tenth Avenue S., Birmingham, AL. 975-2787. Admission.
                                    Web site: www.alysstephens.org
    Alabama Symphony Orchestra, 3621 Sixth Avenue S., Birmingham, AL 35205. 251-7727. Admission.
    Arlington Antebellum Home and Gardens, 331 Cotton Avenue, Birmingham, AL 35211. Tue.-Sat., 10 A.M.4 P.M.; Sun., 1 P.M.-4 P.M. 780-5656. Admission.
    Birmingham Museum of Art Gift Shop, 3809 Clairmont Avenue, Birmingham, AL. Mon.-Sat., 10 A.M.-6 P.M.; Sun., 1 P.M.-5 P.M. 254-7715.
    Barber Vintage Motorsports Museum, 2721 Fifth Avenue S., Birmingham, AL 35233. Wed.-Fri., 9 A.M.-3 P.M. 252-8377. Admission.
    Birmingham Public Library, Southside Branch, 1814 Eleventh Avenue S., Birmingham, AL 35205, Mon.-Sat., 9 A.M.-6 P.M. 933-7776.
    Charlie Boswell Golf Course, Highland Avenue, Birmingham, AL. 322-1902.

Charlie Boswell Tennis Center, Highland Avenue, Birmingham, AL. 251-1965.

Robert R. Meyer Planetarium, Birmingham Southern College, 900 Arkadelphia Road, Birmingham, AL 35254. First and third Sat. and following Sunday at 2 P.M. each month. 226-4770. Admission.

Ruffner Mountain Nature Center, 1214 Eighty-first Street S., Birmingham, AL 35206. Tue.-Sat., 9 A.M.-5 P.M.; Sun., 1 P.M.-5 P.M. 833-8112.

Southern Environmental Center, Birmingham Southern College, 900 Arkadelphia Road, Birmingham, AL 35254. Mon.-Fri., 9A.M.-5 P.M.; Sat.-Sun., 1 P.M.-5 P.M. 226-4770. Admission.

Smith and Hardwick Book Store, 3900 Clairmont Avenue, Birmingham, AL 35222. Mon.-Fri., 9 A.M.-6:30 P.M.; Sat., 9 A.M.-5:30 P.M. 591-9970.

Information:

Alabama Golf Association, 1025 Montgomery Highway, Suite 210, Birmingham, AL 35216. 979-1234.

Birmingham City Park Information. 254-2391.

Birmingham Convention and Visitors Bureau, 2200 Ninth Avenue N., Birmingham, AL 35203. 458-8000; (800) 458-8085.

Web site: www.birminghamal.org

Birmingham Fun Line, 458-8000.

Hotel Special Rates. Weekends, Thanksgiving-Christmas. 458-8000; (800) 458-8085.

Traveler's Aid Society. 322-5426.

Restaurants:

Anabel & Lulu's Café, 2222 Highland Avenue, Birmingham, AL 35210, Mon.-Wed., 10 A.M.-10 P.M.; Thurs.-Sat., noon-midnight. 933-5355.

Anthony's, 2131 Seventh Avenue S., Birmingham, AL 35233. Tue.-Thurs., 11 A.M.-2:30 P.M.; 5 P.M.-9:30 P.M. Fri.-Sat., 5 P.M.-10 P.M.; Sun., 11 A.M.-3:30 P.M. 324-1215.

Assagio!, 2015 Highland Avenue, Birmingham, AL 35210, Mon.-Fri., 11:30 A.M.-2:30 P.M.; Mon.-Thurs., 5 P.M.-11 P.M.; Fri.-Sat., 5 P.M.-midnight. 933-6605.

Azalea (now Kane's Chop House), 1218 Twentieth Street S., Birmingham, AL 35210. Mon.-Thurs., 5 P.M.-10:00 P.M.; Fri.-Sat., 5 P.M.-10:30 P.M.; Sun., 5 P.M.-10 P.M. 933-8600.

Beth Maynor Young's Photography Gallery, 700 Twenty-eighth Street S., Suite 204, Birmingham, AL 35233. Call for appointment. 324-1900.

Bottega Café, 2242 Highland Avenue S., Birmingham, AL 35205, Mon.-Thurs., 11 A.M.-10:30 P.M.; Fri., 11 A.M.-11 P.M.; Sat., 11:30 A.M.-11 P.M. 933-2001.

Bottega Italian Restaurant, 2240 Highland Avenue S., Birmingham, AL 35205, Mon.-Thurs., 6 P.M.-10 P.M.; Fri.-Sat., 6 P.M.-10:30 P.M. 939-1000.

Cobb Lane, #1 Cobb Lane, Birmingham, AL 35205, Mon.-Sat., 11 A.M.-2:30 P.M., 933-0462.

Demetri's, 1901 Twenty-eighth Street S., Homewood, AL 35209. Mon.-Sat., 5 A.M.-8:30 P.M. 871-1581.

Dreamland BBQ, 1427 Fourteenth Avenue S., Birmingham, AL 35205, Mon.-Thurs.,10 A.M.-10 P.M.; Fri.-Sat., 10 A.M.-midnight; Sun., 11 A.M.-9 P.M. 933-2133, (800) 752-0544; Web site: www.dreamlandbq.com/ribs.

Highlands Bar and Grille, 2011 Eleventh Avenue S., Birmingham, AL 35205. Tue.-Thurs., 6 P.M.-10 P.M.; Fri.-Sat., 6 P.M.-10:30 P.M. 939-1400.

O'Henry's, 2831 Eighteenth Street S., Birmingham, AL 35205, Mon.-Fri., 7 A.M.-11 P.M.; Sat., 8 A.M.-midnight; Sun., 1 P.M.-6 P.M. 870-1198.

Original Pancake House, 1931 Eleventh Avenue S., Birmingham, AL 35205, Mon.-Fri., 6:30 A.M.-2 P.M.; Sat.-Sun., 7 A.M.-3 P.M., 933-8837.

Savage's Bakery, 2916 Eighteenth Street S., Homewood, AL 35209, Mon.-Fri., 7:30 A.M.-5:30 P.M.; Sat., 9 A.M.-5 P.M. 871-4901.

Silvertron, 3813 Clairmont Avenue, Birmingham, AL 35222. 591-3707.

Sol Azteca Mexican Restaurant, 1459 Montgomery Highway, Vestavia Hills, AL 35216, Mon.-Thurs., 11 A.M.-10 P.M.; Fri., 11 A.M.-10:30 P.M.; Sat.-Sun., 11 A.M.-10 P.M. 979-4902.

Surin West, 1918 Eleventh Avenue S., Birmingham, AL 35209. Mon.-Sun., 11 A.M.-2:30 P.M.; Sun.-Thurs., 5:30 P.M.-9:30 P.M.; Fri.-Sat., 5:30 P.M.-10:30 P.M. 324-1928.

Taj India, 2226 Highland Avenue S., Birmingham AL 35205. Mon.-Sat., 11 A.M.-2 P.M.; 5 P.M.-10 P.M.; Sun. 11 A.M.-2 P.M., 5 P.M.-9 P.M. 939-3805.

Pita Stop, 1106 Twelfth Street S., Birmingham, AL 35205, Mon.-Thurs., 11 A.M.-9:30 P.M.; Fri.-Sat., 11 A.M.-2:30 P.M. and 5 P.M.-10 P.M. 328-2749.

V Richards Café, 3908 Clairmont Avenue, Birmingham, AL 35222. Mon.-Sat., 11 A.M.-2 P.M.; 5 P.M.-10 P.M.; Sun., 11 A.M.-2 P.M., 5 P.M.-9 P.M. 591-7000.

Veranda, 2220 Highland Avenue, Birmingham, AL 35210, Mon.-Thurs., 5:30 P.M.-10:30 P.M.; Fri.-Sat., 5:30 P.M.-11:30 P.M. 933-1200.

Major Annual Events:

Do Dah Day, Rushton and Caldwell Parks, Birmingham—May. 833-3522.

Greek Orthodox Cathedral of Holy Trinity-Holy Cross Festival, Birmingham—October. 716-3080.

Yellow-shafted flicker (yellowhammer), the Alabama state bird. (Photo
courtesy Helen Kittinger)

20

WE LOVE
HOMEWOOD

Summer Jazz Festivals and Friday Flicks in the Park. Fourth of July and Christmas parades. Does that sound like a friendly hometown atmosphere to you? If it does, then Homewood is definitely a place you want to visit.

In 1926 the neighborhoods of Rosedale, Edgewood, and Oak Grove came together under the name **Homewood** to signify that the dream of owning a home and providing a good family life could be realized here. The Hollywood area, a residential section of Spanish mission-style homes and eighteenth-century French wrought iron, was annexed three years later. Now a city of 25,000, Homewood maintains its small-town flavor in a metropolitan setting.

From north to south, Homewood fits between Red Mountain and Shades Mountain. From east to west, the visitor experiences the shift from small established neighborhoods to interstates and new construction. You could stay in one of the many hotels on the west side off Lakeshore Drive at Wildwood. A selection of restaurants and well-known stores lines both sides of the interstate, but one stop for the golfer should be the **Edwin Watts Golf Shop.** Whether the golfer reading this plans to play at a public or semiprivate or state park or **Robert Trent Jones Golf Trail** course, a wide selection of pro-shop necessities and more can be found in this central location. Best tip: pick up a Golf Map. For under $5 you will have a list of every golf course in the state with phone numbers and addresses. The map cannot be found in every pro shop, so get yours now.

Huge shopping areas are often dominated by familiar chain restaurants. We had to hunt for a family-owned business in this area, but we found one. When you leave the Watts Golf Shop, cross Lakeshore Parkway and turn right into the shopping complex. The All you Can Eat Daily Grand Lunch Buffet and the Daily Grand Seafood Dinner Buffet at **Mr. Wang's Chinese Restaurant** are exactly that—grand.

Oxmoor Valley Golf Course is the Robert Trent Jones Trail in this area, and it is made interesting by the peaks and valleys of the Appalachians. Golfers will have their Saturday planned.

Alpine Ice Arena, is close, too, and is a popular spot for all ages. To keep your cool, rent a pair of skates and glide to your heart's content.

On the east side of Homewood, four hotels are close by, and each has its own personality and amenities. The **Embassy Suites** overlooks the north edge of Homewood. It has the sophistication often found in large city hotels. The **Hampton Inn** is next door to **Rossi's,** an Italian restaurant ideal for special occasion dinners, and The **Mountain Brook Inn** has its own dining room that serves three meals daily. The Hampton and the Mountain Brook Inn are close together on U.S. 280. **Courtyard by Marriott,** on Lakeshore Drive across from **Brookwood Mall,** serves a full Southern breakfast. If you enter Homewood from U.S. 280, don't get on the Red Mountain Expressway, but continue west on Rosedale Drive, turn left on Eighteenth Street, and you will be in position to drive through several blocks of a pedestrian-friendly area. Drive to any store door, park, and stroll. Window shopping allowed! Take note for your next day's shopping ventures.

The first "over the mountain" community has given its shopping area facelifts over the years, and the famous Homewood curve is now a reconstructed intersection where Eighteenth Street and Twenty-ninth Avenue meet. It's been landscaped with park benches and street lamps. Yes, people actually sit on the benches. Unusual gift and antique shops and restaurants are so numerous you could spend an entire weekend ambling down the pleasant streets. Outdoor movies, or "Friday Flicks," take place on summer nights in the Homewood Park, on the corner of Oxmoor Road and Central Avenue. This is across the street from **Nabeel's** Market, a retail gourmet and ethnic Mediterranean foods store. Here you will find all the ingredients needed to make an authentic Greek, Italian, Russian, or Middle-Eastern dish—or put together a picnic to eat in the park.

If the night air is nippy, slip into a booth in Nabeel's Restaurant and let the warmth of a European café envelope you. Nabeel's owners, Olivia and Anthony Krontiras, have recalled the friendly hearthside feeling of their own homes in Italy and Greece and recreated it for their American friends and family. Try the spanakopita (spinach pie) or pastitsio (macaroni pie). Treat yourself to spumoni or baklava. Ah!

To begin your Saturday, use the Homewood Park as your landmark. Note the handsome building at the edge of the park. This is the **Exceptional Foundation,** a social and recreational facility for the mentally and physically handicapped. Call two to three weeks ahead of your trip to this area and speak with the director, Jill Miree (say MIree), about scheduled activities. Ages five and up can attend on a drop-in, one-day fee basis. This is a world-class recreation facility that hosts baseball, soccer, basketball, and bowling teams, offers arts and crafts, and sponsors dances. So far this facility is one-of-a-kind and makes coming to Homewood a special treat for families with members who have special needs.

Continue west on Oxmoor Road. You will pass two large churches on your right and arrive in a quaint section of shops and small cafés. Turn right on Church Street and park in the lot across from **V Richards** café and market. The doors open into the fruit section of the market, and you'll think you are sleepwalking in an orchard. Hurry to the café and order a rich cup of cappuccino or a double latte. Add scones slathered with homemade preserves and you'll be revved up and ready to sample Homewood's shops. Across the street you'll see **Trilogy Leathers,** where you can breathe in the smell of fine leather while you browse among high-quality handmade belts, bags, caps, hats, and wallets. Down the street a few doors you will see **Broadway Old Fashioned BBQ.** Their over-stuffed baked potatoes are monstrous in size and flavor. Remember this when it's time to eat again.

After you have explored this section of town, drive back up the hill past the park to **Prime Time Treasures.** Under the sponsorship of the Assistance League, which staffs the store with volunteers, this unusual store sells the handiwork of skilled senior citizen artists and craftspersons. Colorful quilts, handmade wood furniture, and toys that adults will collect too, are handsomely arranged throughout the spacious rooms.

Backtrack to the **Homewood Public Library.** Lunch catered by **Franklin's Homewood Gourmet** adds a nice twist to expected library offerings, and the courtyard is perfect for enjoying your deli choices.

Last night you took notes as you drove up Eighteenth Street. It's time to return. Book people enjoy hanging out at the **Little Professor Book Store.** At lunchtime everybody who just happens to be in the neighborhood stops by **Crepe Myrtle,** a café inside the bookstore owned and operated by writer Jim Muir. Sandwiches and soups can be carried upstairs to tables and chairs near the magazines. Bookstore owner Paul Seitz trusts patrons not to spill anything.

At the other end of Eighteenth Street, you'll want to be sure to pop into **Argent,** which has small keepsakes like Christmas ornaments and antique frames or large elegant pieces such as chandeliers and mirrors. Many more gift and antique stores in this area will keep you on the move until you are ready to cross the street to **Savage's Bakery,** a destination of wedding and birthday party planners for years. Enjoy a bear claw and coffee before you take a side trip to Vestavia Hills, just up the mountain on U.S. 31 (Montgomery Highway).

In **Vestavia Hills,** use the Temple of Sybil on your right as a landmark. Two traffic lights after that white gazebo, turn into the shopping strip on your left and drive up to **Klingler's European Bakery and Café** and **Jewels by Rose,** a gift shop that specializes in custom jewelry designs and offers a large selection of estate and gemstone jewelry. Klingler's carries imported deli products and serves authentic German cuisine. Delicious European tortes, tender pastries, and warm breads fill the bakery case. This Old World café is small, and lunch often spills out onto the wrought-iron tables and chairs on the sidewalk. Sunday brunch is popular and worth strategizing about how to get there at the best time. Keep this in mind for tomorrow.

If you have been too busy shopping to eat, you may at last be ready for lunch. How about a picnic? From Jewel's by Rose go south on U.S. 31 about two miles until you see **Pier 1 Imports** on your left. **Diplomat Deli** is at the north end of the shopping area, and the list of subs and salads will make you want to sample a little of each. Even if you're not a vegetarian, you'll like the Hawaiian sub. Make your decisions, and head for the Temple of Sybil again, where you'll find three levels of picnic areas. Choose your favorite view. The first group of tables will be close to your car, but you'll have to carry your lunch up concrete steps to reach the other two levels or to go inside the gazebo.

Spend your afternoon shopping, ice skating, or playing golf, and when dinnertime comes you may already have several ideas of where you would like to eat. If you're in the mood for Chinese, many consider The **Great Wall** the great place to go. Believe the menu. If the food is described as hot and spicy, it will be. Teriyaki beef is a popular appetizer, and cashew shrimp and kung pao chicken are favorites.

If you'd like to sample authentic Mexican cuisine, **Sol Azteca** is a gathering place for singles, couples, and families with babies and toddlers. The service is prompt and friendly, even if you have trouble with accents (yours and the pleasant waiter's). Delicious food will find a way!

After Sunday brunch at Klingler's, drive across the **Samford University** campus. You've seen it from above, now enjoy the stately buildings up close. Wright Hall is the site of many outstanding musical events. You may want to plan your time in this area to coincide with a famous opera or ballet.

On the north and east edges of Homewood are Vulcan Park and Mountain Brook. Vulcan Park, just outside of Homewood, will be closed while the Iron Man is not on his pedestal. He has been removed and is undergoing a million-dollar repair. On the border between Mountain Brook and Homewood you can find gravestones dating from the mid-1850s in **Union Cemetery.** While you are there, you could travel a little farther and visit the **Birmingham Botanical Gardens** and the **Birmingham Zoo.** They will be described in the next chapter.

Homewood is well-known for its festivals. In July, the We Love Homewood Day brings out everybody in town. It just might bring you back.

Area Code: (205)

Getting There:

From Birmingham, Homewood can be reached by going south on Twentieth Street past Vulcan or on the Red Mountain Expressway (U.S. 280/U.S. 31) and by Interstate 65 South.

Where and When:

Alpine Ice Arena, 160 Oxmoor Road, Homewood, AL 35209. Fri., 1 P.M.-6 P.M.; Fri.-Sat., 7 P.M.-10:30 P.M.; Sun., 1 P.M.-3:30 P.M. 942-0223. Admission.

Argent, 2924 Eighteenth Street S., Homewood, AL 35209. Mon.-Sat., 10 A.M.-5 P.M. 871-4221.

Edwin Watts Golf Shop, 189 State Farm Parkway, Birmingham, AL 35209. Mon.-Fri., 9:30 A.M.-6 P.M.; Sat., 9:30 A.M.-5 P.M. 942-7083.

Web site: www.ewgs.com/bhm

Exceptional Foundation, 1801 Oxmoor Road, Homewood, AL 35209. 870-0776.

Homewood Library, 1721 Oxmoor Road, Homewood, AL 35209. Mon.-Tue. and Thurs., 9 A.M.-9 P.M.; Wed., Fri.-Sat., 9 A.M.-6 P.M.; Sun., 1 P.M.-6 P.M. 877-8661.   Web site: www.bham.net/hpl

Jewels By Rose, 619 Montgomery Highway, Birmingham, AL 35216. Mon.-Fri., 10 A.M.-5:30 P.M.; Mon.-Sat., 11 A.M.-2:30 P.M.; 5 P.M.-9 P.M.; Sat., 10 A.M.-4 P.M. 979-5611; (800) 269-2467.

Little Professor Book Center, 2717 Eighteenth Street S., Homewood, AL 35209. Mon.-Sat., 9 A.M.-9 P.M.; Sun., 9 A.M.-6 P.M., 870-7461.

Mountain Gallery, 2902 Eighteenth Street S., Homewood, AL 35209. 871-2092.

Pier 1 Imports, 1441 Montgomery Highway (U.S. 31), Vestavia Hills, AL. Mon.-Sat., 9 A.M.-10 P.M.; Sun., 10 A.M.-8 P.M. 822-1208.

Prime Time Treasures, 1755 Oxmoor Road, Homewood, AL 35209. Mon.-Sat., 10 A.M.-4:30 P.M. 870-5555.

Oxmoor Valley, Shannon-Wenonah Road, Birmingham, AL 35211. 942-1177.

Trilogy Leathers, 1001 Oxmoor Road, Homewood, AL 35209. Mon.-Fri., 9 A.M.-5:30 P.M.; Sat., 9 A.M.-4 P.M.; Closed Wed. 871-9468.

Union Cemetery, Hollywood Boulevard at U.S. 280, Homewood, AL.

Vestavia Hills-Scrushy Library, 1112 Montgomery Highway, Vestavia Hills, AL 35216. Mon.-Thurs., 9 A.M.-8 P.M.; Fri.-Sat., 9 A.M.-6 P.M.; Sun., 1 P.M.-5 P.M. 978-0155.

Information:

Alabama Vacation Guide. Call 1-800-ALABAMA (252-2262).

Alabama Golf Association, 1025 Montgomery Highway, Suite 210, Birmingham, AL 35216. 979-1234.

Birmingham City Park Information, 254-2391.

Birmingham Convention and Visitors Bureau, 2200 Ninth Avenue N., Birmingham, AL 35203. 458-8000; (800) 458-8085.

Web site: www.birminghamal.org

Birmingham Fun Line, 458-8000.

Homewood Chamber of Commerce, 1721 Oxmoor Road, Homewood, AL 35259. 871-5631.

Hotel Special Rates Weekends, Thanksgiving-Christmas. 458-8000; (800) 458-8085.

Traveler's Aid Society. 322-5426.

Vestavia Hills Chamber of Commerce, 2031-R Canyon Road, Vestavia Hills, AL 35216. 823-5011.   Web site: www.vestaviahills.org

Accommodations:

Courtyard by Marriott, 500 Shades Creek Parkway, Homewood, AL 35209. Buffet breakfast, Mon.-Fri., 6:30 A.M.-10 A.M.; Sat.-Sun., 7 A.M.-11 A.M. 879-0400.

Embassy Suites, 2300 Woodcrest Place, Birmingham, AL 35209. 879-7400; (800) 362-2779.

Hampton Inn, 2731 U.S. 280, Birmingham, AL 25223. 870-7822; (800) 426-7866.

Mountain Brook Inn, 2800 U.S. 280, Homewood, AL 35209. 870-3100.

Restaurants:

Crepe Myrtle Café, 2721 Eighteenth Street S. (inside Little Professor Book Center), Homewood, AL 35204. Mon.-Fri., 10 A.M.-8 P.M.; Sat.-Sun., 10 A.M.-2:30 P.M. 879-7891.

Courtyard by Marriot, 500 Shades Creek Parkway, Homewood, AL 35209. Buffet breakfast, Mon.-Fri., 6:30 A.M.-10 A.M.; Sat.-Sun., 7 A.M.-11 A.M. 879-0400.

Café Savannah, 2800 U.S. 280 (in the Mountain Brook Inn), Homewood, AL 35209. Daily, 6:30 A.M.-10 A.M., 11 A.M.-2 P.M., 5 P.M.-10 P.M.; Sun. brunch starts at 11:30 A.M. 870-3100.

Demetri's, 1901 Twenty-eighth Street S., Homewood, AL 35209. Mon.-Sat., 5 A.M.-8:30 P.M. 871-1581.

Broadway Old Fashioned BBQ, 1008 Oxmoor Road, Homewood, AL 35209. 879-1937.

Diplomat Delicatessen and Spirits, 1413 Montgomery Highway, Vestavia Hills, AL 35216. Mon.-Fri., 9 A.M.-8 P.M.; Sat., 9 P.M.-9 P.M.; Sun., 11:30 A.M.-3:30 P.M., 979-1515.

Franklin's Homewood Gourmet, 1919 Twenty-eighth Avenue S., Homewood, AL 35204. 871-1620.

Great Wall, 706 Valley Avenue, Birmingham, AL 35209. Sun.-Fri., 11 A.M.-2:30 P.M.; Sun.-Thurs., 5 P.M.-10 P.M.; Fri.-Sat., 5 P.M.-11 P.M. 945-1465.

Klingler's European Bakery and Café, 621 Montgomery Highway, Vestavia Hills, AL 35216. Mon.-Sat., 7 A.M.-5 P.M.; Sun., 8 A.M.-2 P.M. 823-4560.

Mr. Wang's Chinese Restaurant, 217 Lakeshore Parkway, Homewood, AL 35209, Sun.-Thur., 11 A.M.-9:30 P.M.; Fri.-Sat., 11 A.M.-10 P.M. 945-9000.

Nabeel's Restaurant and Market, 1706 Oxmoor Road, Homewood, AL 35209, Mon.-Sat., 9:30 A.M.-9:30 P.M. 879-9292.

Web site: www.nabeels.com

Rossi's, 2737 U.S. 280, Birmingham, AL 25223. Mon.-Fri., 11 A.M.-3 P.M.; 5 P.M.-10 P.M.; Sat., 5 P.M.-9:30 P.M. 879-2111.

Ruth's Chris Steakhouse, 2300 Woodcrest Place, Homewood, AL 35209. Daily, 11 A.M.-11 P.M. 829-9995.

Savage's Bakery, 2916 Eighteenth Street S., Homewood, AL 35209. Mon.-Fri., 7:30 A.M.-5:30 P.M.; Sat., 9 A.M.-5 P.M.

Sol Azteca, 1459 Montgomery Highway, Vestavia Hills, AL 35216. Mon.-Thurs., 11 A.M.-10 P.M.; Fri., 11 A.M.-10:30 P.M.; Sat.-Sun., 11 A.M.-10 P.M. 979-4902.

V Richards, Oxmoor Road and St. Charles Street, Homewood, AL 35204. Mon.-Sat., 7 A.M.-7 P.M.; Sun., 9 A.M.-5 P.M. 879-8010.

Major Annual Events:

We Love Homewood Day—Fourth of July.

21

GARDENIAS, GIFTS, AND GIRAFFES

A **Mountain Brook** address has been prized for generations. Drive leisurely through the opulent neighborhoods and you will understand that living here signifies success. By now you have toured many antebellum homes. The palatial homes guarding great sloping expanses of green lawn in Mountain Brook are surely the house museums of the future, but at present these elegant columned mansions are private residences.

As you learned in the last chapter, Homewood and Mountain Brook border each other. The same hotels that gave you easy access to the east side of Homewood will serve you well again. So will many of the same restaurants.

Residents who are morning people begin their day in the **Birmingham Botanical Gardens** with a stroll through fragrant dew-sparkled gardens. No wonder artists set up their easels here. Wander through the woods, sit a while on a swing, and while cardinals serenade, plan which path to follow.

The gardens grow lovelier with age. However, the main building has taken on a new look with the addition of a $4.5 million, 25,000-square-foot education wing, relocation of the lobby, and an enlargement of the elegant Gatehouse Gift Shop. This is the largest municipally-owned botanical garden in the southeastern United States, and the oldest municipally-owned botanical garden in the state.

You could anchor a summer weekend around this area with an early walk in the gardens, a visit across the street to the **Birmingham**

Above and below: *Magnolia blossom.*
(Photos courtesy Charlene Wells)

Zoo in the morning when the animals are as excited about a new day as you are, Saturday dinner at the always charming **Café de France** (in the main Botanical Gardens building), and a unique and delightful outdoor evening theater experience, **Garden Variety Shakespeare.** All performances of the "Shakespeare for the Squeamish" summer season are held in the Botanical Gardens. The next day enjoy Sunday Strolls, a free and focused hour in the gardens with a knowledgeable volunteer guide, or step into the gigantic greenhouse and visit the orchids, gardenias, cacti, and other plants that thrive in the moist warmth. And what would you do in-between? Shop! Three distinct villages offer an enticing array of gift shops.

Parking is free at the zoo. Go to the gate and pick up the *Birmingham Zoo News* at the gate to see what is happening inside. Ride the train for an overview, and then choose which exhibits you will most enjoy. There are 100 acres of wooded areas and over 800 animals including elephants, tigers, bears, playful otters, people-watching monkeys, and the slim, haughty giraffes who look down on everybody. You can walk a lot or a little, but if you come in the summer, early is best since the temperatures can soar and make both man and beast uncomfortable. The same climate makes visiting the zoo a pleasant possibility all year. In December, when the zoo is trimmed in tiny lights for the annual Zoolight Safari, most people are happy wearing a sweater.

To avoid the restaurant rush, plan to eat lunch around 11:30. **Mountain Brook Village** is the closest of the three shopping and eating areas waiting for your happy discoveries.

Browdy's has been a neighborhood tradition since 1913. You'll be glad you came early. If you already have a favorite Reuben sandwich, stack Browdy's Gourmet Reuben Special against it. It's hard work being a judge. Reward yourself with dessert and choose chocolate cheesecake or step up to the bakery case and pick out a pastry.

After lunch, make your way down the sidewalk to **Smith's Variety,** a toy and gift shop that will be enjoyed by people who claim they detest shopping. There are fun gifts, ideas for parties, and doo-dads you didn't know you needed until you saw them there. Take your time walking the aisles. There are more shops across the street, each one scented, beribboned, and overflowing with treasures. Pace yourself around both blocks. Don't miss **White Flowers** across Cahaba Road. Its whiteness is almost ethereal.

Ready for more? Before you move on, pop into the **Big Sky Bakery** for a chewy cookie and then go east on Montevallo Road to Church Street. Turn left and drive toward the clock tower in **Crestline Village.** Park, walk, and enjoy! **Michelle's** offers an eclectic selection of women's clothing, gift items, and jewelry in medium, moderate, and high-end price ranges. **Villa Nova** offers a complete selection of Judaica, including kinetic mixed-media dreidel sculptures. Face the clock tower, and you are facing Euclid Avenue. You are also looking at **Harvest Glen Fresh Market,** a grocery filled with fragrant fruit and gleaming bottles of jam and jelly. Proceeds benefit the handicapped.

Climb back into your car and go west on Euclid. You will arrive in **English Village** next. The statue of the young girl is a representation of **Carolyn Cortner Smith,** the first woman architect in Alabama. **Armand's,** a fine dining establishment, is on your left. Those whose tastes run to the finest antiques will want to spend several hours exploring the collections gathered in this area.

You can stay in Mountain Brook and enjoy a traditional full-course dinner, or you can exercise your pioneer spirit and look for new territories to conquer. Go back to U.S. 280 East, pass the water works, and turn left on Green Valley Road. Go to Crosshaven Lane and turn right. Turn right again at Cahaba Heights Road. **Cahaba Heights** is on the southern side of Mountain Brook, and it, too, has many shops to mine for treasure. Since some of the gift stores are closed on Sunday, try to arrive in this area by 3 P.M. You won't want to miss **Lamb's Ears,** across from the Cahaba Heights United Methodist Church. This assemblage of laces, china, silver, pillows, and frames will keep you reaching out to touch, and the atmosphere will remind you of your great aunt's front porch—comfortable and cozy.

For dinner in an hour or so, you may want to come back to this area and step into another culture at **Antoine's,** a Lebanese restaurant. Among the specialties are tabbouleh and kibbeh. Another choice is the **Heights Café,** which serves favorite Southern vegetable casseroles. You are not far from the **Bagel Factory,** which is probably the only place in the country where you can find a Southern bagel. Owner Jay Epstein says a Southern bagel is softer and sweeter. His bagels are also hole-less, so the cream cheese, which he flavors and changes from plain to extraordinary, won't get all over your fingers. Keep this place in mind for a Sunday morning treat.

Return to Crosshaven Lane, turn left and go to **Crosshaven Bookstore.** Check the sign out front to see whether a favorite author is signing today. **David's Art and Frames** next door features original art. Have you discovered the **Summit** yet? You are on the edge of it.

Yucca plant at Birmingham Botanical Gardens. (Photo courtesy Charlene Wells)

If you had turned right on Crosshaven Lane, that is where you would be. This multiplex is an extravagance of leading department stores, specialty shops, and well-known restaurants. A Sunday afternoon foray into this area will enable you to recall this weekend as a true "shop 'til you drop" experience.

Area Code: (205)

Getting There:
Mountain Brook can be reached from downtown Birmingham via U.S. 280.

Where and When:
Birmingham Botanical Gardens, 2612 Lane Park Road, Birmingham, AL 35223. Open sunrise to sunset. 414-3900.

Birmingham Zoo, 2630 Cahaba Road, Birmingham, AL 35223. Daily, 9 A.M.-7 P.M.; winter until 5 P.M. 879-0408. Admission.

Bromberg's, 2800 Cahaba Road, Mountain Brook, AL 35223. Mon.-Sat., 9:30 A.M.-5:30 P.M. 871-3276.

Christine's, 2822 Petticoat Lane, Mountain Brook, AL 35223. Mon.-Sat., 10 A.M.-5 P.M. 871-8297.

Crosshaven Bookstore, 3916 Crosshaven Drive, Cahaba Heights, AL 35243. Mon.-Fri., 9 A.M.-6 P.M., Sat., 9 A.M.-5 P.M. 972-8778.

Dande Lion, 2701 Culver Road, Mountain Brook, AL 35223. Mon.-Sat., 9 A.M.-5:30 P.M. 879-0691.

David's Art and Frames, 3920 Crosshaven Drive, Cahaba Heights, AL 35243. Mon.-Sat., 9 A.M.-6 P.M. 967-0480.

Emmet O'Neal Library, 50 Oak Street, Mountain Brook, AL 35213. Mon.-Tue. & Thurs., 9 A.M.-9 P.M.; Wed., 9 A.M.-6 P.M.; Fri.-Sat., 9 A.M.-5 P.M.; Sun., 1 P.M.-5 P.M. 879-0459.

Gallerie Alegria, 600 Olde English Lane, Suite 128, English Village, Mountain Brook, AL 35223. Tue.-Sat., 10:30 A.M.-5 P.M. 868-9320.

Harvest Glen Fresh Market, 100 Euclid Avenue, Mountain Brook, AL, 35213. Summer, 9 A.M.-6 P.M.; winter, 9 A.M.-5:30 P.M. 879-1678.

Hen House, 1900 Cahaba Road, English Village, Mountain Brook, AL 35223. Mon.-Fri., 9:30 A.M.-5 P.M., Sat., 1 P.M.-5 P.M. 918-0505.

King's House Antiques, Gifts and Flowers, 2418 Montevallo Road, Mountain Brook, AL 35223. Mon.-Fri., 10 A.M.-5 P.M., Sat., 10 A.M.-4 P.M. 871-5787.

Lamb's Ears, 3138 Cahaba Heights Road, Birmingham, AL 35243. Mon.-Sat., 10 A.M.-5 P.M. 969-3138.

Michelle's, 81 Church Street, Crestline Village, Mountain Brook, AL 35213. Mon.-Sat., 10 A.M.-7 P.M. 870-3366.

Smith's Variety Toy and Gift Shoppe, Mountain Brook Village, Mountain Brook, AL 35223. Mon.-Sat., 8:30 A.M.-5:30 P.M. 871-0841.

Springhouse Interiors, 2841 Culver Road, Mountain Brook, AL 35223. Tue.-Fri., 10 A.M.-4 P.M. 870-1244.

Table Matters, 2409 Montevallo Road, Mountain Brook, AL 35223. Mon.-Fri., 10 A.M.-6 P.M., Sat., 10 A.M.-4:30 P.M. 879-0125.

Villa Nova, 81 Church Street #107, Mountain Brook, AL 35223. Mon.-Sat., 10 A.M.-5 P.M. 870-3400.

White Flowers, 2824 Cahaba Road, Mountain Brook, AL 35223. Mon.-Sat., 10 A.M.-5 P.M. 871-4640.

The **Summit,** U.S. 280 at Interstate 459.

Accommodations:

Courtyard by Marriot, 500 Shades Creek Pkwy., Homewood, AL 35209. Buffet breakfast, Mon.-Fri., 6:30 A.M.-10 A.M.; Sat.-Sun., 7 A.M.-11 A.M. 879-0400.

Embassy Suites, 2300 Woodcrest Place, Birmingham, AL 35209. 879-7400; (800) 362-2779.

Hampton Inn, 2731 U.S. 280, Birmingham, AL 25223. 870-7822; (800)426-7866.

Mountain Brook Inn, 2800 U.S. 280, Homewood, AL 35209. 870-3100.

Restaurants:

Antoine's, 3144 Green Valley Road, Cahaba Heights, AL 35243, Mon.-Sat., 1 A.M.-2:30 P.M., 5 P.M.-10 P.M. 969-3629.

Arman's, 2117 Cahaba Road, Mountain Brook, AL 35223. Mon.-Wed., 5 P.M.-10 P.M.; Thurs.-Sat., 5 P.M.-11 P.M. 871-5551.

Armand's at Parklane, 99 Euclid Avenue, English Village, Mountain Brook, AL 35223. Mon.-Wed., 5 P.M.-10 P.M., Thurs.-Sat., 5 P.M.-11 P.M. 871-5551.

Bagel Factory, 3118 Cahaba Heights Road, Birmingham, AL 35243. Mon.-Sat., 6:30 A.M.-5 P.M.; Sun., 6:30 A.M.-3 P.M. 969-0000.

Big Sky Bread Company, Mountain Brook Village, Mountain Brook, AL 35223. Tue.-Fri., 7 A.M.-5 P.M.; Sat., 7 A.M.-5 P.M. 870-1935.

Bongiorno, 68 Church Street, Mountain Brook, AL 35213. Mon.-Sat., 11 A.M.-2:30 P.M.; Fri.-Sat., 5 P.M.-10 P.M. 879-5947.

Browdy's Restaurant and Deli, 2713 Culver Road, Mountain Brook, AL 35223. Tue.-Sat., 9 A.M.-7:15 P.M.; Mon., 9 A.M.-2 P.M. 879-8585.

Café de France, 2612 Lane Park Road, Birmingham, AL 35223. Mon.-Sat., 11 A.M.-2 P.M., 6 P.M.-8 P.M. Reservations preferred. 871-1000.

Gilchrist Drug Company, 2805 Cahaba Road, Mountain Brook, AL 35223. Mon.-Fri., 8 A.M.-5 P.M.; Sat., 8:30 A.M.-5 P.M. 871-2181.

La Paz Ristorante and Cantina, 99 Euclid Avenue, Mountain Brook, AL 35213. Mon.-Fri., 11 A.M.-2 P.M.; 5 P.M.-10 P.M.; Sat. 11 A.M.-11 P.M.; Sun., 11 A.M.-10 P.M. 879-2225.

Mauby's, 121 Oak Street, Mountain Brook, AL 35213. Mon.-Thurs., 5 P.M.-10 P.M.; Fri.-Sat., 5 P.M.-11 P.M.; Sun., 11 A.M.-2 P.M., 5 P.M.-9 P.M. 870-7115.

Mary Ann's Village Diner, 75 Church Street, Mountain Brook, AL 35213. Mon.-Thurs., 6:30 A.M.-8 P.M.; Fri., 6:30 A.M.-3 P.M.; Sat., 7 A.M.-10 A.M.; Sun., 11 A.M.-2 P.M. 871-7281.

Surin of Thailand, 64 Church Street (Crestline Village), Mountain Brook, AL 35213. Mon.-Sun., 11:15 A.M.-2 P.M.; Sun.-Thurs., 5:15 P.M.-9 P.M.; Fri.-Sat., 5:15 P.M.-9:30 P.M. 871-4531.

Heights Café, 3134 Cahaba Heights Road (Cahaba Heights Village), Birmingham, AL 35243. Daily, 11 A.M.-3 P.M., 5 P.M.-8:30 P.M. 967-3132.

Major Annual Events:

Garden Variety Shakespeare, Birmingham—933-2609.

Zoolight Safari, Birmingham Zoo—December.

Bridge and creek. (Photo courtesy Charlene Wells)

22

SIR HENRY'S NAMESAKE

The first settlers arrived near what is now the city of **Bessemer** in 1815. John Jones settled there and the valley named for him, Jones Valley, would later become the town lot of Birmingham. Pennsylvanian **Daniel Hillman** built a forge on the banks of Roupes Creek in 1830, and by the early 1860s the nearby blast furnaces at Tannehill were turning out twenty tons of iron a day. After the Civil War, British inventor Sir Henry Bessemer built several steel mills near Jones' early settlement and experimented with new ways to convert pig iron to steel. Birmingham was founded in 1871, and after **Henry Fairchild DeBardeleben,** the son of wealthy industrialists, visited Bessemer's steel mills, he decided to build a city to rival the size and success of Birmingham. In 1887 DeBardeleben transformed the woods into a city, which he named for Sir Henry.

That's a partial timeline for steel production, but you can have a lot more fun with the dates and places by visiting **Tannehill Ironworks Historical State Park,** which will take you back to the early days, and **VisionLand** amusement park, which adds a theme-based creative twist to the historical past.

If you really want to immerse yourself in the experience, haul your camper, tent, or RV to Tannehill. Improved and primitive sites are available. This could be your base of operations for the entire area. So could hotels and motels along I-20/59 and I-459. Plan to sleep well no matter where you lay your head. Fresh air and exercise abound!

Tannehill Ironworks Historical State Park has grown up around the ruins of the ironworks. In the 1860s the industrial center at Tannehill came into its finest hour as a great producer of weapons to fuel the Confederacy. The mighty 20-ton daily production of the huge blast furnaces did not go unnoticed by the Union. The furnaces made the list of war industry sites that General James H. Wilson and his famous raiders were determined to destroy. On March 31, 1865, they accomplished this goal. It took only three companies of the Eighth Iowa Cavalry to reduce the foundry, tannery, sawmill, grist-mill, and cabins that had housed 600 slave laborers to smoking ruins.

Today visitors to the Iron and Steel Museum in the park can see exhibits that explain ironmaking and revisit the lives of the people, white pioneer and Native American families, who lived there and were the backbone of the industry. Sit in a rocking chair on the front porch of the museum and imagine the family that shared the covered wagon parked nearby. How far did they travel with that fragile con-veyance as their home?

If you are a shopper or a swapper, you won't want to miss the **Trade Days,** which take place the third Saturday of each month from March through November. You'll find tools, clothing, jewelry, knives, rugs, and furniture for indoors and out. Friendly sellers, buyers, and bystanders mill among booths and concessions.

The train station is near the campground, and you can ride the train to the large grassy area where the trade days take place. Walking on the smooth, shaded pathway and crossing the bridge on foot is pleasant, too. From spring through late fall, the blacksmith, miller, and other craftsmen demonstrate their trades in restored pioneer cabins, and they will chat with you from the front porches. The cotton gin, pioneer farm, and working gristmill recall a long-ago way of life, and hiking trails take your feet where many have gone before you.

Not far from Tannehill, on Eastern Valley Road, you'll find three historic plantation homes. You'll need an appointment to see inside, but a lot can be understood from the outside. The **Sadler Plantation Home** was built first, in 1817. The original part of the home was con-structed of hand-hewn logs by a furniture maker, John Loveless. In 1836 Isaac Sadler purchased the home and built a bigger house around the log structure. In 1860 this was one of the most productive farms in Jefferson County. It has been restored to its 1840s appear-ance and contains some of the original furnishings.

The **Owen Plantation Home** began as a honeymoon cottage for Thomas Owen and his bride, Melissa Sadler. It was built in 1833. Owen

Winter at Oak Mountain State Park. (Photo courtesy Lynard Stroud)

operated a foundry near Tannehill during the Civil War, and his son was involved in the founding of Birmingham Southern College.

The **McAdory Plantation Home** was built around 1840 and was the center of a 2000-acre plantation. The first mayor of Bessemer was born there.

While you are on a hunt for history, take I-20/59 to Exit 112 into the city of Bessemer and head for the railroad tracks. The **Bessemer Hall of History Museum** is housed in the renovated Southern Railway terminal, which was built in 1916 at a cost of $30,000 and is on the National Register of Historic Places. See the antique telephone exhibit and artist James H. Walker Jr.'s mural of early Bessemer on display in the Pioneer Room. Don't disturb the prim and proper lady in the waiting room! Trains pass routinely, rattling the old depot and giving those with active imaginations a taste of the old times.

A drive through the town, around the park and courthouse, will take you down Nineteenth Street, and you'll see the **Bright Star,** a restaurant that opened in 1907 and has built a well-known and well-deserved reputation for fine dining. The ambiance is understated, hushed, and expectant. Ceiling fans whirr and the mirrored, marbled walls reflect images of contentment. The specialties are tenderloin of beef and broiled snapper—both are prepared Greek style. Seafood is brought in from the Gulf and is not even breaded until it is ordered. In spite of the formal feeling, casual dress is acceptable, and well-behaved children feel welcome here. There is a children's menu, and we spotted many grandparents making the most of a special luncheon. On Friday and Saturday only, you can reward yourself (you'll think of a reason) with Bananas Foster Short Cake: sliced fresh bananas in a caramel sauce served over a homemade banana shortcake, dusted with powdered sugar, and topped with homemade whipped cream.

Sunday is funday. Look for breakfast along the interstates if you have opted not to cook it over your campfire at Tannehill, or have an early lunch at the Bright Star. Then take Interstate 20/59 to **VisionLand**. This theme park links the area's iron and steel history to whirling, swirling fun rides and amusements. The **Steelwaters Waterpark** consists of the Mine Shaft, Quarry Bay, and Warrior River for tubing enthusiasts who don't mind getting wet. The **Wild River Gorge** rapids ride features a whirlpool, cave, geysers, waterfalls, and waves generated by a wave machine. This ride cost a cool $4.9 million to build and will keep kids and adventuresome adults cool on hot days.

The park's centerpiece is a giant $4.3 million wooden roller coaster, the **Rampage.** The ride on the Rampage takes only a minute, but the coaster goes 60 miles an hour and has a 120-foot plunge. Track its progress by listening to the rise and fall of riders' screams. If you are on it, your stomach will gauge the distance from start to stop, top to drop.

You cannot bring a picnic into the park, but concession stands will keep you from going hungry. While you are getting your land legs back after riding the Rampage, note the wall of sculptured brick that pays tribute to the contribution of steel industry workers and the Commemorative Wall, which recognizes the cooperation of 11 cities that helped make the vision of the park's founding father, **Fairfield** mayor Larry Langford, a reality.

Now look up. The Ferris wheel rises 106 feet. It is a Mondail Ferris wheel, and the first of its kind to be placed in a theme park in the United States. It's larger than carnival-size Ferris wheels.

At present the park covers 75 acres, but it seems like more because acreage doesn't include vertical space.

One last ride on the carousel and you'll be headed home with the sound of VisionLand ringing in your ears.

Area Code: (205)

Getting There:
Bessemer can be reached via Alabama Interstate 20/59, Exit 112.

Where and When:
Bessemer Hall of History Museum, 1905 Alabama Avenue, Bessemer, AL 35020. 426-1633.

Birmingham Public Library, Bessemer Branch, 400 Nineteenth Street N., Bessemer, AL 35350. Mon.-Thurs., 9 A.M.-8 P.M.; Tue., Wed., and Fri., 9 A.M.-6 P.M.; Sat., 10 A.M.-4 P.M.; Sun., 2 P.M.-5 P.M. 428-7882.
Web site: bessemer.lib.al.us

Historic Plantation Homes, (Sadler, Owen, McAdory), Eastern Valley Road, Bessemer, AL 35020. By appointment. 426-1633. Admission.

Tannehill Ironworks Historical State Park, 12632 Confederate Parkway, McCalla, AL 35111. Daily, 7 A.M.-dark. 477-5711. Admission.
Web site: www.tannehill.org

VisionLand Theme Park, Academy Road. Exit from Interstate 20/59, Bessemer, AL. 481-4750. Admission.
Web site: www.visionlandpark.com

Information:

Bessemer Chamber of Commerce, 321 N. Eighteenth Street, Bessemer, AL 35350. 425-3253; (888) 423-7736.

Restaurants:

Bright Star, 304 N. Nineteenth Street, Bessemer, AL 35203. Mon.-Fri., 11 A.M.-3:30 P.M.; Sat.-Sun., 11 A.M.-10 P.M. 424-9444.

Major Annual Events:

Southern Appalachian Dulcimer Festival, Tannehill Ironworks Historical State Park, McCalla—May. 477-5711.

Tannehill Trade Days, Tannehill Ironworks Historical State Park, McCalla—Third weekend each month, March-November. 477-5711.

23

DINNER BY
DESTINATION

You can go around the world without leaving **Hoover** if you do it with a fork and spoon or a set of chopsticks. What a variety of ethnic restaurants! To put you in the middle of your culinary world, check into the **Wynfrey Hotel** and set up a planning session at the hotel's **Chicory Grille,** where frequent patrons say the pasta bar is "to die for." The Wynfrey has more than 400 guestrooms, so unless you choose a most unusual weekend, there should be a place for you to enjoy the amenities of this four-star hotel.

The Wynfrey is part of the **Riverchase Galleria** office, hotel, and retail multiplex, which covers 2.4 million square feet. The Galleria mall is the number-one tourist attraction in the city. 186,000 square feet of glass give the atrium a claim to being the largest in the Western Hemisphere, and some say the skylight is the largest in the world.

Do you hear cash registers singing? Shoppers spend well over one million dollars a day in the seventeen restaurants and 200-plus stores in this, the country's twentieth-largest mall. Eighty of the stores are exclusive to the area.

After you recover from the overwhelming enormity of the window above your head, you might wonder just how the glass stays so clean. This is how: it takes four professional window washers, wearing safety equipment, ten days twice a year to wash the skylight. They walk on the exterior wearing safety belts and use a hose, brush, and window-cleaning solution. Cleaning the archway is similar to cleaning a sliding board. Due to the expansion and contraction of the glass and metal, resealing takes place periodically to deal with leaks.

Riverchase Galleria, as seen from Oak Mountain State Park. (Photo by Neal Broerman)

Presumably the fall cleaning chores are complete when it's time to kick off the holiday season on the second Friday in November, when the Grand Lighting Ceremony sets the entire atrium aglow. From November to March, kids of all ages are enchanted by the whirling mirrored musical replica of Gustav Dentzel's Carousel. Every February the mall hosts a circus to celebrate its anniversary. The winter events are dizzying!

Surrounded by a small city under a glass roof, you could stay indoors for the entire weekend. But if global dining appeals to you, choose your itinerary from the following list: Go south on Montgomery Highway to the Riverchase Wal-Mart Shopping Center—it will be on your left—and you will find a touch of Italy in **La Dolce Vita.** Warm, fresh-baked bread and a salad are enough for a meal. Waiters parade with a pepper mill and a cheese grinder. Then the main dishes arrive. They are fragrant, steaming, and much too generous for a diner who has already savored the bread and crisp, cheddar-sprinkled romaine. This is one of those times when you will want to ask the waiter to split your order and bring two plates. There is a split fee, but it saves you from feeling guilty and leaves you with room for dessert.

In the same shopping center, you will see **Grandma's Attic,** which has many booths filled with the creations of local artists. Of special note is the **Southeastern Mineral Market,** which features minerals, rocks, fossils, jewelry, and natural gift items. The booths seem to overflow at Christmas time, but any time you are close by is a good time to stroll through the variegated displays.

If you go north on U.S. 31 (Montgomery Highway), the first shopping center on your left after the Galleria is the Center at Riverchase. Persia and Mexico await in this small group of stores.

Guadalajara is an authentic Mexican restaurant featuring a fun atmosphere with occasional live bands. The food is excellent, the service is swift, and the family atmosphere is casual and relaxed. This is definitely a jeans place. **Ali Baba's** Restaurant serves Middle Eastern dishes with a concentration on Persian food. Bastani is Persian ice cream. Appetizers of baba ghannouj or kashk o'bademjan make a new dish out of eggplant, and Popeye would never recognize his favorite vegetable as it is treated in borani-e esfenaj.

From the Center at Riverchase, make a right and take the next left at Municipal Drive and turn into the **Hoover Public Library** parking lot. This ever-expanding facility has its own theater series and its annual Southern Voices literary event is a sell-out. Leave the library lot and turn left. You'll see the walking track around the Hoover Lake on your right. Park beside the Lake House and spend a pleasant half-hour ambling and observing the ducks and swans.

When you leave the Lake House, continue away from U.S. 31 toward Lorna Road. Across Lorna you will spot **Costa's,** a Mediterranean café that offers excellent service and presentation as well as delicious entrées. The moussaka is lighter than most moussakas, and one serving of the succulent souvlaki is generous enough for two. The Greek salad is more than ample. Ask about splitting both main dish and salad. If you have never eaten tiramisu, a spongy chocolate dessert, this is the place to try it.

You could leave Costa's, go left, and reach the Galleria again. Instead, go right, take the first left (Patton Chapel Road North), and when you get to U.S. 31 again, go right or north toward Birmingham. Ahead on the right you will see the Original Golden Rule. Turn left on Greenvale Road. You are approaching, on your left, **Green Valley Drug Co.,** which, in addition to its pharmacy, houses a one-stop gift shop (tasteful gifts, cards, and wrapping paper), and a popular soda fountain and grill. At least two generations of Hooverites have court-ed over chocolate milkshakes and, reportedly, "the best cheeseburg-ers anywhere."

Note the spot on your map for a future tryst, and continue to the stop sign just past the Hoover Florist. At the stop sign, turn right on Spruce, continue into the shopping center. The **Mandarin House** is on your left. Here is a taste of the Orient served in a red-and-gold atmosphere softened by wind chimes and whispering flutes. The steamed rice clings well enough that even a novice with chop sticks can eat a few bites successfully.

Retrace your steps to the Green Valley Drug Co., which has been standing on that spot since 1961 (and is still owned by its founder, Dr. Joseph Box, and his son, William) and drive in front of it, past its shopping center neighbors, through Hoover Court. Turn right. Follow the sizzle to **La Fiesta,** another authentic Mexican restaurant that will lift your spirits. Vegetarians and meat eaters alike will be happy here, and so will children.

Now that you've had a whirlwind tour of so many tempting menus, you need time to think about your dinner choice. From La Fiesta, return to Greenvale, go left to the end of the street, and turn left again. At the bottom of the hill lies **Star Lake,** circled by a favorite neighborhood jogging/walking track. Two and a half times around equals a mile. Walk as long as you need to.

After your evening meal is a memory, return to the Galleria and pass in front of it to U.S. 150. Turn right and go about two miles to Stadium Trace Parkway, then turn left and follow the spacious neigh-borhood streets to the **Hoover Metropolitan Stadium.** This is where the Birmingham Barons moved when they left Rickwood Field. The seating capacity of the Met is 10,000, and there are 60 acres of park-ing. If the Barons are playing, you can probably walk right up and get a ticket. Enjoy!

Sunday morning arrives and you still have eating choices. This time they are Southern. Go south on U.S. 31, one block from the Galleria, and turn left on Lorna Road. Turn left at the second light into Lorna Brook Village shopping center. **Chef's Café** will be ahead on the left. The café is small and has a friendly, cup-of-coffee, neigh-borly feel to it. Add the chef's rich and fluffy omelets, biscuits, and fresh fruit, and you'll be convinced this is the way life should be; unhurried, with time to relax and enjoy the beginning of a new day.

Cherry trees at Star Lake. (Photo by Neal Broerman)

The chef, Richard Tasich, is carrying on a family tradition. When his aunt was a store owner, she gave her customers calendars at holiday time. When Tasich opened his cafe, he framed one of his aunt's calendars and placed it above the cash register. You'll see it when you check out. The calendar date is 1936, and you'll be glad, along with all the other café patrons, that the Tasich family tradition continues.

Around the corner on Lorna Road, near Costa's, you'll find another popular brunch spot, the **Original Pancake House.** If the name sounds familiar, it's because there is another one on Southside, and you may have stood in line there on an earlier getaway. You may have to stand in line here, too, but the end result is the same—an amazing array of choices and a very satisfied you when the meal is over. The servings are monstrous. Each omelet has at least four eggs in it, plus the fillings and sauce. One order could serve several people. For seniors, children, and people with small appetites, bear this in mind. Ask for extra plates. From your table or booth, you can see into the kitchen, which is spotless and busy. How do they avoid running into each other?

By now you and your children could be ready for a few restful, creative hours. From the Galleria, get on Interstate 459 North, go to

Acton Road (Exit 17), and turn left. Follow Acton Road to Dolly Creek Station, which is just inside Vestavia Hills. At the shopping area across from the Alabama Automobile Association Building, you will see **Painted By U.** This is a great pottery studio for ages three and up. There is a studio fee plus the cost of your choice of bisqueware. It's your personalized handpainted touches that transform your piece into a family heirloom. Leave your work for glazing and firing. If you are in the area a few days later for pickup, fine. If not, shipping arrangements can be made. Saturdays after school starts and before or after the holiday shopping season are the best times to plan a visit here.

How could you spend a weekend pondering international cuisine and not include Southern barbecue? Not to worry. **Richard's BBQ and Grill** is steps from Painted By U. Home-owned and operated by the Cairnes family, this is not a paper plate and napkin place. The napkins are cloth and the plates and flatware would stand up to cutting the meat if you had to, but you don't. All the barbecued meats are fall-apart tender. A model train runs at ceiling height through a tunnel and in and out of two dining rooms, and television sets tuned to the current sports event make up a relaxed, informal atmosphere. Save room for chocolate chip chess pecan pie.

Are you ready for a breathtaking view? Get back in your car and get on Interstate 459 South. Go to Interstate 65 North, get off at the Alford exit, and turn left. Cross the expressway and turn right. Go one block to Shades Crest Road. Drive along Shades Crest and enjoy the view of the valley. This is especially lovely at twilight.

You are driving through **Bluff Park,** which is the most historical section in Hoover. In the early 1900s this was a mountaintop retreat. The **Park Avenue Historic District** is on the National Register of Historic Places.

By Bluff Park standards, Hoover is very young. When Hoover was incorporated in 1967, the total population was 410. Now it is almost 60,000 and ranks sixth in size in the state. Hoover is also the fastest-growing city in Alabama, probably because everyone eats so well.

Area Code: (205)

Getting There:
Hoover can be reached via Interstate 65, Exits 247, 250, or 254.

Where and When:
Grandma's Attic, 1853 Montgomery Highway, Hoover, AL 35244. Mon.-Thurs., 10 A.M.-5 P.M.; Fri.-Sat., 10 A.M.-6 P.M.; Sun., 1 P.M.-5 P.M.

Cherry trees. (Photo by Neal Broerman)

987-9505.

Hoover Metropolitan Stadium, 100 Ben Chapman Drive, Hoover, AL 35226. 988-3200. Admission. Web site: www.barons.com

Hoover Public Library, 200 Municipal Drive, Hoover, AL 35216. Mon.-Thurs., 9 A.M.-9 P.M.; Fri.-Sat., 9 A.M.-6 P.M.; Sun., 2 P.M.-6 P.M. 444-7800. Web site: www.hoover.lib.al.us

Painted By U, 2409 Acton Road, Suite 165, Birmingham, AL 35243. Tue.-Thurs., 11 A.M.-9 P.M.; Fri., 10 A.M.-10 P.M.; Sat., 10 A.M.-6 P.M. 823-4407.

Riverchase Galleria, 3000 Riverchase Galleria, Hoover, AL 35244. Mon.-Sat., 10 A.M.-9 P.M.; Sun., 1 P.M.-6 P.M. 985-3020; (800) 476-7006.

Southeastern Mineral Market (Inside Grandma's Attic), 1853 Montgomery Highway, Hoover, AL 35244. Mon.-Thurs., 10 A.M.- 5 P.M.; Fri.-Sat., 10 A.M.-6 P.M.; Sun., 1 P.M.-5 P.M. 987-9505.

Information:

Hoover Chamber of Commerce, 3659 Lorna Rd. (Lorna Brook Village), Hoover, AL 35236. 988-5672.

Web site: www.hooverchamber.org

City of Hoover, Municipal Drive, Hoover, AL 35236. 444-7630.
North Shelby Chamber of Commerce, P.O. Box 324, Pelham, AL 35124. 663-4542.   Web site: www.nscoc.com
Vestavia Hills Chamber of Commerce, P.O. Box 660793, Vestavia Hills, AL 35266. 823-5011.   Web site: www.vestaviahills.org

Accommodations:

Wynfrey Hotel, 1000 Riverchase Galleria, Hoover, AL 35244. 987-1600; (800) 476-7006.

Restaurants:

Ali Baba's, 110 Centre at Riverchase, Hoover, AL. Tue.-Fri., 11 A.M.-2:30 P.M., Sat.-Sun., 11:30 A.M.-2:30 P.M.; Sun., Tue.-Thurs., 5 P.M.-9:30 P.M.; Fri.-Sat., 5 P.M.-10:30 P.M. 823-2222.
                                        Web site: www.alibabarst.com
Chef's Café, 3659 Lorna Road, 147 Lorna Brook Village, Hoover, AL 35216. Mon.-Fri., 10 A.M.-2 P.M.; 5 P.M.-8 P.M.; Sat.-Sun., 9 A.M.-3 P.M. 988-9112.

Chicory Grille, Wynfrey Hotel, Galleria Circle, Hoover, AL 35244. Mon.-Sat., 6 A.M.-2 P.M., 5 P.M.-11 P.M.; Sun., 6 A.M.-2 P.M., 5 P.M.-10 P.M., 987-1600.

Costa's Mediterranean Café, 3443 Lorna Road, Hoover, AL 35216. Mon.-Thur., 11 A.M.-9:30 P.M.; Fri.-Sat., 11 A.M.-10:30 P.M. 978-1603.

Green Valley Drug Co., 1915 Hoover Court, Hoover, AL 35226. Mon.-Fri., 8A.M.-8P.M.; Sat., 9A.M.-5 P.M.; Sun., 1P.M.-5 P.M.

Guadalajara, 142 Center at Riverchase, Hoover. AL 35244, Mon.-Thurs., 11 A.M.-9:30 P.M.; Fri., 11 A.M.-10:30 P.M.; Sat., 11 A.M.-10 P.M.; Sun., 11 A.M.-9:30 P.M. 823-9549.

La Dolce Vita, 1851 Montgomery Highway, Hoover, AL 35244. Mon.-Thurs., 5 P.M.-10 P.M.; Fri.-Sat., 5 P.M.-11 P.M. Reservations preferred. 985-2909.

La Fiesta, 1941A Hoover Court, Hoover, AL 35216. Mon.-Fri., 11 A.M.-2 P.M.; Fri., 5 P.M.-10:30 P.M.; Sat.,11:30 A.M.-10 P.M.; Sun., 11 A.M.-2 P.M., 5 P.M.-9 P.M. 979-7314.

Mandarin House, 1550 Montgomery Highway, Hoover, AL 35216. Tue.-Sat., 11 A.M.-2:30 P.M.; Tue.-Thurs., 5 P.M.-10 P.M.; Fri., 5 P.M.-11 P.M.; Sat. 2:30 P.M.-11 P.M.; Sun., 11:30 A.M.-9 P.M., 822-1761.

MoonBreaks, 757 Shades Mountain Plaza, Hoover, AL 35260. Tue.-Sat., 6 A.M.-2 P.M. 823-8027.

Original Golden Rule BBQ, 1571 Montgomery Highway, Hoover, AL 35216. Mon.-Sat., 10:30 A.M.-9 P.M.; Sun., 11 A.M.-8 P.M. 823-7770.

Original Pancake House, 3305 Lorna Road, Hoover, AL 35216. Mon.-Fri., 6:30 A.M.-2 P.M.; Sat.-Sun., 7 A.M.-3 P.M. 823-5828.

Richard's BBQ and Grill, 2409 Acton Road, Birmingham, AL 35243. Mon.-Thurs., 7 A.M.-9 P.M.; Fri., 7 A.M.-10 P.M.; Sat., 8 A.M.-10 P.M.; Sun., 8 A.M.-7 P.M. 979-6057.

Winston's, Wynfrey Hotel, Galleria Circle, Hoover, AL 35244. Mon.-Sat., 6 P.M.-10 P.M. 987-1600.

Major Annual Events:

Southern Voices Conference, Hoover Public Library, Hoover— February. 444-7810.

Battle of Bibb Furnace, Brierfield Ironworks Park, Brierfield— March 665-1856.

Birmingham Barons Baseball, Hoover Metropolitan Stadium, Hoover—April-Sept. 988-3200.   Web site: www.barons.com

Bluff Park Art Show, Bluff Park—October. Phone: 822-0078

Peavine Falls at Oak Mountain State Park. (Photo courtesy Lynard Stroud)

24

THE BIRD WITH
THE SKY ON ITS BACK

Drive into **Oak Mountain State Park** and follow Findlay Boulevard. Look for a flash of bright blue flitting in and about the scattered trail of bluebird boxes along the road. You'll soon know that the bluebird fits Henry David Thoreau's description, "the bird with the sky on its back."

John Findlay came to Alabama in his retirement years to escape the harsh northern winters and found a calling. A dedicated birder, he was determined to bring the bluebirds back to this part of the country. Creeping suburbs and competition from aggressive house sparrows and starlings had reduced the nesting spaces available to bluebirds. Findlay set about building and mounting nesting boxes specifically designed for the small birds, and he held classes and taught others to build bluebird boxes, too. In tribute, he was called "Mr. Bluebird," and the main road into Oak Mountain, the largest Alabama state park, was named for him.

The cabins at Oak Mountain have been updated and are just what a work-weary vacationer needs. This could be your center of operations for the entire weekend.

The 10,000-acre park is part of the Appalachian chain. You will get an appreciation of this if you drive, hike, bike, or ride a horse up the scenic road to the top of Double Oak Mountain. Stop at an overlook to take pictures or listen to sounds usually lost in the hubbub of daily living. Off in the distance you might hear a train. The glass Galleria is barely a spot in the deep green of summer or the confetti colors of fall foliage. The road changes from asphalt to dirt, and this is the longest part of the drive, but there are many wonderful surprises at the end of little dirt roads in Alabama. Let yourself become one in spirit with the first Native American to set foot here.

Are you traveling with a family of different ages and stages and a wide variety of interests? Golfers will find the **Oak Mountain State Park Golf Course** to their liking and yes, children can really ride horses here. Ages three to eight can ride around a ring or on ponies. The minimum age for a guided trail ride is eight. These guided trail rides can be of varying lengths, up to an hour and a half. If you bring your own horse, overnight lodging is available.

Boating enthusiasts can rent canoes, pedal boats, and flat-bottom boats by the hour during the season. Two 85-acre lakes stocked with bream, bass, and catfish will keep fishermen (and fisherwomen?) happy. Bait, tackle, and fishing licenses are sold at the fishing center store, and you can rent boats there, too.

Hikers can explore about 50 miles of trail. Ask for trail maps when you arrive.

The **BMX dirt trail** and the **Bicycle Moto Cross Track** are designed for fun and also for the serious rider. Sanctioned races are held throughout the summer.

Animal lovers can begin with petting gentle creatures at the demonstration farm and then visit wild ones, too. Follow the **Tree Top Nature Trail** at the top of Oak Mountain to see birds of prey and other injured wildlife at the **Alabama Wildlife Rehabilitation Center.** Watch the volunteers feed orphaned birds and set broken wings. The volunteers nurse the animals back to health so owls, beavers, raccoons, and other wildlife can go back to doing what they do best— being wild animals. Bring your binoculars and scan the treetops!

Take a little of the Wildlife Center home with you. Visit the **Backyard Habitat Demonstration Area** and find out what kinds of plants and feeders you can put in your yard to send an invitation to native birds. You'll find out how to attract rabbits and raccoons, too.

Nearby the **Oak Mountain Amphitheater** brings in well-known musical groups for outdoor summer concerts. A schedule of events will demonstrate the wide appeal. When leaving Oak Mountain State Park, turn left on Amphitheater Drive before you reach Alabama 119. Close to U.S. 31, on the same road as the Amphitheater, is the **Pelham Civic Center,** which hosts year-round hockey and ice and figure skating in its twin Olympic-size skating rinks. Call first. Hours and programs are varied and when other events are not scheduled, the

Bottle-brush buckeye at Oak Mountain State Park. (Photo courtesy Lynard Stroud)

public can rent skates and practice double and triple toe loops, or just put one foot in front of the other.

Hungry? From the Civic Center go to U.S. 31; turn right. Take U.S. 31 to Valleydale Road and turn right again into the Riverbrook Plaza Shopping Center, immediately on your right. The tantalizing aroma of sizzling hot peppers and onions greets you at the **Zapata Mexican Restaurant,** and the hostess is not far behind to usher you to smoking or nonsmoking sections. Guitars strum softly in the background. The smiling waitress returns with chips and salsa for munching while you look over a menu that is, thankfully, not overwhelming with choices yet includes fine fare for vegetarians. Charo and Leovi Castro have been welcoming guests to this touch of Mexico for three years. You won't forget where it is.

While you are in this part of the state, you must not miss the opportunity to visit with your family, the one that preceded you by a couple hundred years. Living history parks and interactive museums are making our past an exciting place to visit and an easier time to remember. The newest one is an eighteenth-century village north of Montevallo on Alabama 119 called the **American Village.** If there is another one in the country like it, we don't know where it is. Costumed interpreters of great moments in the founding of our country facilitate the entry of visitors into those moments. You can actually participate as a patriot, loyalist, or neutral in the debate over declaring independence from Great Britain. At the colonial courthouse you could become justice, juror, or defendant. Rally, march, drill, protest, debate. This could engage the entire family for several hours and only later will everyone realize how much they have learned.

Washington Hall, inspired by Mount Vernon, is the centerpiece of the village. A reproduction of Jean Antoine Houdon's life-size statue of George Washington presides over the Grand Foyer. The Mount Vernon Room replicates Washington's dining room, and the Assembly Room recalls the legislative chamber in Independence Hall in Philadelphia. In this room the Rising Sun Chair is an arresting symbol of the new American Republic. Visitors move outside, down a covered rampway, and into a faithful recreation of the Oval Office as it is today. In traveling from one room to another and from one era to another, participants consider the impact of decisions made in George Washington's day on today's government.

The American Village, founded by Executive Director Tom Walker, and supported wholeheartedly by a host of history buffs from the

American Village craft-demonstration cottages. (Photo by Neal Broerman)

Above and left: *American Village Revolutionary War encampment.* (Photos by Joan Broerman)

University of Montevallo and surrounding towns, is more than an opportunity to tie dates and places together. Stepping into the lives of the people who plotted the course for this new nation binds the generations. It's difficult to leave the village without a determination to keep the country as bold and strong as the founding fathers intended when they spoke of "We the people..." Experiences like this will place apathy on the endangered list. Plan to come often. The American Village will continue to evolve and expand for the next decade.

When you leave the American Village, turn right on Alabama 119 S., and drive into the charming town of **Montevallo.** Park and walk across the brick streets of the University of Montevallo campus, or drive up to the president's home, Flowerhill, and enjoy the rose bushes beside the long tree-lined brick drive.

Continue west through Montevallo to **Brierfield Ironworks** on Alabama 25 S. This is an historic ironworks park similar to Tannehill, also a Confederate gun production site, burned by Union soldiers the same day Tannehill was destroyed. Brierfield was revived by railroad man Thomas Jefferson Peter, who arrived in the early 1880s, and the furnaces soon roared to life again. The boom—which earned Brierfield the name "Magic City of Bibb County"—was short-lived, because the huge metal furnaces in the new city of Birmingham could produce ten times as much iron per day as the old brick furnace at Brierfield.

Hurry back through Montevallo to Alabaster before The **Fossil Site** closes. The owner, David Frings, is a professional geologist, and he teaches nature classes for children in a corner of his store. A large aquarium and bubbling fountain will mesmerize the kids and free you to purchase fossils, minerals, and natural gift items.

In addition to lodging at the state park, there are many hotels and motels along U.S. 31 and Interstate 65. Twenty miles south of Alabaster, the **Jemison Inn** draws rave reviews from previous guests. At the urging of those who have sampled her cooking, innkeeper Nancy Ruzicka has written a cookbook. Nancy, her husband, Joe, and the family cat, Dingle, oversee the gardens, fountain, and swimming pool. Leave the children and pets at home and enjoy a romantic weekend.

For an afternoon of shopping concluded by a perfect dinner for two, go to downtown **Helena** and browse to your heart's content through two long blocks of gift shops, each one more inviting than the last. Your biggest problem will be deciding where to start.

Dinner at **Fox Valley** Restaurant should be next on your itinerary.

Continue on Helena Road, Alabama 261, to Shelby County Road 17 S., then to the Shell Station. You'll spot the restaurant's name in the row of stores on your left. The building is nondescript, but it's only a building. You'll forget about outward trappings once you step through the door. Reservations are not taken, but since a new dining room has been added, the waiting time may be less than in the past. Even if you must wait, do so.

Owner Susan Lemieux and her partner and co-owner, chef Anthony Mangold, bring many years' experience in all aspects of the business to this successful blend of gourmet food and ease. Jackets and ties are acceptable, but starched collars are out of place. Most diners are comfortably dressed and free to enjoy such delights as roast apple-wood, bacon-wrapped grouper fillet served in a broth of coconut milk, Chardonnay, lump crab, and fresh spinach. Carpetbagger steak is popular and not just because the name is shorter. This is a char-grilled petite filet mignon stuffed with fried oysters with sauce choron. Presentation is artful, candles and fresh flowers create a romantic atmosphere, and the service seems choreographed. Owners and staff have worked together as a team for many years, and harmony is evident. Both owners specialize in desserts and this, too, is evident. Can anyone resist a dessert with a name like white chocolate raspberry amaretto marble cheesecake?

May Sunday bring you lovely weather for more outdoor activities. If you camped at Oak Mountain, you probably brought a cooler. Fill it with sandwiches and soda and let the day begin.

Shelby County is the fastest-growing county in the state, but there are stewards at work to protect the natural treasures. The Cahaba River is Alabama's last free-flowing river, and it supports 131 different species of fish, more than any river of comparable size in North America. The river is ideal for canoeing, fishing, hiking, and bird-watching. Contact the **Cahaba River Society** for information.

Lay Lake, a 12,000-acre lake that was the site of the 1996 Bass Masters Classic, is another popular fishing area. Guides are available. For maps of the lake and lists of launch sites and marinas, check the Alabama Power Web site and click on "Lakes and Waterways."

After a day on the water, you are sunburned, pleasantly tired, and ready to go home. If you feed the kids first, they might sleep while you drive. **Uncle Bud's** features country cooking, and at night, heading toward Birmingham, the well-lighted family restaurant stands out like a beacon in a strip of familiar fast food places lining Highway 31 in Alabaster, just outside Pelham. Uncle Bud's has been in business 16 years, and the sign at the door lets you know these are local people and proud of it.

While you are waiting for supper, look around the table and ask what was the most fun this weekend. After all, you learned the value of personal opinion at the American Village.

Area Code: (205)

Getting There:

From Interstate 65 S. take Exit 246 and turn right. Immediately turn left on Oak Mountain Parkway. Oak Mountain State Park is about two miles down the parkway.

Where and When:

Alabama Wildlife Rehabilitation Center, Oak Mountain State Park, Pelham, AL 35124. 663-7930.

American Village, Alabama 119 N., Montevallo, AL. Daily, 9:30 A.M.-4 P.M., but hours are variable, so call first. 665-3535, (877) 811-1776. Admission.   Web site: www.americanvillage.com

Brierfield Ironworks, Route 1, Box 147, Brierfield, AL 35205. 665-1856.

Fossil Site, 1614 Kent Dairy Road, Alabaster, AL 35007. Mon.-Fri., 10 A.M.-5 P.M.

Oak Mountain Amphitheater, 1000 Amphitheatre Road (off Interstate 65, Exit 246), Pelham, AL 35124. Apr.-Oct. 985-0703. Admission.

Oak Mountain State Park, 200 Terrace Drive (off Interstate 65, Exit 246), Pelham, AL 35124. 620-2520. Admission.

Web site: www.bham.net/oakmtn/

Oak Mountain State Park Demonstration Farm, 200 Terrace Drive (off Interstate 65, exit 246), Pelham, AL 35124. 620-2526. Admission.

Web site: www.bham.net/oakmtn/

Oak Mountain State Park Fishing, 200 Terrace Drive (off Interstate 65, Exit 246), Pelham, AL 35124. 620-2528.

Web site: www.bham.net/oakmtn/

Oak Mountain State Park Golf Course, 200 Terrace Drive (off Interstate 65, Exit 246), Pelham, AL 35124. 620-2522.

Web site: www.bham.net/oakmtn/

Oak Mountain State Park Trail Rides, 200 Terrace Drive (off Interstate 65, Exit 246), Pelham, AL 35124. 621-0123. Admission.

Web site: www.bham.net/oakmtn/

Water Course, 2030 Seventh Street, Clanton, AL. 280-4442; (800) 544-6328. Admission.

Pelham Civic Center Complex, 500 Amphitheater Road, Pelham, AL 35214. Open for skating, Mon.-Fri., 9 A.M.-11 A.M., 4 P.M.-6 P.M., 7 P.M.-9 P.M.; Sat., 10 A.M.-noon, 1 P.M.-3 P.M., 4 P.M.-6 P.M., 7 P.M.-9 P.M.; Sun., 1 P.M.-3 P.M., 4 P.M.-6 P.M. 620-6448. Admission.

Information:

Alabama Small Boat Rentals, 424-3634.

Cahaba River Society, 322-5326.

Fish Habitat Enhancement Map. Write Alabama Power Co., P.O. Box 160, Montgomery, AL 36101.

Maps of Alabama Power Company Hydrogeneration, Lakes, Launch Sites, and Marinas. Web site: www.alapower.com/hydro

North Shelby Chamber of Commerce, P. O. Box 324, Pelham, AL 35124. 663-4542.   Web site: www.nscoc.com

South Shelby Chamber of Commerce, P. O. Box 396, Columbiana, AL 35051. 669-9001.

Accommodations:

Jemison Inn, 212 Alabama 191, Jemison, AL 35085. 688-2055.

Web site: www.bbonline.com/al/jemison

Oak Mountain State Park, 200 Terrace Drive (off Interstate 65, Exit 246), Pelham, AL 35124. 620-2520.

Web site: www.bham.net/oakmtn/

Restaurants:

Fox Valley Restaurant, 5745 County Road 17 at County Road 44, Maylene, AL 35114, Tue.-Thurs., 5 P.M.-9 P.M.; Fri.-Sat., 5 P.M.-10 P.M. 664-8341.

Uncle Bud's, 1201 First Avenue N., Alabaster, AL 35007, Mon.-Thurs., 5:30 A.M.-8 P.M.; Fri., 5:30 A.M.-8:30 P.M.; Sat., 5:30 A.M.-2 P.M. 664-3565.

Zapata Mexican Restaurant, 2005 Valleydale Road #3, Hoover, AL 35244. Sun.-Thurs., 11 A.M.-10 P.M.; Fri.-Sat., 11 A.M.-11 P.M. 733-1115.

25

CHOICES, CHOICES!

You can spend a lot of time sitting on the section of U.S. 280, the focus of this chapter, which will carry you from **Cahaba Heights** to **Chelsea.** Fortunately, you will not be contending with the weekday rush hours, when "rush" seems to be a misnomer because the lanes are clogged with traffic and definitely not "rushing." No, on the weekend, your time will be spent making choices. Buildings of brick and glass stand alone or dot shopping strips arranged artfully at the ends of squares of asphalt parking lots. As you travel east on this bustling thoroughfare, from Birmingham, Homewood, or Cahaba Heights, collections of businesses, stores, and restaurants stretch out toward each other until there is little break in the mercantile connection. Then, just after you pass Alabama 119, the scenery shifts from brick and glass to green, the road curves and ascends. Ahead lies a contrast with the glamour of new commerce and the serenity of a wooded retreat. You can have a little of both, but your first choice will be your base of operations, hotel or hideaway.

To simplify, zoom in on the space between Valleydale Road and Alabama 119. Centrally located and positioned above this busy corridor is the **Wingate Inn,** which serves corporation executives during the week, but understands the pursuit of leisure on weekends, too. This hotel is set far enough away from the busy-ness that when you sign your name in the guest book, you feel as though you have checked your load of responsibility at the front door. If you've come during warm weather, take a quick dip in the pool and consider your options for dinner.

Anyone who has ever eaten at **Lloyd's Restaurant** remembers it and returns. It lies just a mile and a quarter east of Valleydale Road on U.S. 280 on the left. This place is so popular, they stop letting people in after 9 P.M. The only time you won't have to wait for a table is when Auburn and Alabama are playing football. Lloyd's restaurant owners have not given in to the temptation to place a large TV in either of the two large dining rooms crammed with tables and booths. Friendly waitresses wave you in with a "sit where you can." The focus is on great food and friendships that are celebrated here at every lunch and dinner. So generous are the hamburger steak and fish platter servings that you may want to ask for a half order and save room for one of the homemade desserts. The lemon icebox pie is tart enough to offset the sugary crust. Together it's a good marriage.

Lloyd's has been a landmark since 1937 and is the only restaurant of its kind in the area. If the lines of fans outside the door have anything to say about it, people will continue to give directions to the rest of the commercial strip as "down the road from Lloyd's" for years to come.

Saturday morning you can stay at the Wingate and relax. Every breakfast appetite can be satisfied by the extensive offerings at the sumptuous breakfast buffet served from 6 A.M. to 9:30 A.M. Just because the world outside is in a hurry doesn't mean you have to be.

When you are ready to explore the shops and stores, start with the Brookhills Shopping Center on 280, next to Lloyd's. On the right-hand side of the center, look for **Moore Frames & Art,** an unusual frame shop where framing is considered an art, too. The surprise is that you can buy a **Daniel Moore** painting in this little shop that glistens with mirrors and handsomely displayed artwork of Moore and other artists. You might catch a glimpse of Moore himself. He is one of Alabama's most well-known and well-loved artists. If you visited the Paul Bryant Museum in Tuscaloosa, you saw several Moore paintings on display there. Moore's talent is in capturing and painting great moments in football so realistically that the onlooker feels the rush of adrenaline, too. Throughout the state, in homes, restaurants, sports grills, and cafés, wherever Alabama fans gather, look for a Moore painting or print.

Explore the length and breadth of this shopping extravaganza all the way to the Summit. When you turn around to head back toward the Wingate Inn, be sure to drive into the shops of **Colonnade.** Swoop around the drive and past the cinema and see the eateries and shops. Keep **Connie Kanakis'** in mind for Saturday dinner, if you can wait that long.

After hours of shopping up and down the U.S. 280 corridor, you may be ready for another setting. You could take a right on Alabama 119 and drive to **Oak Mountain State Park.** The many activities available there are described in the last chapter.

If you'd rather have lots of outdoors punctuated by a few shopping trips, you might prefer staying at **Twin Pines Resort & Conference Center,** considered one of the nine great rustic retreats in America. From Alabama 119 on U.S. 280, continue east on a drive that becomes more and more scenic. Go to Shelby County Road 43 North and turn left. Five minutes later turn right on 45 South. Two minutes later turn right again. The sign says it is one mile to Twin Pines. Three minutes later, you are there. Allow yourself about an hour and a half if you make this trip from downtown Birmingham. However, you may want to stop and look at wildflowers on the way.

Those who stay on the grounds of the 200-acre retreat center enjoy log cabin lodges, canoeing, paddle boats, tennis, softball, volleyball, hiking, fishing, and an ever-changing vista of the mountains across Lake Laura Lee. Hike out to the **Bob Saunders Family Covered Bridge,** featured in the World Guide of Covered Bridges. Listen to the sound of crickets and birds, feel the crunch of dirt and gravel under your feet, and breathe in the pines. Twin Pines is aptly named. You might catch a whiff of smoke coming from the creekstone fireplaces in the large dining room, which hosts corporate meetings but is also the scene of weddings. It's open to the public for Thanksgiving dinner, too.

To go a little deeper into the countryside, leave Twin Pines and turn right on Shelby County Road 43, go to Vandiver, and turn left on Alabama 25, which crosses Coosa Mountain from Vandiver to Dunavant. This is a 15-minute trip across the mountain on a serpentine road. It takes about 22 minutes to drive from Twin Pines to U.S. 78 West at Leeds. From there you could go left on Alabama 119 and return to U.S. 280. The mountain views are breathtaking. So are the hairpin turns. This is not a good trip for anyone who gets carsick easily, but careful drivers who love to "ooh" and "aah" around each bend will be glad they took time to explore.

If you are not in a hurry to return to U.S. 280, and you are ready to eat, retrace your steps, cross U.S. 280 on Shelby County Road 43. This will take you to Old U.S. 280. Ahead on the left you should see the new **Bernie's Grill.** If the new restaurant has not been completed by the time you read this, you can drive out to the old Bernie's and

Fountain and lake at Twin Pines Conference Center. (Photo by Joan Broerman)

Sanders covered bridge. (Photo by Neal Broerman)

enjoy homemade salads and desserts plus pork so tender it has to be hand-pulled because it can't be sliced. The new restaurant will replace the old one, but as long as Bernard Tamburello is the owner and chef, the food will be terrific. To get to the original Bernie's, continue east on Old U.S. 280 until you are one block from the light at Chelsea Corners. Turn left on Chesser Road before you get to the light. If you miss the first turn, you can turn left at the light and go toward the fire station, then turn left and you will pass in front of Bernie's. Another landmark is the post office on your left. The fire station and Bernie's are behind it.

After lunch at Bernie's, drive east on U.S. 280 about 40 miles to Alexander City and turn left on Tallapoosa County 22, then right on Tallapoosa County Road 49. You'll arrive at **Horseshoe Bend National Military Park,** where General Andrew Jackson defeated the Creek Indians in the Battle of Horseshoe Bend in 1814. The Creeks then ceded almost half of present-day Alabama to the United States. The museum has an electric map for plotting the progress of the bloody battle. By some accounts, it was here that Chief Junaluska shielded General Jackson and saved his life. Later, as the Trail of Tears wound its painful way west, it's said the chief regretted his heroics. Write to the park for a schedule of living history programs and come prepared to learn about the hardships and sacrifices of camp life.

You could save the military park for Sunday and take either the 3-mile driving tour or the 2.8-mile hiking trail. Both trails follow the tour stops. Audio tapes that you can rent or purchase augment the historical markers.

If you return to U.S. 280 for one last glimpse of the glittering galaxy of eating and shopping opportunities, the only problem you will have is deciding where to eat supper. Choices, choices!

Area Code: (205)

Getting There:

U.S. 280 runs from its start at Interstate 20/59, Exit 126A, in Birmingham to the Georgia border near Phenix City. The section described in this chapter lies just east of Interstate 459, Exit 19, and extends into Shelby, Coosa, Tallapoosa, and Lee Counties.

Where and When:

Twin Pines Resort & Conference Center, 1200 Twin Pines Road (Shelby County Road 45), Sterrett, AL 35147. 672-7575.

Web site: www.twinpinesresort.com

The Goal Line Stand. (Original painting by Daniel A. Moore, courtesy NewLife Art, Inc.)

Horseshoe Bend National Military Park, 11288 Horseshoe Bend Road, Daviston, AL 36256. Daily, 8 A.M.-5 P.M. (256) 234-7111.

Moore Frames & Art, 5287 U.S. 280 S., Suite 263, Birmingham, AL 35242. Mon.-Fri., 10 A.M.-6:30 P.M.; Sat., 10 A.M.-5 P.M. 991-1560.

Information:

Alabama Vacation Guide. Call 1-800-ALABAMA (252-2262).

North Shelby Chamber of Commerce, P. O. Box 324, Pelham, AL 35124. 663-4542.   Web site: www.nscoc.com

Accommodations:

Wingate Inn, 800 Corporate Ridge Drive, Birmingham, AL 35242. Breakfast buffet, 6 A.M.-9:30 A.M. 995-8586.

Web site: www.wingateinns.com

Restaurants:

Bernie's Grill, 1330 Chesser Drive (off U.S. 280), Chelsea, AL 35043. Tue.-Thurs., 6:30 A.M.-8:30 P.M.; Fri.-Sat., 6:30 A.M.- 9 P.M.; Sun., 11 A.M.- 2 P.M.; Mon., 6:30 A.M.-2 P.M. 678-6513.

Connie Kanakis' Café, 3423 Colonnade Parkway, Shops at the

Colonnade, Birmingham, AL 35243. Mon.-Fri., 11 A.M.-2:30 P.M.; 5 P.M.-10 P.M.; Sat., 5 P.M.-10 P.M. 967-5775.

Heavenly Ham, 120 Inverness Corners, Hoover, AL 35242. Mon.-Fri., 10 A.M.-6 P.M.; Sat., 10 A.M.-4 P.M. 980-0501.

Lloyd's Restaurant, 5301 U.S. 280 S., Birmingham, AL 35242. Daily, 11 A.M.-9 P.M. 991-5530.

Ragtime Café, 2080 Valleydale Road, Hoover, AL 35244. Mon.-Sat., 11 A.M.-10 P.M. 988-5323.

Tin Roof BBQ, 4524 Valleydale Road, Southlake Village, Hoover, AL 35244. Mon.-Sat., 11 A.M.-9 P.M.; Sun., 11 A.M.-3 P.M. 987-4002.

Major Annual Events:

Black History Exhibit, Sylacauga—February. (256) 245-4016.

Horseshoe Bend National Military Park, Anniversary of the Battle of Horseshoe Bend—May.

Bruno's Memorial Classic Senior PGA Tour, Greystone Golf Club, Birmingham—May. 991-4747.

Horseshoe Bend National Military Park, Anniversary of the park opening—August.

Clarkson Covered Bridge. (Photo by Neal Broerman)

26

CATCHING
THE DREAM

Dreams have a history in this part of the state. For German refugee Col. John G. Cullmann, the dream was to establish a colony for his countrymen in America. It was the early 1870s and for Cullmann, Alabama became home.

For this weekend getaway, bring shoes that will carry you comfortably over pavement and pebbles. In jeans paired with a sweater or jacket, you'll make transitions easily from indoor to outdoor sightseeing. Few days will be cold enough to require more layers of clothing. Long pants, even in hot weather, will protect your legs from stickers, prickers, and bugs on trails or jaunts into the unspoiled countryside. A picnic cooler filled with sandwiches and cold drinks will be a welcome companion, too. You'll be able to replenish your supply throughout the next two days. Of course, you'll want to bring binoculars and a camera.

Knowledgeable hikers carry the following: maps, compass, whistle, flashlight, sharp knife, fire starter, waterproof matches, first-aid kit, extra food, and warm clothing. We hope you won't need the whistle, but if you do, three sharp blasts mean you need help. A layer of warm clothing could prevent hypothermia if you get wet or lost or if the temperature drops suddenly. For short trips, carry bottled water. Never drink it from a lake or stream, no matter how pure it looks.

The interstate assortment of hotels, motels, and restaurants near **Cullman** stand ready to serve you. Choose your lodging along Interstate 65 and get ready for a range of experiences.

The **Cullman County Museum** will give you a fine acquaintance with the life in Cullman as the good colonel lived it, but the museum is not open on Saturday, so begin your day by traveling to **Smith Lake,** a fisherman's dream. You can get there from Interstate 65 via several exits south of Cullman. This 21,200-acre lake is 315 feet deep in places. Thirty-pound fish are commonplace, and trophy fish become stars in exciting stories. Fly-fishing at night has become popular here, and it's said the pier lights bring out the largemouth bass, spotted bass, striped bass, and bream. You will want to take a look at the lake in daylight first, however. The cold waters below Smith Lake Dam are ideal for fly-fishing for rainbow trout, which are restocked every 60 days by the Alabama Game and Fish Department. **Riverside Outfitters and Fly Shop** has been on the lake for 10 years, and owners John and Elizabeth Eisenbarth have thought of everything from the needs of novices, elderly, and disabled adventurers to the skilled sportsman looking for the only trout-fishing stream in the state. Another eagerly sought catch is red-eye bass, which Elizabeth says is found only in Alabama in this water system.

All you need for fly-fishing is provided in a four-hour tour that John leads weekly. Wear comfortable clothes, sunglasses and a hat, and carry your Alabama fishing license. John will bring the necessary fishing equipment, including the waders and boots. He'll even supply sunscreen and insect repellant. His happy clients include octogenarians. If you really want serenity, talk to Elizabeth about renting the farmhouse on the lake. This could be an entire weekend of hiking, fishing, and canoeing, all in the hands of knowledgeable guides. Birdwatchers and photographers should also take note that scenery, wildlife, and a wide variety of birds offer excellent photo opportunities.

More astonishing sights lie ahead. Take Alabama 157 (Interstate 65, Exit 310) to the **Bankhead National Forest Trading Post,** near Moulton at the head of the **Bankhead Forest Heritage Trail.** You can pick up maps and supplies here and see lots of interesting pottery and local artwork at the same time.

For now your goal will be to see wildflowers and waterfalls in as short a hike as possible. Ask at the trading post for a short-term plan, but take notes for later weekends. Camping options are superb, from car and pop-up sites in **Brushy Creek** to primitive areas in **Sipsey Wilderness.** Bring your own horse or canoe. Rentals are not yet available.

The **Corinth Recreation Area** has swimming, fishing, and boating. Tents and other recreational vehicles can set up here and be close to water and hot showers. This section, including the shooting range, is also fully accessible for those with disabilities. Corinth Recreation Area is located on Smith Lake in Winston County. Take U.S. 278 East from Double Springs for four miles, then turn right (south) and go three miles on Winston County Road 57. Joe Nicholson, who oversees the recreation program for the four national forests in Alabama, says that with every upgrade they are trying to make facilities accessible. The Forest Service is working to eliminate barriers "so that people with disabilities can have the experience of a primitive camping trip without feeling like they are camping in a parking lot."

Additionally, Clear Creek and Brushy Lake Recreation Areas are accessible, but Brushy Lake's paved walk has moderate to steep inclines. The Sipsey Wilderness has about 34 miles of hiking trails. Some are challenging. This range of difficulty should be a warning to seniors, families with young children, and weekend wanderers who don't want to spend the next few days rubbing sore muscles.

If you dream of quiet places, **Dream Valley Ranch** in **Blountsville,** back near Cullman, is another good place to seek them. About 50 miles from Huntsville, Gadsden, or Birmingham, this 740-acre spread is owned by D. W. Hart and has 12 miles of trail for riding horses (yours) from 8 A.M. to dusk. Mountain bikes are welcome, too. The view and silence enjoyed from a rocking chair on the porch of the red cedar cabin, built in 1820 is worth the trek. There is a bathhouse with water near the wooded picnic grounds, but this is a back-to-basics place. Pack lightly with necessities, including insect repellent.

For you who characterize a hunting trip as a search for bargains, set aside a few hours to shop the **Warehouse District** in Cullman. We were there when the town was decorated for Christmas. The glitter-sparkled windows showcased gorgeous clothes and sturdy antiques. Park in the side lot. Other parking areas are restricted. Enter the shops from the street, not the end of the building.

Two blocks from the Warehouse District, step through the door of **A Touch of German** and be greeted by a wall of German clocks celebrating time with music, chimes, and soft cuckoo calls. Owner Peggy Grobe (pronounce the "e") says the originator of this delightful store wanted to honor Colonel Cullmann and his German roots. Other countries are represented too, however. Handsome nutcrackers stand guard over delectable chocolate that calls the name of every chocoholic who ambles in. European willow baskets hang from the rafters. A selection of Christmas ornaments and Fontanini nativities beckons holiday shoppers. Dutch Blue Delft and nested dolls from Poland are always appropriate gift choices.

Whenever you are in the mood for lunch or dinner, two excellent menus are waiting for your perusal. **Provence Market** is at the end of the Warehouse District. Service and food are excellent. I feasted on the signature chicken salad, called the entrée salad, with fresh fruit and sweet bread. My husband ordered the corn chowder and discovered it was a meal in itself. We talked with owner Kim Calvert as we left and understood why the waitresses were so enthusiastic and eager to please. The owner's bubbly personality is pervasive.

A second dining choice is the **All Steak** restaurant, so called because more than 60 years ago there was no room on the sign for the rest of the name, All Steak Hamburgers, and no money to make the sign bigger. There is more than steak here, however, and the hours of business mean you can eat every meal here every day except Sunday supper. It would be out of place to lick your fingers in the midst of formal tablecloths and centerpieces, but the orange rolls, for which the restaurant is known, will tempt you to do just that. The All Steak is located downtown, above the Cullman Savings Bank. Don't be shy about driving up the parking ramp to the third floor.

All that being said, you may want to begin your Sunday with breakfast at All Steak, followed by a visit to the **Ave Maria Grotto.** The peaceful, sloped walks meander for about two blocks among 125 small stone and cement structures designed and brought into artistic being by Brother Joseph Zoettel, O.S.B. A monk of St. Bernard Abbey, the only Benedictine monastery in Alabama, Brother Joseph constructed the miniature reproductions of beloved churches, shrines, and other famous buildings from discarded pieces of building materials. He built the first replica around 1912 and the last one, the Lourdes Basilica miniature, in 1958 when he was 80. Since your tour will be self-guided, take as much time as you need. Allow at least 30 minutes.

Leave the peace of the abbey and go back through town to cross Interstate 65. You'll soon come to the **Cullman Flea Market,** which bills itself as the "nicest and cleanest in the South." Here you will see all kinds of fresh vegetables, dolls, knives, computers, tools, furniture, and just about everything else. Most displays are housed indoors, where the temperature is comfortable. Restrooms are well marked, and you can find a snack here and there or a cup of coffee. Carry your bargains to the car and travel U.S. 278 W. (Interstate 65,

Exit 308) to the **Clarkson Covered Bridge,** site of the 1863 Battle of Hog Mountain. This is one of Alabama's largest covered truss bridges, and it is on the National Register of Historic Places. Picnic here or hike, but be wary. We watched a snake sun himself on a rock in the creek. If snakes make you think about running, you will appreciate the talents of world-record setter Jesse Owens.

In the 1936 Olympics in Berlin, **Jesse Owens** became the first athlete to win four gold medals in a single year. Take Alabama 157, just west of the intersection with Alabama 36; turn right onto County Road 81 and see the **Jesse Owens Memorial Park and Museum.** High above the neighboring cornfield, a bigger-than-life Owens runs through the Olympic rings, forever bronzed by Birmingham sculptor **Branko Medenica.** A replica of Owens' boyhood Alabama home is on the grounds and looks out on cotton fields just as Owens must have, too. Listen to creaking sounds in the old cabin and imagine the triumphs of this son of a black sharecropper who made a mockery of Hitler's dream of a master race.

Turn right when you leave, then left, and go about half a mile to the **Oakville Indian Mounds** park and museum, which features the largest 2,000-year-old Woodland Indian Mound in Alabama. The museum is a replica of a seven-sided, 8,000-square-foot Cherokee Council House. You'll see a 12-foot-tall statue of **Sequoyah** carved by **David Goodlett** and thousands of artifacts dating as far back as 10,000 B.C.

The seven sides of the council house represent the sacred **Cherokee** number seven. Seven directions were recognized by the Cherokee: North, South, East, West, up, down, and inside the person. Cherokee clans numbered seven: Blue, Bird, Deer, Wolf, Paint, Long Hair, and Wild Potato.

A descendent of the Blue clan supplies the gift shop with dream catchers. It's said that if you hang a dream catcher over your bed, it will catch the bad dreams and let the good ones through. In the morning, the sun will burn up the bad dreams.

To conclude your weekend, return to Cullman and the **Cullman County Museum.** A seven-foot-tall Indian warrior carved from a sweet gum tree dominates the first room to the right of the lobby, and you know you are in for a trip through another era. Although the museum is a replica of Colonel Cullmann's home—the original burned in 1912—it is a repository of thousands of artifacts from Cullman's history. Cullman, the city, is one man's dream come true.

Jesse Owens Memorial. (Photo by Neal Broerman)

Oakville Indian Mound & Museum. (Photo by Neal Broerman)

Area Code: (256)

Getting There:

Cullman is located at Interstate 65, Exit 308.

Where and When:

A Touch of German, 218 First Avenue S.E., Cullman, AL 35055. Mon.-Sat., 9:30 A.M.-5:30 P.M. 739-4592. Admission.

Web site: www.cullmanchamber.org

Ave Maria Grotto, St. Bernard Abbey, 1600 St. Bernard Drive S.E., Cullman, AL 35055. Daily, 7A.M. to dark. 734-4110. Admission.

Web site: www.sbabbeyprep.org

Bankhead National Forest, P. O. Box 117, Moulton, AL 35650. 974-6166.

Bankhead National Forest, Wild Alabama Trading Post and Cultural Headquarters, Alabama 33 at Alabama 36.

Clarkson Covered Bridge Park, 1240 Cullman County Road 1043 (off U.S. 278), Cullman, AL 35056. Daily, 9 A.M.-sunset. 734-3369.

Corinth Recreation Area (Bankhead National Forest), Winston County Road 57, Double Springs, AL 35553. 832-4470.

Cullman County Museum, 211 Second Avenue N.E., Cullman, AL 35055. Mon.-Wed., Fri., 9 A.M.-4 P.M.; Thurs., 9 A.M.-noon; Sun., 1:30 P.M.-4:30 P.M. 739-1258. Admission.

Cullman Flea Market, U.S. 278 at Interstate 65, Exit 308, Cullman, AL 35055. Sat.-Sun., 8 A.M.-5 P.M. 739-0910.

Dream Valley Ranch, 1137 Moore Road, Hanceville, AL. (205) 429-3760. Admission.

Jesse Owens Museum, Lawrence County Road 187, off Hwy 157 at Moulton, Danville, AL 35619. Tue.-Sat., 11 A.M.-3 P.M.; Sun., 1 P.M.-5 P.M. 974-3636. Admission.

Lewis Smith Dam, 640 Powerhouse Road (off Walker County Road 43), Jasper, AL 35504. Mon.-Fri., 7 A.M.-2 P.M. 387-2567.

Miguel's Gift Shop, 273 Schwaiger Road (Interstate 65, Exit 304), Good Hope, AL 35055. Sun.-Thurs., 11 A.M.-9 P.M.; Fri.-Sat., 11 A.M.-10 P.M. 734-5200.

National Forests in Alabama, 2946 Chestnut Street, Montgomery, AL 36107. 832-4470.

Oakville Indian Mounds Park and Museum, 1219 Lawrence County Road 187, off Alabama 157, Danville, AL 35619. Fri. 9 A.M.-5 P.M.; Sat., 10 A.M.-6 P.M.; Sun., noon-5 P.M. 905-2494.

Riverside Outfitters and Fly Shop, 17027 Alabama 69 N (2 miles south of Lewis Smith Dam on Alabama 69), Jasper, AL 35504. 287-0050.

Web site: www.1flyfish.net

Warehouse District, 100 Second Avenue N.E., Cullman, AL 35055.
Woodland Ceremonial Mound and Copena Burial Mound, 1219 Lawrence County Road 187, Danville, AL 35619. Mon.-Fri., 8A.M.-4:30 P.M.; Sat.-Sun., 1 P.M.-4:30 P.M. 905-2494.

Information:
Maps of Alabama Power Company Hydrogeneration, Lakes, Launch Sites, and Marinas.   Web site: www.alapower.com/hydro
Alabama Vacation Guide. Call 1-800-ALABAMA (252-2262).
Cullman Area Chamber of Commerce, 211 Second Avenue N.E., Cullman, AL 35056. 734-0454.
                                    Web site: www.cullmanchamber.org
Cullman Convention and Tourism Bureau, P. O. Box 1104, Cullman, AL 35056. 734-0454.
Fish Habitat Enhancement Map. Write Alabama Power Company, P. O. Box 160, Montgomery, AL 36101.
Riverside Outfitters and Fly Shop, 17027 Alabama 69 N, Jasper, AL 35504. 287-0050.   Web site: www.1flyfish.net

Accommodations:
Chain and independent motels are available along Interstate 65. See the Alabama Vacation Guide. Call 1-800-ALABAMA (252-2262).

Restaurants:
Miguel's, 273 Schwaiger Road (Interstate 65, Exit 304), Good Hope, AL 35055. Sun.-Thurs., 11 A.M.-9 P.M.; Fri.-Sat., 11 A.M.-10 P.M. 734-5200.
Provence Market, 105 First Avenue N.E., Cullman, AL 35055, Mon.-Sat., 11A.M.-2 P.M.; Wed.-Sat., 4 P.M.-8 P.M. 734-8002.
All Steak, 314 Second Avenue S.W., Cullman, AL 35055. Mon.-Wed., 6 A.M.-9 P.M.; Thur.-Sat., 6A.M.-10P.M.; Sun 6:30A.M.-9 P.M. 734-4322.

Major Annual Events:
Mid-Summer Jam, Smith Lake Park.
Oktoberfest, Cullman—October. 734-0454.

27

GO WEST!

Red Bay is the kind of town where people sit on the front porches a few yards back from the oak-lined streets and wave to passersby. The wave is not a perfunctory dismissal kind of wave, but a "Hey, how are you?" greeting, as if they really care. The town of 3,100 has its own arts center, unusual in a town this size, and thereby hangs a tale.

In the early nineties, the Community Spirit Bank sponsored a "Breakfast With Santa" event, held inside the bank. The crowd grew. Children had to sit down with Santa in shifts. Then one December so many children showed up that when the bank closed at noon, some youngsters had to be turned away. This did not sit well with the bank's executive vice president, Pat Nelson, who is especially Christmas-minded. It bothered her all winter, and then she and the bank president, Billy Bolton, had a vision that involved a bowling alley in the center of town. The building was empty that hot, sticky July day when the two bank officers walked through it, but they pictured it filled with children at holiday time, all of them having breakfast with Santa together, not in shifts. Then they took the vision one more step. Why not turn this building next to the library into an arts center the whole town could enjoy all year?

Major obstacles had to be overcome, but if you walk into the **Arts and Entertainment Center** today, you will see the happy ending that came six months after the idea took hold. Two entrances lead into a well-appointed lobby furnished with antiques and comfortable chairs. The elegant banquet hall glitters with chandeliers and mirrors, a

Nelson's Arboretum. (Photo by Neal Broerman)

proper setting for the talents of local caterers. Not only do the people of Red Bay celebrate anniversaries and hold large parties in this room, but groups from outside the city schedule events here, too. The intimate theater is the scene of community and area productions, and a third room is the Garden Room, so named because of the realistic mural running the length of it. Do you smell perfume or the flowers in the garden?

When Pat Nelson isn't turning discarded buildings into artistic endeavors or handling her tasks at the bank, she and her husband, Tommy, the town mayor, run a relaxing home-away-from-home bed and breakfast, **Nelson's Arboretum Inn.** Breakfast is served early, at 7 A.M., and often includes chocolate gravy. During summer months this hearty meal will be served poolside. Thanks is given for each meal. Blessings are many here, and guests become friends.

The house is filled with antiques and furniture upholstered in white, the perfect foil for the mirrors and baroque accents. The guesthouse across from the pool accommodates retreats.

Every Christmas, Pat brings 30 bales of hay into her home and builds a nativity scene in the atrium. While carols play softly in the background, ethereal angels turn their heads toward the stable. Golden wise men approach.

Throughout the house, Santas and glistening ornaments trim the tables in the hall, the formal dining room, breakfast room, and all the bedside tables in the stylishly decorated bedrooms. Gilded gold-and-white ceramic animals populate the hearth.

When you are ready to explore the town of Red Bay, you may wonder where the bay is. Actually, the town is named for the red-berried bay tree.

Golfers can make arrangements to play at the **Redmont Country Club,** and gift shop browsers can choose a few quiet blocks in the middle of town to window shop or speak to pleasant store clerks. It's estimated that Red Bay's homegrown motor home industry brings in 8500 travelers annually to order, upgrade, or service their homes on wheels. Voices with accents from around the world blend at the shop counters and cafés.

Swamp John's is the place to eat in Red Bay. Although the ladies behind the steam tables in the back of this gas station and sundry store serve meatloaf and gravy and all kinds of stick-to-your-ribs dishes throughout the week, Thursday is catfish day. John Shewbart is Swamp John. All he set out to do was cook up some catfish for his buddies. This became a weekly ritual until someone said it was so good he ought to sell it. On Thursday, which is the only day catfish is served, 700-800 plates of fried catfish, potatoes fried or baked, and cole slaw or baked beans pass over the counter to eager customers. Some stay to eat in the small dining room or the booths that line the side of the store. Others drive up to the gas pumps, yank down the lever, run inside and fill up large cardboard boxes with dozens of hot carry-out boxes, dash back outside, finish the transaction and take off. One can only imagine the crowd of hungry people they will soon make happy. If there is any way you can start your weekend on Thursday, you will congratulate yourself on walking through Swamp John's door by 4:30 P.M. Everything about this experience is unique, and the cashier's low total will amaze you.

To start a new day, after you've enjoyed breakfast with the Nelson's, a side trip to the **Coon Dog** Cemetery will give you a new perspective on the family pooch. Key Underwood buried his famous coon dog "Troop" there on Labor Day, 1937. This was a favorite hunting area and seemed a fitting place for the old dog's last resting place. Since then, over 100 coon dogs have been buried there by

Swamp John's Restaurant & Gas Station. (Photo by Neal Broerman)

*Coon Dog Monument at Coon
Dog Memorial Graveyard.*
(Photo by Neal Broerman)

*Old Tip grave marker at Coon
Dog Memorial Graveyard.*
(Photo by Neal Broerman)

mourning owners. Each Labor Day a celebration is held in the park, including bluegrass music, buck dancing, and a liar's contest. To get there, take Alabama 24 E. to Alabama 247 N. Go about 13 miles and turn left at the sign to the cemetery. Just when you think you have taken a wrong turn and will never get there, you *are* there.

Return to Red Bay and head for **Russellville** on Alabama 24. Franklin County was named in honor of Benjamin Franklin. After a number of political skirmishes, which always make good stories, especially when told on a front porch, Russellville became the county seat. The courthouse sits in the center of town. Also of interest are two lovely Victorian-style private residences on the main street. Pass these homes and drive up the hill to **Pilgrim's Place** BBQ, where you can put together a lunch to take to several picnic spots.

Pilgrim's Place is named for its owners, Fred and Sue Pilgrim. Sue has numerous specials to her credit, and she names many of them for her grandchildren. Although not named for a grandchild, the Mayflower Brownie is a treat you must sample. Sue tops a fudge brownie with marshmallows and pecans then frosts it with melt-in-your-mouth chocolate frosting.

You have several choices for your picnic place. Down U.S. 43 you'll come to the **Dismals Canyon**. This is a privately owned and operated national landmark of the National Park Service named for tiny creatures called dismalites that light up the canyon at summer twilight. The only other place you are likely to see this phenomenon is New Zealand.

The Indians consider this sacred ground, and *Reader's Digest* called it one of America's most interesting and yet uncrowded places to visit. Staff shortages on the edges of the season make park openings uncertain, but at the height of summer, mountain biking and canoeing enthusiasts revel in this area, and so do fishermen.

Bear Creek Lakes is another choice destination, whether you want to picnic, fish, or float. The system was originally built to aid in flood control, but the recreation possibilities are endless. Hundreds of thousands of vacationers come every year to swim, ski, camp, and fish in the four lakes—Cedar Creek, Little Bear, Upper Bear, and Bear Creek. The **Bear Creek Floatway** is rated one of the best canoe trips in Alabama. If fishing is not your favorite thing to do, bring a camera. Your pictures will make a fine "catch."

If you elected to eat your brownie at Pilgrim's instead of packing a lunch, you could be hungry by now. Back in Russellville, **Speedy Pig** has been a local favorite for about 20 years. The dipping sauces developed

Treetops at Horseshoe Bend on Bear Creek. (Photo by Joan Broerman)

Cowcomber leaf (wild magnolia) with fountain pen. (Photo by Joan Broerman)

here now enjoy a worldwide reputation and are distributed through chain stores. But why buy them when you can try them here first?

From Bear Lakes turn the car toward Haleyville and follow the winding country roads through fields of corn, cotton, and soybeans to **Natural Bridge of Alabama,** the longest natural bridge east of the Rockies. U.S. 278 will take you to the town called Natural Bridge. Privately owned by Barbara and Jimmy Deaton, the bridge is actually two arches, side by side. The largest arch is 148 feet long, 33 feet wide, 8 feet thick, and 60 feet high. Atop the sandstone bridge is the fossil of a tree that has been traced back millions of years. The trail leads underneath the double arches and around a loop behind them to the other side. Even though the path is easy to follow, good walking shoes are important here. Watch for the high steps. It takes about half an hour to walk through, and you'll see 27 varieties of ferns and several large, old Canadian hemlocks. Unusual is the wild magnolia or cowcomber, which has a leaf cluster up to one yard wide and blooms one foot in diameter. You'll hear the soothing sound of water falling over rocks. Relax. The natural setting is so blissful, some people even get married here.

The gift shop features crafts by Alabama artisans such as **Morris Barber**, who made his first potter's wheel from the gear box of a cotton picker when he was 71. His message is it's never too late to do what you have always wanted to do.

Have you always wondered about the free state of Winston? When states were seceding from the Union, Winston County folks decided to secede from the state. You'll enjoy learning about these sturdy independent thinkers at **Looney's Tavern,** where Alabama's Official Outdoor Musical Drama takes place. *Incident at Looney's Tavern* is about young **Winston County** schoolteacher Christopher Sheats. A talented cast drawn from neighboring towns brings Christopher and his friends to life. As events progress, you'll come to care about each proud family member struggling against the horror of the times.

First things first. From Natural Bridge, take U.S. 278 to Interstate 65 outside Cullman and choose a motel. Call ahead for play tickets, and make a dinner cruise reservation on the *Free State Lady,* too. Captained by Neal Shipman, the boat plies the water of Lewis Smith Lake on each show date. Captain Shipman is a Civil War historian, an entertainer whose tall tales will keep you chuckling, and he will get you back to the theater in time for the show.

Your motel should be about a half hour from Looney's Tavern. If you can't get there in time to board the boat, you can eat in **Sister Sara's Kitchen,** near the outdoor auditorium, which is a satisfying, reasonably priced buffet. Take a few minutes to visit **Carolyn's Gifts** downstairs. Bring a cushion and take your time descending the steep concrete steps to your seat. Make any special needs known when you call for tickets.

If you can spend Sunday in the William B. **Bankhead National Forest,** count yourself fortunate. From Cullman take Alabama 157 W. about 24 miles to Alabama 36 W. It's about 8 miles to the Trading Post at Alabama 33. Pick up a map of the recreation areas scattered throughout the forest. Camp, picnic, fish, hike, hunt, ride horseback, or swim. **Smith Lake** lies partially within the 21,000 acres of pine and hardwoods. The lake is bordered by many bluffs and outcroppings, with over 500 miles of shoreline. Native birds sing their appreciation. All a poet needs is a pen and paper.

Go south of Cullman and you'll feel south of the border at **Miguel's** Mexican restaurant. Choices and servings should match your outdoors appetite. Families return often because the fare is consistently delicious. Waiting for a table is a pleasant opportunity to explore the gift shop, but it's never as much time as you need.

Area Code: (256)

Getting There:
Red Bay can be reached from Interstate 65 by going to Decatur, Exit 334, and taking Alabama 24 W. Red Bay is about 65 miles from Decatur.

Where and When:
Bankhead National Forest, South Main Street, Double Springs, AL 35553. 489-5111.

Barber's Pottery at Belgreen, 2490 Cotton Gin Road, Russellville, AL 35653. 332-4017.

Bear Creek Lakes, Bear Creek Development Authority, PO Box 670, Russellville, AL 35653. Apr.-Oct. 15th. 332-4392; (877) 367-2232.

Bear Creek Scenic River, Bear Creek Development Authority, PO Box 670, Russellville, AL 35653. 332-4392; (877) 367-2232.

Carolyn's Gifts in **Sister Sara's Kitchen,** 22400 U.S. 278, Double Springs, AL 35553. 489-3500.   Web site: www.bham.net/looneys

Coon Dog Memorial Graveyard, Alabama 247, Coondog Cemetery Road, Tuscumbia, AL 35674.

Dismals Canyon, 901 Franklin County Road 8, Phil Campbell, AL 35581. Memorial Day-Labor Day, open daily; closed Dec.-Feb. 993-4559; (800) 808-7998. Admission.   Web site: www.dismalscanyon.com

Lewis Smith Dam, 640 Powerhouse Road (off Walker County Road 43), Jasper, AL 35504. Mon.-Fri., 7 A.M.-2 P.M. 387-2567.

Looney's Outdoor Theater and Park, 22400 U.S. 278, Double Springs, AL, 35553. 489-5000; (800) 566-6397. Admission.

Web site: www.bham.net/looneys

Miguel's gift shop, 273 Schwaiger Road (Interstate 65, Exit 304), Good Hope, AL 35055. Sun.-Thurs., 11 A.M.-9 P.M.; Fri.-Sat., 11 A.M.-10 P.M. 734-5200.

Natural Bridge of Alabama, U.S. 278, West of Alabama 13, Natural Bridge, AL 35577. 486-5330. Admission.

Red Bay Arts and Entertainment Center, Community Spirit Bank, P.O. Box 449, Red Bay, AL 35582.

Redmont Country Club, Country Club Drive, Red Bay AL. 356-9971.

Information:

Alabama Mountain Lakes Tourist Association, 25062 North Street, Mooresville, AL 35649. 350-3500.

Bankhead Heritage Trail System Map, Wild Alabama, P.O. Box 117, Moulton, AL 35650. 974-6166.

Fish Habitat Enhancement Map. Write Alabama Power Company, P. O. Box 160, Montgomery, AL 36101.

Franklin County Chamber of Commerce, P. O. Box 44, Russellville, AL 35653. 332-1760.

Web site: www.getaway.net/fklcoc

Maps of Alabama Power Hydrogeneration, Lakes, Launch Sites, and Marinas.   Web site: www.alapower.com/hydro

Guide Services:

Dwight Hargett, Guide to Big Bear Lake, Russellville, AL. 332-2390.

Gary Fleming, Guide to Big Bear Lake, Russellville, AL. 331-0509.

Accommodations:

Chain and independent motels are available along Interstate 65. See the **Alabama Vacation Guide.** Call 1-800-ALABAMA (252-2262).

Nelson's Arboretum Inn Bed & Breakfast, 201 Tenth Avenue N.W., Red Bay, AL 35582. 356-2681.

Restaurants:

Free State Lady Riverboat, 22400 U.S. 278, Double Springs, AL 35553. By reservation only. 489-3500.

Web site: www.bham.net/looneys

Miguel's, 273 Schwaiger Road (Interstate 65, Exit 304), Good Hope, AL 35055. Sun.-Thurs., 11 A.M.-9 P.M.; Fri.-Sat., 11 A.M.-10 P.M. 734-5200.

Pilgrim's Place, 1314 Jackson Avenue, Russellville, AL. Wed.-Sat., 10 A.M.-7 P.M. 332-1007.

Sister Sara's Kitchen, 22400 U.S. 278, Double Springs, AL 35553. 489-3500.   Web site: www.bham.net/looneys

Speedy Pig, 13670 U.S. 43, Russellville, AL. Mon.-Sat., 10 A.M.-8 P.M. 332-3380.   Web site: www.speedypig.com

Swamp John's, 5181 Alabama 24, Red Bay, AL 35582. Mon.-Fri., 10 A.M.-7 P.M. 356-2300.

Major Annual Events:

Watermelon Festival, Russellville—Third weekend of August.

Christmas Open House, Natural Bridge of Alabama—Weekend before Thanksgiving.

28

THE MOOD IS BLUES

In August, the town of **Florence** gives in to the blues. Notes squeezed through a golden horn reach out from the pen and piano of a man long gone but never forgotten. The **Handy Festival** remembers Florence native W.C. Handy as the "Father of the Blues." His music flows from cafés, pubs, parks, lawns of libraries and churches, malls, and parking lots. Wherever musicians gather, eager listeners settle on a bench, a blanket, or a folding chair, or simply stand and sway, their moments transformed by rhythmical magic. It's Handy Week.

Throughout the first week of August, a talented roster of local and nationally known musicians weave their blend of blues, jazz, and spirituals through the coordinated events of Street Strut, Riverside Jazz, Sweetwater Swing, Handy Nights, and the ABC's of Jazz. Even the Web page sets toes a-tapping as the long list of parades, receptions, movies, and even sports events scrolls by. It's safe to say any day or night (or all week) you choose, will be right.

Those who live in the Quad Cities—**Florence, Sheffield, Muscle Shoals,** and **Tuscumbia**—already have a place to stay, but you will need to make your plans early. A good central location for attending the Handy Festival or for making the **Quad Cities** a weekend getaway on its own is the **Holiday Inn** in Sheffield. The big hotel feeling is minimized by small sitting areas in a warm, welcoming lobby. Fresh-perked coffee wafts an invitation to enjoy the dining room just steps away from the front desk. Hang your bathrobe in the closet of your home away from home and hurry out to see the sights.

View from the roof of the Renaissance Tower. (Photo by Neal Broerman)

The view from the top is always heady, and the sights you will see from the dining room at the top of the 300-foot **Renaissance Tower** are dizzying. The night sky glows with the lights of the Quad Cities and weekend promises. Enjoy steak or seafood at the **Renaissance Grille** or dive into the triple cheese concoction smothering chicken Rotel and plan your days ahead.

Sheffield, where you are staying, began as a trading post in 1815. It was developed in 1816 by a group of land speculators including General Andrew Jackson and General John Coffee. However, the speculators switched their attentions to Florence, across the Tennessee River. Later, in 1885, Sheffield was named for the iron-manufacturing city in Yorkshire, England. By 1900 five blast furnaces announced the city's intentions of capitalizing on the same natural resources undergirding Birmingham's industrial success. Florence, where you are dining, was named for the hometown of the Italian architect who laid out the town. Tuscumbia was the site of a Chickasaw town that was burned by white settlers and Cherokee Indians in 1787, then named for a famous Cherokee chief.

Your spot in the dining room overlooks **Wilson Dam,** the largest conventional hydroelectric plant in the **Tennessee Valley Authority** (TVA) power system. With the completion of Wilson Dam, the treacherous shoals that gave Muscle Shoals its name were buried under a new lake. The Wilson Dam has one of the highest single-lift locks in the world, is a national historical landmark, and is the cornerstone of TVA's plan to develop the Tennessee Valley region.

Following that brief history lesson, you will be ready to sleep well, enjoy a breakfast to order at the hotel, and get an early start. Wear your comfortable walking shoes and take along your camera. A notepad and pencil might be a good idea. A record of which pictures you took where is always helpful when it comes time to share your trip with friends back home.

Turn the car toward the river and go to and through Florence to the new **Pettus Museum** at **Killen.** This is both a dream and a practical solution. Ronald and Brenda Pettus are retired teachers. She taught English and Spanish for 27 years, and Ronald taught history for 30 years. Like most history buffs, Ronald could not throw anything away. For 40 years he collected items he recognized as valuable. Finally, as any wife will understand, Brenda urged Ronald to clean out the basement, the attic, the garage, and all those other nooks and crannies bursting with pieces of the past. Ronald's solution was to build a separate building and open a museum. When possible, Ronald will lead tours and talk about the various displays, which effectively coordinate the Civil War, World Wars I and II, the Korean War, the Vietnam Conflict, and Desert Storm with the political history and climate of the time period. Postal memorabilia is especially interesting and may inspire you to write letters again.

While you are pondering the first person you'd like to surprise with a handwritten note, go toward Florence, but stop just outside the city limits in **St. Florian** to visit **St. Michael's Catholic Church.** Served by Benedictine fathers since 1876, the parish was established over 100 years ago. The present church—don't miss looking up at the arched ceiling—was built in 1912, and the 22 stained-glass windows were lovingly donated by the members, most of whom were descendants of the original German community.

Hungry? Place your order at the deli counter in **Eva Marie's,** which specializes in breads so fragrant you'll want to slip behind the glass display to help the friendly clerk slice your wheatberry, sourdough pumpernickel, or rye for your sandwich. Fortunately, making choices will keep you too busy to get in the way of lunchtime preparations.

Mrs. Pearley Woods and W. C. Handy's trumpet. (Photo by Neal Broerman)

Crocks of freshly prepared tabbouleh, basmati, and Mediterranean pasta will keep your attention and then you must decide which fruit flavored tea will complement your veggie burger. Or did you decide the Reuben would suit your yen for something tart and crunchy? Dessert choices will take time, too.

For your afternoon's enjoyment, the first stop will be the **W.C. Handy Birthplace, Museum and Library.** When William Christopher Handy decided to follow his inner musical voice, he caused conflict within the Handy household. His father was a minister, the son of a minister, and he expected his son to be a minister, too. The younger Handy left home at the age of 18.

The museum holds the most complete collection of Mr. Handy's personal papers and artifacts anywhere. His famous trumpet, his personal piano, his handwritten sheet music, his library, citations from famous people, photographs, household furnishings, and other memorabilia are explained carefully by **Mrs. Pearley Woods,** who clearly admires the subject of her many tours and lectures.

Mr. Handy wrote the "Saint Louis Blues" in 1914 and opened a publishing firm in New York in 1918. He wrote all the arrangements of his famous song and thereby collected all the royalties. You'll want to buy a copy of the sheet music in the small gift shop and pick out the melody on your piano at home. Maybe.

Cross the river back to Sheffield and go to the TVA Visitors' Center, about 15 minutes away. TVA is one of America's largest producers of electric power. It also manages the Tennessee River—the nation's fifth-largest river system—for flood control, navigation, recreation, water quality, and water supply. **Wheeler Dam,** about 15 miles upstream from the Quad Cities, was the first of eight dams built by TVA on the main stream of the Tennessee River. Wilson Dam, between Florence and Muscle Shoals, had been built earlier by the Corps of Army Engineers. It was turned over to TVA when it was created in 1933. Wilson and Wheeler Dams helped flood historic Muscle Shoals, a series of rock formations that had blocked navigation on a 37-mile stretch of the Tennessee River since colonial days.

Wheeler Dam was named for General Joseph Wheeler, a general in the Army of the Confederacy, and later a U.S. congressman who introduced the first in a long series of bills for development of Muscle Shoals that eventually culminated in the creation of TVA. You will see General Wheeler's name throughout this area. Wheeler Lake, Joe Wheeler State Park, and the Joe Wheeler National Wildlife Refuge are major recreation and tourist centers.

From Sheffield, take U.S. 43 South to U.S. 72 West in Tuscumbia. Stop by the Colbert County Tourism and Convention Bureau and take a quick peek at the ornate musical instrument in the parlor. You'll see another just like it in the Decatur Convention and Visitors Bureau. Both are crafted by a local artist.

Next, be on the lookout for **72 Choices,** a specialty catalog returns outlet. Furniture, decorative accents, and designer clothing pack this shop with exciting discoveries you can take home and enjoy with a bit of smugness. After all, you saved enough to fund your next shopping trip. All the displayed items were featured in upscale department store catalogs and ordered by buyers who changed their minds before they used the merchandise. Shipments arrive sporadically. If you see what you like, buy it. It will probably not be there the next time you come.

For another shopping treat, venture into downtown Tuscumbia to the **Carousel Shop** at Sixth Street and Main. We discovered this by accident because the owner, Lisa Littrell, had placed a richly ornamented carousel horse on the sidewalk in front of her store. That is

St. Johns Episcopal Church. (Photo by Neal Broerman)

all it takes to lure carousel collectors in to circle the shelves and counters of carousel displays as if they've been caught up on a merry-go-round of another sort. Take several turns around among miniature carousels, tiny carved horses, jeweled carousel pins, and tea sets with a carousel motif. Is your head spinning? It will be!

Hold onto the armrest in your car and take in the **Colbert County Courthouse District,** which is on the National Register. This includes **St. John's Episcopal Church,** which survived the Civil War and a tornado, and the **Colbert County Courthouse.** The courthouse was built in 1881 and gutted by fire in 1908, then rebuilt in 1909 on Main Street. When each state was asked to choose one courthouse to feature in a book of United States courthouses, this one was selected to represent Alabama.

Cross the river back to Florence and take the walking tour, which is actually two tours. The **North Court and College Tour** includes lovely **Wilson Park** and its fountain, a statue of W.C. Handy, and the **University of North Alabama,** which began in 1830 as the first college chartered by Alabama. Some say General Sherman slept there during the Union occupation of Florence. He wasn't the only famous man to stay in the city. The tour also takes you to **Trowbridge's,** a soda shop frequented by entertainer George "Goober" Lindsey when he was a student at the University of North Alabama, and **Pope's Tavern,** which may have been a stopover for General Andrew Jackson. The **Historic Downtown Tour** is shorter and leads you through the National Register Historic District, all commercial buildings, but there isn't any name-dropping to be enjoyed there. Call the Florence/Lauderdale Tourism Bureau for a map.

The walk will put you in a great mood for the festive atmosphere at the **Court Street Café,** which is not on Court Street. It's across from the post office and surrounded by cars with out-of-state licenses. Obviously, the word is out that this is the "in" place. Greg (Jake) Jacobs, the president who is also a hands-on chef and manager, says he wants the café to be the kind of place where people celebrate family occasions. He stocks custom-brewed beer in small batches and will stock favorite wines for regular customers. The waitress's enthusiastic endorsement of Jamaican steak and Cajun salad pleased us so much that we trusted her suggestion that we'd enjoy an apple crunch brownie with ice cream. It had just been delivered to the café, still warm from a local creative cook's oven. If you eat as well as we did, now is probably a good time to take that second walking tour before your return to your hotel.

You could eat Sunday breakfast at the hotel or drive to the **Joe Wheeler State Park** for the day. There are more museums to see and although this bit of information will not affect a traditional weekend, it is interesting to note that museums on the Florence side of the river are closed on Mondays. Museums on the Tuscumbia side of the river are open all week. Three must-see museums in Tuscumbia are also open on Sunday afternoon. Area churches welcome visitors, or you could take that Florence walking tour in the morning and eat lunch before you head for Tuscumbia. **Stephano's** serves the herbed Italian dishes local college students savor.

To get to **Ivy Green,** internationally known birthplace of **Helen Keller,** cross the river on U.S. 72 S. to Avalon Avenue and turn right. Go to Main and turn left. Go five blocks to Common Street and turn right. You are two blocks from Ivy Green, where Helen Keller was born in 1880. *The Miracle Worker,* a famous play, is staged annually on the grounds.

Write for tickets because orders are not taken over the phone, and quick sellouts of Alabama's official outdoor drama are not uncommon.

Considered "America's First Lady of Courage," Helen Keller as a child is made warm and loveable through the family photos and anecdotes told by guides at her family home. The house has been

Helen Keller's pump at Ivy Green. (Photo by Neal Broerman)

Judge Almon Tour House (ca. 1888). (Photo by Neal Broerman)

completely restored and is a permanent shrine on the National Register of Historic Places. Step outside and see the pump where Helen and **Annie Sullivan,** her devoted teacher, experienced the miracle of communication. Come away with a new appreciation of the obstacles Helen Keller overcame and the hurdles still ahead. Her legacy is a challenge, and she is honored every June when over 50,000 people participate in the Helen Keller Festival.

Not far from the Keller home is the Almon House. It is a rescued Victorian. The owners wanted to prove that a married couple of moderate means could add modern conveniences, refurbish, and enjoy living in a home built in the 1800s. The home is listed on the National Register of Historic Places and tours are given more often during the months that school is out. High ceilings, rich woodwork, brightly patterned fabrics, and touches of white paint and wicker will soon have you wondering about the aging Victorians in your own city. What if . . . ?

While you are fantasizing about a new house project, here is another whimsical consideration. Have you ever wanted to walk into a jukebox? This you can do. The **Alabama Music Hall of Fame** gives you that chance. Opened in 1990 and dedicated to over 500 musical achievers in all types of music from rock, rhythm and blues, gospel, to country and western, opera, and contemporary, the glittering displays lend credence to the claim that this area was once known as the "Hit Recording Capital of the World." Every other year new Alabama performers are inducted in the Hall of Fame, and the ceremony can be attended by the public. Ask about this when you visit the museum. Then wander through the jukebox, wonder how all those football-player-size guys in the famous group Alabama managed to tour on that not-so-big bus, and hum a few of your favorite tunes as you visit displays of Tammy Wynette, Lionel Richie, Emmylou Harris, the Commodores, Nat King Cole, W.C. Handy, Hank Williams, and others. You can even make your own recording and take it home.

Now it's time to go in search of one attraction named after General Joe Wheeler, **Joe Wheeler State Park.** The dining room in the three-story redwood and stone lodge has a commanding view of the Tennessee River. A marina, 18-hole golf course, campground, cabins, tennis courts, and a boat launch dot the 2,500-acre park. You can swim, picnic, hike, or rent a boat and fish in Wheeler Lake. Even wintry months offer exciting opportunities to enjoy the outdoors. Ask about Eagle Awareness January lodging packages. Now that's a weekend unlike any other!

Area Code: (256)

Getting There:

The Shoals can be reached from Interstate 65 through Decatur on U.S. 72 ALT, from Cullman on Alabama 157, or from Athens on U.S. 72. Florence is about 40 miles west of Decatur.

Where and When:

72 Choices, 1110 U.S. 72 W., Tuscumbia, AL 35674. Mon.-Sat., 9 A.M.-5 P.M.; Sun., 1 P.M.-5 P.M. 383-7271.

Alabama Music Hall of Fame, U.S. 72 W., Tuscumbia, AL 35674. Mon.-Sat., 9 A.M.-5 P.M.; Sun., 1 P.M.-5 P.M. 381-4417; (800) 239-2643. Admission.   Web site: www.alamhof.org

Florence Main Street Program, 301 N. Pine Street, Florence, AL 35630. 760-9648.

Ivy Green, Home of **Helen Keller,** 300 W. North Commons, Tuscumbia, AL 35674. 383-4066. Admission.

Joe Wheeler State Park Lodge, 4401 McLean Drive, Rogersville, AL 35652. 247-5461; (800) 544-5639.

Judge Almon 1888 Tour House, Almon and Water Streets, Tuscumbia, AL 35674. Mon.-Sat., 9 A.M.-5 P.M.; Sun., 1 P.M.-5 P.M. 383-1642. Admission.

Lisa's Carousels, 121 S. Main Street, Tuscumbia, AL 35674. Mon., Wed., Fri.-Sat., 9 A.M.-5 P.M. 383-8532.

Pettus Museum, U.S. 72, Killen, AL. Tue.-Sat., 10 A.M.-5 P.M. 757-9229. Admission.

Renaissance Tower, One Hightower Place (off Veteran's Drive), Florence, AL 35630. Gift shop, Mon.-Sat., 10 A.M.-5 P.M.; Sun., 11 A.M.-5 P.M. 764-5900.

St. Michael's Catholic Church, Church Road, St. Florian, AL 35630. 764-1885.

Tennessee Valley Art Center, W. North Commons, Tuscumbia, AL 35699. 383-0533.

Tennessee Valley Authority, Wilson Dam, Visitors' Center, Alabama 133 (off U.S. 43), Muscle Shoals, AL. 386-2451; (800) 467-1388.

Web site: www.tva.gov

W. C. Handy Birthplace, Museum and Library, 620 W College Street, Florence, AL 35630. Tue.-Sat., 10 A.M.-4 P.M. 760-6434. Admission.

Information:

Alabama Mountain Lakes Tourist Association, 25062 North Street, Mooresville, AL 35649. 350-3500.

Colbert County Tourism and Convention Bureau, 719 U.S. 72 W., Tuscumbia, AL 35674. 383-0783; (800) 344-0783.

Web site: www.shoals-tourism.org

Florence/Lauderdale Tourism, One Hightower Place, Florence, AL 35630. 740-4141, (888) 356-8687.   Web site: www.flo.tour.org

Shoals Chamber of Commerce, 612 S. Court Street, Florence, AL 35631. 764-4661.   Web site: www.shoalscc.org

Tennessee Valley Authority, Lake Level Information, Muscle Shoals, AL.   Web site: lakeinfo.tva.gov

Accommodations:

Holiday Inn, 4900 Hatch Boulevard, Sheffield, AL 35660. 381-4710.

Joe Wheeler State Park Lodge, 4401 McLean Drive, Rogersville, AL 35652. 247-5461; (800) 544-5639.

Limestone Manor Bed & Breakfast, 601 N. Wood Avenue, Florence, AL 35630. 765-0314; (888) 709-6700.

Web site: www.bbonline.com/al/limestone

Restaurants:

Bunyan's BBQ, 901 W. College Street, Florence, AL 35630. Mon.-Sat., 10 A.M.-8 P.M. 766-3522.

Court Street Café, 201 N. Seminary Street, Florence, AL 35630. Sun.-Thurs., 11 A.M.-10 P.M.; Fri.-Sat., 11 A.M.-11 P.M. 767-4300.

Eva Marie's, 106 N. Court Street, Florence, AL 35630. Mon.-Fri., 8 A.M.-5:30 P.M.; Sat., 9 A.M.-4 P.M. 760-0004.

Joe Wheeler State Park Lodge, 4401 McLean Drive, Rogersville, AL 35652. Mon.-Sat., breakfast, lunch, and dinner; Sun. brunch, 11:30 A.M.-2 P.M. 247-5461; (800) 544-5639.

Renaissance Grille, One Hightower Place (off Veteran's Drive), Florence, AL 35630. Mon.-Thurs., 11 A.M.-10 P.M.; Fri.-Sat., 11 A.M.-11 P.M.; Sun., 11 A.M.-9 P.M. 718-0092.

Stephano's, 218 N. Court Street, Florence, AL 35630. Mon.-Wed., 11 A.M.-8 P.M.; Thurs., 11 .am.-9 P.M.; Fri.-Sat., 11 A.M.-10 P.M.; Sun., 11 A.M.-2:30 P.M. 764-7407.

Major Annual Events:

Eagle Awareness, Joe Wheeler State Park—January. 247-5461; (800) 544-5639.

Recall LaGrange, Tuscumbia—Third weekend in May. 383-0783.Frontier Days, Florence—First weekend in June. 383-0783.

Waterloo Heritage Days, Waterloo—Memorial Day Weekend. 383-0783.

Helen Keller Festival, Tuscumbia—Fourth Weekend in June. 383-0783.

The Miracle Worker, Tuscumbia—June-July. 383-4066.

W.C. Handy Music Festival, Florence—August. 383-0783.

Web site: www.wchandyfest.org

Trail of Tears Commemoration and Motorcycle Ride, Waterloo—Third weekend in September. 383-0783.

Alabama Renaissance Faire, Wilson Park, Florence—October. 740-4141.

Festival of the Singing River, Florence—October. 383-0783.

Native American Festival, Florence—October. 383-0783.

Tennessee Rivers Fiddlers Convention, Florence—Second week in October.

29

LIFT-OFF!

Scattered across a verdant field still wet with dew, patches of color swell into bright bubbles. First one bubble breaks free of the earth, then another. Suddenly the sky is filled with a kaleidoscope of bobbing, glorious, hot air balloons. The **Alabama Jubilee** has launched the summer season one more time.

The biggest free-admission hot air balloon rally in the South is held at **Point Mallard Park** in **Decatur** on Memorial Day weekend. The popularity of this hot-air balloon classic has earned Decatur the title of "Ballooning Capital of Alabama."

Ballooning is a team sport that minimizes age and ability differences. It brings families together, too. Beneath the balloons, as the pilots hitch a ride on the wind and sail above the neighborhoods, kids in pajamas, teens glued to cell phones, and adults toting that first cup of coffee tumble from their houses to look up and wave.

After the first magnificent lift-off in the early morning, the balloons return to the field. A few pilots give tethered flights to first-timers, kids, and apprehensive adults. The crowd wanders among rows of concessions, displays and demonstrations, musical acts, Boy Scout exhibits, a collection of antique and classic cars, and many other events scheduled throughout the warm spring day.

Since Jubilee is the perfect opportunity to explore the rest of Point Mallard Park, kids who count days until the swimming pool opens head for the 35-acre water theme park and the wave pool, the first in the country. The championship 18-hole golf course along the banks

Above and below: *Hot-air balloons.* (Photos by Neal Broerman)

of the Tennessee River may be affected somewhat by the Jubilee, but it's been open all year, so golfers are understanding. Other attractions at the park, a top tourist destination, include a gymnasium complex and a three-mile-long riverside hiking/biking trail.

The day drifts by and then comes the evening balloon glow. The soft hush-hush sound of the burners spreads across the field. Voices of neighbors and new friends fade away as the seven-story-tall balloons lift off again, this time against a sky streaked by the rays of a setting sun. A peace settles in. Does it get any better than this?

Decatur demonstrates the friendly hometown atmosphere that is the strength of Alabama. You feel it at the Jubilee. Smiles turn strangers into welcome guests. If you choose to use Jubilee to introduce you to this warm town, tuck a long-sleeve shirt and face-shading hat, insect repellent, sunscreen, and bottled water into your day pack. Campers arrive days early to reserve a space. Call weeks ahead to make room reservations. The Decatur-Morgan County Convention and Visitors Bureau is a valuable source of help.

Country Inns and Suites by Carlson in Decatur is centrally located within walking distance of historic Bank Street, gift shops, and **Simp McGhee's** restaurant. The hotel also serves a complimentary continental breakfast with bakery-fresh pastries, and the staff prides itself on "country hospitality." If this is not a step beyond "Southern hospitality," it's certainly equal to it. You will feel at home.

But first things first. You must fortify yourself for any weekend, whether or not you come for one of the many Decatur festivals. A visit to **Big Bob Gibson's** Bar-B-Q will do just that.

Big Bob Gibson's Championship Red Sauce was crowned "The Best Sauce on the Planet" at the 18th Annual American Royal Barbecue Cookoff and International Sauce Contest in Kansas City, Kansas. Nearly 1,000 judges rated the more than 500 entries. (How do you get a job like that?) It's estimated that in the United States there are more than 10,000 barbecue cooking teams and an average of six competitions take place every weekend. The Kansas City Barbecue Society is the premier sanctioning body in the country. There are four other organizations that have formed their own cooking circuits and can sanction networks and competitions.

"Big Bob's" has been the comfort food of choice for generations of Decatur families since 1925 and is internationally acclaimed, as you will see from the trophies competing for space in front of the cash register. Owner Don McLemore had no place else to put these

Bob Gibson trophies. (Photo by Neal Broerman)

prestigious symbols of excellence. His office is overflowing with awards. Now it's your turn to judge. Ribs, pork, chicken, turkey? Where will you begin?

Saturday morning, if you don't have the "Walking Tour of Historic Decatur," run by the Decatur-Morgan County Convention and Visitors Bureau when it opens at 9 A.M. and get one. This will give your morning shape. There are two tours. One is the **Old Decatur Historic District** and the other is the **New Decatur/Albany Historic District.** If you follow the numbers on your tour guide consecutively, each tour will take less than one hour.

During the Civil War, Decatur was a frequent target for troops on both sides. Only four of its major buildings remained when the war ended. A number of houses on the walking tour were built to replace those destroyed during the war. These homes comprise the most intact Victorian-era neighborhood in Alabama. They are also private residences, and the homeowners take turns participating in the Christmas open house events. You'll notice both Confederate and Union generals have streets named for them. This was a gesture of peace.

The **Old State Bank** is the first stop on the tour, and it has many stories to tell. This fine example of Classical Revival architecture was built in 1833 by slaves, who were freed upon its completion. President Martin Van Buren attended the dedication ceremony. The bank was used as a hospital during the Civil War, and is on the National Register of Historic Places.

As you walk down Bank Street, gift shop windows will catch your interest, and you will want to come back and see what is inside. **The Shop,** owned by Dorothy Schwuchow (say "Swoko"), is a spacious store that welcomes tour groups with lemonade and cookies. Daughter Sandra was minding the store the day I stopped by and pointed out displays of small art items and gift books. **Susan's Fine Ladies' Apparel** is a shop for ladies who enjoy relaxed fashions. The **Riverwalk Antique Mall** is so vast a person could get lost. This is a sampling of the variety along one block of a brick-paved street. Exploring will work up an appetite, and you'll be more than ready to cross the railroad track running down the middle of Bank Street and find a table at Simp McGhee's.

Simp McGhee was a flamboyant river man whose legendary exploits are kept alive in this restaurant that bears his name. You'll enjoy reading about him as you wait for your lunch. The chef has a way with shrimp. Try the New Orleans shrimp remoulade or the marinated shrimp salad. There's a soup and salad combo for light eaters.

Now it's drive time. Head for Hillsboro, 15 minutes west of Decatur on Alabama 20, to the **General Joe Wheeler Plantation.** You've already heard some of General Wheeler's exploits. This is a look behind the scenes at a man who graduated from West Point when he was 19. At age 26, he became one of the youngest lieutenant generals in the Confederate Army, was nicknamed "Fightin' Joe Wheeler" by General Robert E. Lee, and survived many battles (16 horses were shot out from under him!) to become a United States congressman and major general of volunteers in Cuba during the Spanish-American War.

When you cross the threshold and notice that the table is set for the next meal, you get the feeling that the good general and his wife are close by, waiting to greet you themselves. Guide Mary Morris is devoted to Wheeler's daughter, the famous "Miss Annie," who inherited her father's stamina and feistiness, much to the doting father's consternation.

Miss Annie's concern for the needs of others endeared her to generations. In Cuba **Clara Barton** put the young woman in charge of a newly organized hospital, and grateful soldiers called her the "Angel of Santiago." How she happened to be in position to get this appointment is a story that will delight every father's daughter. Her presence is still felt in the family homestead where Miss Annie spent her last years. Pay a visit to Miss Annie's grave and you will smell the boxwood she planted to outline the backyard walkway.

Between the trip from Wheeler's home to the Wildlife Refuge named for him, stop by **Cook's Natural Science Museum** and see the animals you'd most likely come across in Miss Annie's backyard. Kids especially enjoy the close-up view of insects and the 30- to 45-minute tour is short enough to maintain their interest. Start with the 12-minute film.

Another close-up view of wildlife awaits you at the **Wheeler National Wildlife Refuge** on Alabama 67, two miles west of Interstate 65. A flock of snowy white egrets might greet you as they did us. Going toward Decatur from Interstate 65, take Exit 334 to go to the refuge. You'll pass fields of corn planted for ducks and geese and then see the **Givens Wildlife Interpretive Center** on your left. The center contains exhibits of waterfowl, bats, and wildlife. Begin with the movie that takes 10 to 15 minutes and has subtitles for the hearing impaired.

Dab on insect repellent for your trip to the two-story observation deck. The deck is enclosed, but the pathway is not. Inside the glass-enclosed observatory you will enjoy the spectator sport of birdwatching in comfort. Canadian geese, mallards, and wood ducks frolic in the 18-acre pond. If your eyes are sharp, you might spot a muskrat or mink near the water. This 35,000-acre refuge is one of the South's largest educational centers for waterfowl and wildlife study.

Ranger Daphne Moland tipped us off to winter prime times for seeing migratory waterfowl. Come between 1 and 5 P.M. Thanksgiving Day and Christmas Day are the only days the center is closed. For the other seasons, pick up a U.S. Fish and Wildlife Service brochure in the center.

Shadows are lengthening across the ponds and fields. It's time to think of feeding your own flock. Families might prefer making a speedy choice from the restaurants spread along the interstate. For a romantic dinner for two, an excellent choice is **Curry's on Johnston Street.** Meg and Scott Curry combine the management responsibilities of this fine dining establishment with the joy of parenting twin daughters. Look for the chalk drawing of the girls while you wait for your meticulously prepared dinner. Crab cakes are a specialty, but the cowboy ribeye has its fans. White chocolate mousse and strawberry parfait is a mix of cream and white chocolate that adds up to one thing: rich! If you have to ask for a to-go box in order to have dessert, do it. Your room at the Country Inn has a refrigerator.

On Sunday morning pick up a steaming cup of coffee to accompany you to **Rhodes Ferry Park,** beside the Tennessee River. This is at the edge of the Old Decatur Historic District. While you sip your coffee, watch a train cross the bridge on your left, or measure the progress of boats on the river. Toss the cup in a nearby receptacle and—to walk off that parfait from Curry's—follow the markers on the Civil War Walking Tour. During the Civil War, Decatur changed hands many times due to the railroad bridge across the river. Strategy dictated that the army with control of the bridge would control transportation and supply shipments. A tactic of the conquering army was to rid the city of snipers by burning the buildings. Few of Decatur's buildings survived this drastic tug-of-war. Eleven historic markers trace an important "Battle of Decatur" at the end of 1864.

Rhodes Ferry Park. (Photo by Joan Broerman)

Mooresville Post Office. (Photo by Neal Broerman)

Railroad bridge across the Tennessee River. (Photo by Neal Broerman)

For a Sunday dinner that is a tradition with locals, check out of your hotel and drive toward **Mooresville Village,** about six miles from Decatur on Interstate 565. Take Exit 2 to Mooresville, which is a town one year older than the state. Incorporated November 16, 1818, this small village with a population of 62 people covers only 160 acres, and it's proud of its post office, which is the oldest in the state and has been operating continuously since 1819. At least half the structures in this town date back more than a century. The railroad is north of town because the citizens fought plans to put it through their town in 1855. Park the car and swing your feet onto the country road. This little town is like a time capsule and it can best be appreciated by walking. Listen to the birds, and let the serenity relax you.

The first settlers arrived in Mooresville in 1805 and settled on land belonging to the Chickasaw Indians. During even-numbered years, residents dress in period costumes and bring early America to life with an autumn "Walking Tour of Mooresville." If you want to live here, your best opportunity exists if you are related to someone who already owns property. The homes are usually handed down within the family.

Limestone County is the biggest cotton-producing county in Alabama, and you are not far from **Belle Mina,** a small cotton growing community. From mid-September to mid-October, you can watch cotton being picked.

Return to Interstate 565 and take Exit 3. Turn left and follow the signs to **Greenbrier Restaurant,** a Sunday dinner tradition with the locals. In the early days, country music stars used to sit on top of the building and sing to bring in the crowds. Now the combination of tasty country cooking, an endless supply of great hushpuppies, and super service keeps the throngs coming whether anybody sings or not.

It could be a great afternoon to spend at Point Mallard Park. The golf course is always open, and from Memorial Day to Labor Day, you can cool off in the water park that introduced the first "wave activated" pool for public recreation in America way back in 1970.

Another pleasant way to spend an afternoon is a quiet drive through Athens, which also has lovely Victorian homes, many on the National Register of Historic Places. See early 1800s churches and Athens State College, Alabama's oldest. When you are ready to eat again, the entire family will be happy at the **Hungry Fisherman.** After the seafood platter, celebrate a successful weekend with a slice of apple walnut pie. It comes with ice cream. The vacation feeling will last through supper.

Cotton field in Lawrence County. (Photo by Neal Broerman)

Boll weevil trap in Lawrence County. (Photo by Neal Broerman)

Area Code: (256)

Getting There:
Decatur is about five miles west of Interstate 65 at Exit 340.

Where and When:
Cook's Natural Science Museum, 412 Thirteenth Street S.E., Decatur, AL 35601. Mon.-Sat., 9 A.M.-5 P.M.; Sun., 2 P.M.-5 P.M. 350-9347.

General Joe Wheeler Plantation, 12280 Alabama 20, Hillsboro, AL 35643. Sun., 1 P.M.-5 P.M.; Daily by appointment. 637-8513. Admission.

Mooresville Village, Interstate 565, Exit 2, Mooresville. 350-3500; (800) 648-5381.

Old State Bank, 925 Bank Street N.E., Decatur, AL 35601. Mon.-Fri., 9:30 A.M.-4:30 P.M. 350-5060.

Point Mallard Park, 1800 Point Mallard Drive S.E., Decatur, AL 35601. Mid May-Labor Day, Mon., Tue., Thurs., 10 A.M.-9 P.M.; Wed., Fri.-Sun., 10 A.M.-6 P.M. 350-3000; (800) 669-9283. Admission.

Rhodes Ferry Park, Wilson Street (Alabama 20), Decatur, AL

Riverwalk Antique Mall, 818 Bank Street N.E., Decatur, AL 35601. Mon.-Sat., 10 A.M.-5 P.M.; Mon.-Sun., 1 P.M.-5 P.M. 340-0075.

Susan's Fine Ladies' Apparel, 708 Bank Street, Decatur, AL 35601. Mon.-Sat., 10 A.M.-5 P.M. 301-9944.

The Shop, 810 Bank Street, Decatur, AL 35601. Mon.-Sat., 9 A.M.-5:30 P.M. 350-5770.

Wheeler National Wildlife Refuge, 2700 Refuge Headquarters Road, Decatur, AL 35603. Mar. Sept., Wed.-Sun., 10 A.M.-5 P.M.; Oct.-Feb., daily, 10 A.M.-5 P.M. 350-6639.

Information:
Alabama Mountain Lakes Tourist Association, 25062 North Street, Mooresville, AL 35649. 350-3500.

Alabama Vacation Guide. Call 1-800-ALABAMA (252-2262).

Decatur-Morgan County Convention and Visitors Bureau, 719 Sixth Avenue S.E., Decatur, AL 35602. 350-2028; (800) 524-6181.

Web site: www.decaturcvb.org

Accommodations:
Country Inns and Suites by Carlson, Decatur, 807 Bank Street N.E., Decatur, AL 35601. 355-6800; (800) 456-4000.

Restaurants:
Big Bob Gibson's Bar-B-Q, 2520 Danville Road S.W., Decatur, AL 35603. Daily, 9 A.M.-8:30 P.M. 350-6969.

Big Bob Gibson's Bar-B-Q, 1715 Sixth Avenue S.E., Decatur, AL 35601. Daily, 9 A.M.-8:30 P.M. 350-6969.

City Café, 101 First Avenue S.E., Decatur, AL 35601. Mon.-Fri., 5:30 A.M.-2:30 P.M.; Sat., 5:30 A.M.-11:30 A.M. 353-9719.

Curry's on Johnston Street, 115 Johnston Street S.E., Decatur, AL 35601. Mon.-Fri., 8:30 A.M.-5:30 P.M.; Sat., 11 A.M.-2 A.M. Thurs.-Sat., 6 P.M.-10 P.M. 350-6715.

Greenbrier Restaurant, Old Alabama 20 at Greenbrier Road (Interstate 565, Exit 3), Madison, AL 35758. Daily, 10 A.M.-9 P.M. 351-1800.

Hungry Fisherman, 1124 U.S. 72 E, Athens, AL 35611. Sun.-Thurs., 10:30 A.M.-8:30 P.M.; Fri.-Sat., 10:30 A.M.-9 P.M. 233-4433.

Simp McGhee's Restaurant, 725 Bank Street N.E., Decatur, AL 35601. Mon.-Fri., 11 A.M.-1:30 P.M.; Mon.-Sat., 5:30 P.M.-10 P.M. 353-6284.

Major Annual Events:

Racking Horse Spring Show, Celebration Arena, Decatur—April.

Spring Pilgrimage, Athens—April.

Alabama Jubilee Hot Air Balloon Festival, Point Mallard Park, Decatur—May.

Historic Decatur Garden Tour, Old Decatur and Albany Historic Districts, Decatur—May. (800) 524-6181.

Somerville Wagon Train and Campout, Somerville—Third Weekend of June.

Spirit of America, Point Mallard Park, Decatur—July.

Racking Horse World Celebration, Celebration Arena, Decatur—September.

Riverfest, Founders Park and Rhodes Ferry Park, Decatur—September.

September Skirmish, Point Mallard Park, Decatur—September. (800) 524-6181.

Tennessee Valley Old-Time Fiddlers Convention, Athens State University, Athens—October. 233-8205.

Christmas Tour of Homes, Albany and Old Decatur Historic Districts, Decatur—December.

30

BLAST OFF!

You've climbed and plunged aboard the Rampage in Bessemer and drifted lazily across the sky over Decatur in a hot air balloon. Is that all there is? How about weightlessness? Strap yourself into the **Space Shot** at the **U.S. Space and Rocket Center** in **Huntsville** and take off. You'll feel more G-forces than the astronauts do during a space shuttle launch, and you'll experience brief weightlessness at the top of the ride. The entire trip of 30 seconds includes two to three seconds of weightlessness, but it sounds like a minute of sheer terror to me.

Huntsville, often called the Rocket City, began quietly when John Hunt, a Revolutionary War veteran, built his cabin near a big spring in 1802. (This site is now part of the Big Spring International Center in downtown Huntsville.) During the Creek War, Andrew Jackson bought large tracts of land here, too. While Alabama's first capitol was being built at Cahaba, Huntsville served as temporary state capital in 1819, and the townsfolk entertained thoughts of winning that prize for themselves permanently. However, those who argued that Cahaba was more centrally located won out. During the antebellum period, cotton fields and manufacturing flourished and a railroad was built to transport products to markets. When Union troops captured Huntsville in 1862, they cut off the Memphis and Charleston Railroad, the South's only major east-west railroad. Actually, Union occupation protected the city from the fires that ravaged other Southern cities. For that reason, today Huntsville has the largest number of pre-Civil War homes of any city in the state.

The Space Shot Simulator, U.S. Space & Rocket Center. (Photo by Joan Broerman)

From Reconstruction until the end of World War II, the town was quiet again. Then Dr. **Wernher von Braun,** a German-born scientist, was assigned, along with members of his team, to Redstone Arsenal. Von Braun and his associates developed the first Redstone rocket, launched at Cape Canaveral, Florida in 1953. In 1958, the first U.S. satellite, *Explorer One,* was boosted into orbit around the earth by a Jupiter-C rocket developed at Redstone. The major accomplishment of the von Braun team was the huge Saturn V rocket that propelled the Apollo spacecraft to the moon in 1969. A full-size replica of the Saturn V is on display at Huntsville. The **George C. Marshall Space Flight Center** was part of the arsenal until it was separated from the army. It was at the Marshall Center that the moon buggy, in which astronauts explored the moon's surface, was developed, and Marshall engineers also worked on the original space shuttle.

Visitors to the U.S. Space and Rocket Center can spend at least half a day wandering among the displays and participating in the hands-on exhibits. Visit an outpost in space and find out how to take a shower when the water doesn't follow its expected path. Take a sim-ulated flight to Jupiter. Then if you'd like to feel like an astronaut but have no intention of climbing aboard the Space Shot, grip the arm-rests in the Spacedome **IMAX** theater and watch the earth slip away as you speed toward the stars.

In spite of the fact that the Space Center dominates Huntsville, there are other attractions to visit there. For a weekend getaway, visi-tors can stay at one of many hotels in downtown Huntsville or in one of the motels along the interstate. Many serve complimentary conti-nental breakfasts. For memorable mini-vacation accommodations, travel to **Toney,** 30 minutes north of Huntsville, and fly a kite.

Gretchen and Jim Rider are part of the high-tech world in Huntsville and can probably give tips about kite flying, a pastime they recommend at their unusual bed and breakfast, the **Church House Inn.** However, kite-flying aside, a feeling of peace lifts your spirits and stays with you long after you leave this place.

When the Riders first saw their home, they knew immediately that if they were ever going to operate a bed and breakfast, this would be it. A country church inspired the look of the house. In fact the win-dows and entry tower of a church in Tennessee were incorporated in the structure. As Gretchen put it, they bought the house, breathed loving life into it, and the Church House Inn was born.

An Air Force family, the Riders raised their family and carried

Space station mockup, U.S. Space & Rocket Center. (Photo by Joan Broerman)

home with them from one post to the next. They were always hosting family and friends, so their role in this, their third career, doesn't seem so different. They entertain guests who often become friends.

Since many fascinating history museums in Huntsville are not open on Sunday but the Space Center is, arrange your weekend so you can see both. Begin by visiting **EarlyWorks at the Center for Early Southern Life,** which is a history complex containing four com- pelling adventures for those who look at dates and see the lives of people. EarlyWorks takes visitors down the river on a life-size floating keelboat (see if you can figure out how it floats) and introduces them to a talking tree that tells folktales and a clock that turns time back- wards. Invited to participate in the "do touch" experience, kids drag a bale of cotton, sack crops at the General Store, and sign a copy of the Alabama Constitution. Studying Alabama history in school should be much easier after a tour of EarlyWorks. Students will think they "lived" what they read about in the history books. Most families spend about an hour and a half in this time warp.

Alabama Constitution Village whisks visitors to 1819, when

Alabama became a state. Costumed interpreters in period dress demonstrate butter churning and candle dipping, and guests get to help. Stop by the Sweet Shop and sample the homemade fudge before you go to the next stop, the **Historic Huntsville Depot.** The building was there when the Union soldiers rode into town and severed the Memphis and Charleston Railroad from the rest of the Confederacy. At the Depot from March through December you can ride the Huntsville Trolley, a 1920s-era streetcar that will take you through the historic district, including Alabama's largest grouping of antebellum homes. You can hop on and off the trolley for a longer visit in some areas.

The last stop in the complex is the **Humphreys-Rodgers House-Alabama Decorative Arts Center.** In this fully restored 1848 house, you will see period rooms and an 1850s Voss concert grand piano.

It's decision time.

Dedicated shoppers may want to take Interstate 565 to Interstate 65 South, cross the Tennessee River and take Exit 328 to **Hartselle.** The town owes its 1860 beginnings to the railroad, and a renovated depot anchors the downtown shopping area. Enjoy a strawberry pretzel salad at the **Corner Café** and browse through 29 shops lining Railroad Street and Main Street.

Families with children might prefer having lunch at the **Greenbrier Restaurant** and then touring the **Harrison Brothers Hardware** and the **Huntsville/Madison County Botanical Gardens.**

The Bergett family has owned and operated the Greenbrier for over 30 years. Seafood is a specialty, as well as barbecue, and a children's menu featuring chicken tenders makes this a family-friendly place to eat lunch or dinner. You'll come back again.

The Harrison Brothers Hardware has been operating longer than any other in the state, since 1897. Buy marbles by the pound. When you get to the Huntsville/Madison County Botanical Gardens, ask at the gift shop for a children's map so your youngsters can see nature's wonders on their level. Look for the butterfly display. At the **Center for Biospheric Education and Research,** learn how astronauts will grow food in space.

For a special Saturday dinner, dress up a little to enjoy the **Jazz Factory.** Or treat the kids to milkshakes and hamburgers in the fifties atmosphere of the **Zesto Diner.**

Sunday at the **Church House Inn** could be the second morning you are awakened by the sensory message that one of the Riders' favorite breads is about to come out of the oven. A second sniff will tell you that a just-perked cup of coffee is ready to sample. Spoiled yet?

No matter how early you arrive at the Huntsville Space and Rocket Center, you are not alone. Excited voices speak many languages, and tour groups and families queue up to get in. My husband and I have taken our children through the complex several times, but one of the most enlightening tours was with two teenagers from Russia. I pointed out the **Apollo Soyuz** to one young man and said proudly, "Look. We did that together." He was silent, pondering the language, I thought. Then he answered, "Yes, but we call it the Soyuz Apollo."

Over the years the food concessions have improved and the cafeteria has a good selection of salads and sandwiches. After lunch you can take the bus to the NASA Marshall Space and Flight Center. The bus schedule can be unreliable when tour groups run late, but the tour guides are knowledgeable and entertaining.

Save the gift shops for your return to the main building. This will give you a chance to tour one more time and be sure you haven't missed anything.

If you didn't make it to the Botanical Gardens yesterday, it's right next door. To combine more nature with history, take U.S. 431 S. (Governor's Drive) to Monte Sano Boulevard and follow the signs to the **Burritt Museum and Park.** Tour the 14-room mansion and the restored farm buildings in the park and gulp in the panoramic view of the Tennessee Valley.

Golfers probably already know about **Hampton Cove,** on the **Robert Trent Jones Golf Trail,** the last course in the famous trail. The Highlands Course is reminiscent of a Scottish links course. On the other side, laid out on former soybean fields in the flood plain of the Flint River, is the River Course. Standing among the trees left undisturbed by course developers is a 250-year-old black oak.

What have you not seen in Huntsville? Lots. There are art and history museums, gift shops featuring Godiva chocolates, Swarovski crystal, and handcrafted treasures by local artisans, restaurants and cafés to suit a wide range of tastes, more tours, more nature trails to hike, more, more, more. Take your pick of the restaurants along Pratt Avenue and Andrew Jackson Way, and while you rest your feet and wait for supper, plan your next trip.

Area Code: (256)

Getting There:

To reach Huntsville, take Interstate 565 from Interstate 65, Exit 340. Huntsville is about 17 miles east of Interstate 65.

Robot, Huntsville Space & Rocket Center. (Photo by Neal Broerman)

Where and When:
Alabama Constitution Village, 320 Church Street, Huntsville, AL 35801. Mon.-Sat., 9 A.M.-5 P.M. 535-6565; (800) 678-1819. Admission.
Burritt Museum and Park, 3101 Burritt Drive (off U.S. 431 E.) Huntsville, AL 35801. Mar.-Dec., Tue.-Sat., 10 A.M.-4 P.M.; Sun., noon-4 P.M. 536-2882. Admission.

EarlyWorks at the Center for Early Southern Life, 404 Madison Street, Huntsville, AL 35801. Mon.-Sat., 9 A.M.-5 P.M. 564-8100; (800) 678-1819. Admission.   Web site: www.earlyworks.com

Hampton Cove, 450 Old U.S. 431, Owens Crossroads, AL 35763. 551-1818.

Harrison Brothers Hardware, 124 South Side Square, Huntsville, AL 35801. Mon.-Fri., 9 A.M.-5 P.M.; Sat., 10 A.M.-5 P.M. 536-3631.

Historic Huntsville Depot, Jefferson Street (Interstate 565, Exit 19), Huntsville, AL 35801. Mar.-Dec., Mon.-Sat., 9 A.M.-5 P.M. 535-6565; (800) 678-1819. Admission.

Huntsville/Madison County Botanical Garden, 4747 Bob Wallace Avenue, Huntsville, AL 35805. May-Oct., Mon.-Sat., 8 A.M.-6:30 P.M.; Sun., 1 P.M.-6:30 P.M.; Nov.-Apr., Mon.-Sat., 9 A.M.-5 P.M.; Sun., 1 P.M.-5 P.M., 830-4447. Admission.

Huntsville Art League Gallery, 2801 Memorial Parkway (Parkway City Mall), Huntsville, AL 35801. 534-3860.

Huntsville Municipal Golf Course, 2151 Airport Road, Huntsville, AL 35815. 880-1151.

Huntsville Museum of Art, 300 Church Street S., Huntsville, AL 35801. Tue.-Sat., 10 A.M.-5 P.M.; Sun., 1 P.M.-5 P.M. 535-4350; (800) 786-9095.

Interstate Antiques Mall, Interstate 65, Exit 322, Falkville, AL. 784-5302.

Lawren's Gift Shop, 809 Madison Street S.E., Huntsville, AL 35801. 539-3812.

Monte Sano State Park, 5105 Nolen Avenue (off U.S. 431 E.), Huntsville, AL 35801. Open daylight hours. 534-3757.

Monterey Gifts and Collectibles, 700 Airport Road S.W., Huntsville, AL 36802. 882-1775.

North Alabama Railroad Museum, 694 Chase Road, Huntsville, AL 35815. Call for hours. 851-6276. Admission.

Web site: www.dnaco.net/~gelwood/other/narm/

Pagnano's Gifts and Collectibles, 7500 Memorial Parkway, Huntsville, AL 36802. 883-2005.

Shaver's Bookstore, 2362 Whitesburg Drive S., Huntsville, AL 35801. 536-1604.

Signature Gallery, 2364 Whitesburg Drive S., Huntsville, AL 35801. 536-1960.

Theatre 'Round the Corner, 214 Holmes Avenue, Huntsville, AL 35801. Call for schedule. 539-7529; (800) 811-7202. Admission.

Web site: www.trtc.com

Twickenham Historic District, 700 Monroe Street, Huntsville, AL 35801. 551-2230.

U.S. Space and Rocket Center, One Tranquility Base, Huntsville, AL 35805. Daily, 9 A.M.-5 P.M. 837-3400; (800) 637-7223. Admission.

Web site: www.spacefun.com

Von Braun Civic Center, 700 Monroe Street, Huntsville, AL 35801. Call Huntsville/Madison County Convention and Visitors Bureau for events. 533-1953.

Weeden House Museum, 300 Gates Avenue, Huntsville, AL 35801. Mar.-Dec., Tue.-Sun., 1 P.M.-4 P.M. 536-7718. Admission.

Transportation:

Historic Huntsville Trolley Tour, 320 Church Street, Huntsville, AL 35801. Mar.-Dec., Mon.-Sat., 10 A.M.-4:30 P.M. 535-6565. Admission.

Information:

Alabama Mountain Lakes Tourist Association, 25062 North Street, Mooresville, AL 35649. 350-3500.

Alabama Welcome Centers, Interstate 65, Exit 364, Elkmont.
Athens/Limestone County Chamber of Commerce, 101 S. Beaty Street, Athens, AL 35612. 232-2600.
Hartselle Area Chamber of Commerce, P.O. Box 817, Hartselle, AL 35640. 773-4370; (800) 294-0692.
Web site: www.hiwaay.net/chamber/hartselle
Huntsville/Madison County Convention and Visitors Bureau, 700 Monroe Street, Huntsville, AL 35801. 551-2230; (800) 772-234.
Web site: www.huntsville.org
Tourist Information Center, 700 Monroe Street, Huntsville, AL 35801. 533-5723.

Accommodations:

Bibb House Bed & Breakfast, 11 Allen Street, Madison, AL 35758. 772-0586.
Huntsville Hilton, 401 Williams Avenue, Huntsville, AL 35801. 533-1400.
Church House Inn, 2017 Grimwood Road, Toney, AL 35773. 828-5192. Web site: www.bbonline.com/al/churchhouse
Wisteria Inn, 2218 Indian Hills Road, Hartselle, AL 35640. 773-9703.

Restaurants:

Corner Café, Main Street, Hartselle, AL 35640. Mon.-Sat., 11 A.M.-2:30 P.M.; Fri.-Sat., 5 P.M.-9 P.M. 751-0054.
Green Bottle Grill, 975 Airport Road S.W., Huntsville, AL 35802. 882-0459.
Greenbrier Restaurant, Old Alabama 20 at Greenbrier Road (Interstate 565, Exit 3), Madison, AL 35758. Daily, 10 A.M.-9 P.M. 351-1800.
Jazz Factory, 109 Northside Square, Huntsville, AL 35801. Mon.-Thurs., 11 A.M.-10 P.M.; Fri., 11 A.M.-11 P.M.; Sat., 5 P.M.-11 P.M.; Sun., 10 A.M.-2:30 P.M., 5 P.M.-11 P.M. 539-1919.
Pauli's Bar and Grill, 7143 U.S. 72 W., Madison, AL 35758. Mon.-Sat., 5 P.M.- 10 P.M. 722-2080.
Velma's Country Diner, Alabama 67 and Alabama 36, Somerville, AL 35670. Mon.-Sat., 5:30 A.M.-9 P.M.; Sun., 6 A.M.-9 P.M. 778-7824.
Zesto Diner, 720 Pratt Avenue N.E., Huntsville, AL 35801. Daily, 10 A.M.-10 P.M. 534-8801.

Major Annual Events:

Hartselle Depot Days, downtown Hartselle—First Sunday in November, last Saturday in September.
Hartselle Tour of Homes, downtown Hartselle—First Saturday in December.

Gazebo at Lodge at Gorham's Bluff (Photo by Steven Brooke Studios)

31

WHERE IN THE WORLD IS PISGAH?

You may think **Pisgah** is in the middle of Nowhere. Then you travel from **Scottsboro** to Pisgah to Gorham's Bluff and you know you have arrived at Somewhere, somewhere special.

For couples who enjoy being away in a time and place belonging only to them, there is no more idyllic place in Alabama than the **Lodge at Gorham's Bluff.** A bed and breakfast that takes the definition of a getaway to new heights, this could be the only destination you'll need for the entire three days. An elegant gourmet dinner is served to the public by reservation. Add this to the full Southern breakfast provided guests and the well-stocked guest kitchen, and leaving this mountain retreat becomes unthinkable.

From your private balcony, the view of the Tennessee River valley is an ever-changing panorama of seasons and light. Your richly furnished room is a setting for romance. A fireplace, whirlpool tub, aromatic bath salts, fluffy robe, and soft music conspire to pamper and soothe you.

When hints of a new day stir your consciousness, contemplate a walk across the town growing up around the lodge, a new town a-building in Appalachia. You could wave to a neighbor puttering in a garden or just listen to a chorus of early songbirds. Maybe the best plan is to move to a rocking chair on the lodge porch. Watch an eagle soar on an updraft. Measure the progress of a barge inching its way along the river. Or stay where you are, warm and content. The world will wait.

Clara and Bill McGriff and their daughter, Dawn, are the visionaries building a town in tune with life's rhythms. Each fills the role best played. Bill is a retired accountant, Clara oversees every aspect of hospitality, and Dawn's marketing background is the foundation for savvy business decisions. They've set up a foundation to handle the cultural development of the community.

Practically speaking, the town residents' basic needs will be satisfied within walking distance. Over the next decade Gorham's Bluff will expand to 350 homes served by a downtown with a meeting house, post office, shops, restaurants and professional spaces, an area for assisted living, and a workshop district and artists' colony. While the beauty of the bluff is maintained, serenity and community will blend.

Clara's father recognized the aesthetic value of the land when he purchased it from the original owner, a Civil War veteran, and inspired his daughter and her husband, who own it now, to become stewards. To the McGriffs, Gorham's Bluff has become a legacy to future generations. They are living their dream.

Those who have already invested in the vision recognize that it is a lifestyle change. To come for a weekend is a taste of the good life.

To get to Gorham's Bluff see "Getting There" at the end of this chapter. There are several turns in the directions, but the road signs are very clear. It's only two hours from Birmingham or Atlanta, but it's a world away from the stress and tension of those cities.

The Scottsboro area attracts families with children, too. Golfers, fishermen, and hunters choose their favorite cottage or campsite and return often. Lakes and mountains create a powerful magnet.

There is only one **Crow Creek Cottage,** but someday there may be more. For now this sturdy, picturesque cottage built by Charles K. Loyd will be a prized weekend location if you are lucky enough to call when it is available. Loyd is a house builder by trade, and along with his father, Charles "Bo" Loyd, owns the grounds surrounding the house. The modern two-bedroom cottage in the woods has all the amenities of home. A comfortable screened porch overlooks Crow Creek, part of Lake Guntersville, snuggled among two state wildlife management areas and the Tennessee River.

Send the goose and duck hunters off with a thermos of coffee. Pack a lunch for the fisherman heading out to pursue bass, crappie, and bream. Take your book to the porch and spend the day. Through traffic will not disturb you. There isn't any. To get there, you'll go through the horse pasture on the Loyd's farm. Wave to the friendly children and the dogs that greet you with wagging tails.

Is Crow Creek Cottage booked? **Goose Pond Colony** in Scottsboro

Lodge at Gorham's Bluff (Photo by Steven Brooke Studios)

Crow Creek Cottage. (Photo by Neal Broerman)

Blue heron at Goose Pond Colony. (Photo by Neal Broerman)

Swing at Goose Pond Colony. (Photo by Neal Broerman)

has plenty of room. If the lakefront cottages are taken, there are 116 paved camping sites. Surrounded on three sides by 69,000-acre Lake Guntersville, this 360-acre family recreation complex has a view of the foothills of the Appalachian Mountains. World championship golf is available year-round, and the decks of cottages are pock-marked with golf cleats, showing there's lots more than fishing to this resort area.

Stash your stuff. Pull on a pair of jeans and your favorite sweat-shirt, and watch the wildlife putting on a show at sunrise or sunset. While the birds glide across the water, your cares will lift off. Listen to the squawk of the birds and forget the raucous noises of the work-a-day world.

In this north Alabama climate, Mother Nature changes the scenery with the seasons. Locals who keep an eye on Goose Pond Colony have developed another way to tell the seasons apart. In the spring they see hunters and fishermen tramping through the woods and golfers heading for the greens. In the summer families come to swim, camp, boat, hike, and fish. The golfers play extra rounds. In the fall the hunters are back. The golfers are still swinging. Winter? There's bound to be a golfer out there somewhere ready to tee off. When resort manager Joe Reed Brumbley says golf is great all year long, all he has to do is point to the Colony or the Plantation Course. There are plenty of people on the links to prove him right.

Stock your kitchen at Crow Creek or Goose Pond and cook in all weekend if you wish. Don't even think about leaving your rocking chair at the Lodge on Gorham's Bluff. But what if you want to eat out?

Have you noticed how the personality of the owner or manager of a restaurant affects the entire feeling of the place? At **Crawdaddy's, Too** everyone knows jovial Ron Harrison. He's always smiling. Crawdaddy's, Too is right on the river, and the combination of scenery, atmosphere, and succulent seafood is unbeatable. If you've never eaten crawdads, this is the place to learn. Ask a local to demon-strate to get you started!

Are you looking for good Southern cooking and plenty of it? **Liberty Restaurant** will fill the bill. This is a longtime local favorite run by longtime resident Edna Talley. Save room for the banana pudding.

Make the short trip to Rainsville at the crossroads of Sand Mountain, and you'll find a new restaurant that is building a base of satisfied regulars. The town isn't very big, but it's easy to miss **Buena Vista Mex-Mex Grill,** because it blends in with the buildings around it. It's just south of the main part of town on Alabama 35, and if you don't find it the first time, turn around and go back. Slip into a booth, and look over the menu that describes the Mexican dishes. Servings are generous and prices are reasonable. A fajita salad is a substantial meal.

While you're driving around to see area restaurants, you might want to see area attractions, too. Six blocks from the Courthouse Square is Scottsboro's claim to fame, the **Unclaimed Baggage Center.** It's been featured on Oprah and David Letterman, and truly dedicated bargain hunters make this a regular stop. When luggage, cameras, clothing, jewelry, and luxury items languish in airport storage, they are one step from shipment to Scottsboro. Unclaimed does not mean unwanted. Unclaimed Baggage Center staff have what they call "unique buying relationships" and truck in lost and unclaimed airline property, which they sell for much less than replacement value. Media attention has generated an increase in crowds and may change Oprah Winfrey's quote that this is "One of the country's best-kept shopping secrets . . ." It isn't a secret. Last year it rivaled the number of visitors to the U.S. Space and Rocket Center in Huntsville. Shoppers needn't worry that more customers will mean fewer bargains. The supply of lost airline passenger property seems endless. No wonder carry-on luggage is so prevalent.

From the Unclaimed Baggage Center, go to South Houston Street and drive around the **Scottsboro-Jackson Heritage Center.** Unless you are there during the week or attend the annual Southeastern Native American Festival held on the grounds, driving around is as close as you can get. However, this is a must-see whenever you can manage it.

You'll recall the political skirmishes that took place around the placement of the state Capitol from statehood in 1819 until the Alabama State Capitol in Montgomery opened its doors in 1847. That's 28 years. Scottsboro is the county seat of Jackson County, but it took 49 years to make that happen. The struggle for the location of the county seat is detailed in the tour of **Sagetown,** the Heritage Center's pioneer village.

Each of the buildings in the village date between 1820 and 1880, and the 1868 Jackson County Courthouse is part of the complex. A complete tour places emphasis on the various Native American tribes that were in the area when the first explorers arrived and later when the first settlers arrived. The center has also become an important source of genealogical information.

Jackson County Court House (ca.1868). (Photo by Neal Broerman)

Sage Town Pioneer Village. (Photo by Neal Broerman)

Diorama at Russell Cave National Monument. (Photo by Neal Broerman)

Sagetown dates to the early 1800s, but Alabama Highway 72 between Bridgeport and Scottsboro traverses approximately the same route along which De Soto and his men passed over 450 years ago. De Soto was a late arrival.

Nine thousand years ago, the first "bed and breakfast" in Alabama opened in Bridgeport. **Russell Cave National Monument** has been scientifically dated as the oldest known site of human occupation in the southeast United States. Using carbon dating of ancient carbon found in the cave, scientists have determined that nomadic bands of Indians lived in and around the cave during the autumn and winter seasons from 7,000 B.C. to A.D. 1,000, before Egypt and the Far East built the first true civilizations.

Now a National Historic Landmark operated by the National Park Service, the cave offers one of the longest and most complete archaeological records in the eastern United States. Our guide demonstrated how the Indians practiced "forest efficiency" using all the resources of the land. He used an antler to flake a rock into an arrowhead or hide scraper. Then he made a drill using the arrowhead, a stick, and twine made from deer hide. The museum has an interesting array of gifts and books to further build respect for our ancient ancestors.

There are 3500 caves in Alabama, and almost half of them are in Jackson County. Greg McGill, recently retired director of the Alabama Cave Survey, says cavers are motivated to explore caves so they can see sights that no one else has seen. He also says cavers are careful to have a light source available no matter where they are. If you meet a caver on the street, McGill thinks he would have a flashlight in his pocket.

Alabama has a law against breaking off a cave formation, and experienced cavers respect and protect precious underground resources. Responsibility for the safety of each person on a caving trip is shared. The **National Speleological Society** (NSS) is located in Huntsville, and that is a starting point for future cavers. Privately-owned **Sequoyah Caverns Campground** and **De Soto Caverns** have short guided tours open to the public, and they are covered in future chapters. In case you are wondering, a cave is formed by water, and a cavern is created by movement of the earth.

To get to Russell Cave, take U.S. 72 to Jackson County Road 75 north from **Bridgeport** for about four miles, and turn right on Jackson County Road to 98. Russell Cave is about three miles on the left.

This is the north side of the Tennessee River, and you can see Gorham's Bluff above and beyond Mud Creek. The valley is surrounded by the small bumps of the foothills of the Appalachians. Off 72 to 79, 75 snakes around fields of watchful cows. You'll see cars buzzing down the new highway.

While cavers are intrigued by the world underground, hikers might be interested in the **Rivermont Cave Historic Trail,** which is open February through November. This has been approved as a historic trail by the National Council, Boy Scouts of America. I did not hike this but was so impressed by the historical spots marked on the trail that I decided to let the BSA approval convince me to list it here. It is open to the public with permission. Write to the trail chairman to make reservations and receive necessary directions and permission. The trail is 15 miles long and takes about six and a half hours.

Not far from Bridgeport is the **Stevenson Railroad Depot Museum,** which is on the Register of Historic Places. The old Stevenson Hotel, built in 1872, was a stopover point so train passengers could eat while the "Iron Horse" replenished steam engines with

Above and below: *Civil War reenactment, Jere McCraw's farm, Big Oak.*
(Photos by Neal Broerman)

water from a stone reservoir built in 1852. The **Choo Choo Restaurant** next door is the oldest restaurant in Alabama and dates from 1862. The owner, Sarah Gamble, is a Stevenson native who has owned the restaurant since 1981. The cafeteria serves Southern vegetable casseroles and Mrs. Gamble creates her own recipes. One of them is Hawaiian pudding, a creamy, fruity dessert. Keep this restaurant in mind if you come to the Civil War reenactment, which is held every year at Jere McCraw's farm, Big Oak.

"The Siege at Bridgeport" has become the largest Civil War reenactment of its kind in the state. It's a somber reminder of the sacrifices made by the men who fought and the families who struggled to survive this terrible conflict. The McCraw farm is an ideal setting, and the graveside service in the family cemetery is especially moving.

When you return from Stevenson to Scottsboro, you will probably wonder about the two tall structures that look like the ceramic creation of a giant potter. These are power plant cooling towers and are part of the incomplete **Bellefonte** TVA Power Plant.

A trip to this part of the state would not be complete without a visit to **Crow Mountain Orchard.** Owners Carol and Bob Deutscher are genial proprietors of a country store that sells the produce grown on their mountaintop farm. The trip up the mountain is an experience in itself, and you will greet each directional sign with a sigh of relief that you are not lost—not yet. Your nose will tell you when you pull up to the brown metal building at the end of a gravel drive that you are in the right place. The fragrance of apples and pears wafts through the doors and into the yard. Inside you'll see stacks of baskets and boxes piled with luscious fruit. The apple-ripening schedule begins in June and runs through Dec 15. Peaches and plums are ready in June, nectarines, grapes, and pears, in mid-July. Of course, ripening times are approximate. The mountaintop climate and soil work together in their own time.

Here are the directions: From the light at Five Points in Scottsboro (where Alabama 229, 279, and 35 merge), stay on Tupelo Pike (Jackson County Road 21) for about six miles. At the "Y" in Pikeville, Jackson County Road 21 goes left and Jackson County Road 470 goes straight. Stay on 470 about two miles to a stop sign and go left on Jackson County Road 33. Travel up a steep and scenic two-lane road about 8 miles to the top of the mountain. At the cut made by the power lines, you will get a breathtaking view of the valley. Watch for signs to the orchard. When you see Jackson County Road 39, turn right. Go about three and a half miles and you are there and in for a treat that will dribble down your chin and make your hands sticky, but you won't care. Your pocketknife will come in handy for slicing samples, which you're invited to do. The trip down the mountain is still ahead. Set aside about two hours for enjoying this adventure. Yes, you have the time.

The mountain air and a sample of Crow Mountain apples have probably set off your appetite alarm. When you return to Scottsboro, take the John T. Reid Parkway and watch for the sign to the **Jackson County Park,** land owned by the TVA that overlooks Lake Guntersville and the Tennessee River. You could spend a weekend here, easily. The park has a camping area, a walking trail, a great playground and pool pavilion, and swings on the water's edge just waiting for a body in need of relaxing. A restaurant that had just been open three weeks when we were in the area serves a buffet lunch that is more than satisfying. Take your plate to the screen porch that overlooks the water. Go before noon. Everyone who has a lunch hour goes here. You'll see the insurance office staff, church secretaries, and bank officers. Everybody knows everybody. They won't know you, but it doesn't matter. They will speak to you anyhow. No wonder people visit here and come back to stay.

Area Code: (256)

Getting There:

From Interstate 65, Scottsboro can be reached by going through Huntsville on Interstate 565 and continuing on U.S. 72. Scottsboro is about 80 miles from Huntsville. From Birmingham, take Interstate 59 to exit 218, and follow Alabama 35 to Scottsboro.

Directions to **Gorham's Bluff**: From Scottsboro, take U.S. 35 South toward Fort Payne. Cross B.B. Comer Bridge, then take the first left up the mountain on Alabama 40. Follow Alabama 40 to the four-way stop and turn left on Alabama 71 north. Follow Alabama 71 to Jackson County 58, take a left at the Kountry Korner market, and follow Jackson County Road 58 to Pisgah. Follow Jackson County Road 58 through the heart of Pisgah for 2.2 miles and turn left on Jackson County Road 357 (left turn is .3 of a mile past Blow Gourd General Store). Follow Jackson County Road 357 for 1.2 miles and turn left on Jackson County Road 457. Follow Jackson County Road 457 for .7 of a mile and turn right onto Main Street in Gorham's Bluff.

Where and When:
Crow Mountain Orchard, 6236 Jackson County Road 39, Fackler, AL 35746. Open daily, 8 A.M.-5 P.M. Closed in winter season. 437-9254.
Goose Pond Colony, 417 Ed Hembree Drive, Scottsboro, AL 35769. 259-2884; (800) 268-2884. Web site: www.goosepond.org
Rivermont Cave Historic Trail, Trail Chairman, Courtney Coffman, 102 Carl Maynor Lane, Bridgeport, AL 35740. 495-2667.
Russell Cave National Monument, 3729 Jackson County Road 98, Bridgeport, AL 35740. Daily, 8 A.M.-4:30 P.M. 495-2672.
Web site: www.nps.gov/ruca/
Scottsboro-Jackson Heritage Center, 208 S. Houston Street, Scottsboro, AL 35768. Tue.- Fri., 11 A.M.-4 P.M. 259-2122. Admission.
Stevenson Railroad Depot Museum, Main Street, Stevenson, AL 35772. Mon.-Fri., 9 A.M.-5 P.M. Open Sat., Apr.-Dec. 437-3012.
Unclaimed Baggage Center, 509 W. Willow Street, Scottsboro, AL 35769. Mon.-Thurs., 8 A.M.-5 P.M.; Fri.-Sat., 8 A.M.-6 P.M. 2591525.
Web site: www.unclaimedbaggage.com

Information:
Alabama Mountain Lakes Tourist Association, 25062 North Street, Mooresville, AL 35649. 350-3500.
National Speleological Society, 2813 Cave Avenue, Huntville, AL 35810. 852-1300. Web site www.caves.org
Rainsville Chamber of Commerce, P.O. Box 396, Rainsville, AL 35986. 638-7800.
Rivermont Cave Historic Trail, Trail Chairman, Courtney Coffman, 102 Carl Maynor Lane, Bridgeport, AL 35740. 495-2667.
Scottsboro-Jackson County Chamber of Commerce, 407 E. Willow Street, Scottsboro, AL 35768. 259-5500; (800) 259-5508.
Web site: www.sjccchamber.org

Accommodations:
Crow Creek Cottage, 367 Jackson County Road 287, Stevenson, AL 35772. 437-2535; (800) 344-5573.
Goose Pond Colony, 417 Ed Hembree Drive, Scottsboro, AL 35769. 259-2884; (800) 268-2884. Web site: www.goosepond.org
Lodge at Gorham's Bluff, 101 Gorham Drive, Pisgah, AL 35765. Call for reservations. 451-3435. Web site: www.thebluff.com

Restaurants:
Buena Vista Mex-Mex Grill, Alabama 35 S., Rainsville, AL 35986, Mon.-Thurs., 11 A.M.-9 P.M.; Fri.-Sun., 11 A.M.-10 P.M.

Choo Choo Restaurant, Main Street, Stevenson, AL 35772, Mon.-Fri., 5 A.M.-2 P.M.; Sun., 11 A.M.-2 P.M. 437-8736.

Crawdaddy's, Too, 417 Ed Hembree Drive, Scottsboro, AL 35769. Winter, Wed.-Sat., 4:30 P.M.-10 P.M.; summer, Wed.-Thurs., 4:30 P.M.-10 P.M.; Fri.-Sat., 11:30 A.M.-10 P.M. 574-3071.

Jackson County Park, County Park Road, Scottsboro, AL 35768. Mon.-Tue., 6 A.M.-2 P.M.; Wed.-Sun., 6 a.m-8 P.M. 259-3877.

Liberty Restaurant, 907 E. Willow Street, Scottsboro, AL 35768. Mon.-Thurs., 6 A.M.-7:30 P.M.; Fri.-Sat., 6 A.M.-8 P.M., 574-3455.

Western Sizzlin, 23980 John T. Reid Parkway, Scottsboro, AL 35768. Mon.-Thurs., 10:30 A.M.-10 P.M.; Fri.-Sun., 10:30 A.M.-11 P.M. 259-6888.

Major Annual Events:

First Monday Trade Days, Jackson County Courthouse Square, Scottsboro—First Mon. and preceding Sat. and Sun. 259-5500; (800) 259-5508.

Russell Cave Native American Festival, Bridgeport May. 495-2672.

Gerhart Chamber Music Festival, Gorham's Bluff, Pisgah June. 451-3435.

Stevenson Depot Days, Main Street, Stevenson—June. 437-3012.

Independence Day Celebrations, Goose Pond Colony—July 4th. 259-2884; (800) 268-2884.

Alabama Ballet Residency, Gorham's Bluff, Pisgah—July. 451-3435.

Summer Theater Festival, Gorham's Bluff, Pisgah—August. 451-3435.

Storytelling Festival, Gorham's Bluff, Pisgah—Last weekend in September. 451-3435.

Southeastern Native American Festival, Scottsboro-Jackson. Heritage Center, Scottsboro—October. 259-2122.

32

PILLOW TALK

The **Mentone-Fort Payne** area has two state parks, at least eight bed and breakfasts, a golf and ski resort, a dude ranch, and a newly re-opened inn. No matter whether you are considering lodge accommodations, cottage alcoves, bed and breakfast suites, camp sites, or a bunkhouse, that's a lot of places to lay your head when you visit this paradise hidden away at the Southern gateway to the Appalachian Mountain region.

Where you stay will have some bearing on your schedule for this weekend getaway. Restaurants and activities will be closer to one bed and breakfast than another. If it's too hard to decide where to stay, just keep coming back until you've tried every one.

Mentone has six bed and breakfasts, and three of them are "havens." **Raven Haven, Rock Haven,** and **Summer Haven** may share the same second name, but each has a personality of its own.

When Anthony and Eleanor Teverino merged their talents to develop **Raven Haven,** the project became a creative endeavor, too. Like many innkeepers, Tony and Eleanor had other careers and raised a family before they became partners in the full-time business of running a bed and breakfast. Tony's stained-glass craftsmanship brightens several rooms in the house. Eleanor is a quilter, doll collector, and artist. Her quilts complement the color scheme. Small surprises she has painted in unexpected places delight guests.

Each of the four guestrooms is decorated to carry out a theme. The old-fashioned eighteenth-century boudoir feeling in the "Queen

DeSoto Falls. (Photo courtesy Helen Kittinger)

Anne" is completed with a stained-glass window above the bed. Sturdy furnishings in "The Nautical" are softened by light from a porthole above a rope hammock, perfect for a good book and a long afternoon. "Casablanca" is a Bogie and Bacall trip down Memory Lane. Or was that Ingrid Bergman? "The Little Room on the Prairie" is more secluded and has a "buttoned up against the storm" cozy feeling.

Hang your clothes in the closet and visit with the Teverinos and Running Horse, the cat who really runs the house, by the Franklin stove in the living room. Settling into the custom-crafted rocker could defeat your plan to go to your room early.

In the morning soft music plays throughout the house, inviting guests to gather around the picture-perfect table set with linen and lace, flowers, fresh fruit, homemade jams and jellies, just-baked specialty breads, and a steaming breakfast casserole. Early risers are best prepared to enjoy such a hearty meal. They have already been outside wandering among the gardens and flowerbeds.

Rock Haven is a separate house large enough for a family of four to stay for a week or two. Instead of serving breakfast, the owner stocks the kitchen so guests can prepare their own. A play yard outside the cottage entertains youngsters for hours.

When Cristina Wise toured her husband's family home the first time, she was completely unprepared for what she saw when she stepped out the back door: the breathtaking view of thundering De Soto Falls. One of the two **Summer Haven Cottages** enjoys the same majestic view.

The main house was built in 1925, about the same time Bill Wise's grandfather built the dam and first hydroelectric power plant in North Alabama. In 1926 this plant lit up the small towns around Mentone. You can see the pad where the generator stood, but you won't want to leave the deck and the view of the falls. "Awesome" is the apt description.

Along with sustenance, innkeepers are eager to serve their guests a healthy dollop of knowledge about the area. They can give you directions to miles of hiking trails and scenery that inspires artists. Business hours of restaurants and stores are seasonal and sometimes sporadic. The call of the outdoors on an unexpected glorious day is pretty hard to resist. Can you blame anyone for closing up shop and going fishing? B&B owners have an idea as to what will be open.

Two more charming places to stay are the **Mountain Laurel Inn** and **A Little Village Called Valhalla.** Both have separate cabins, but

DeSoto Falls from Summer Haven Cottages. (Photo by Neal Broerman)

guests eat in the family house. Sarah Wilcox does all the cooking at **Mountain Laurel Inn** and might serve zucchini, carrot, or lemon bread in the light-filled breakfast and library. Later, choose a good book and a comfortable chair or hike along the bluff. De Soto Falls is a 10-minute walk away.

Valhalla borders Little River Canyon National Preserve. Together the four cottages comprise "A Little Village Called Valhalla." Karen Ormstedt's main house is a 1930s farmhouse with a big-family feeling. Imagine the kitchen alive with happy voices and the sounds of chopping and stirring.

Two larger B&Bs are located in the center of Mentone, within walking distance of shops and several restaurants. You could spend the entire weekend within the boundaries of two blocks.

Ro's Kreations has a Christmas room the year-round, and the **Crow's Nest,** one of several shops inside the **Hitchin' Post,** is influenced by its owner, Bernise Crow, a writer with a Christmas attitude. The building is on the National Register of Historic Places, and the second floor was a turn-of-the-century dance hall. Now you can find wonderful old books there. Owners of the **White Elephant Galleries,** Judy and Louis Pierce, have filled the many rooms of their rambling building with art and collectible antiques. Scented candles and crystal bowls of muscadine potpourri perfume both floors, keeping browsers in a mellow mood.

The **Mentone Inn** was built in 1927, but it was closed for most of 1999. It has just re-opened and is waiting for you to try it out. New owners are Michael and Sarah Campbell, and their hostess, Daisy Anne Elliott, affectionately called "Ms. Daisy," is already charming guests. Across the street, **Mentone Springs Hotel** Bed and Breakfast, next door to the White Elephant, is the oldest hotel in Alabama still in use. It was built in 1884. Claudia and Dave Wassom bought this graceful Queen Anne Victorian about four years ago. They welcome pets and kids. **Caldwell's** Restaurant in the Hotel serves a popular Sunday buffet open to the public. Breakfast for bed and breakfast guests is made to order and served in the dining room or on the veranda that overlooks a rolling lawn and clusters of rhododendron.

Wherever you stay on Friday, Saturday morning breakfast is assured, and it will be substantial. Now you are ready to spend Saturday touring Mentone. Don't worry about your appetite. By the time you finish touring the antique and craft shops, you will be ready for lunch. You won't have far to travel.

Mentone Springs Hotel. (Photo by Neal Broerman)

Log Cabin Deli was an Indian Trading Post from 1800-1835. It was the only one for 150 miles. Collette Kirby has owned the historic restaurant for a dozen years and makes delicious soup from home-grown veggies. How long has it been since you had a fried bologna sandwich? The Cabin Hobo is made up of this old favorite plus onion, lettuce, and tomato. De-stress by pulling up a rocking chair in front of the stone fireplace. It's been watching people snooze for almost 200 years.

Rumor has it that **Dessie's Kountry Chef** serves the best catfish in the world, and that just might be true. Dessie is also an artist, and her paintings are on display. Her son built the doll's spinning wheel in a showcase by the desk. This is the only restaurant in Mentone open on Monday. Along with the catfish, Dessie Newberry's Sunday dinner chicken and dressing has earned quite a reputation, too.

The **Bistro** is a new restaurant only a half mile from the Georgia line, but Mentone residents are happy to claim it. The décor has a French country garden feeling, and the shrimp sandwich, chef salad, and hamburgers are receiving rave reviews.

You are not far from **Valley Head** and two more unique bed and breakfasts. **Woodhaven** is a working farm sprawled in a valley below Lookout Mountain. Take Alabama 11 E. toward Chattanooga. Judith and Kaare Lollik-Andersen invite guests to have a snack before breakfast and stroll out to the pasture to take a look at the cattle, sheep, and goats. Then enjoy a homemade breakfast and, if you like, carry your book to the creek or swing gently on the front porch, shaded by 200-year-old trees. In cool months, a fire in the sitting room, or even in your own room, will keep you toasty.

Kaare is from Norway, and he chose Valley Head because the climate made him think of home. Reminders of his life at sea decorate the house.

Winston Place, on the National Register of Historic Places, is where Jane Matthews grew up. She enthralls guests with fascinating tidbits about each room and almost every piece of furniture. Alabama fans will enjoy highlights of All American **Jim Bunch**'s football career in the basement museum and video viewing room.

Dolly Madison's grandmother and the mother of Patrick Henry are part of the family of Winston. The house pre-dates the Civil War and has always offered gracious hospitality with the single exception of the time more than 30,000 Union troops camped around the Winston Spring in the fall of 1863.

Sequoyah taught his alphabet under the Cherokee Council Tree near Winston Place, and Sequoyah Caverns, named for the revered educator, is also in Valley Head. You will see many pictures and statues of Sequoyah in this area, and because he wore a turban, not feathers, and walked with a cane, he is easily recognized. Sequoyah is considered a genius, as he was the only man in history to conceive and perfect an alphabet. He also walked with his people in 1838 on the Trail of Tears.

Saturday afternoon is a great time to visit **Sequoyah Caverns and Campground.** As you approach, you will cross a stream and see pastures dotted with old red barns. "See Rock City," one proclaims. These barn signs are now considered an art form.

You'll see the campground first and get a rare glimpse of the buffalo that used to storm across our earth in large herds. Pygmy goats graze the fields beside shy white fallow deer. Sally, George, Jack, and Judy Eastman, who own the caverns, brought the deer from Germany. Bring a picnic lunch. You can eat and enjoy the animals from a distance.

The guided tour of the caverns takes about half an hour and is an

Bikers at Sequoyah Caverns. (Photo by Neal Broerman)

Sequoyah Cave stalagmites. (Photo by Neal Broerman)

Shady Grove Dude Ranch. (Photo by Neal Broerman)

easy walk for every age. Rainbow falls, looking-glass lakes, and majestic columns, formed when stalactites and stalagmites meet, create an underground palace, so stunning that weddings have taken place in the "ballroom." Imagine the flickering light of torches while the wedding march echoes through the chambers!

From the depths of the earth to the top of it, take DeKalb County Road 89 from the De Soto State Park toward Mentone for about three miles and turn right on DeKalb County Road 614 to **Cloudmont Ski and Golf Resort** and **Shady Grove Dude Ranch.** Both are owned and operated by **Jack Jones,** who gives new meaning to the term "colorful character." Eighty years young, Jack grew up going to children's summer camps on Lookout Mountain. He always knew the mountain was where he wanted to live. Now he owns lots of it. Jack runs the southernmost ski resort in the United States. Guests can ski in the wintertime or play golf in the summertime at Saddle Rock Golf course, which he also owns. Most of the time guests can ride horses while they soak up the rustic atmosphere at the Shady Grove Dude Ranch. With a twinkle in his eye, Jack will tell you the life history of every horse and mule in the barn.

Jack raised eight kids, wrote a book, and still rides and paints. He's always somewhere on the ranch, but that's a big place. If you can't find him, pick out a rocking chair on the bunkhouse porch and read his book, *Come Sit a Spell.*

For supper, you are in for a treat. No matter how cool the mountain air may be outside, the **Little River Café** will warm your bones. Next door to **Lookout Mountain General Store,** the café is in Fischer Crossroads, a European settlement established in 1856 by Gustavia Fischer of Hugelheim, Germany. It is atop Lookout Mountain and is two and one half miles south of De Soto State Park.

An early Sunday morning drive along scenic **Little River Canyon** Rim Road, Alabama Highway 176, is reverential. Little River Canyon is the fifth-largest canyon east of the Rockies. Canyon Rim Road is part of Lookout Mountain Parkway and follows the west rim of Little River Canyon. You'll peek over the edge at drops of 600 to 700 feet that will take your breath away. A glimpse of tiny wildflowers will squeeze your heart. Listen to the roar of Little River, one of the few rivers in the country that rises and runs its course atop a mountain. It flows out of the canyon and leaves Lookout Mountain at Canyon Mouth Park.

At **Wolf Creek Overlook** you'll see the bluffs that challenge rappellers and the fast-moving, treacherous water that canoers and kayakers love. Nearby is **Mushroom Rock,** a sandstone formation that sparks imaginations.

DeKalb County contains 1,700 miles of country road, and nearly all of it is scenic. You can do a lot of hiking and exploring in the undeveloped sections, but plan ahead. Write or stop by the Dekalb County Tourism office and pick up maps and guidance.

Check your watch. You may have time to make the 10 A.M. service at the **Sallie Howard Memorial Chapel,** just outside De Soto State Park. The pulpit is made of stones from Little River and the back of the chapel is a large boulder. Even if you miss the service, you can visit at other times. The chapel is always open.

Sunday afternoon in Fort Payne offers a range of sights to enjoy. Music fans will delight in the **Alabama Fan Club Museum.** Members of the world-famous group grew up in Fort Payne, and fans flock to see personal items such as **Randy Owen**'s bottle collection and **Teddy Gentry**'s first guitar, as well as the musical awards amassed by the "Entertainers of the Decade." The souvenir shop is well stocked with everything from shirts to CDs.

Theater and music lovers and history buffs, too, will appreciate the **Fort Payne Opera House,** the oldest theater in Alabama still in use. It's on the National Register of Historic Places and the National Register of Nineteenth Century Theaters in America. Legendary performers Jenny Lind and Sarah Bernhard have captivated audiences there.

Private tours of the Opera House can be arranged, and seeing this grand old lady of the theater is worth the extra effort. Of special note are the Opera House murals by artists **Jeff Wright** and **John Hill, Jr.**

The murals are a timeline of life in the area from the signs of earliest habitation in the cliff caves below De Soto Falls through the country's bicentennial celebration in 1976. Indians, explorers, frontiersmen, British agents, pioneers, traders, and missionaries stand tall. Friends and brothers part to fight on opposite sides in the Civil War. The end of the war did not end the division of opinion, and eruptions of anger and bitterness made some homecomings difficult. In the latter half of the nineteenth century, the discovery of coal and iron ore fueled a Fort Payne "boom" that lasted for about four years. Developers from the northeast descended and laid out city streets and parks. The Opera House was opened in 1889, the year after the industrial boom began. Modern farming, new industry, and the region's growing attraction for tourists mark the completion of the mural.

The next stop on the history trail is the **Depot Museum,** a short

Sallie Howard Chapel at DeSoto Fall State Park. (Photo by Neal Broerman)

Fort Payne Opera House. (Photo by Neal Broerman)

walk away. You'll spot the turret and peaked roof. This building was used as a passenger station until 1970. It's on the National Register of Historic Places, and the history of the families of the area can be read in the articles on display.

DeKalb County was created from Cherokee lands. **Fort Payne** was named for the fort built by a captain named Payne, sent by the federal government in 1837 to build a fort to protect the white settlers in case the Indians didn't want to move west. The Cherokees who left DeKalb County were among the last to leave their native country. Forced to march on the **Trail of Tears,** some of the Cherokees' hastily-left-behind possessions could be included in the pottery, baskets, weapons, tools, and clothing assembled in the Depot Museum. Household items, farm equipment, tools, and early machines from the 1800s and early 1900s have been donated by longtime Fort Payne residents. A jewelry collection from the 1930s and 1940s is growing. An old player piano from the 1920s and a collection of hand-blown glassware known as whimsies are especially interesting. The gift shop will whet your appetite for **Big Mill Antique Mall.**

Items you saw on display in the Depot Museum are apt to have "cousins" for sale in the Old Mill. Wander the aisles of the building that was, indeed, an old mill built in 1889 and listed on the National Register of Historic Places. Clocks, jewelry, china, toys, tools, books, and an amazing array of collectibles and reproductions fill every nook and cranny. Local artist **Jimmy Frazier** memorialized the mill and the way of life it supported in his paintings. The Mill carries note cards featuring Frazier's well-known work.

Did you know Fort Payne is the sock capital of the world? At this writing, the hosiery mills were not open to the public, but ask at the Dekalb County Tourism office if it's possible to set up a private tour. Watch for sock outlet stores scattered throughout shopping areas.

To end your weekend with an awesome experience, get closer to **De Soto Falls** than you have been already. From Fort Payne, take Alabama 35 S. up the mountain, and follow the signs to the falls. The road is like a ribbon running up and down and across Lookout Mountain. It will take you about 10 minutes to reach the Falls. If heights bother you, ease yourself onto a bench and let others grasp the railing and descend the steep steps. The thunderous sound of water cascading 100 feet is as overwhelming as the view. This is not the place to let toddlers loose.

Whether you hike to the edge of the water or sit and admire, you

Shugart Sock Mill. (Photo by Neal Broerman)

are going to work up an appetite. It's time for supper and you are not far from the lodge at **De Soto State Park.** You could spend a weekend there, too, hiking, picnicking, playing tennis, swimming, or boating. The restaurant in the lodge serves three meals a day, a good fact to remember if you are unable to find a place to eat in Mentone or Fort Payne.

After supper, if it is still light, enjoy the short boardwalk trail between the lodge and the information center. It's comfortable for small wheels as well as feet. Strollers and wheelchairs glide easily. The trail follows a rock-pocked stream to a cluster of benches. Rest awhile and enjoy the serenade of the falls.

Sand Mountain is the site of **High Falls County Park,** and that's a scenic adventure to include on any weekend you spend in this area. Try to reach the falls by 10:30 A.M. and you just might see a rainbow. The High Falls Bridge on Town Creek was dedicated in October 1998. It replaced a covered bridge that burned in 1955. Park Ranger John Mitchell and his buddy Charlie Putnam recalled their boyhood in the area. On Sunday nights the church held a dinner on the grounds and then went to a baptism hole 100 yards beyond the

Pedestrian bridge at High Falls Park. (Photo by Neal Broerman)

Waterfall at High Falls Park. (Photo by Neal Broerman)

bridge. "If you wanted to see the girls, you went to the baptizing," the men said. They also told what they'd heard of life before the covered bridge was built. Wagons forded the creek, and it was a tricky business. If a wagon wheel dropped into a crevice in the rock, property and lives could be lost.

Town Creek flows into **Lake Guntersville.** While we hiked along the creek and shouted to each other above the gurgle of the water, we threaded our way through dogwood and wild azaleas. Bring your camera and a pen and paper if you are one whose fingers itch to sketch or make notes. Not many people know about this secluded park. Enjoy!

When you leave High Falls Park, take Alabama 75 to Rainsville and go right on Alabama 35 to **Katy's Catfish Cabin** in a log cabin that dates from the early 1800s. Randy Moore is the proud owner, and the specialty of the house is Cajun catfish.

At this point you are on the Trail of Tears Corridor. *Nunna daul tsuny* is "the trail where they cried." The annual motorcycle ride from Chattanooga to Waterloo brings attention to this sad chapter in American history, and more markers are springing up on the highway that traces the route across the northern part of the state. Fort Payne native **Jerry Ellis,** a Cherokee descendant, walked the 900-mile trail backwards from Oklahoma to his Alabama home and wrote a book about it, *Walking the Trail.* His book is one man's way to help us remember.

Area Code: (256)

Getting There:

Fort Payne lies in the valley between Sand Mountain and Lookout Mountain. Interstate 59 between Birmingham and Chattanooga also follows this valley. Fort Payne can be reached from Exits 218 and 222.

Where and When:

Alabama Fan Club Museum, 101 Glenn Avenue, Interstate 59, Exit 218, Fort Payne, AL 35967. Mon.-Sat., 8 A.M.-4 P.M.; Sun., noon-4 P.M. 845-1646.

Alabama Souvenir and Gift Shop, 101 Glenn Avenue, Interstate 59, Exit 218, Fort Payne, AL 35967. Mon.-Sat., 8 A.M.-4 P.M.; Sun., noon-4 P.M. 845-1646.

Big Mill Antique Mall, 151 Eighth Street N.E., Ft. Payne, AL 35967. Mon.-Sat., 10 A.M.-4 P.M.; Sun., 1 P.M.-4 P.M. 845-3380.

Buck's Pocket State Park, 393 DeKalb County Road 174, Grove Oak, AL 35975. 659-2000.

Cherokee County Historical Museum, 101 E. Main Street, Centre, AL 35960. Mon.-Sat., 8:30 A.M.-4 P.M. 927-3633. Admission.
Shady Grove Dude Ranch, 721 DeKalb County Road 614, Mentone, AL 35984. 634-8028. Admission.
Cloudmont Ski and Golf Resort, 721 DeKalb County Road 614, P.O. Box 435, Mentone, AL 35984. 634-4344. Admission.
Crow's Nest Antiques, 6081 Alabama 117, Mentone, AL 35984. 634-4548.
Depot Museum, 105 Fifth Street N., Ft. Payne, AL 35967. Mon., Wed., Fri., 10 A.M.-4 P.M.; Sun., 2 P.M.-4 P.M. 845-5714.
De Soto State Park, 265 Jackson County Road 951, Ft. Payne, AL 35967. 845-0051; (800) 568-8840.
Fort Payne Opera House, 510 Gault Avenue, Ft. Payne, AL 35699. Open by appointment. 845-3137.
Little River Canyon National Preserve, 2141 Gault Avenue N., Ft. Payne, AL 35967. Open year-round. 845-9605.
Web site: www.nps.gov/liri/
C. J.'s Wholesale Socks, 504 Gault Avenue N., Ft. Payne, AL 35967. Mon.-Fri., 9 A.M.-5 P.M.; Sat., 10 A.M.-4 P.M., 845-7986.
Lookout Mountain General Store, De Soto Parkway at Fischer Crossroad, Mentone, AL 35984. Mon.-Sat., 8 A.M.-5 P.M. 844-6500.
Ro's Kreations, 5889 Alabama 117, Mentone, AL 35984. 634-4456.
High Falls County Park, DeKalb County Road 144, Geraldine, AL.
Sallie Howard Memorial Chapel, 70 Green Valley Center, Fort Payne, AL 35967. Open 24 hours. Sunday services, 10 A.M. 845-1986.
Sequoyah Caverns and Campground, 1438 Jackson County Road 731, Valley Head, AL 35989. Mar.-Nov., daily, 8:30 A.M.-5:30 P.M.; Dec.-Feb., weekends only. 635-0024; (800) 843-5098. Admission.
Web site: www.bham.net/sequoyah/caverns/
White Elephant Galleries, 6152 Alabama 117, Mentone, AL 35984. Mon., Wed.-Sat., 10 A.M.-5 P.M.; Sun., 1 P.M.-5 P.M. 634-4529.

Information:
Alabama Mountain Lakes Tourist Association, 25062 North Street, Mooresville, AL 35649. 350-3500.
Alabama Welcome Centers, Interstate 59, Exit 241, Valley Head, AL.
DeKalb County Tourist Association, 1503 Glenn Boulevard S.W., Fort Payne, AL 35968. 845-3957.
Web site: www.hsv.tis.net/~dekbtour
Fort Payne Chamber of Commerce, 300 Gault Avenue, Ft. Payne, AL 35968. 845-2741.   Web site: www.fortpayne.com

Franklin County Chamber of Commerce, 500 N. Jackson Avenue, Russellville, AL 35653. 332-1760; Web site: www.getaway.net/fklcoc/

Accommodations:

A Little Village Called Valhalla, 672 Jackson County Road 626, Mentone, AL 35984. 634-4006.   Web site: www.virtualcities.com

De Soto State Park, 265 Jackson County Road 951, Ft. Payne, AL 35967. 845-0051; (800) 568-8840.

Mentone Inn, P. O. Box 290, Mentone, AL 35984. 634-4836; (800) 455-7470.

Mentone Springs Hotel, 6114 Alabama 117, Mentone, AL 35984. 634-4040; (800) 404-0100.   Web site: www.virtualcities.com

Mountain Laurel Inn, 624 Jackson County Road 948, Mentone, AL 35984. 889-4244.   Web site: www.bbonline.com/al/mli

Pruett's Fish Camp and Cabins, Cherokee County Road 16/22, Centre, AL 35960. 475-3950.

Raven Haven, 651 Jackson County Road 644, Mentone, AL 35984. 634-4310.

Sequoyah Caverns and Campground, 1438 Jackson County Road 731, Valley Head, AL 35989. Mar.-Nov., daily, 8:30 A.M.-5:30 P.M.; Dec.-Feb., weekends only. 635-0024; (800) 843-5098. Admission.
          Web site: www.bham.net/sequoyah/caverns/

Summer Haven Cottages, 132 DeKalb County Road 935, Mentone, AL 35984. 634-6025.

Winston Place, P.O. Box 165, Valley Head, AL 35989. 635-6381; (800) 494-6786.   Web site: www.virtualcities.com

Woodhaven, 390 Lowry Road, Valley Head, AL 35989. 635-6438.

The **secret bed and breakfast,** 2356 Alabama 68 W., Leesburg, AL 35983. 523-3825.
          Web site: www.bbonline.com~bbonline/al/thesecret

Restaurants:

Bistro, 1630 Alabama 117, near the Georgia state line, Mentone, AL 35984. Fri.-Sun., lunch and dinner.

Caldwell's, Mentone Springs Hotel, 6114 Alabama 117, Mentone, AL 35984. Thurs.-Mon., 11 A.M.-2 P.M., 5 P.M.-8 P.M.; Sun., 11 A.M.-3 P.M. 634-4040; (800) 404-0100; Web site: www.virtualcities.com.

Cragsmere Manna, Lookout Mountain Parkway, Mentone, AL 35984. Fri.-Sat., 5 P.M.-9 P.M. 634-4677.

Dessie's Kountry Chef, 5951 Alabama 117 S., Mentone, AL 35984. Mon., Wed.-Sat., 10 A.M.-8 P.M.; Sun., 11 A.M.-2 P.M. 634-4232.

Katy's Catfish Cabin, 1382 Main Street, Rainsville, AL 35986. Mon.-Thurs., 11 A.M.-9 P.M.; Sat.-Sun., 11 A.M.-10 P.M. 638-7200.

Little River Café, 4608 De Soto Parkway N.E. at Fischer Crossroad, Mentone, AL 35984. Mon.-Fri., lunch; Fri.-Sat., dinner. 997-0707.

Log Cabin Deli, 6080 Alabama 117, Mentone, AL 35984. Tue.-Thurs., 11 A.M.-7 P.M.; Fri.-Sat., 11 A.M.-9 P.M. 634-4560.

33

A FRIENDSHIP REWARDED

Rarely does anyone notice the dark-eyed young man in the picture in the **Gadsden** Public Library. He's the man for whom the town is named, but few know why. When James Gadsden sailed up the Coosa River to visit his friends at their Double Springs settlement, he rejoiced with them at the beauty and promise of their land. Pleased with his enthusiasm for their choice, they decided to name the town for him.

This is not the only place you will find the Gadsden name. The man was a key figure in the settlement of Florida, and a county and federal highway in that state bear his name. **Jefferson Davis** influenced President Franklin Pierce to appoint Gadsden to negotiate a land purchase that is noted in the history books as the Gadsden Purchase, in the states of Arizona and New Mexico. Gadsden, Arizona, is named for **James Gadsden,** too.

From such a friendly beginning, Gadsden, Alabama has grown and prospered. Gadsden's reunion with his friends can't be too far from the spot where the marble statue of **Emma Sansom** stands. This monument to a teenage girl recalls a later arrival in the town's history, an unwanted visit from Union troops. They burned a bridge to delay pursuing Confederate cavalry, but Emma helped General **Nathan Bedford Forrest** and his men find a way to ford Black Creek and continue the chase.

Near Emma's statue is a memorial to **John Wisdom,** who rode all night from Gadsden to Rome, Georgia, to warn that Union raiders were on the way. For his long ride and lost sleep, Wisdom is called the "Paul Revere of the Confederacy."

The middle of downtown Gadsden may not be as James Gadsden and his friends knew it, but the wooded slopes and hillocks of Shinbone Ridge are as green and unspoiled as they were 175 years ago. From that ridge, guests in Diane and Bill Cruickshank's mountaintop mansion, the **secret bed and breakfast,** enjoy a commanding view of the valley and its treasure, **Weiss Lake.** This priceless treasure is guarded by a patrolling peacock while bed and breakfast guests relax in the rooftop pool.

Diane and Bill recently completed the Sugar Shack, a honeymoon cottage, not far from the mansion. It has its own private view of the lake.

The Cruickshank's serve a full Southern breakfast on a ten-foot revolving tabletop in the two-story great room. After such an auspicious beginning to the day, guests can swim, swing, loaf, or stroll the grounds, all under the watchful eye of that peacock. They might also drive into Gadsden for a morning of museums.

While a just-for-two weekend is unfolding at the secret, a family could be climbing out of a tent or camper at **Noccalula Falls Park** and Campground on the edge of Gadsden, about three miles from Interstate 59. The city owns the park, which offers all the expected campground amenities, and the location is ideal for those who can't decide between a campout and the cultural offerings of a small city. Why not have it all?

Botanical gardens surround the park, and every spring over 25,000 azaleas burst into bloom, competing for the attention of winter-weary eyes. Explore the ravine below the 90-foot falls and see historic sites and unusual rock formations. Does the legend of the luckless Noccalula stir your sympathy? The Pioneer Village will tax your feet less, but it will fire your imagination just the same.

Crave a little culture? A morning in the museums should satisfy. Leave your tree-shaded campsite and head for the city.

Community helpers work hard at the **Imagination Place Children's Museum** at the **Center for Cultural Arts.** With appropriate motor and siren sounds, the rescue squad swings into action. In another part of the "let's pretend" town, storekeepers and librarians ask politely, "May I help you?" While the children are role-playing in their make-believe city, adults can take the escalator to the second floor and see nationall-known exhibits.

The **Gadsden Museum of Art** is now city-owned and is at a temporary location. It will soon move to the same block as the Cultural Arts

Center and Imagination Place, and its focus will be on local artists and craftspersons.

John Solomon Sandridge is a local artist who designs **Luv Life Collectibles,** paints, sculpts, and writes lyrics and children's books. This multi-talented artist makes his home in Gadsden with his wife and six children. He describes his work as "African American Life in America in Revolutionary Progress," progress that shows in the faces of his subjects, from slave portraits to successful modern women. His painting "Delicious and Refreshing" is the first art work with a black theme authorized by Coca-Cola. John has been called "a black Norman Rockwell." Call to visit his gallery. You just might get to meet him, too.

Farther down the road, in east Gadsden, headed toward **Glencoe,** you'll see the growth of another artistic vision, **All God's Children,** the collectibles designed by Miss **Martha Root.** Since the showroom is closed Friday through Sunday, you'll have to stay over until it opens at 7 A.M. on Monday. The best way to plan this short side trip is to call for directions before you go. Miss Martha's handcrafted figurines capture the joy and delight of childhood. They'll put a smile on your face, too.

A scenic drive before lunch will kick appetites into high gear, and **Muffins Café** will be worth the wait. For some, the 1950s atmosphere at Muffins will be pure nostalgia. For others it will be an introduction to the happy times that get better as television reruns embellish the memories. Atmosphere aside, the luncheon specials are sure to nurture. From downtown Gadsden, take U.S. 411 East to **Centre.**

After lunch, travel east on U.S. 411 and continue your trek back in time with a visit to the **Cherokee County Historical Museum.** From dolls to books to local farm equipment, the rooms are crammed with displays of items pertinent to the history of the area.

As you drive along U.S. 411, the sun bouncing off the crystal lake waters is bound to lure you to the side of the road to take pictures. However, fishermen may receive signals of a different sort. Weiss Lake calls itself "The Crappie Capital of the World." That claim can be tested by a weekend in a cabin, trailer, room, or campsite at **Pruett's Fish Camp** and Cabins. Rates are reasonable, and the camp overlooks the clear water of Cowan Creek.

At the other end of the pamper scale, a new bed and breakfast in **Hokes Bluff** will have you humming "Tara's Theme" as you wend your way toward it. Although it wasn't quite open for business when we stopped by, **Cove Creek** Bed and Breakfast is right in the middle

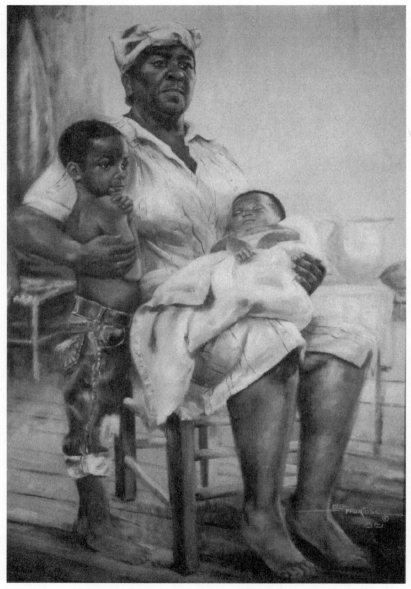

My Mama Yo Mama. (Original painting by John Solomon
Sandridge, courtesy LUVLIFE Collectibles, Inc.)

Cove Creek Bed & Breakfast. (Photo by Neal Broerman)

of things on U.S. 278. It's not far from golf at **Silver Lakes,** fishing at Weiss Lake, or downtown Gadsden. Cheryl Wright owns this elegant home and has decorated the rooms to perfection in taste, yet spared no effort on comfort. Guests can swim, hike, or just claim the chair and ottoman in the spacious breakfast room and read a good book.

Silver Lakes is another **Robert Trent Jones Golf Trail,** and this one was named by *Golf Digest's Places to Play* as one of the nation's Great Value courses in the public category. Set at the edge of **Talladega National Forest,** Silver Lakes boasts three championship nines and a nine-hole short course some golfers consider the most challenging on the Trail.

Whether you set up camp at Noccalula, drop a line at Pruett's, snuggle into a comfortable chair at Cove Creek, or loaf by the pool at the secret, dinnertime is inevitable. Although we did not eat dinner in Gadsden, we have two restaurants to suggest.

We entered the **Olde Warehouse** at noon on a workday, never a good time to arrive at a downtown restaurant. It seemed that every possible space was filled with happy diners, but the hostess managed to seat us promptly. A waitress rushed by, helped us choose two of the specials, savory vegetable casseroles, which arrived steaming hot and delicious, and 35 minutes later we were outside again. If it's that good when the place is mobbed, what must it be like when it is not so busy? Or does that ever happen? We'll have to go again to see. Judging from the bandstand set up at one end of the dining room, there must be live music in the evenings.

Top O the River Restaurant is surely another excellent choice. Our experience at the family-owned Top of the River in Anniston is described in a future chapter. What we learned there applies here. Be early—before the five o'clock opening so you will be called for the first seating—and ask your waitress about splitting appetizers and entrées. Portions in the Anniston restaurant were beyond bountiful. Local residents say they starve themselves all day before settling down in front of the generous seafood platter served at the Gadsden location.

Sunday is another day filled with numerous possibilities. You haven't gone shopping yet. Yard sales and flea markets flourish in the Gadsden area. The third weekend in August, the **World's Longest Yard Sale** begins at Noccalula Falls Park. The **Lookout Mountain Parkway,** one of the most scenic drives in America, begins there, too. If the yard sale is not of interest, the overlooks will be.

On any of the other 51 weekends, Sunday is the day to head for the **Mountain Top Flea Market.** Janie and Milton Terrell see that this bargain bonanza runs smoothly 52 days a year. Five A.M. is the starting time. Early birds, start your engines. The entire flea market is all on one level, and admission and parking are free. The only thing you need money for is your bargains. Come to think of it, the best time to come to this flea market might be while everyone else is at the 450-mile-long yard sale. Ah, shopping strategy!

Make room in the car for more treasures, and drive into **Attalla,** directly off Interstate 59. In 1903 Attalla became home to the first hydroelectric generator in the world and the birthplace of Alabama Power. It was the first city to be completely powered by water. The first foothill of the Appalachian Mountains is located there. So are 15 richly endowed antique shops. All are in the center of town, presumably well lit.

There's even more good news for shoppers and bargain hunters. More than 100 factory stores and 5 outlet shopping centers are 13 miles away down U.S. 31 in **Boaz.** Not every town can claim that it has been written up in both *Time* and *Newsweek.* Boaz can. The community has celebrated its 100th birthday and **Snead State Community**

College, within the town's borders, just had its 100th anniversary, too, making it the oldest two-year college in the state. The Snead College cafeteria is open to the public, and on Sunday shoppers get in line with the townsfolk who eat there after church. Those with numerous church pot luck suppers in their past will have an edge when it comes to juggling sweet potatoes, green bean casseroles, several meats, and salads and dessert, but take it slowly and you'll manage just fine. No one will rush you.

For a separate weekend, the antique and art stores of **Springville,** 30 miles from Gadsden or Boaz, at Interstate 59, Exit 156, are open on Saturday, and the old-fashioned log cabin bedrooms of **Capps Cove** Bed and Breakfast in Oneonta are close enough to replenish energy stores. **Springville Café** charms its diners with nostalgia, and the **Springville House Tea Room** and **Café DuPont** are described by recent enthusiastic visitors as "upscale and new."

On Sunday afternoon, especially when fall colors are at their most intense, ride through Blount County, the "Covered Bridge Capital of Alabama." **Old Easley Covered Bridge,** built in 1927 and 1928, is the county's oldest surviving bridge, and, at 96 feet, is the shortest. **Swann Bridge,** a three span bridge 324 feet long, is the longest covered bridge in the state and the ninth-longest in the United States. It was built in 1933. **Horlon Mill Bridge** is one of the highest covered bridges above water in the United States. 220 feet long and 14 feet wide, it was built in 1934 and 1935 and was the first in the South to be listed on the National Register of Historic Places. All three are listed now.

You are not far from **Chandler Mountain,** which has the same reputation for tomatoes as Crow Mountain does for apples. Did you see signs for **Horse Pens 40**? You will if you take Asheville Exit 166 off Interstate 59 and turn left on U.S. 231. Cross U.S. 11 and go to St. Clair County Road 35. Watch for signs on the right, and follow the steep drive up Chandler Mountain to see rock formations that had many uses. Described in the first deed of ownership in the early 1900s as the "lower 40 . . . the farming 40 . . . and the horse pens 40," the horse pens section of the 120-acre spread was used by the Indians for shelter and to corral wild horses in spaces between the rocks. Later, valley settlers stored horses and provisions there during the Civil War. Pick your way among the boulders and outcroppings. Listen to the sounds of the wind. Or was that the wind?

Area Code: (256) Springville and (205) Oneonta

Getting There:

Gadsden can be reached from Interstate 59 at Exit 182 to Interstate 759. For Attalla and Boaz, use Exit 183.

Where and When:

Accents, 2101 First Avenue N., Pell City, AL 35125. Tue.-Sat., 11 A.M.-2 P.M. (205) 338-7499.

All God's Children Showroom, 1119 Chastain Boulevard, East Gadsden, AL. Mon.-Thurs., 7 A.M.-5 P.M. 492-0221.

Center for Cultural Arts, 501 Broad Street, Gadsden, AL 35902. Mon., Wed.-Fri., 9 A.M.-6 P.M.; Tue. 9 A.M.-9 P.M.; Sat., 10 A.M.-6 P.M.; Sun., 1 P.M.-5 P.M. 543-2787. Admission.

Web site: www.culturalarts.org

Charlotte's Web, 7162 U.S. 11, Springville, AL 35146. Closed Mon. and Tue. (205) 467-7243.

Cherokee County Historical Museum, 101 E. Main Street, Centre, AL 35960. Mon.-Sat., 8:30 A.M.-4 P.M. 927-7825.

Gadsden Museum of Art, 2829 West Meighan Boulevard, Gadsden, AL 35904. Mon.-Wed., 10 A.M.-4 P.M.; Thurs., 10 A.M.-8 P.M.; Fri., 10 A.M.-4 P.M.; Sun., 1 P.M.-5 P.M. 546-7365.

Web site: www.bham.net/gadsden/gma/

Horlon Mill Bridge, Alabama 75 N., Oneonta, AL 35121.

Horse Pens 40, 3525 St. Clair County Road 42, Steele, AL 35987. Open year-round for camping, hiking, and picnics. 570-0002; (800) 421-8564. Admission.   Web site: www.horsepens40.com

House of Quilts, 530 Main Street, Springville, AL 35146. Closed Mon.-Tue. (205) 467-6072.

John Solomon Sandridge Gallery, P.O. Box 1628, 225 S. Fourth Street, Gadsden, AL 35902. Open by appointment. 549-1534.

Mountain Top Flea Market and Country Mall, 11301 U.S. 278 W. at mile marker 101, Attalla, AL 35954. Open Sun., 5 A.M.; (800) 535-2286.

Noccalula Falls Park, 1500 Noccalula Road, Gadsden, AL 35902. Daily, 8 A.M.-dusk. 549-4663. Admission.

Web site: www.bham.net/nocca/falls/

Old Easley Covered Bridge, Alabama 160, Oneonta, AL 35121.

Silver Lakes Robert Trent Jones Golf Trail, Oak Grove Road, Glencoe, AL 35905. 892-3268.

Swann Bridge, Alabama 79, Cleveland, AL.

Information:

Alabama Mountain Lakes Tourist Association, 25062 North Street, Mooresville, AL 35649. 350-3500.

Albertville Chamber of Commerce, P. O. Box 1457, Albertville, AL 35950. 878-3821; (800) 878-3821.
Web site: www.albertvillechamber.com
Arab Chamber of Commerce, P. O. Box 626, Arab, AL 35016. 586-3138; (888) 403-2722.   Web site: www.arabcity.com
Blount/Oneonta Chamber of Commerce, P. O. Box 1487, Oneonta, AL 35121. 274-2153.   Web site: www.coveredbridge.org
Boaz Chamber of Commerce, P. O. Box 563, Boaz, AL 35957. 593-8154; (800) 746-7262.   Web site: www.boazalabama.com
Fish Habitat Enhancement Map. Write Alabama Power Company, P. O. Box 160, Montgomery, AL 36101.

Gadsden-Etowah Convention and Visitors Bureau, One Commerce Square, Gadsden, AL 35901. 547-9181; (800) 320-1692.

Gadsden-Etowah Tourism Center, 90 Walnut Street, Gadsden, AL 35901. 549-0351.   Web site: www.cybrtyme.com/Tourism/

Maps of Alabama Power Hydrogeneration, Lakes, Launch Sites, and Marinas.   Web site www.alapower.com/hydro

Miss Martha's Originals, Inc., P. O. Box 5038, Glencoe, AL 35905.

Springville Chamber of Commerce, P. O. Box 250, Springville, AL 35146. (205) 467-6072.

Guide Services:
Thornton Lakes Outdoors, 576 Thornton Lake Road, Gadsden, AL 35903. 492-0403.

Accommodations:
Capps Cove Bed and Breakfast, 4126 Blount County Road 27, Oneonta, AL 35121. 625-3039; (800) 583-4750.
Web site: www.bbonline.com/al/cappscove/antiques
Cove Creek Bed and Breakfast, 5595 U.S. 278, Hokes Bluff, AL. 442-5275.
Noccalula Falls Park and Campground, 1500 Noccalula Road, Gadsden, AL 35902. 549-4663.
Web site: www.bham.net/nocca/falls/
Pruett's Fish Camp and Cabins, 5360 Cherokee County Road 22, P. O. Box 507B, Route W, Centre, AL 35960. 475-3950; (800) 368-6238.

Restaurants:
Arbor House, U.S. 75, Oneonta, AL 35121. Mon.-Thurs., 11 A.M.-2:30 P.M.; Fri., 11 A.M.-9 P.M. 625-6666.
Café DuPont, 619 Main Street, Springville, AL 35146. Wed.-Sat., 11 A.M.-2 P.M., 5 P.M.-9 P.M., (205) 467-3339.

City Grill, Fifth and Broadway, Gadsden, AL. Tue.-Fri.,11 A.M.-2 P.M.; Tue.-Thurs., 5 P.M.-9 P.M.; Fri.-Sat., 5 P.M.-10 P.M. 546-8555.

Muffins Café, U.S. 411 S, Centre, AL. Mon.-Thurs., 10 A.M.-9 P.M.; Fri., 10 A.M.-10 P.M., Sat., 11 A.M.-10 P.M.; Sun., 11 A.M.-8:30 P.M. 927-2233.

Olde Warehouse, 315 S. Second Street, Gadsden, AL. Mon.-Fri., 11 A.M.-2 P.M.; 4 P.M.-10 P.M.; Sat., 5 P.M.-10 P.M. 547-5548.

Snead State Community College, 220 N. Walnut Street, Boaz, AL 35957. Mon.-Fri., open for lunch; Sun., buffet lunch. 593-5120.

Web site: www.snead.cc.al.us

Springville Café, 6204 U.S. 11, Springville, AL 35146. Mon.-Sat. 6:30 A.M.-10:30 A.M.; daily, 11 A.M.-2 P.M. (205) 467-7360.

Springville House Tea Room, 518 Main Street, Springville, AL 35146. Tue.-Sat., 11 A.M.-3 P.M., 467-6488.

Top O the River, 1606 Rainbow Drive, Gadsden, AL. Mon.-Thurs., 5 P.M.-9 P.M.; Fri., 5 P.M.-10 P.M.; Sat., 4 P.M.-10 P.M. 547-9817.

Major Annual Events:

Homestead Hollow Festival, Springville—Two times a year.

Riverfest, Gadsden—Spring., 543-3472. Admission.

Web site: riverfest.cybrtyme.com

Hot Rod Car Show, Noccalula Falls Park—June. 549-4663.

Summerfest, Homestead Hollow—Springville. June. 467-6403.

World's Longest Yard Sale, Gadsden—Third weekend in August.

World's Longest Outdoor Sale, Lookout Mountain Pkwy., Gadsden—Third week in August. 549-0351; (800) 320-1692.

Cherokee Pow Wow and Green Corn Festival, Noccalula Falls Park—September. 549-4663.

Antique Car Show, Noccalula Falls Park, 1500 Noccalula Road, Gadsden, AL 35902—Late fall. 549-4663.

Alabama's Covered Bridge Festival, Oneonta—October. 274-2153.

Harvest Festival, Homestead Hollow—October. 467-6403.

Harvest Festival, Boaz—October.

Native American Indian Festival Pow Wow, Boaz—October. 593-7336.

Christmas in the Country, Homestead Hollow—November. 467-6403.

Web site: members.aol.com/hmhollow

34

HOOKED
BY ONE LOOK

Azure waters mirrored in a summer sky blend into soft curves, then fade into the distant violet hues of the majestic Appalachian Mountains. The golden light of fall sharpens the focus. Winter's brief shadow dissolves into spring pastels and soon summer tints the world again. This is Alabama's picture postcard, **Guntersville.**

Located on Alabama's largest lake, Guntersville's 8000 residents support more than 40 civic organizations. Parks and trails are marked with signs of their support. For example, the Civitan Park has a 900-seat amphitheater with a lighted stage, and next to it is a 1.5-mile paved public walkway along the lake. To further embellish the quality of life, city parks have boat launch facilities, picnic areas, tennis and handball courts, a public pier, beach, and swimming. On our first night in Guntersville, we followed the **Sunset Drive Walking Trail** and saw a farmer's market, picnic tables in the park, and well-groomed (and busy) soccer fields. At the end of Sunset Drive we spotted **Adrian's** and began our weekend with a relaxing dinner and our first taste of the town's hospitality, a warm welcome.

Historical references list the town's founder as John Gunter, a Scotsman or a Welshman who married an Indian maid or an Indian princess. One account says he lived among the Cherokees, mined salt, and traded salt for his wife. He set up the first ferry on the river at Gunter's Landing in 1818 or 1820.

One hundred nineteen years later, the town underwent a drastic change, and those events are, happily, more clearly recorded. On

Hydrangea, Alabama state wildflower. (Photo courtesy Lynard Stroud)

January 15, 1939, the TVA dammed the Tennessee River. In 30 days Guntersville became a peninsula, and a lovely lake resort was born.

Lake Guntersville is the largest body of water wholly within Alabama and contains 68,000 acres of water and almost 1,000 miles of shoreline. There are seven public launch areas on the lake, and they are all free. As you cross the causeway into town, you'll grasp the popularity of boating immediately. Rows of tall masts with furled sails bob in marinas and outline private docks. A good day is heralded by billowing sails. Of course, all types of water activities flourish.

Because Guntersville is a resort area, there are many fine places to stay. My husband and I found many treasures at the end of little dirt roads in Alabama, and **Ivy Creek Inn** is one of them. Although the mailing address is Scottsboro, the Inn is five minutes closer to Guntersville. Guests at Ivy Creek can enjoy the best of both towns. Call ahead and innkeepers Kathy and Hess Fridley will set up a tee time at a nearby championship golf course in Scottsboro or Guntersville or engage a fishing guide to navigate Lake Guntersville's coves and creeks, streaked with silver and gold-flecked trophy catches.

The Fridley's greeting committee is made up of two cheerful collies,

Waterfall at Ivy Creek Inn. (Photo courtesy Lynard Stroud)

Lucky and Lucy, who bound over to welcome you, but have to wait for your reappearance on the porch. They are not allowed inside. You, however, will cross the threshold and feel at home immediately.

In mild weather, celebrate a special occasion with a candlelight dinner by the Fridley's creek. This must be arranged several days ahead of time, and Kathy's staging reflects artfulness and thoughtful preparation. When it's time to be seated, guests travel a torch-lined pathway to a romantic table glistening with candles. Violins blend with the song of the rocks and water. Dinner arrives in courses. Savory soup, crisp salad, yeast rolls, and jam made from berries picked on the mountain begin the meal. Your imagination can create the rest of the scene.

In the morning, pour a cup of just-perked coffee from the carafe on the hall table and slip outside to stroll the woodsy paths. Lucy will accompany you, but Lucky will wait on the porch. Watch for the noisy flight of geese turning neon in the sun as they flap their way toward the state park. Kathy says they fly by at 6:30 every morning. Bid the collies goodbye and step back into the house that, in your absence, has become fragrant with the smell of bacon and baking bread. Breakfast, included in the bed and breakfast package, is fully Southern and irresistible.

Don't rush headlong into the day. Browse through the country store Kathy and Hess set up for their guests so they can "take a little something home." Kathy's friend, Peggy Whitaker, who runs her own shop, **Peg's Posies,** out of her home, manages the country store and stocks it with jams, jellies, and pickled vegetables that preserve the memories of neighbors' gardens. A line of skin care products and bath salts mixed from locally grown natural ingredients by Jona Moody will keep you sniffing and dabbing little bits of cream on your wrists.

After trekking the woods, do you wonder where the sidewalks in Guntersville might lead you? For an in-town setting, you can't get a better location than **Lake Guntersville Bed and Breakfast.** What could be more soothing than a quiet stroll around a friendly town in the mountains? When your feet get tired, claim one of the hammocks on the porch. The resident Himalayan cat might curl up nearby and purr your worries away.

Innkeeper Carol Dravis was once a guest but returned to live in this glorious setting above the water.

In spite of the small-town feeling you'll get when you amble the blocks around Carol Dravis's B&B, the lengthy stretch of gift and

Marina and swing on Lake Guntersville. (Photo by Neal Broerman)

antique shops through the center of town can best be enjoyed by driving and parking. We sampled three and they are representative. Let them draw you next door and down the street and . . .

The owners of **Southern Pines,** Suzanne and Dennis Goldasich, go on buying trips to Europe and bring back antiques and reproduction furniture to fill their showrooms. Native Teresa Gilliland and her husband place an emphasis on the unusual in their display of fine gifts at the **Sugar Plum.**

The **Rock House** had just been open a few days when we stopped by. If there are gardeners on your gift list, hunt there for handy, helpful, or just plain delightful surprises. Sit on a garden bench in the back room and listen to a bubbling fountain while you mull over your choices.

As you drive down the 300 and 400 blocks of Gunter Avenue, you'll see many gift and clothing stores, and all of them display wares that you must see and touch. Every shopper knows this is true. To pacify the non-shoppers in your car, stop by **Wanda's** and order an ice cream treat. Of course, you could also stay for lunch. You are only blocks away from the **Guntersville Museum and Cultural Center.** We happened by on a day that board member George Newman was enthralling a class of first-graders with his tour of local exhibits. The children waved to us as they trooped out, and Mr. Newman and volunteer tour guide Mary Isom provided running commentary as we drifted in and out of the galleries and browsed the well-captioned exhibits. Guntersville is proud of its Cherokee and Creek heritage, and a framed picture of Will Rogers indicates Rogers' pride in his local Cherokee ancestry. The Indian Room pays further tribute. Archaeologists know that the Guntersville Basin has been inhabited for over 10,000 years. It is said that the Cherokees, Creeks, and whites lived here harmoniously, and choosing the Guntersville port as a place of embarkation for shipping the Indians westward on the Trail of Tears did not sit well with the town and area residents. The River Room details Gunter's Landing as a major port on the Tennessee River and the impact of the steamship on the town's economy.

In the TVA room you'll see a permanent educational exhibit on the construction of the Guntersville Dam, from the earliest surveys in 1929 through the actual flooding of the valley in January 1939. What was life like in the valley before and after the flooding? Some mourned the loss of farmlands, but this grief was lessened as the recreational possibilities blossomed.

Spanning the decades always builds an appetite. If you haven't eaten lunch yet, drive south on U.S. 431 and turn left at the huge billboard for **Mac's Landing.** Your destination is **Willie J's.** Ask for a table outside, an unhurried vantage point for all kinds of observations. Watch the children climbing trees, birds swooping along the water's edge, and cars like small buzzing beetles on the causeway across the lake. Crunch your way through a salad or sandwich and make afternoon plans.

Buck's Pocket State Park is talked about a lot, especially after elections. Presumably, defeated politicians go there to lick their wounds. The park lies in three counties. You've visited two, Jackson (Scottsboro) and Dekalb (Fort Payne and Mentone). The third one is Marshall, the one you are in now, and you are only 19 miles from the park. Take Alabama 227 and turn left on DeKalb County Road 402. On the way, you'll see Lake Guntersville Recreational Area, an inviting grove of trees beside the lake dotted with picnic tables. It looks secluded and could be a perfect place for a quiet picnic.

When you reach Buck's Pocket, you'll get that other-world feeling that intimidating boulders inspire. Rock climbers will rejoice at the cliffs looming over the roads and valleys. Others will be awed by the sheer size of the craggy formations.

The park's 2000 acres are not highly developed, but we saw a couple of people riding along the pathway to the office in electric wheelchairs, always a good sign of accessibility. I talked with campers who spend several weekends a year boating, fishing, and hiking while based at the modern campsites. One set of grandparents claimed 18 years of seasonal camping trips with their children at Buck's Pocket. They are carrying on the tradition with their grandchildren.

Now, here is a question to ponder as you drive back to Guntersville: If the magnificence of this mountainous Buck's Pocket retreat is what election losers get, why would anyone want to win? Alabama politicians are a canny bunch.

All that political philosophizing will put you in the mood for barbecue, and **Clarence's Rib Shack** has the perfect combination of panoramic lake views and the thick, rich aroma of wood-smoked, flame-seared ribs. Alabama football fans will warm to the colors of red and grey and framed pictures of team victories, plus several prints by sports artist **Daniel Moore**. This is a Roll Tide place. Check any other team regalia at the front door and ask if you can sit on the screened porch. With barbecue to sustain you, you'll survive.

Sunday is a good day to see what **Lake Guntersville State Park** is all about. The famous **Eagle Watch** in January makes great demands on the lodge, cottages, chalets, and surrounding accommodations, so early arrangements are the best plan. Ask as you drive into the park for maps and information on weekend packages. You don't have to stay in the lodge to participate in the eagle-centered field trips.

The emerald expanse of the mountaintop golf course is an impressive sight. Except for Christmas Day, the course is open all year. To get a tee time for the weekend, call after 7 A.M. on Wednesday. Early reservations are encouraged. Weekday tee times are assigned on a first-come basis.

The park sits on a 500-foot bluff overlooking Lake Guntersville, and the cottages have a lake view, too. Golf is not the only activity. You can swim, boat, hike along 31 miles of marked trails, play tennis, or drop into the Nature Center, which is under the direction of a trained park naturalist. Bass and crappie fishing tournaments are also held all year.

Sometimes it's a challenge to find a restaurant open on Sunday. However, **Bruce's Restaurant** (or **Bruce's Kountry Buffet**) is open only on weekends, a testimony to the popularity of Lake Guntersville as a weekend getaway. Whatever you call Bruce's and however you

Marina and boats on Lake Guntersville. (Photo by Neal Broerman)

spell it—and it is known by both names—this has some of the best country cooking anywhere. The friendly folks at Bruce's will wish you a safe trip home, and when you pull out of the parking lot and take a farewell look at the lake, your mind will snap the picture you'll take home. It's even prettier than a post card.

Area Code: (256)

Getting There:
Guntersville lies on U.S. 231, midway between Gadsden and Huntsville. A more direct and scenic route from Birmingham would be Alabama 79 from Interstate 20/59, Exit 128.

Where and When:
Guntersville Museum and Cultural Center, 930 O'Brig Avenue, Guntersville, AL 35976. Tue.-Fri., 10 A.M.-4 P.M.; Sat.-Sun., 1 P.M.-4 P.M. 571-7597.

Habana 1512, 382 Gunter Avenue, Guntersville, AL 35976. Mon.-Sat., 11 A.M.-2 P.M.; Thurs.-Sat., 6 P.M.-10 P.M. 582-0210.

Lake Guntersville State Park, 1155 Lodge Drive (Alabama 227), Guntersville, AL 35976. 571-5440; (800) 548-4553.

Peg's Posies, 2214 Lugenia Drive S.W., Guntersville, AL 35803. By appointment only. 881-3035.

Rock House Flowers, Gardens, Gifts, 1201 Gunter Avenue, Guntersville, AL 35976. Mon.-Sat., 9 A.M.-5 P.M. 582-7391.

Southern Pines Antiques and Reproductions, 336 Gunter Avenue, Guntersville, AL 35976. Tue.-Sat., 10 A.M.-5 P.M. or by appointment. 582-1300.

Sugar Plum Fine Gifts and Antiques, 801 Gunter Avenue, Guntersville, AL 35976. Mon.-Sat., 9:30 A.M.-5:30 P.M. 582-6004.

Information:

Alabama Mountain Lakes Tourist Association, 25062 North Street, Mooresville, AL 35649. 350-3500.

Lake Guntersville Chamber of Commerce and Welcome Center, 200 Gunter Avenue, Guntersville, AL 35976. 582-3612; (800) 869-5253.
Web site: www.lakeguntersville.org

Marshall County Convention and Visitors Bureau, 200 Gunter Avenue, P.O. Box 711, Guntersville, AL 35976. 582-7015; (800) 582-5282.   Web site: www.marshallcountycvb.com

Guide Services:

Doug Campbell, Fishing Guide, Waterfront Grocery, Guntersville, AL. 582-6060.

Tee Kitchens, Tee's Bait and Guide Service, Ossa-Win-Tha, U.S. 79 N, Guntersville, AL 35976. 582-4595.

Accommodations:

Ivy Creek Inn Bed and Breakfast, 985 Carlton Road, Guntersville, AL 35976. 505-0722; (800) 379-4711.
Web site: www.bbonline.com/al/ivycreek

Lake Guntersville Bed and Breakfast, 2204 Scott Street, Guntersville, AL 35976. 505-0133.
Web site: www.bbonline.com/al/lakeguntersville

Mac's Landing Motel and Marina, 7001 Val Monte Drive, Guntersville, AL 35976. 582-1000.

Restaurants:

Adrian's, 1405 Sunset Drive, Guntersville, AL 35976. 582-3106.

Bruce's Restaurant, 21235 U.S. 431 N., Guntersville, AL 35976. Fri.-Sat., 10:30 A.M.-9 P.M.; Sun., 10:30 A.M.-8 P.M. 582-8261.

Clarence's Rib Shack, 3370 Alabama 69, Guntersville, AL 35976. Mon.-Thurs., 11 A.M.-8:30 P.M.; Fri.-Sat., 11 A.M.-9 P.M.; Sun., noon-8 P.M. 582-3935.

Wanda's, 392 Gunter Avenue, Guntersville, AL 35976. Mon.-Sat., 7 A.M.-4 P.M. 582-5842.

Willie J's at Mac's Landing Motel and Marina, 7004 Val Monte Drive, Guntersville, AL 35976. Mon.-Thurs., 6:30 A.M.-10 P.M.; Fri.-Sat., 6:30 A.M.-11 P.M.; Sun., 11 A.M.-3 P.M. 582-2245.

Major Annual Events:

Art on the Lake, Guntersville—June.

Eagle Awareness, Lake Guntersville State Park—June.

Christmas Parade/Parade of Lights, Guntersville—December.

35

ANNIE'S TOWN, HOW YOU'VE GROWN!

It's Friday night on Noble Street. The sweet strains of a jazz medley drift lazily on the summer air. **Chris Culver** and the Jazz Ensemble from JSU are holding forth in the **Coffeehouse Café**. A daytime deli and a gourmet restaurant at night, the Coffeehouse is always a coffeehouse where interesting people hang out. Convivial owner David Magil keeps Friday and Saturday nights lively with blues by Billy Abbott from Memphis, classic rock and oldies by **Danny Slick** and **Benny Pitsinger,** and the always popular Culver and **Jackson State University Jazz Ensemble.** These talented musicians turn an evening into an event.

Was it prophetic? **Anniston** was first called Woodstock. That had no musical connotations, however. Woodstock was the name of a local iron company. To honor Annie Scott, the wife of Alfred L. Tyler, a founder of both the iron company and the company town, the name was soon changed to Annie's Town. Days later, when the post office application was submitted, the name was shortened to Anniston, and Anniston it has been since 1873.

Created after the Civil War, the town was intended by its founders, the Noble and Tyler families, to be an industrial center of the New South. The two families used their company's profits for community improvements such as parks, schools, and churches. They even built an opera house. The Woodstock Iron Company's control of city development resulted in the segregation of residential areas according to who did what within the company. It took the coming of the

railroad in 1883 to open the city to more businesses and attract people who did not work for the iron company. Competition weakened
Woodstock's control and turned Anniston into the fastest-growing
community in the state.

What really put the name of the town on the industrial map?
Railroad cars. Anniston's plants manufactured engines, cattle cars,
coal cars, cabooses, and everything in between. You'll think of
Anniston the next time you have to wait at a crossing for a long train.

Iron continued to drive the town's expansion. Forty years after the
Georgia Pacific Railroad chugged into town, Anniston became the
world's largest producer of cast iron pipe.

From whatever direction you approach Anniston, you will find a
wide range of well-known hotels and motels along Interstate 20 and
U.S. 431. Slip on your favorite casual slacks and shirt and then look
ahead to an evening of easy listening while you savor gourmet fare at
the **Coffeehouse Café.**

We found the shrimp scampi to be a perfect marriage of butter and
herbs. From the looks on the faces of the diners around us, the clams
and mussels met with favor, too. Ask your waitress about splitting an
order, however, because the servings are generous and you won't want
to waste a morsel or an opportunity to order dessert. Sample one of
David's mother's masterpiece confections and you'll know where he
got his culinary gifts. Special dishes and desserts keep customers
returning, because they expect the unexpected. You'll return to your
motel humming. What put you in such a great mood? Was it the music
or the meal? You'll fall asleep working out the answer.

If you are in search of breakfast or want to put together a picnic
lunch to store in your cooler, sip a cup of custom-blended coffee and
munch on a fresh bagel while you wait for your sandwiches and salads to be made to order. **Big Apple Bagels** has a good morning wake-
up aroma about it every day all day. The wide choice of coffees and
caffeine content gives you the power to set your nervous energy level.

When you leave the bagel shop, turn left and go about two miles
to Museum Drive. You'll see **Lagarde Park** on your right, a perfect
place to spread your picnic later in the day. Your first stop, however,
will be the **Anniston Museum of Natural History,** the only natural history museum in the state accredited by the American Association of
Museums.

Unless you want to walk through the exhibits three times on your
first visit, slow down and take your time. This is not a left side, right

side museum. Tilt your head back and look at the ceiling. Look deeply into each scene for small creatures or telling details about the habitat.

Pause in the exhibit known as Underground Worlds, one of only a few man-made indoor caves in the Southeast, and listen. Can you hear the sound of time passing? Since a man-made cave is so rare, I spoke with **Jim Loftin,** who built the cave. How, I wondered, did he get this job? "Well," and he smiled modestly, he was "an artist who could weld."

Loftin is also an avid and competent caver. As you already know, there are 3600 caves in the **Alabama Cave Survey.** To qualify as a cave, the underground space must be 50 feet long or the caver must be able to get so far inside that he is in total darkness. This mandates that part of the caver's equipment is three sources of light. For those who want to experience caves without an arduous climb or a wiggle through small spaces in the dark, the cave Loftin created feels real.

The museum's changing exhibit gallery hosts several temporary shows each year and one, River Walk, written by journalist **Jennifer Greer** and illustrated by the stunning photographs of naturalist **Beth Maynor Young,** was organized at the museum under the direction of Susan Robertson. This exhibit is still traveling across Alabama, Georgia, Mississippi, and South Carolina. Young thinks of herself as an environmental pilgrim, and her artistic camera shots rivet attention to the beauty and importance of Southern rivers and inspire concern for the future. To fully experience the role of rivers in Alabama's history, take your own river walk. Call upon the **River Network** for information.

Most people spend an hour or more in the museum on a first visit. Before you leave, notice the German Black Forest clock with its military figures in the lobby. This clock strikes five minutes *before* the hour.

If hunger pains are also striking, you have several choices before you venture next door to the **Berman Museum.** You may take your picnic lunch to the park, or you could run into town for a true cure for hunger: barbecue. **Betty's Barbecue,** on the main drag in Anniston, will pull the famished into the warmest down-home atmosphere anywhere. If you're not a meat eater, order the vegetable plate. Everybody in the family will leave this place happy.

You may have noticed The **Original Old Smokehouse BBQ** across the street from Big Apple Bagels. This is owned by Gershon and Patricia Weinberg, and at some point in your day you will want to stop by and have peach or apple cobbler. Of course, this is another excellent barbecue choice in a town that takes such pleasures seriously.

A third possibility is **Café LeMamas!**, set in an 1885 railroad freight house. Open only during the week, this is for non-traditional weekenders, who should be there at 11 A.M. when the doors open. Chef's specials and vegetable casseroles are so popular that they run out before the café closes.

Having fortified yourself for more walking and looking, return to the **Berman Museum,** an international collection of paintings, bronze sculptures, books, weapons, and historical artifacts representing world cultures. The preservation of these items and their histories is due to the generosity of Colonel and Mrs. Farley L. Berman, who spent more than 70 years amassing this collection. Now deceased, their legacy to the state of Alabama is displayed in this handsome modern museum. Each item begs the onlooker to stop and enter the life of its former owner. Our guide, Joey Crews, pointed out the brass whale oil chandelier that hung in Napoleon's bedroom on the island of St. Helena, where he lived in exile until his death in 1821. What do you suppose the former emperor thought as he stared at this lamp for nearly six years?

After speculating on the uses of so much treasure, you may be in the mood for touring gift shops. In addition to downtown Anniston's jewelry stores and boutiques, you can browse through a row of antique and gift shops across from the Oxford Civic Center on a road called U.S. 78, U.S. 431, and Snow Street, between Interstate 20, Exits 185 and 188. Lug your packages to the car, and reward the patience of sports enthusiasts with a trip to the **International Motorsports Hall of Fame and Museum,** adjacent to the **Talladega Superspeedway** and only 20 miles from Anniston.

Racing enthusiasts will already hold tickets for the Diehard 500 in April or the Winston 500 in October, but those new to the sport or who want to immerse themselves in the great moments of racing will feel the energy surging through the eight halls of fame. The receptionist at the museum says an hour is enough time for some to tour the museum; others spend several hours reliving moments of triumph with Bobby Allison, Richard Petty, Bobby Unser, and many other Hall of Famers. To avoid the press of huge crowds, skip the great race weekends, but don't skip the museum. Note: for race weeks, accommodations are booked for more than 100 miles around Talladega. If you plan to stay anywhere in the area during this time, a year ahead is not too early to make reservations. Check the Web site for firm dates of race weeks.

Talladega Superspeedway. (Photo by Dan Brothers, courtesy Alabama Bureau of Tourism & Travel)

The receptionist at the Motorsports Museum had another tip for the weekend traveler. Her grandfather built the original stone steps that afforded many the opportunity to visit the Great Onyx Cathedral in **De Soto Caverns** in Childersburg, 15 miles from Talladega and 37 miles from Anniston. The cathedral is said to be larger than a football field and higher than a 12-story building. Those stone steps made the trip a test for the hardy, limiting the sightseers to a fit few. A renovated entrance has changed all that. More ages and stages can now enjoy the laser light and sound show inside the cathedral.

Check your watch. Hurry to the **Top O the River Restaurant.** We were warned to get to the restaurant before it opened or risk a long wait. Our advice was correct. We arrived before 5 P.M. and found a line inside. At exactly 5 an orderly progression to tables began. Then the food arrived: fried dill pickles, onion rings, fried cheese, coleslaw, and the largest seafood platter in the world. That's what they called it, and we were too busy eating to argue. Ask your waitress about splitting orders.

After such a satisfying meal, a walk would be a good idea, but a driving tour through a Victorian neighborhood is the next best thing. Tyler Square Park and its surrounding two-story Queen Anne Victorian homes in the **Tyler Hill Residential District** will give you an idea of the town founders' early esthetic and architectural planning. These gracious homes date from the 1880s and 1890s. View them in the setting sun and you can almost picture early residents peeping out the windows, wondering who *you* are and why you are wandering their private avenues.

You can indulge yourself further in the Victorian atmosphere with a night or two at the **Victoria Inn** and dinner at the Victoria Inn Restaurant. The walking is easy from the dining room to the **Wren's Nest,** an art gallery located down the hill. The inn is a combination of bed and breakfast rooms, inn rooms and suites, and a honeymoon cottage. The Wren's Nest is the exclusive international distributor of works by acclaimed artist **Larry K. Martin.** His paintings and prints of wildlife line the shelves and counters of the gallery and charm the onlooker. Domestic animals receive their due, too. You'll chuckle at the pigs and their personality.

Opportunities to appreciate art in Anniston continue at the church of **St. Michael and All Angels,** which was built in the late 1800s and is open to the public when services are not being held. The altar is 12 feet high and made of white Carrara marble. If you do not know what a reredos is, it means "screen behind an altar," and this one is surmounted by seven angels holding symbols of events in Christ's life. Stained-glass windows filter the sunlight through their ancient stories. Look up to the rose window, high above the south entry. Don't miss the Tiffany Madonna and Child.

On Sunday morning, a 30-minute drive down Interstate 20 will take you into **Pell City,** the largest city in St. Clair County and the gateway to Logan Martin, known as the lake of a thousand coves. You can eat an early lunch at the **Pell City Steak House** or pass through Pell City to Cropwell and breakfast at the **Big Bull Restaurant.** You could also bring a picnic lunch to **Lakeside Park** and spend time hiking the nature trail.

Lake **Logan Martin** was created in the 1960s when Alabama Power built Logan Martin Dam. It was host to the Bass Masters Classic in 1992, 1993, and 1997. Marinas and boat ramps are scattered about the 245 miles of shoreline.

If you spend the afternoon fishing or boating on the lake, you will be more than ready to enjoy dinner at the **Barbecue Shack.** Just look for an old railroad car, which is part of the Shack's charm.

As you drove through **Pell City,** you may have noticed a variety of gift shops. If you'd like to see what's inside, you'll have to come back on a Saturday, when they are open. One way to do that is to stay at **De Soto Caverns Park.** Shop in Pell City on Saturday and see the museums in Anniston on Sunday. There's more than one way to do it all and see it all.

Area Code: (256), Pell City and Childersburg, (205)

Getting There:
Anniston lies just north of Oxford along U.S. 431 and can be reached by taking Exit 185 from Interstate 20.

Where and When:
Anniston Museum of Natural History, 800 Museum Drive in Lagarde Park, Anniston, AL 36202. Mon.-Sat., 10 A.M.-5 P.M.; Sun., 1 P.M.-5 P.M.; closed Mon. Sept.-May. 237-6766. Admission.
Web site: www.annistonmuseum.org
Berman Museum, 840 Museum Drive in Lagarde Park, Anniston, AL 36202. Mon.-Sat., 10 A.M.-5 P.M.; Sun., 1 P.M.-5 P.M.; closed Mon. Sept.-May. 237-6261. Admission.
Web site: www.annistonmuseum.org
De Soto Caverns Park, 5181 De Soto Caverns Parkway (Alabama 76), Childersburg, AL 35044, Mon.-Sat., 9 A.M.-5 P.M.; Sun., 12:30 P.M.-5 P.M., (256) 378-7252. Admission.
Web site: www.cavern.com/desoto/
International Motorsports Hall of Fame and Museum, 3366 Speedway Boulevard, Talladega, AL 35160. Daily, 8 A.M.-5 P.M., 362-5002. Admission.   Web site: www.motorsportshalloffame.com
Lakeside Park, 2801 Stemley Bridge Road, Cropwell, AL 35054. March-April, 8 A.M.-6 P.M.; May-August, 8 A.M.-8 P.M. 338-9713.
St. Michael and All Angels Church, 1000 W. Eighteenth Street, Anniston, AL 36202. Daily, 9 A.M.-4 P.M. 237-4011.
Web site: www.brasenhill.com/stmikesaa/
Talladega Superspeedway, 3366 Speedway Boulevard, Talladega, AL 35160. Daily, 8 A.M.-5 P.M., (256) 362-7223, (800) 748-7467. Admission.
Web site: www.talladegasuperspeedway.com
Tyler Hill Historic Residential District, East Sixth and Seventh Streets off Leighton Avenue, Anniston, AL.
Wren's Nest Gallery, 1604 Quintard Avenue, Anniston, AL 36201. Mon.-Sat., 10 A.M.-6 P.M. 238-0710; (800) 833-9736.
Web site: www.larrykmartin.com

Information:

Alabama Vacation Guide. Call 1-800-ALABAMA (252-2262).
Alabama Welcome Center, Interstate 20, Exit 213, Abernathy, AL.
Calhoun County Chamber of Commerce, 1330 Quintard Avenue,
Anniston, AL 36202. 237-3536.   Web site: www.calhounchamber.org
Calhoun County Convention and Visitors Bureau, P.O. Box 1087,
Anniston, AL 36202. 237-3536; (800) 489-1087.
   Fish Habitat Enhancement Map. Write Alabama Power Company,
P. O. Box 160, Montgomery, AL 36101.
   Maps of Alabama Power Lakes, Launch Sites, and Marinas.
                         Web site: www.alapower.com/hydro
   Pell City Chamber of Commerce, 1610 Cogswell Avenue, Pell City,
AL 35125. 338-3377.   Web site: www.pellcitychamber.pell.net
River Network. (503) 241-3506.
                         Web site: www.teleport.com/~rivernet
Talladega Chamber of Commerce, P. O. Drawer A, Talladega, AL
35161. 362-9075.   Web site: www.talladega.com

Accommodations:

DeSoto Caverns Park Campgrounds, 5181 De Soto Caverns
Parkway, Childersburg, AL 35044. Open year-round. 378-7252; (800)
933-2283.
   Victoria Inn, 1604 Quintard Avenue, Anniston, AL 36201. 236-0503.

Restaurants:

   Accents Tearoom, 2101 First Avenue N, Pell City, AL 35125. Tue.-Fri.,
10 A.M.-5 P.M.; Sat., 10 A.M.-3 P.M. 338-7499.
   Ark, U.S. 78 E., Riverside, AL 35135. Mon.-Thurs., 11 A.M.-9 P.M.; Fri.-
Sat., 11 A.M.-10 P.M.; Sun., 11 A.M.-8:30 P.M. 338-7420.
   BBQ Shack, 7744 Stemley Bridge Road, Talladega, AL 35160.
Mon.-Thurs., 10 A.M.- 7 P.M.; Fri.-Sat., 10 A.M.-8 P.M.; Sun., 10 A.M.-4 P.M.
268-2005.
   Betty's Barbecue, 401 S. Quintard, Anniston, AL 36201. Mon.-
Thurs., 10:30 A.M.-8:30 P.M.; Fri.-Sat., 10:30 A.M.-9 P.M. 237-1411.
   Big Apple Bagels, 101 Greenbrier-Dear Road, Anniston, AL 36201.
Mon.-Thurs., 6 A.M.-8 P.M.; Fri.-Sat., 6 A.M.-11 P.M.; Sun., 7 A.M.-5 P.M.
231-0070.
   Big Bull Restaurant, 4300 S. Martin Street, Cropwell, AL 35054.
Mon.-Thurs., 10:30 A.M.-9 P.M.; Sat., 6:30 A.M.-10 p.m; Sun., 6:30 A.M.-
2:30 P.M., (205) 338-7172.
   Café LeMamas!, 1208 Walnut Avenue, Anniston, AL 36201. Mon.-
Fri., 11 A.M.-2 P.M. 237-5550.

Coffeehouse Café, 919 Noble Street, Anniston, AL 36201. Mon.,10:30 A.M.-2 P.M.; Tue.-Fri., 10:30 A.M.-9 P.M.; Sat., 5 P.M.-midnight. 236-7000.

Original Old Smokehouse BBQ, 631 S. Quintard Avenue, Anniston, AL 36201. Sun.-Thurs., 10:30 A.M.-8 P.M.; Fri.-Sat., 10:30 A.M.-9 P.M. 237-5200.

Pell City Steak House, 215 N. Comer Avenue, Pell City, AL 35125. Daily, 10:30 A.M.-9:30 P.M. (205) 338-7714.

Top O the River, 3220 McClellan Boulevard, Anniston, AL 36201. Mon.-Thurs., 5 P.M.-9 P.M.; Fri.-Sat., 5 P.M.-10 P.M.; Sun., noon-9 P.M. 238-0097.

Victoria Inn Restaurant, 1604 Quintard Avenue, Anniston, AL 36201. Mon.-Sat., 6 P.M.-10 P.M. 236-0503.

Major Annual Events:

Indian Dance Festival and Country Crafts Festival, DeSoto Caverns Park, Childersburg—April. 378-7252; (800) 933-2283.

Tomato Festival, Horse Pens 40, Steele—July. 570-0002; (800) 421-8564. Admission.   Web site: www.horsepens40.com

September Fest, De Soto Caverns Park, Childersburg—September. 378-7252; (800) 933-2283.

International Motorsports Hall of Fame Race Week—October. 362-5002.   Web site: www.daytonausa.com

Leukemia Cup Regatta, Lake Logan Martin, Vincent, AL—November (mini-regattas every Sunday).

Christmas Festival of Lights, DeSoto Caverns Park, Childersburg—Thanksgiving through December. 378-7252; (800) 933-2283.

Bluettes in bloom at Cheaha State Park. (Photo by Neal Broerman)

Water bird at Cheaha State Park. (Photo courtesy Charlene Wells)

36

SUNSET ON TOP
OF THE WORLD

"There it goes. 3-2-1." The young family seated in the corner of the restaurant cheers. A waitress whisks away the curtains that moments before shielded diners' eyes from the glare. A hush falls over the room. It's sunset atop **Mount Cheaha,** the highest point in Alabama. A wall of windows at the **Cheaha State Park** Resort Restaurant over-looks **Talladega National Forest** from a vantage point of 2,407 feet and seems to float above the mountain peaks. Those wise enough or lucky enough to have their evening meal at this moment see what one witness to this spectacular event called the sun kissing the mountains goodnight.

Groundwork for the resort at Cheaha, the Choctaw word meaning "high," was begun by the Civilian Conservation Corps (CCC) in the 1930s, and the restaurant and other accommodations were renovated and refurbished in the 1990s. Rooms, cabins, and chalets have air conditioning, fireplaces, and showers, but not all have bathtubs. None have TVs, but guests may bring their own.

After a night of sleeping well in the Appalachian Mountain air and returning to the dining room for breakfast, the refreshed traveler can wander down to the Country Store and pick up a map of hiking trails and information on group tours of the park, the Nature Center, the CCC Museum, and special events. This family-friendly resort has a picnic and play area, wildflower garden, mountain bike trail, fishing, and pool and lake swimming. Fees for a day-use permit include park entrance, picnicking, fishing, and swimming.

Even the drive to and from Cheaha has its rewards. Photographers of all levels of experience delight in the season's scenery while traveling through Talladega National Forest. Non-photographers simply "ooh" and "ah."

Spend an entire weekend hiking Cheaha's trails and relaxing in the lodge or use your campsite or A-frame as a base and see what else is in the area. Anniston, which you toured in the last chapter, is simply down the mountain.

Although you could spend hours or days on the state park trails, these are not the only ones in the area. New ones are constantly being developed, and one of the first links to the national Rails-to-Trails program is the **Chief Ladiga Trail.** Rails-to-Trails is a conversion of abandoned railroad corridors to paths for public use, whether it be bicycling, walking, or in-line skating. When this trail is completed, wheel chairs will roll comfortably, too.

Already in place to smooth wheelchair access is a raised boardwalk that extends to the spectacular view at Bald Rock. It is constructed in sections that alternate from flat to an easy ramp, enabling a person in a wheelchair to negotiate the walk without assistance. For those who are not taking along their own chairs but welcome a chance to rest, sheltered areas with benches are scattered along the walkway.

In the Talladega division of the Talladega National Forest, the **Coleman Lake Recreation Area** offers accessible, up-close views of nature. Above the Loop Trail, on Coleman Lake, a boardwalk leads to the water. The Warden Station Horse Camp is made user-friendly with a firm ground surface and an accessible rest room. **Lake Chinnabee Recreation Area** also has accessible restrooms in the day-use area and campground, but pea gravel on the campsites may hinder wheelchair users.

Hikers can spend the entire weekend on the **Pinhoti National Recreation Trail,** which is the longest hiking trail in the national forests of Alabama. Camping is allowed along the trail, but there is a charge for camping in developed areas. The trail length is marked with diamond-shaped metal markers tacked to trees. There are side trails in the Cheaha Wilderness and Cheaha State Park that are a part of the Pinhoti Trails system. Sections of Cheaha Mountain trails may be blazed with blue paint. You should be able to see markers at any point along the trail, except for a portion inside the Cheaha Wilderness. These were left unmarked to keep the feeling of a wilderness experience.

Gravel road in Talladega National Forest. (Photo courtesy Lynard Stroud)

Ferns at Cheaha State Park. (Photo courtesy Charlene Wells)

Snow-covered rock at Cheaha State Park. (Photo courtesy Charlene Wells)

Above and right: *Winter at Cheaha State Park.* (Photos courtesy Charlene Wells)

As you read in an earlier chapter, experienced hikers carry a compass, whistle, flashlight, sharp knife, fire starter, waterproof matches, first-aid kit, extra food, bottled water, and warm clothing. Double-check with the park ranger about safety precautions.

Every season is lovely at Cheaha. In spring the woods burst into vibrant color that yields to a sea of deep green washing over the valleys and spreading up the mountains. Viewed from the trails or the lodge dining room, fall is a riot of crimson and gold. Winter calms the world with an unexpected hush. How fortunate are the few who get snowed in on Cheaha Mountain. Stir the crackling fire in your cabin, and add another log. Snuggle closer together. The company is exclusive.

Outside the white flakes swirl. Winter in Alabama is short, but your memories will be long.

Area Code: (256)

Where and When:

Cheaha State Park, 19644 Alabama 281, Delta, AL 36258. 488-5111. Admission.   Web site: www.americasroof.com/ah.html
Talladega National Forest. Daily, 9 A.M.-5 P.M. 362-2909.

Information:

Rails to Trails Information, P.O. Box 112, Piedmont, AL 36272. 447-3363.

Accommodations:

Cheaha State Park Lodge, 2141 Bunker Loop, Delta, AL 36258. 488-5115; (800) 846-2654.

Restaurants:

Cheaha State Park Restaurant, 2140 Bunker Loop, Delta, AL 36258. Daily, 7:30 A.M.-10:30 A.M., 11:30 A.M.-3 P.M., 4:30 P.M.-8 P.M. 488-5115.

REFERENCES

Alabama Atlas & Gazetteer by DeLorme

Alabama: Off the Beaten Path by Gay Martin

Alabama's Historic Restaurants and Their Recipes by Gay Martin

Birmingham for Families by Joseph Billingsley

"Birmingham Neighborhoods" (*Birmingham Family Times*, October 1999) by Dr. Marvin Whiting

Downtown Birmingham Architectural and Historical Walking Tour Guide— 1971 (Birmingham Historical Society) edited by Marjorie Longnecker White

Gaineswood and the Whitfields of Demopolis by Jesse George Whitfield

The Ghost in the Sloss Furnaces—Birmingham Historical Society

Guntersville Remembered (Guntersville Historical Society) edited by Larry J. Smith

History of Eufaula, Alabama 1930 by Eugenia Persons Smartt; reprint from the 1933 edition

A History of Tallassee by Virginia Noble Golden

Images of America: Birmingham and Jefferson County—Jefferson County Historical Commission

Let the Good Times Roll! by Emily Staples Hearin

Mardi Gras—Mobile's Illogical Whoop De Do by Bennett Wayne Dean

Mardi Gras, New Orleans by Henri Schindler

A Mobile Mardi Gras Handbook by Bennett Wayne Dean

Moundville: An Introduction to the Archaeology of a Mississippian Chiefdom by John A. Walthall

Place Names in Alabama by Virginia O. Foscue

Rivers of History by Harvey H. Jackson III

Seeing Historic Alabama by Virginia Van der Veer Hamilton and Jacqueline A. Matte

The Story of Mobile by Caldwell Delaney

13 Alabama Ghosts and Jeffrey by Kathryn Tucker Windham and Margaret Gillis Figh

True Tales: Weekly Columns in the Birmingham News (Birmingham Historical Society) compiled by Larry Ragan

Yesterday's Birmingham by Malcolm C. McMillan

INDEX

D

E

H

P